Fragonard

Fragonard

ART AND EROTICISM

Mary D. Sheriff

THE UNIVERSITY OF CHICAGO PRESS
CHICAGO AND LONDON

Mary D. Sheriff is an associate professor in the art department at the University of North Carolina at Chapel Hill.

Published with the assistance of the Getty Grant Program.

The University of Chicago Press, Chicago 60637
The University of Chicago Press, Ltd., London

Printed in the United States of America

99 98 97 96 95 94 93 92 91 90 54321

Library of Congress Cataloging in Publication Data

Sheriff, Mary D.
Fragonard : art and eroticism / Mary D. Sheriff.
p. cm.
Includes index.
1. Fragonard, Jean-Honoré, 1732–1806—Criticism and interpretation. 2. Erotic art—France. I. Fragonard, Jean-Honoré, 1732–1806. II. Title.
ND553.F7S53 1990
759.4—dc19 89-4783
ISBN 0-226-75273-9 (alk. paper) CIP

This book is printed on acid-free paper.

For Rose Sheriff

Contents

Illustrations

Plates follow page 146

Figures

Acknowledgments

I believe in luck, in being at the right place at the right time. And I've been in two right places at two right times—at the University of Delaware as a graduate student when Barbara Stafford joined the faculty there, and at the University of North Carolina as an assistant professor when Richard Shiff was completing his book, *Cézanne and the End of Impressionism.*

With her powerful intellect and unabashed enthusiasms, Barbara Stafford brought me into the eighteenth century. Not only have I benefited from her profound mastery of art theory and intellectual history, but since my first year as a graduate student she has supported my work while allowing me the freedom necessary for an independent intellectual development. If I have never felt constrained by the orthodox boundaries of art history it is because I had the good fortune of working with Barbara Stafford. It is with admiration and affection that I thank my Doktormutter.

It is also with admiration and affection that I thank Richard Shiff whose inquiring mind, challenging ideas, and wry humor stimulated my intellectual growth at Chapel Hill. Through discussions with him, my understanding of critical theory broadened and deepened; I become more attuned to the assumptions underlying my own work. His best teaching, however, was by example. I learned much from watching Richard Shiff tackle a problem, from seeing him pursue it relentlessly, prod it, probe it, write it, rewrite it, and never be content with the obvious questions and answers.

Yes, I have had good luck.

Fortune has also graced me with generous friends and colleagues, many of whom have made significant contributions to this book. Bernadette Fort I thank for many things: for her careful reading of the manuscript and many helpful suggestions, for sharing with me her forthcoming work, for invaluable assistance in my French translations, and, most of all, for her friendship, conversation, and confidence. To Mary Pardo I am grateful for similar kindnesses; for reading and commenting on parts of the manuscript, for editing my translations, and for the day-to-day support of a personal friend and valued colleague. I am also indebted to Patricia Crown for her close and knowledgeable reading of the manuscript, for her pertinent observations on Fragonard paintings, and for her encouragement and support, which reach back to a time when we two were downright unusual (although not alone) in taking rococo painting seriously. Other friends read and commented on parts of this manuscript; many stimulated my thinking about the issues raised here. I much appreciate the help of Ann Bermingham, Jane Burns, Jack Censer, Candace Clements, Dena Goodman, Dorothy Johnson, Jerrine Mitchell, Ann Peterson, Neil Siegel, and Vivian Cameron.

I am particularly indebted to the J.-P. Getty Foundation for a Postdoctoral Fellowship that allowed me to complete the writing of my manuscript. Financial support for this project also came from the University of North Carolina at Chapel Hill. The Faculty Research Council awarded me a research grant in 1985 and a publication grant in 1988, and from the College of Arts and Sciences I received a Junior Faculty Development Award in 1986. With these awards came the funding for research assistants who have provided invaluable service. Luck played no part here for I knew well the abilities of Andrea Bolland and Margaret Farr. They participated in all stages of the project, acting not only as investigative reporters, but also as readers and editors. For Andrea Bolland, who was my lifeline to research facilities while I was off writing in solitude, and for Margaret Farr, who suffered with me those long hours of reading aloud the galleys, I reserve much heartfelt appreciation.

Last, but not least, I am especially thankful to Herb Silverman who has weathered this author's ups and downs and has listened patiently to her obsessions and fixations. By trade a mathematician, Herb Silverman has acted as my final safeguard against faulty reasoning, gratuitous jargon, and obfuscating prose. He contributed no small share to the completion of this manuscript.

Preface

It is easy to remain on the surface of Fragonard's paintings; the artist, it would seem, holds us there with his sensuous strokes of paint and playful subjects. We roam freely over his surfaces but any thought of moving beyond them, of resisting the artist's seductive power, is stifled by our image of Fragonard as a lighthearted painter temperamentally suited to love themes. This image, however, was established by writers writing with particular political objectives at particular historical moments. In the introduction to this book I explore their writings not to survey the literature, but to strip bare the mythic Fragonard constructed from the motivations, assumptions, and prejudices of those who fabricated him.

In the chapters that follow I break the surfaces of a few, carefully selected works; I was brought to this by a disagreement with the commonly held views of Fragonard's paintings. Looking beneath their surfaces I saw what should have been obvious from the beginning, that although Fragonard's work does not often speak directly to issues we might define as "significant," his works are, nevertheless, cultural products invested, saturated, and embellished with meanings. Those meanings are, strictly speaking, neither "in" the painting nor "in" the eye of the beholder; they come alive in the interaction between painting and beholder, and thus are infinitely varied and variable.

This book is concerned with both historical and contemporary interactions and with the meanings produced by those interactions. In the first case I am overtly interested in what meanings an eighteenth-century viewer of a certain type—the elite viewer versed in aesthetic codes—might have seen in Fragonard's paintings. I freely admit that I can never read these works from the native's point of view, and that any elite viewer I imagine is a construct synthesized from my various researches. Yet I can and do suggest a range of possible, even probably readings through my investigation of how meaning in rococo art was constructed and understood. In the second case, the case of contemporary interactions, my interests may be less obvious, for, in writing from the eighteenth-century premise that art should hide art, I have not foregrounded (so to speak) my engagement with contemporary critical theory and its applications. Recent critical debates, however, have colored my interactions with the paintings by suggesting the specific issues that I explore in terms of the eighteenth century. I have also borrowed many analytic tools from recent thinking about representation.

I note in my epilogue that I have tried to clarify some of the junctures where the concerns of rococo artists and theorists cross those of their twentieth-century interpreters, and that in so doing I have tried to give Fragonard's paintings a place in the past and present. I have also tried, in many instances, to match my rhetorical structures to the paintings I analyze. This strategy sometimes brings me dangerously close to the works, seeming to negate the necessary critical distance. Yet I think it is worth the risk, since this strategy also allows me to represent more effectively the self-conscious eroticism, wit, and irony of Fragonard.

Introduction: Presenting Fragonard

The rococo artists have never recovered from a revolution that left them despised and forgotten.[1] More properly said, there were two revolutions, and the combination of a radically changed aesthetic with a sociopolitical upheaval determined the later fortunes of those painters associated with the *ancien régime.* By 1792 rococo paintings, already condemned as mannered luxury products, were taken as symbolic of the oppressive system being crushed by the revolution. This interpretation coincided with a collapsing market; many patrons of rococo art lost their fortunes, others emigrated, some went to the guillotine. In contrast to the virtuous heroes painted by David, the shepherds of Boucher and the nymphs of Fragonard were instruments of corruption bearing the indelible stamp of Pompadour. To denounce, to exile, even to obliterate such works was to condemn the enemies of civic virtue in republican France. It is small wonder, then, that many eighteenth-century masterpieces, disgrace of a nation, were banished to closets and cellars, scarcely mentioned and rarely seen.

Although the rococo seemed to vanish during the First Republic, it reappeared under various guises in the Empire and Restoration. Prud'hon, Schall, Mallet, Boilly, and Debucourt were among those painters who continued the earlier traditions almost without interruption.[2] Some *amateurs,* such as La Caze and the brothers Marcille, amassed early collections of rococo art, their purchases stimulated by admiration and a deflated market. The larger revival of rococo forms, however, moved more slowly, beginning among a few poets, painters, and critics, and gradually spreading to the bourgeois public.

By 1830 many of the painted exiles had already emerged from cellars and closets; their authors were greeted with renewed recognition. Fragonard came forward slowly when the repatriation began. Although his works had been hidden for a time, his person remained more permanently concealed by silence; he had written nothing and his contemporaries had said little about him. His history would depend on scant information: a few recorded anecdotes, some questionable family traditions. Speculation based on current theories of artistic development filled some of the gaps—and left much to be intuited from his paintings.

The Rococo Condemned: Assessments of Fragonard before 1820

The rococo was high fashion in 1862 when Charles Blanc lamented that Fragonard remained almost completely forgotten. The national collections, Blanc maintained, owned nothing or nearly nothing by him, and his great history painting *Coresus Sacrificing Himself to Save Callirhoe* (1765) was hung in an obscure gallery of the Louvre that few visited. Criticizing this official neglect of Fragonard, Blanc reminded his readers that the French traditionally took their national painters more seriously.[3] But Fragonard had not been neglected on all counts—he was well remembered as France's great example of wasted talent.

Only two years after his death, Fragonard had been so characterized in P.-M. Gault de Saint-Germain's *Les trois siècles de la peinture en France,* 1808. Gault's brief comments on Fragonard and his general opinions about rococo art typify early nineteenth-century writings based on ethical, aesthetic, and social ideologies inherited from the previous century. As represented by Gault, Fragonard began with much promise. His *Coresus* announced a "brillant career in history painting as a superior athlete, but . . ."[4]—what follows is a conventional view: Fragonard's art was ruined by the prevailing taste of his time. Gault abhorred the rococo for its excessive license and disregard of antique models, and placed Fragonard in the sphere of Boucher, whom he believed fostered such undesirable qualities. Although admitting that Fragonard showed inspired genius and bold expression, Gault also described his art as "bizarre, mannered, and false."[5] It is not surprising that Gault should take this position since the stated purpose of his writing was to demonstrate how culture (in particular, manners and politics) influences the progress and decline of the arts.[6]

Along with his theory of cultural causes, Gault held a cyclical view of the historical process in which art rose to high peaks only to fall into inevitable decline. He argued that after the élan of the great seventeenth-century painters was exhausted, imitation ruled, and artists were mastered by fashion and caprice. In this state of inertia artists "did not dare to overthrow the prejudices under whose yoke they were obliged to bend."[7] Yet with a view to both personal and national glory a few painters—Vernet, Chardin, Greuze, and La Tour—did dare to inspire society with moral art. Most artists chose instead to cater to debauched taste, and in their decision Gault found another criticism of the rococo. He censured those greedy artists who cultivated the fast and easy execution most expedient for a "time when each hoped for an extraordinary profit."[8]

Gault's assessment of Fragonard, then, offered three related explanations for the artist's decline: he worked during a period when painting, given over to imitation, was at the nadir of a natural cycle; he was corrupted by the prevailing taste; he abandoned the noble genres to seek financial rewards. These indictments were repeated by Alexandre Lenoir in the *Biographie universelle, ancienne et moderne* (1816 and subsequent editions), where, highlighting Fragonard's financial success in a less than flattering way, Lenoir concluded that the artist "marched to his fortune on a path strewn with roses."[9] Lenoir's entry also demonstrates how Fragonard's failure could be attributed to cultural causes, this time by pointing to the painter's already-corrupted teachers as well as his libertine patrons. Nature, Lenoir contended, had given Fragonard all the qualities proper to a good painter, but the young artist was malformed by frivolous mentors who led him to neglect the elevated subjects and the *beau idéal.* To prove the painter's deficient preparation, the biographer called Fragonard himself as witness. Lenoir reported that upon seeing the old masters in Rome the young artist despaired of ever attaining their excellence. Depressed by the paintings of Raphael and Michelangelo, his brush was stilled. It was then that Fragonard realized the limitation of his training and sought his inspiration in the degenerate Italian masters—Pietro da Cortona, Tiepolo, and the lesser painters of the seventeenth and eighteenth centuries. This theme is then transferred to Paris where Fragonard presented his acclaimed *Coresus* in 1765. The reader is told that the lukewarm reception of his next history painting *The Visitation* (now lost) again reminded Fragonard of his poor training; and believing himself incapable of great works, he turned to the erotic genres where he was assured easy success.[10]

By 1820 Fragonard was considered primarily a painter of frivolous subjects, of love scenes à la mode. This characterization had been given a positive cast in the great painter's obituaries of 1806: in the *Courrier des Spectacles* he was called renowned in the graceful and erotic genre; in the *Decade philosophique,* successful in elegant and erotic subjects; and in the *Journal de Paris,* a name linked with the very idea of charm.[11] But later biographers were not so kind, and the following remark by Lenoir typifies a moralist critique of his works:

> One cannot evade the fact that the licentious compositions of this painter have often shocked virtue and alarmed modesty. In regard to this one will say: Fragonard is guilty, and one should not approve, even in admiring the painter, the genius whose product inflames the dangerous passions and leads to the corruption of morals.[12]

For those writing in the years after the artist's death, Fragonard, master of the erotic genre, was the great disappointment of French painting. He began his career with exceptional promise, he could have become the nation's foremost history painter, but . . . . Motivated by greed and corrupted by degenerate patrons and teachers, Fragonard, instead, became a corruptor of morality, an artist who traded elevating subjects for licentious ones.

The assessment of Fragonard common to the early nineteenth century and exemplified here by the statements of Gault de Saint-Germain and Lenoir was founded in attitudes toward art in general and rococo art specifically that developed in the second half of the eighteenth century. For example, Gault's suppositions are dependent on theories such as those propounded by Winckelmann in his *Geschichte der Kunst des Altertums,* 1764.[13] There Winckelmann established the Greeks as the measure of perfection and set down the fundamental principle that art forms develop within natural cycles of birth and decay. Reading rococo art through Winckelmann's analysis, Gault adopted his cyclical view and chastised the masters of the *ancien régime* for imitation. But even the application of these theories to the eighteenth century had been anticipated by Winckelmann himself, who used the model to elucidate both ancient and modern art. In regard to the latter, Winckelmann argued that decline had been notably accelerated since the High Renaissance.[14]

It was also in Winckelmann that Gault could find a justification for concentrating on the cultural causes of progress (and decline) in the arts. In his *Geschichte* the German writer had asked why the Greeks, of all civilizations, developed such perfection. His twofold answer, climate and custom, would have already been familiar from the Abbé Du Bos' 1719 *Réflexions critiques sur la poësie et sur la peinture.* Du Bos emphasized climate, but Winckelmann established culture as an equal, if not greater, partner. He argued that Athenian democracy was the core of cultural superiority, for it allowed the Greeks a loftiness of thought unattainable by those living under tyranny. He saw that in Athens artists were secure and honored; their reputations were not dependent on the "wretched" taste of the rich, and they were able to elevate their work above all mercenary considerations in conformation with the high ideals of the whole nation.[15] How easily the inverse situation could be seen in eighteenth-century France, where the corrupt taste of well-paying patrons diverted artists from the grand tradition.

The impact of Winckelmann's ideas, however, does not fully account for the strength of antirococo sentiment in France. His writings appealed because his art theory harmonized with the biases of others who criticized the rococo and with the political ideology of a revolutionary generation.[16] For example, where Winckelmann saw the effect of society on art, Diderot posited a mutual interaction between the two with a decline in the arts precipitated by the corruption of society: "If morals are corrupted, do you think that taste can remain pure? No, no, that is impossible, and if you believe it, you ignore the effect of virtue on the fine arts. . . . Oh riches, measure of all worth! Oh deadly luxury child of riches! You destroy everything. . ."[17] Conversely, Diderot argued that morals could be raised if didactic messages were imbedded in art works.

Writing as both critic and *philosophe,* Diderot wrestled with the problems raised in 1750 by Rousseau's *Discours sur les sciences et les arts.* In addressing the question of whether the arts and sciences contributed to the improvement of morals, Rousseau answered a resounding no. By viewing the arts within the social structure, he saw that they were luxury items tied to wealth. Rather than serving a useful social function, these coveted treasures corrupted morals and enervated virtue, encouraging those greedy for them to accumulate wealth voraciously. Rulers could use the arts to subjugate their people, making civilized populations happy slaves to their taste. And what of the artists? As the makers of luxury products they wasted energy that could be directed to activities productive for all of society.[18]

In answering comments about his discourse, Rousseau extended his attack on the arts by using the distinction between the natural (the true) and the artificial (the false) to condemn all representation. Art is challenged in a familiar way—it is appearance that belies reality. For Rousseau an art work stood for the object it represented in the same way that social graces replaced real virtues.[19] Rousseau thus developed a theory that gave art no place in a healthy society. As part of luxury, it corrupted morals; as a tool of the ruling power, it sweetly subjugated the people; as mere appearance, it lied.

Anxious to defend the arts, Diderot believed that even in an age where art had been corrupted by manners, some artists could escape their fate and work to improve society by presenting moral examples. (Recall that Gault allowed Chardin, Greuze, Vernet, and La Tour to rise above the debauched taste.) A luxury product was by definition useless, and art could be rescued from that category if given an important social function. Diderot thus set the goal for art to render virtue admirable and vice odious.[20] Although this end might have been achieved simply through the representation of didactic stories, Diderot also insisted that such subjects be rendered in the proper style. The critic moved his discussion of style into the realm of ethics by equating a natural handling (a handling where the drawing, color, etc. were tied primarily to the appearance of the object represented) with the true, and a mannered one (a handling where the drawing, color, etc. were tied primarily to the acquired habit of the artist) with the false. Thus where Rousseau condemned all art because it substituted for nature, Diderot condemned mannered art, equating mannerism with the decline of virtue: "Manner in the arts is like the corruption of morals in society."[21] In expressing the subjective fantasies of an individual rather than the qualities of the object, manner was tainted; it could be neither natural nor true.

Diderot's critique of the mannered art of delectation, Rousseau's criticism of art as luxury, and Gault's later polemic against the rococo can all be read as condemnations of certain elements of eighteenth-century society. Artists who created luxury products could be taken as parasites living off wealthy aristocrats and *seigneurs,* other parasites who never contributed materially to society. This view of the aristocratic patron was more fully developed during the revolutionary period, and Sieyès dramatized it effectively in the opening of his famous 1789 pamphlet *Qu'est-ce que le tiers-état?* Everything necessary to constitute a complete nation, he argued, was present in the third estate, and those who lived from the labor of the working class—those idle aristocrats set apart by their civil and political prerogatives—were foreign to that nation.[22] Although Sieyès vented his revolutionary ire against the aristocracy, another group throughout the eighteenth century was particularly despised, the so-called financiers and *fermiers généraux* who collected the taxes. "Those vile tax gatherers who corrupted every commodity they touched" grew more hated as they grew more rich and more ostentatious; in seeking the outward signs of status and gentility, they became major patrons of the arts. Thus by the end of the eighteenth century it was possible to claim that the rococo developed from the corrupt morals of corrupt patrons; artists who catered to those patrons traded their talent and promise for financial reward, and in the process they became as useless as the patrons themselves.

Gault's perspective in 1808, then, was derived from late eighteenth-century antirococo attitudes solidified during the revolutionary period, when the art of the *ancien régime* was inextricably associated with tyranny, libertinism, and greed. It is easy to see why he, and others after him, would argue that Fragonard was corrupted by his time, that he had sacrificed his talent to the whims of a public willing and able to reward him financially. Biographers struck these chords most loudly when Fragonard's subsequent career was compared to what the *Coresus* suggested might have been. The painter emerged in the early nineteenth century as a Gallic Hercules failed, one who chose the way of riches and ease rather than the hard path of virtue that led to glory. If the role seemed made for Fragonard, it was because the script had already been prepared in the previous century. Its writing began at the moment in 1765 when Fragonard presented his first reception piece *(The High Priest Coresus Sacrificing Himself to Save Callirhoe)* to the Academy. If a general condemnation of rococo art determined later attitudes toward Fragonard, there were also specific connections between eighteenth-century assessments of the artist and the early nineteenth-century commentaries that followed.

Several contemporary observers recorded how the academicians received Fragonard's *Coresus* with a unanimity and applause rarely seen.[23] In his *Salon of 1765* Diderot lauded the work and speculated that Fragonard would be France's next important history painter. Two years later, however, the young artist disappointed both Academy and public, who had awaited some considerable Salon entry. Instead, they saw naked putti gamboling in the clouds. The work was a sketch for a decorative ceiling commissioned by the *amateur* and *fermier général* Bergeret de Grancourt. Diderot was more than disappointed, he was outraged: "M. Fragonard, when one has a reputation it is necessary to have a little more self-respect."[24] Perhaps Diderot's criticism was particularly pointed because Fragonard was also becoming a name in amorous subjects. Collé says as much describing how *The Swing* (London, Wallace Collection) was commissioned in October of 1767. After Doyen refused the job he mumbled the name of an artist who accepted just such work—Honoré Fragonard.[25]

Fragonard did not appear in an official exhibition after 1767, and his conspicuous absence from the next Salon prompted the following caustic remark in the *Mémoires secrets:*

> M. Fragonard, that young artist who for four years had given us the greatest hope for the genre of history painting, whose talents were little developed at the last salon, has shown nothing at this one. One suspects that the lure of gain has turned

him from the great career that he had entered, and that instead of working for glory and posterity he is content to shine today in the boudoirs and dressing rooms.[26]

Like Diderot, many must have viewed Fragonard's decision to abandon history painting for less edifying subjects as a prostitution of the talents that he had displayed in the Salon of 1765. A young struggling artist might be justified in supporting himself with titillating works. Diderot had done as much by publishing *Les bijoux indiscrets* in 1748. But an artist once established in the public eye had duties beyond providing wealthy patrons with useless luxury products. Believing that a painter interested in material gain was lost, Diderot wrote, "At the moment an artist thinks about money he loses his sense of the beautiful."[27] Diderot was not the only critic to express such sentiments. La Font de Saint-Yenne launched a polemic in 1747 against artists who gave up history painting to make portraits that catered to the whims of the rich patron. Through such a decision the painter would "stifle the voice of genius and turn his brush from the path of glory in order to follow that which leads to ease."[28]

As Diderot and La Font de Saint-Yenne decried the artist who worked for financial gain, their public statements posited their view that the painter (like the poet) had a higher calling and duty to society.[29] Others, particularly the members of the Académie Royale, also had perhaps another reason for deprecating financial motivation. Too obvious a commercial attitude was not consonant with the upward social mobility desired by artists. The establishing of an Academy in 1661 had given them status over the artisan, and in the next hundred years some painters began to vie with poets in the effort to attain the rank of the intellectual. With its founding in 1648, the Academy prohibited its members from keeping an open shop, from displaying their works in shop windows, and from advertising to the public through signboards.[30] The desire for social position might also have lurked behind the lofty motives claimed by Diderot and La Font de Saint-Yenne. The association of the *gens de lettres* and the *grands* was a favorite theme of the *philosophes* at mid-century when, in theory, writing conferred a distinguished "estate" on men of great talent but modest birth.[31]

In considering how a desire for financial reward was seen as incompatible with intellectual status, the case of Falconet is instructive. The sculptor participated in the literary salons of his time, corresponded with his friend Diderot, and generally aspired to be a man of letters. Falconet, as is now well known, frequently engaged in commercial activity to augment his income; he made designs for luxury crafts and models for Sèvres porcelain. However, he kept these enterprises relatively hidden from public view because he liked to give the impression of loftiness and austerity.[32]

Unlike Falconet, Fragonard did not participate in intellectual salon life. By working too openly as a professional artist meeting the demands of a paying clientele, Fragonard left himself vulnerable to serious charges from biographers and contemporaries. Biographers wrote that greed attracted him to the corrupt "taste of the times," and contemporary critics held him in a double bind. Academicians and *philosophes* could (and did) castigate Fragonard because his businesslike approach to art subverted their claims to elite social and intellectual status. On the other hand, many of this same group could consider Fragonard, who produced luxury goods for the wealthy, no better than the useless aristocrats for whom he worked. Thus Fragonard could be chastised because he rejected elitism and because he embraced it.

The antirococo attitudes that allowed Fragonard's biographers to find him greedy, spoiled by the taste of the times, and ill trained for serious art, persisted through the first two decades of the nineteenth century. Even at the height of the rococo revival, when general opinion of that period had changed, the traditional criticisms were voiced. In reviewing works at the Universal Exposition of 1855, Delécluze discussed the development of the genres in French painting. The eighteenth century was accused of having corrupted all of them with "fashion, fantasy, and mannerism."[33] And in his 1855 *Louis David, son école et son temps* Delécluze wrote of the rococo period that never had taste been so perverted, the true doctrines of art so completely neglected, and the purpose of art so thoroughly vain.[34]

Reviving the Rococo: Rediscovering Fragonard

The re-evaluation of the rococo was precipitated by altered political and social ideals as well as changed conceptions of the purposes and goals of art. The July Monarchy saw a revival of aristocratic sentiments among the newly rich bourgeoisie and the old aristocrats, and both coveted art works as emblems of luxury, wealth, and social position. Objects that had decidedly negative associations in a different political climate took on positive value for these groups. By 1836 Watteau and Boucher dominated the Faubourg Saint-Germain, a district inhabited by the aristocracy, who believed themselves the select arbiters of taste. For them the rococo revival was a reassertion of the cultural and social supremacy that by birth or wealth was rightfully theirs.[35]

Whereas the aristocrat and the socially-aspiring bourgeois understood rococo works as symbols of wealth and taste that identified their owners as part of a notable elite, some nationalists adopted the eighteenth century as a truly French school during the short-lived Second Republic. In 1849 Walferdin, an ardent republican and admirer of Diderot, donated Fragonard's *The Music Lesson* to the Louvre because he felt that one of France's great artists was poorly represented there. With the gift went the stipulation that the work could remain in the public collection only as long as France remained a republic.[36] This nationalist taste for the rococo led Delécluze to remark on the "monstrous" (i.e., unnatural) mixture of republican opinions and revived taste for Watteau and Boucher.[37] Such a blend was unnatural to Delécluze who, trained in the school of David, could see the rococo as nothing other than the evocation of the *ancien régime*. For him its meaning was preordained. But symbols are culturally determined; and others who could shift their perspectives found in rococo paintings other meanings convenient to their own ideologies.

The brief moment of associating the rococo with republican sentiments ended as the bourgeoisie assumed social and political power under the Second Empire. To give their social aspirations visible form they usurped the signs of culture, as had their eighteenth-century predecessors, the financiers and tax farmers. Seeking differentiation from, rather than identification with, the larger public, the rich found their emblems of refined taste in rococo paintings that, unlike those of the revolutionary period, had not (theoretically) been intended for "the people."

Although there was no real artistic direction from the state under Napoleon III, the taste of the Empress Eugénie fueled the revival of Boucher's school. She had eighteenth-century paintings installed in her rooms and mixed them with murals painted in imitation of a rococo style. Appropriating the original wardrobe of Marie Antoinette, she commissioned Winterhalter to do her portrait à la Vigée Le Brun. Little differentiation was made, one might add, between the Style Louis XVI and the Style Louis XV. When not emulating Marie Antoinette, Eugénie was busy giving fêtes in the manner of the earlier monarch with details copied from engravings by Cochin.[38]

New attitudes toward art patrons emerged in writings about the eighteenth century and can be discerned in a re-evaluation of Mme de Pompadour published by La Fizelière in the *Gazette des Beaux-Arts* of 1859.[39] Focusing on her influential and beneficial role as art patron, he stressed that the charming and talented Pompadour, chosen only for her merits, was disdained by the court because of her bourgeois origins. The king's mistress showed her mettle, however, by protecting the Physiocrats and encouraging all the arts through her refined taste and generous commissions. Her extravagant expenditures for personal luxury, he argued, had a trickle-down effect that spurred the French economy, for the more she dispensed, the more money circulated to enrich France.[40] Although the author claimed he could not say if Mme de Pompadour used the resources for the good of society, he concluded that she made splendid and often intelligent use of the riches accessible to her. Mme de Pompadour here is something of a bourgeois heroine for the Second Empire; despised by the aristocrats, she shows herself more noble than they by her judicious support of philosophy and arts. Although she was spending from the government coffers, her economics were familiar to La Fizelière's audience; the production of luxury goods enriched the state.

This economic perspective on the arts is not surprising given that as early as 1805 Emeric-David had justified the support of painting and drawing by pointing out that they perfected the commercial arts and created markets by developing the tastes of consumers. Emeric-David even went so far as to admit that art objects themselves could be items of commerce.[41] In 1848 the establishment of the Conseil Supérieur de Perfectionnement des Manufactures Nationales, which oversaw the Sèvres porcelain factory and the tapestry works at the Gobelins and Beauvais, made official the role of the fine arts in providing industry with the best design. And in bringing together all the products of the nation, the International Exhibitions of 1851, 1855, 1862, and 1867 linked the fine and commercial arts in a clearly visible way.[42] These exhibitions had a precedent in the late eighteenth century when art objects and industrial inventions were displayed together at Pahin de la Blancherie's Salon de la Correspondance held monthly in Paris between 1777 and 1792. This enterprise had a clearly commercial purpose as collectors, artists, and entrepreneurs brought works to be displayed, examined, and perhaps purchased.[43]

Throughout the first half of the nineteenth century, the bourgeoisie's attitude toward the arts was two-sided. Sought as signs of nobility, the arts still had to justify their existence in a world dominated by economic concerns. As in the late eighteenth century, the arts were called upon to defend their utility; but where they were once propagators of virtue, they had become spurs to commerce and trade. It was this latter attitude toward the arts, prevalent in both the July Monarchy and Second Empire, that disgusted the circle of writers and critics—Gautier, Houssaye,

Gerard de Nerval—who brought the rococo to public attention in the 1830s. They believed that art was of value precisely because it was useless. In his famous preface to *Mademoiselle de Maupin* of 1836, Gautier registered a scathing disdain for the equation of art with commercial production:

> No, imbeciles, no, cretins and goitrous fools that you are, a book does not make consummé; a novel is not a pair of seamless boots; a sonnet, a syringe with a continuous jet; or a drama, a railway. . . One cannot make a cotton cap out of a metonymy or put on a comparison like a slipper; one cannot use an antithesis as an umbrella.[44]

But the preface was not aimed only at those who demanded material utility; Gautier also railed against the Christians, progressives, socialists, and utopians who called for a morally useful art.[45] As an ideal, uselessness represented freedom for artists who no longer were obliged to direct their art toward aims other than aesthetic ones. Gautier and his circle saw in eighteenth-century painting the epitome of that useless beauty so necessary to the sensual pleasure that can be derived from art.

If Gautier's appreciation of eighteenth-century art was founded on a theoretical position far from sympathetic to the bourgeoisie, his brand of elitisim was equally distant from theirs. Vehemently antibourgeois, Gautier and his associates saw vulgar commerce at the heart of their society. They believed that the arts could only prosper in an aristocracy where the upper class remained untainted by the stain of commerce and had the wealth and leisure to cultivate its sensibilities toward an appreciation of truly subtle art. Many who adopted this position developed a highly fantasized view of the eighteenth century as a culture organized to foster the interests of art and artists. Dandies often tried to recreate the fashionable artist as they imagined him, hobnobbing with aristocrats in a society of refined sensibilities and good taste.[46] As a consequence, texts that rediscovered eighteenth-century artists often dwelled on anecdotes from their seemingly blessed lives. The Goncourts' description of Maurice Quentin de La Tour at the height of his artistic success followed from this sort of idealization:

> He is part of society, of the highest society, of the best company, of Madame Geoffrin's Monday dinners. . . . He belongs to that charming and *operadique* circle of M. de la Popelinère at his house at Passy. He is on the most familiar terms with the Minister Orry. His are the most delightful and the most flattering of relations, ties to the great nobles, the literary men, the savants.[47]

It was a life, as the Goncourts describe it, of opulent simplicity and substantial comfort, a life of rubbing shoulders with all the famous personalities and talents of the age. Even those articles that appeared in periodicals written for a more middle-class audience (*Le Magasin pittoresque,* for example) were a kind of escapist literature interested only in the imaginative description of rococo elegance.[48]

In the vogue for eighteenth-century luxury products and aristocratic life style, two prominent attitudes emerged: that of the bourgeoisie who promoted a utilitarian concept of art while seeking works as emblems of refinement and wealth, and that of artists and critics who pursued the eighteenth century because they believed its values were the antithesis of vulgar bourgeois commerce. Both elitist attitudes were far from that of the republicans who saw in the rococo the French national tradition.

Given the general attitudes of those who advocated *l'art pour l'art,* one might expect that they would treat Fragonard sympathetically. This was not always the case. Arsène Houssaye, the friend of Gautier who participated both privately and publicly in the rococo revival, had few positive sentiments toward Fragonard.[49] The artist merited only two brief references in his history of eighteenth-century painting (*L'Artiste,* 1844), and a dubious distinction was highlighted. He might have been a great history painter: "if he had maintained the promise of his debut, without a doubt he would have arrived at one of the most noble places in painting, but . . ."[50] In explaining Fragonard's defection from the grand tradition, Houssaye relied on inherited opinion: Fragonard was weak and succumbed to the taste of the times.

The author's more extended treatment of the eighteenth century, *Histoire de l'art français au dix-huitième siècle,* 1860, was no more sympathetic to Fragonard, the artist who "threw away more recklessly than Boucher a gifted mind." Houssaye's concentration on anecdote, however, is typical of later nineteenth-century approaches to artist's biographies, and he purports to show a day in the life of the painter. That day was based on an entry in Grimm's *Correspondance littéraire* where Fragonard's revenge on the dancer Mlle Guimard was reported. Quarreling with the painter over the decoration of her salon, she apparently treated him in such an imperious manner that he abandoned the work. According to Grimm, Fragonard returned secretly to his murals and, with a few deft touches, altered the expression of her portrait to depict raving fury. Upon entering the room with a group of friends the dancer saw the metamorphosis; the angrier she became, the more she resembled Fragonard's caricature.[51]

In reporting the story, Grimm's attention was focused not on the artist but on the dancer, who at that time was entirely the rage. Houssaye, on the other hand, imagined Fragonard the main character and gave him motivations that must have seemed consistent with the style and subject of the artist's erotic themes. Agreeing with Buffon that "the style is the man," Houssaye claimed to look for the heart of an artist in his works.[52] In a greatly expanded version of the story, Fragonard was jealous because the dancer refused his amorous advances. The painter, however, could not feel real emotion; his was the mannered artifice depicted in his paintings.[53] Houssaye reported (or fabricated) an incident in which Greuze had the misfortune to confess a true love to Fragonard, who called him an amorous cherub and ridiculed his fine sentiments. The two obviously had been to "different schools."[54]

Houssaye perpetuated old attitudes, added the kind of anecdote loved by nineteenth-century writers, and operated under the logical fallacy that the man is his work. The first nineteenth-century writer who actively defended Fragonard was Charles Blanc, and his account of the artist's career stands apart from those of other early biographers. Sensitive to the plight of the artist dependent on government patronage, Blanc saw Fragonard as a victim of the state's laxity in paying its accounts:

> During the term as Sûrintendant of M. de Marigny, brother of Mme de Pompadour . . . he [Fragonard] met with so many difficulties in the sale and payment of his *Coresus* that he renounced commissioned paintings and the good will of the official world. The favor of the public was offered him and was destined to compensate him generously for this break.[55]

Here is public opinion compensating Fragonard for a significant loss, rather than greed luring him from an expected career. Throughout the article Blanc treats Fragonard's ability to command great prices not as a sign of the artist's cupidity but as a mark of his reputation.[56]

In judging the artist by the value of what he did produce, rather than by the loss of what he did not, Blanc deviates from the accepted view of Fragonard as the great could-have-been. Commonly repeated incidents are reinterpreted as well. For example, although Blanc duly reports that some great Italian monuments depressed the young painter, he subverts the account by noting that Fragonard did draw after all the celebrated paintings of the great masters. No art intimidates his Fragonard who can assimilate all styles and who has the ability to remake the works that he copies—to "fragonardize" them.[57]

Blanc's reassessment of Fragonard offered a broader view of the artist because Blanc considered the whole range of genres handled by the painter rather than attending only to the early historical subjects and the later erotic scenes (as was the case with the earlier biographies). Treating even the most titillating paintings without disdain, Blanc refuted those moralists who would chastise the artist and argued that a renewal of French society had to precede a "purification" of art. When that renewal began (and Blanc located its beginning late in the reign of Louis XVI), Fragonard's art responded. He produced happy family scenes, such as his *Good Mother* (version in the Boston Museum of Fine Arts, engraved by DeLaunay in 1779) dedicated to the nation, and created a great allegorical portrait of Benjamin Franklin (the engraving *Au génie de Franklin,* 1778). Rewarded by the Jacobins for his wide knowledge of art, Fragonard was made a conservator of the Louvre.[58] As an apologist for Fragonard, Blanc was perhaps the first writer to use the cultural explanation of artistic progress to the painter's advantage.

Charles Blanc viewed Fragonard from a perspective within the institutions of the visual arts. His assessment of Fragonard's decision to abandon history painting makes of the artist neither a failure nor a tradesman; it does not depict him (as Houssaye's account did) as naturally predisposed to love themes. That Blanc accepted the artist's financial decisions without reproach might indicate that at least some of those connected with the visual arts were willing to accept that money could be a motivating factor. Certainly the address of Emeric-David, the commissions on commerce and art, and the various other associations of art and industry in the First and Second Empire indicate as much.

Yet as we have seen, any hint of commercialism on the part of artists and writers was criticized by proponents of an independent art *(l'art pour l'art).* Writers such as Houssaye, Gautier, and later the Goncourts maintained a *l'art pour l'art* position, and as revivers of the rococo, they could hardly be happy when an artist seemed concerned with financial gain. Any writer with their philosophy who stated baldly that Fragonard chose to be a comfortable man (what they would consider a bourgeois) rather than a great master, said, in effect, that Fragonard was no artist at all. But his works belied that idea; and as products of fantasy, useless objects made entirely to give pleasure, they could scarcely be termed bourgeois. Any discrepancy between the character of the man and the nature of his art would confound critics who, like Houssaye, wanted to interpret the one through the other. How could a bourgeois mentality (an artist who sought monetary rewards for his work) produce what seemed to be such antibourgeois art? Other explanations must account for his career; older explanations emphasized that he had been corrupted by the age, or that his training had been weak. Newer ones, such as that of the Goncourt brothers, raised the issue of temperament.

Fragonard According to the Goncourts

In their assessment of Fragonard, the Goncourts operate from two basic critical assumptions: that the man is revealed in his art, and that climate determines temperament. The first of these was already present in Houssaye, who, from Fragonard's works, invented a day in the artist's life. The second had an impeccable French pedigree, extending back to the Abbé Du Bos' *Réflexions critiques sur la poësie et sur la peinture* of 1719. There Du Bos observed that all the arts flourished and decayed at the same time in the same place and hypothesized that certain moral and physical conditions were necessary for the seeds of genius to bear fruit. But moral conditions, determined by culture or social milieu, could not by themselves explain genius, for Du Bos could cite civilizations (such as France under François I) in which the arts did not flourish even though the social milieu was right. Therefore he believed the physical causes to be primary; simply put, human genius was like a plant, it had its preferred climatic conditions and preferred years.[59]

In the nineteenth century the influence of climate and geography continued to be cited, even by those authors who seemed most strongly to stress social conditions. For example, although at the outset of his *Philosophie de l'art* Taine wrote that a comprehension of the general social and intellectual condition of the times must precede understanding a work, artist, or group of artists, he also argued that people always received the imprint of the country they inhabited. He began discussing Greek art by describing the geography of Greece and the favorable climate, concluding, "It is a beautiful country which turns the soul towards joy and encourages man to consider life as a festival."[60]

Although not denying cultural influences, the Goncourts see Fragonard as a product of the Midi where his imagination was warmed by Provençal sunlight:

> Every aspect of his art—his palette; his imagination; the best of his ideas, sentiments, and colors—derives from the Midi; and might we not say that all of his painting was improvised beneath a blue sky, upon an easel placed in a garden wrapped in the happiness of the atmosphere, in the summer's breath.[61]

His birthplace was also the clue to Fragonard's character; conditioned by the *dolce far'niente* of the southern clime, Fragonard inherited its indolence and effortless living. The Goncourts use their character analysis to answer the central historical question of why the artist renounced the success of his *Coresus.* His decision, for the Goncourts, was not an abdication but a return, a return to the more authentic qualities of his personality. They imagine that he was bored and fatigued at the idea of a great undertaking and indifferent to gain, to fame, to posterity—to all that usually motivated artists to a fever pitch. He abandoned the grand tradition because he recognized that he was a born improviser suited to the smaller stage. The Goncourts relegate to a footnote the remark that Fragonard was also diverted from the pursuit of heroic subjects by the difficulty of securing payment for the *Coresus.*[62] If their *l'art pour l'art* philosophy prevented them from developing this latter explanation, the still-potent climatic theory of temperament provided a convenient alternative.

The Goncourts' image of Fragonard informed the first major monograph and catalogue devoted to the artist, written by Baron Roger Portalis in 1889. Developing his geography of genius, Portalis agreed with the Goncourts in attributing Fragonard's temperament to the meridional sun: "Let us say, then, that the sunlit Provence, birthplace of Fragonard, has not been without influence on his artistic temperament, and that he has had to draw from the entrails of the earth that irresistible gaiety, that infectious warmth so characteristic of his works."[63] Portalis eliminated both love and money as probable motivating factors and envisioned a Fragonard who did not regret leaving serious work because it was difficult for his exuberant nature to hold to a rigorous path. In painting gallant subjects, Fragonard was only following his natural penchant.[64]

In his adherence to the explanation of temperament Portalis is a student of the Goncourts, and like them he intuited temperament not only from geography but also from a naive reading of the man in his art. For example, in discussing *The New Model* (c. 1770; Paris: Musée Jacquemart-André) Portalis wanted to recognize his hero in the scene, in the bloom of youth, loving women, and "impregnating" himself with them.[65] Unlike the Goncourts, however, Portalis turned Fragonard into a kind of realist whose subjects were an accurate representation of the times, "the mirror of the court, the echo of the theaters and salons."[66] Aside from this deviation in interpreting the paintings, Portalis only validated the image of Fragonard fabricated by the brothers Goncourt.

It is ironic that the Goncourts' myth of Fragonard has so tenaciously persisted, because at points they subverted their own conclusions. For example, although they described Fragonard's temperament and concluded that it conditioned his art, the Goncourts wrote:

> Behind the painter the man hardly appears. What do we know of him? Almost nothing. What has he left? What remains of him in the memoirs and diaries of the time? . . . Newspapers, reviews, the obituary records of the time are silent about this amiable artist who found fame without searching for renown.[67]

The Goncourts readily admit that the real Fragonard is inaccessible, and unlike many subsequent readers, they accept their Fragonard as a beautiful fiction. With characteristic wit and facility the Goncourts bring even the lack of evidence to bear on their fabrication:

> It seems to us that too many documents, too many facts might weigh on this light memory. . . . Let [the facts] of his existence flicker as if in one of his sketches; the half light suits this poet's life; and Fragonard's personality is one of those that we may prefer to envisage as a blessed shade holding a finger to its lips.[68]

Those who have called up the Goncourts' Fragonard in the last twenty-five years have seemed unaware that the image convinces by the power of the writers' colorful, imaginative, and often engaging prose, which makes vivid and lively the master's paintings. Consider, for example, this description of *The Fountain of Love* (c. 1780; London: Wallace Collection; figure 1):

> It is still night, a night of stormy mystery weighing heavily upon the dark trees and richly perfumed groves. A pair of lovers crowned with roses rushes forward. The wind that was cleft by Atalanta's course strikes the woman's throat and draws back her tunic. She and her companion have but a foot poised at the marble lip of the basin, the basin of *The Fountain of Love,* and, both of them hungering, their eyes blazing, they quench the thirst and desire of their lips at the magic cup borne by cupids, cupids flying or tumbling into the basin, their hands mingling, their fingers entwining, their wings dipping into the potion they offer. From the fountain water falls; from the basin vapor rises, and there are only cupids, cupids half-lost in the billows of vapor, cupids half-soaked in the spray, cupids streaming with light, cupids on whose backs the falling stream and the vaporous billows break in cascades, in droplets of pearls.[69]

First let us attend to Fragonard's painting, not to analyze it fully, but as a preliminary step in exploring how the Goncourts recreated Fragonard's representation. An allegorical mode of reading is signaled in action, figures, and surroundings. A pair of youthful lovers, seen in classic profile and antique drapery, approach an overflowing fountain. With transfixed eyes and open mouths they stand ready to drink from a cup offered by attending amors. The ritualistic overtones are clear; just as amors are both (Christian) angels and (pagan) cupids, so the offered cup suggests both the sacred chalice of the Mass—the chalice from which bride and groom drink at the nuptials—and the cup of love potions and magical draughts.

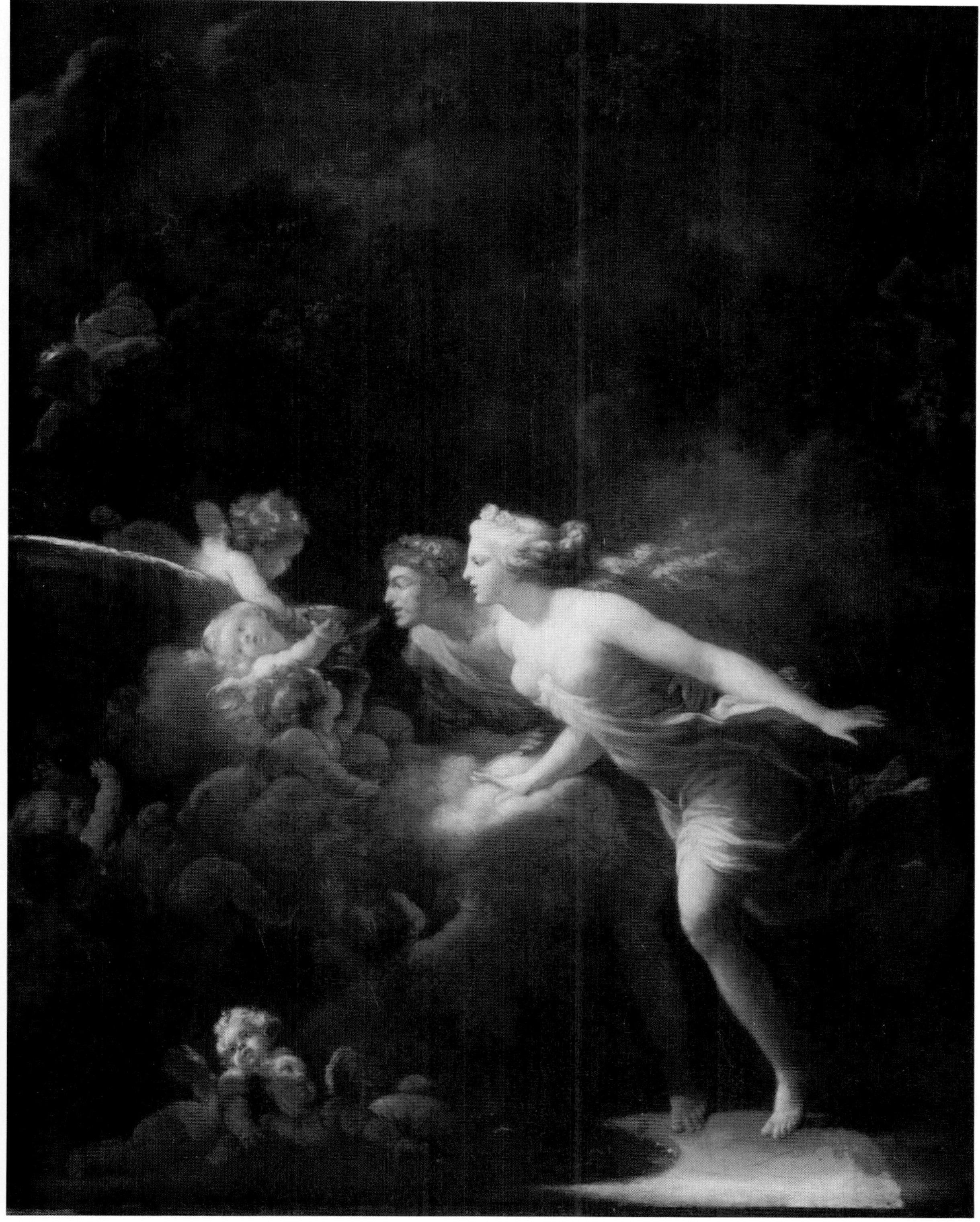

Figure 1 Jean-Honoré Fragonard, *The Fountain of Love,* c. 1780. Reproduced by permission of the Trustees, The Wallace Collection, London.

Ritual actions must be interpreted at a level beyond the literal one; and the suggestion of another meaning in Fragonard's painting is reinforced by the vaporous darkness, which removes the figures from a recognizable contemporary context (for example, a picturesque garden). That the allegory has erotic content is clear. The woman's bared breasts are made prominent—lifted and framed—her belly and navel are emphasized by the clinging transparent drapery, and her long, flowing tresses are adorned with a rose crown.[70]

The Fountain of Love, engraved by Regnault in 1785, belongs with several other allegories by Fragonard that draw upon the principal theme of classicizing erotica: rituals associated with the cult of Venus.[71] The image represents sexual union, or perhaps more precisely the moment of orgasm, in the context of sacred and antique ritual. Symbolic meanings that can be attached to the objects represented indicate as much: the fountain (especially the fountain of love) could in the eighteenth century be read as a conventional sign for the female sex, and the overflowing water as a sign for the seminal fluid called the *eau de vie.*[72] But more compelling than the symbolism of objects represented in *The Fountain of Love* is the display of both desire and satisfaction, for together these suggest a moment of consummation.

Desire is represented both by and in the two lovers who approach the fountain with their eyes focused on the cup. They have barely alighted at their destination; the woman's right leg is raised as if still in the process of moving, and her left heel has not yet touched the ground. Drapery and hair pushed back by the swift motion stream behind the figures. All these suggest great speed on one level and indicate the urgency of desire on another. As the couple leans forward, they seem rigid in their formal profile views and deliberate postures. Their bodies express a dynamic tension as motion in one direction—bodies surging forward—is held in check by an energetic movement in the other—hair and drapery flying behind. The tense, urgent, desiring lovers are set against the amorini who, sporting in the overflowing fountain, suggest release in their activities and arrangement. The head of one putto is thrown back in an ecstatic pose; another lies supine with legs splayed open; a third, like Io, is embraced and penetrated by the vaporous cloud. In contrast to the tension of the main figures, they fall into a gentle cascade down the picture plane and in their seemingly unplanned postures suggest the liberation or release of sexual tension.

Turning to the Goncourts' description, we can see how it recreates the effects of Fragonard's painting. Their prose also suggests an allegorical mode of reading, particularly in phrases such as "night of stormy mystery" *(une nuit de mystère d'orage)* and the "magic cup" *(la coupe enchantée)*. Casting the painting as a love allegory in antique dress, they evoke the mythical Atalanta, image of speed and seduction who, like the young woman represented, severed the wind with her onward course. The idea of sexual consummation is also implicit in the Goncourts' writing, and they use the quenching of thirst as a metaphoric equivalent. In picturing them as "hungering" *(affamés)*, in imagining how they "quench the thirst and desire of their lips" *(tendent la soif et le désir de leurs lèvres)*, the Goncourts recreate Fragonard's representation of the moment before longing is extinguished. The dynamic tension depicted in the painting is suggested by their descriptive language. For example, they place the image of the lovers rushing forward directly against that of the wind flinging back the woman's tunic. And as in Fragonard's painting, orgasmic release is suggested by the amors who immerse, even satiate, themselves in the fountain, "their hands mingling and their fingers entwining" *(mêlant leurs mains, croisant leurs doigts)*. Finally, the sensual atmosphere of *The Fountain of Love* is represented throughout the passage; the grove is heavily perfumed, the rain glistens with light, the vapor undulates, and the water breaks into pearly drops.[73]

The Fragonard Myth Examined

Wildenstein's 1960 *catalogue raisonné* exemplifies the tendency of modern scholars to rely on the Goncourts for facts rather than to appreciate their skill in recreating a painting. Wildenstein assured his readers that he strove for "pure objectivity" and that he would avoid those effusions so characteristic of other, unreadable Fragonard studies.[74] Blind even to the possibility of his own prejudice, Wildenstein proceeded to approach his subject with assumptions inherited from the Goncourts. Chapter 1, line 1 of his text reads, "Jean-Honoré Fragonard was born in Provence." The invocation of geography is followed by a reference to the Goncourts, who, in his opinion, admirably expressed what Fragonard owed to the Midi.[75] After adopting as fact the image of Fragonard skillfully constructed by the Goncourts, Wildenstein went on to ignore their suggestive recreations of Fragonard's paintings. In contrast to the Goncourts' interpretation of Fragonard as a poet, Wildenstein (like Portalis) pictured him as the eighteenth-century Courbet:

> Fragonard, to the great indignation of the art critics of his time, turned his back on antique and mythological subjects in order to produce what since Courbet has come to be called "living art." Thanks to him we have a picture of the life of his age, and ever since the eighteenth century this has been one reason for his success.[76]

Although Wildenstein's comment was probably meant to defend Fragonard's subject matter, the strategy was poorly chosen. Fragonard's suggestive fictions, cast in the conventional language of art, hardly qualify him as a Realist *avant le lettre.* More importantly, no painting is a simple and accurate mirror reflecting the times; no painting is innocent. As an artfully constructed representation, a painting can deny or affirm, exaggerate, understate, distort, or in other ways comment upon what it overtly depicts.

Since the publication of Wildenstein's catalogue, the tendency to view Fragonard in ways dictated by the nineteenth century has persisted. The most extravagant reassertion of the Goncourts' mythical Fragonard appeared in the catalogue of the 1980 Fragonard exhibition held in Tokyo: "Fragonard is the artist of the springtime of love, of the pleasures of the senses, of delight in life, in color and in beauty . . ." and "His love of pleasure is reflected in his work. . . ."[77] This second comment indicates that some have continued to read Fragonard through the Goncourts because they have absorbed nineteenth-century presuppositions about the relation between an art work and its maker.[78]

It is only because of unexamined prejudice that modern readers, like their eighteenth- and nineteenth-century predecessors, assume that an artist's personality is directly "reflected" in the art work. Although that assumption accords well with some twentieth-century myths about art as self-expression (for example, Kandinsky's "inner necessity"), neither approach can be maintained in light of recent thinking about the nature of representation. Because the artist bases the choice of subject and handling on factors that may not be known to the audience, it is necessary to acknowledge that the beliefs and prejudices of the real artist (the historical figure) may not be the same as those of the apparent one (the artist implied by the work).[79]

Apparent artists and real artists may or may not coincide in their beliefs, prejudices, stylistic preferences, and speed of execution. Peasant Breughel, Brouwer the Dutch Boor, and Fragonard, the Cherubino of erotic painting, are all apparent artists, not real ones. Taking the apparent artist for the real one, moreover, directs how we look at paintings. If we believe that Breughel was a simpleton painting his own, we are not apt to look for complex symbolic meanings in his work. And Fragonard's paintings will demonstrate nothing of aesthetic theory if we believe he was a freewheeling sensualist.

The idea that the artist's personality is "reflected" in his or her painting is a variant of the notion that aesthetic preferences are determined by temperament. Indeed, what here is called personality has often been designated by the term *temperament,* used to refer to both the proclivities of the specific individual (as in Fragonard's carefree temperament) and the general disposition shared by the people living in a particular geographical region (as in Fragonard's Provençal temperament).[80] As formulated by the writers quoted here, interpretations based on notions of personality or temperament are far from the insights that could be achieved through rigorously applying the techniques of psychoanalytic criticism. Personality and temperament are often loosely conceived and, in the case of Fragonard, have depended upon a superficial reading of his art works, a knowledge of his birthplace, or both.

Why, then, do explanations of personality and temperament continue to dominate analyses of Fragonard's art?[81] Is it simply that a causal relation between personality and art work is upheld in twentieth-century myths about self-expression? In the case of Fragonard there is another, perhaps unconscious, reason for embracing these explanations. Fragonard's temperament and personality were invoked by writers such as the Goncourts and Portalis in explaining his defection from academic history painting. Modern scholars have, I believe, followed suit because they also find distasteful the alternative suggested by the documentary evidence: that Fragonard worked for those who paid him. As a result we are presented with explanations such as this one: "The reasons for Fragonard's break with the Académie and official art remain unknown. Perhaps he valued his independence and the freedom it gave him to work according to his own rules."[82] The implication is that Fragonard left the Academy because his temperament was unsuited to its rigor. But contrary to wanting the freedom of his own rules, Fragonard readily adapted himself to those who paid him. His striking variety of subject matters and paint handlings suggests a willingness to conform to the task at hand rather than a stubborn attachment to personal preference.

Thus far we have considered only attitudes toward financial motivation, attitudes expressed by a diverse group of writers with differing ideological perspectives. But how can we assess those attitudes in view of what research has uncovered of the actual social and financial situations of artists? Our understanding of a painter's economic situation in the eighteenth century is still limited, but it is clear that painters either conceived, produced, and owned the unique object that was later sold to a patron, or they were commissioned to execute a work for a prearranged sum of money.[83] If they wanted their works mass-marketed, they could hire an engraver and specify by contractual arrangement who owned the plate and how many pulls were assigned to each party.[84] The mechanical skill that might lead others to label them artisans gave painters the power to live on their production.[85]

Because painters owned the art objects they made (as opposed to authors, who owned neither text nor books), their Academy could function both as a privilege system defining its members as an intellectual and social elite and as an institutional program of government patronage structured so that its members could make money from the sale of their works. Academic painters did work for the glory of French art, but they also worked to the specifications of a paying patron, the government. Government patronage, alas, was never dependable; and in the mid-eighteenth century the Academy looked elsewhere to encourage the arts. It opened its ranks to wealthy *amateurs,* who formed a cadre of private patrons, another buying public.[86] In seeking the support of private patrons, artists acted in a mode tacitly sanctioned by the Academy itself. Thus during the eighteenth century the Académie Royale provided both intellectual status and financial reward, ends theoretically incompatible.

Many academic artists received free lodging in the Louvre and some, like writers, were afforded sinecures and pensions. Most, however, depended on selling their works. If artists did not turn to private patrons, if they concentrated exclusively on the machines of history painting, they most likely could not expect the ten to twenty thousand livres that Darnton shows was provided yearly for the writer Suard, who rarely wrote.[87] Artists might produce at their own expense one or two large-scale history paintings every year and often had to depend on the government to buy them.[88] If this noble work was the only source of income, an artist might have financial difficulties. A major piece might bring only the twenty-four hundred livres that Fragonard was paid for four years of work on his *Coresus.*[89] And if Fragonard's experience was typical, the artist could wait as long as seven years for full payment.

Although the government had supported Fragonard as a student and awarded him lodging in the Louvre, it seems that it could not give him the financial incentive to produce other great Salon machines.[90] In 1765 Cochin, then secretary of the Academy, wrote repeatedly to the Marquis de Marigny to ask for some payment on the *Coresus,* which had been sent to Gobelins tapestry manufacture. Like Diderot, Cochin believed that the reputation of French painting depended on the talent of Fragonard, whom he characterized as "destined to uphold the glory of our school."[91] In arguing Fragonard's case, Cochin stressed that without the financial remuneration needed to sustain him the young artist would turn to minor, but saleable, works.[92] Cochin's pleadings were not enough to secure support for Fragonard, who was not paid in full until January 1, 1773. This experience discouraged the artist from working on government commissions; and even when asked to paint subjects of his own choosing, he neglected the projects.[93]

In the eighteenth century attitudes ran counter to practice. At the same time that writers and artists were making pronouncements about the evils of financial rewards, most were scrambling to earn their living through government stipends and/or private support. After his disappointing experience with official patronage, it seems that Fragonard declined to assume even the guise of high-mindedness. His reputation was damaged because most artists (and writers) wished to maintain the public front his actions too blatantly subverted. Here was an exceptionally talented artist, the author of an extraordinarily acclaimed history painting, the prime protégé of the Academy; and he was not upholding the necessary fictions. From the evidence, however, the interpreter can conclude that Fragonard was less motivated by greed than by the necessity of earning an income in a market not receptive to history painting on a monumental scale. He did what artists before him had always done: he worked for those who would pay him.

Fragonard found a ready market among the wealthy *amateurs* and financiers who regularly bought art, and he had made early contacts with those groups, meeting Bergeret de Grancourt while a student in Boucher's studio. His most important patron, the Abbé de Saint-Non, Fragonard encountered while a pensioner at the French Academy in Rome. The academic authorities completely approved of Fragonard's association with Saint-Non, for the *amateur,* learned in art and aesthetics, could both acquaint the young artist with the masterpieces of Italy and advise him on theoretical principles.[94] In view of Fragonard's early associations and in view of the general influence that *amateurs* wielded in the eighteenth-century Academy (for example, they often took over the task of lecturing to the students on the principles of art), it is hardly surprising that Fragonard should turn to them for support.[95] As he made his reputation, the artist attracted a larger buying public to his work. Fragonard's relation to that public was dynamic; if admirers sought after his paintings, Fragonard tuned his art to their desires.

Recent interpreters who continue to focus on temperament as the primary determinant of Fragonard's artistic career skew our understanding of the principles underlying his art. Recall the comment cited above: "The reasons for Fragonard's break with the Académie and official art remain unknown. Perhaps he valued his independence and the freedom it gave him to work according to his own rules." If Fragonard worked "according to his own rules," how was he understood, even by his contemporaries? It seems more likely that Fragonard worked within the codes of eighteenth-century art, especially as those codes were explicated in academic theory, and that he modified them according to his audience.

That Fragonard mastered the principles of academic art there can be no doubt, even though the tendency to underestimate the importance of an academic training in Fragonard's art has a long history. (Recall, for example, how Lenoir cited his inadequate training, his frivolous teachers, and his inability to master the difficulties of his art.) Examining the record we find that after winning the 1752 Prix de Rome with his *Jeroboam Sacrificing to the Idols* (Paris, Ecole des Beaux-Arts), Fragonard studied at the Ecole Royale des Elèves Protégés from May, 1753 until September, 1755. The school had been part of an effort to reform the Academy, to make its training more rigorous; and the curriculum included reading the great works of history and literature, copying the masterpieces in Paris collections, and drawing from models.[96] The six pupils allowed to attend the school at any given time worked closely with their professors.[97] During Fragonard's tenure these included Carle Van Loo and Michel Dandré-Bardon, whose *Traité de peinture* of 1765 provides a comprehensive exposition of the principles of painting as they were understood in the eighteenth century. Much of the treatise explained to the artist how to choose the formal properties that would produce the desired effect on the viewer. After his years with Van Loo and Dandré-Bardon, Fragonard completed his training with four years at the French Academy in Rome. It seems implausible that when Fragonard left academic history painting he rejected all his training and produced intuitive paintings that "reflected" his lighthearted temperament. More probably, what had become intuitive by then were the academic responses themselves.

Attitudes toward Fragonard; Attitudes toward the Rococo

As we have seen, some partisans of Fragonard continue to consider his work as the spontaneous outpourings of a lighthearted temperament. This argument has maintained its appeal in part because it accords well with attitudes among the general population of art historians toward rococo painting, attitudes that often devalue the rococo for just those qualities its admirers praise.[98] Although many sophisticated and intelligent readings of eighteenth-century art works are available, American students and budding scholars continue to learn about the insignificance of French painting during the reign of Louis XV. Many who become professional art historians never revise these early prejudices, which often lurk just below the surface even if an appreciation of the rococo is later acquired. Such attitudes are inculcated early by our art history survey books. Given that surveys typically simplify and distort all periods, it is the particular skew of the distortion that interests us here. In such texts the rococo is afforded a minimum of attention and is usually treated as the last gasp of the baroque, as a degeneration of previously virile forms. The argument smacks of Winckelmann and his cyclical view of art, but it has a more direct ancestry in the writing of Jacob Burckhardt, who generalized the term *rococo* and used it to describe the dissolution he saw in the late phases of all periods and styles. Rococo, in other words, was synonymous with degenerate. That this attitude toward the eighteenth-century rococo is still widespread in general assessments of painting will be evident from the following comments taken from the most recent editions of widely-used survey texts.[99]

About Boucher's painting, one scholar noted that " *powerful* Baroque curves are dissected into a multiplicity of *decorative* arabesques and Baroque drama *dissipates* into sensual playfulness" (emphasis added).[100] "Decorative," "sensual," and "playful" characterize the rococo style here, but these terms are qualified negatively by the use of the word "dissipates." A similar analysis marks a discussion of Clodion's rococo style in another survey text. Clodion is coquettish, his art a "miniature Baroque," a "playful dissolution" of the "ecstasies of Bernini and Puget."[101] Taken alone, "coquettish," "miniature," and "playful" are not necessarily pejorative; however, the term "dissolution" here provides the negative twist. A third survey text includes this assessment:

> In European cultural history the eighteenth century is a unique period in that it did not produce a single figure in the visual arts to rank with the universal masters of previous epochs. The seventeenth century can boast Caravaggio, Bernini, Borromini, Rubens, Rembrandt, Vermeer, and Velazquez, all artists of the highest stature. . . . Paradoxically it [the eighteenth century] was a period of intense creative activity, with countless artists of talent, many delightful, yet all limited. Nothing completely new was created except the Rococo style, and even that was a lighthearted version of Baroque grandiloquence.[102]

As conceived here, the eighteenth century *is* a unique period in the history of art; it is the only period in which the author has not seen fit to designate a master as "universal." It is prudent to remember that "universal master" (like genius) is a culturally determined category, and the selection of those artists one places in this category varies from age to age and writer to writer. For example, Bernini and Borromini were not always considered "universal masters," as a reading of the eighteenth-century classicist critics (Winckelmann, for example) will confirm.[103]

Conceived as a degenerate (or lighthearted) version of the baroque, rococo painting has been compared negatively to both the baroque painting that preceded it and the neoclassical painting that followed it. And these comparisons are dominated by a bipolar contrast in which rococo paintings are perceived to have qualities traditionally associated with the feminine; they are called personal, frivolous, diminutive, decorative, lighthearted. Although baroque and neoclassical paintings might be vastly different from one another, in comparison to rococo works they both are designated as public, meaningful, heroic, vigorous, powerful—masculine.[104] This prejudice against what is conceived as feminine even finds its way into the writing of those who would support Boucher, Pompadour, and French rococo painting. One partisan has noted, "Boucher's art suggests an interpretation of the world of Louis XV and the court which is only partially true. It was not all frills; it was a *manly* place" (emphasis added).[105] From there he goes on to describe hunting (a prototypically male preoccupation) and painters who depicted trophies of the hunt. Clearly the writer implies that the frills (read frivolity) belong to the feminine side of the rococo, and that there is another, more weighty component that is masculine.

What I am getting at here is that any revision of Fragonard is complicated by the attitudes toward the rococo held by many art historians (including some specialists in the eighteenth century) and perpetuated in textbooks used to introduce students to art history. But even more than the prejudices cited above, there is another assumption about painting that has made it especially difficult to undertake a rigorous study of rococo art in general and Fragonard's painting in particular. That assumption locates the meaning and importance of a painting in "significant" subject matter. Consider this recent comment on Boucher's *Triumph of Venus* (1740; Stockholm: National Museum) taken from a survey text written by a prominent scholar of nineteenth-century painting:

> It would be futile to look for a profound meaning in the picture; attitudes and gestures aim at little more than seductively exposing the bodies of barely nubile young women. Indeed, the lack of significant subject matter is compensated by the lighthearted eroticism.[106]

The two sentences imply two sets of equivalences: profound meaning equals significant subject matter, and seductively exposing the bodies of barely nubile young women equals lighthearted eroticism. We might rewrite the statement: It is futile to look for a profound meaning in Boucher's painting because it lacks (what I would consider) a significant subject. Instead of a significant subject, Boucher has represented the seductive bodies of barely nubile young women, which is (to me) lighthearted eroticism. Leaving aside the implications of the second equivalence and the meaning that a feminist critic might find there, consider the implications of the first one, the association of profound meaning with significant subject.

The contention that a painting's meaning is primarily located in its subject matter (that is, in the story or object depicted) remains a common assumption of many interpreters, even though it has been challenged on various fronts. Art historians have been particularly interested in the analysis of subject matter ever since Panofsky laid down its theoretical principles. In his essay on iconography and iconology, subject matter was defined as the part of painting that carried meaning, and certain kinds of subjects—narratives and allegories drawn from literary sources—seemed especially meaningful because they were best suited to Panofsky's method.[107] Naive or literal-minded readings of Panofsky that locate meaning entirely within the story or object depicted have quite obviously discouraged the serious consideration of much rococo painting, which because of its overt subject is determined to be frivolous or insignificant even before it is analyzed.

Several major studies of French eighteenth-century art have recently opened the way to new methods of looking at, thinking about, and interpreting the rococo. To name some of these: Michael Fried's *Absorption and Theatricality: Genre and Beholder in the Age of Diderot,* 1980; Norman Bryson's *Word and Image: French Painting of the Ancien Régime,* 1981; Marion Hobson's *The Object of Art: The Theory of Illusion in Eighteenth-Century France,* 1982; and Thomas Crow's *Painters and Public Life in Eighteenth-Century Paris,* 1985.[108] These texts have not only replaced eighteenth-century French art into appropriate social, political, and critical contexts, they have also expanded the range of meanings that can be discerned in rococo painting. Looking beyond ostensible subject, these scholars have asked questions about marketplace, audience, codes of representation, self-referentiality, and ideological meaning. In short, they have cleared an area for a re-evaluation of rococo painting based on new assumptions about the nature of representation. Within this area we will mark out a path for reexamining Fragonard, a path that will lead us from his academic triumph through those paintings that thematize art and eroticism.

1 *The Academic Ideal Represented*

The High Priest Coresus Sacrificing Himself to Save Callirhoe and the Demands of History Painting

Of all Fragonard's paintings, the one most praised by his contemporaries was executed to secure his associate membership in the Academy and was exhibited in 1765 as *The High Priest Coresus Sacrificing Himself to Save Callirhoe* (figure 2). The scene is set within a shadowy, smoke-filled temple. To the surprise and horror of all gathered there, the high priest has plunged a dagger into his own heart rather than slay the intended victim. Callirhoe lies in a faint, the acolytes stare in disbelief, the onlookers gape and tremble. Contemporary reports assure us that Fragonard's painting was a sensation in 1765 when Salon viewers stood transfixed before it. Among those captivated by the *Coresus* was Diderot, who opined that no other painter in Europe could have invented anything so sublime.[1] The response of public and critic concurred with that of the Academy, which had judged this display piece prior to its public exhibition.[2] Receiving Fragonard with "a unanimity and applause rarely seen," the academicians officially recognized the young artist's mastery of narrative history painting.[3]

In a prevailing atmosphere of concern over the highest genre's fate, the presentation and exhibition of Fragonard's *Coresus* were dramatic events. By the middle of the eighteenth century many French academicians and critics believed that history painting languished. Some (Diderot, for example) blamed its decline on the *amateurs* who commissioned only works in the lesser genres. Others had related explanations. La Font de

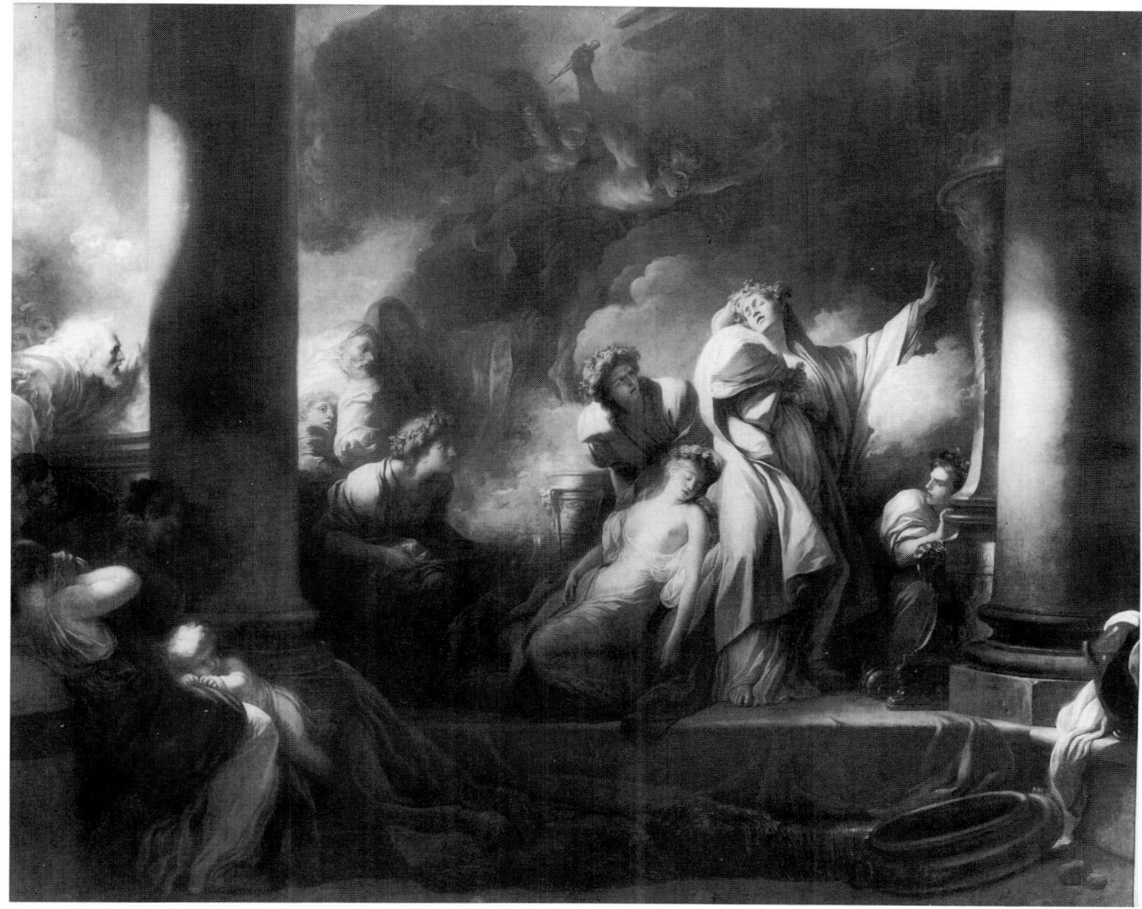

Figure 2 Jean-Honoré Fragonard, *The High Priest Coresus Sacrificing Himself to Save Callirhoe*, Salon of 1765. Paris, Musée du Louvre. Cliché des Musées Nationaux, Paris.

Saint-Yenne, for example, noted that the fashion for setting oversized mirrors in rococo interiors left no room for large-scale history paintings.[4] Academic officials believed that the level of student training had fallen, and so the Ecole Royale des Elèves Protégés was founded in 1748 to prepare the most promising students, the Prix de Rome winners, for the intricacies of history painting.

Fragonard's *Coresus* impressed its audience because it was so unlike those mythologies by Boucher or Lagrenée that signaled to many the highest genre's imminent demise. First of all, the work was conceived and executed on a monumental scale; in comparison with the average size of a reception piece, the dimensions of Fragonard's *Coresus* were extraordinarily large.[5] Equally impressive was the scale of the grand figures with their expansive, operatic gestures. In this they suggest the work of earlier French history painters, perhaps Jean Jouvenet who by 1765 represented superior achievement in that genre. Also reminiscent of works by Jouvenet is the emotional tenor of the *Coresus,* where figures express the more violent passions with a dramatic intensity alien to contemporaneous painting.[6] The much remarked upon handling of light and dark helped raise the emotive faces and gestures to the sublime by endowing the *Coresus* with an eerie, preternatural quality. Shrouded in an aura of mystery and raised to an intense emotional pitch, Fragonard's *Coresus* still seems as singular as it did to Diderot, whose canny recreation of Fragonard's painting remains a showpiece of his Salon criticism.

Although Fragonard's reception piece diverged from contemporaneous history paintings, it also shared with them the basic principles of the genre. To practice the highest genre required erudition, or book learning, because history paintings were textually based; painters were not free to create their own stories but were obliged to illustrate one already known.[7] This restriction developed because painters could show only an instant of an action's duration, and unless the story were already familiar, viewers could not easily fill in the surrounding events or imagine the inner thoughts of a character. How closely a history painter should adhere to the particulars of the text, however, was a matter of debate. Although *littérateurs* such as Félibien or Du Bos were apt to favor an exacting accuracy, by the middle of the eighteenth century many academic theorists argued otherwise. Cochin, for example, contended that a slavish following of the literary text led to pedantry, and he claimed for the painter poetic license, pointing out that a beautiful piece of literature was never rejected because it did not exactly conform to history.[8] Both the poet and the history painter deviated from a source to express more effectively the meaning of a story or event as it was known to the public. Thus, by the middle of the eighteenth century many, like Cochin, conceived of the history painting less as an illustration of a narrative than as a version of it.

When Fragonard represented the tragedy of Coresus and Callirhoe, he represented a story with a classical pedigree. Among the ancient writers, Pausanias recounted the events in conjunction with his description of a sanctuary dedicated to Dionysos and named Calydonian because the god's image had been brought there from Calydon. The cult statue stimulated Pausanias' imagination and inspired him to tell of what it witnessed at distant Calydon, where Coresus, a priest of Dionysos, was enamored of a young girl, Callirhoe, who could only despise him. Unable to change her resolution, the angry priest appealed to his god, and Dionysos responded by striking the Calydonians mad. The unhappy people learned from an oracle that the madness would abate only after Coresus sacrified either Callirhoe or someone in her stead. But Callirhoe found no one to take her place, and

> when the preparations for the sacrifice had been made as the oracle of Dodona had directed, the damsel was brought like a victim to the altar, and Coresus stood ready to offer the sacrifice; but, yielding to the impulse of love rather than of anger, he slew himself instead of her, thus giving proof of the most unfeigned affection that ever was heard of. But when Callirhoe saw Coresus lying dead, she repented, and touched with pity for him and shame at her own treatment of him, she cut her throat at the spring which is in Calydon not far from the harbour, and which has been called Callirhoe after her ever since.[9]

The story of Coresus and Callirhoe was not a subject familiar to eighteenth-century artists; indeed, there are few, if any, known paintings of the theme before Fragonard's famous work.[10] It is not clear if the young artist chose the subject of this first reception piece or if it was assigned to him by the Academy.[11] In either case, however, the general purposes and expectations of such a work allow us to speculate why a novel theme might have been selected. We can think of the preliminary *morceau de reception* as a test in which the artist had to demonstrate a mastery of both art and genre by representing adequately a specific subject. Certain subjects were difficult to execute, and these fell at two extremes: those well known to painting and those unknown to it. A subject known through famous examples by recognized masters might present a direct competition too imposing for a student's first presentation piece.[12] On the other hand, when no examples of the subject were available, the candidate's task was difficult but not overwhelming. With the literary text as a guide, the student had to be resourceful in imagining and inventing the work—in selecting the moment, visualizing it, and choosing the means to portray it. Because there were no obvious pictorial precedents, the artist would be forced to find models in other themes that could be adapted to new purposes, and this process would further try the imaginative powers.[13]

If the story of Coresus and Callirhoe was a new subject for painters, it was not unknown to the educated public. Trying to capitalize on the growing taste for travel literature, the Abbé Gedoyn had translated Pausanias into French in 1731, and editions appeared throughout the century.[14] Theater audiences were also familiar with the story through Antoine de La Fosse's 1702 tragedy *Coresus et Callirhoé* and André-Cardinal Destouches' 1712 opera *Callirhoé* (libretto by Pierre-Charles Roy). In the streets the theme was burlesqued by Lesage in the second act of his 1713 *Arlequin, roi de Serendib*.[15] Encouraged by Fragonard's "theatrical" presentation of the theme, many interpreters have tried to locate the "source" for his *Coresus* in one or the other of these works.[16] Neither stage performance, however, was available to Fragonard between 1761 and 1764 when he conceived the painting, and in neither of them did the scene Fragonard depicted appear.[17] Coresus does not stab himself on stage in La Fosse's tragedy, but the audience hears of the suicide in a *récit*. Destouches' Callirhoe goes to the sacrificial altar with her lover, Agenor, and after Coresus' unexpected self-sacrifice, the two sing a duet while Dionysos arrives with his retinue.[18] More important than demonstrating that neither of these stage performances was copied by Fragonard, however, is the observation that to take the *Coresus* as a portrait (free or exact) of a theatrical performance is to confuse a mode of representation (the theatrical) with a subject represented (a specific scene from a specific play). We will return to this issue of theatricality after a close reading of the painting.

The Expressive Moment Portrayed: Fragonard and the Legacy of Timanthes

Like La Fosse's tragedy and Destouches' opera, Fragonard's painting embroidered the basic story found in Pausanias' text, but unlike those versions, it did so by framing a single narrative moment. The importance of the moment in narrative painting stemmed from the conflict between the nature of the subject (an action) and the nature of the medium. Actions occur in time and assume movement or change; paintings depend on the arrangement of static forms in spatial configurations.[19] In selecting the instant just after Coresus plunged the dagger into his breast, Fragonard chose a moment appropriate to the spatiality of painting, for it allowed him to represent a variety of related actions and responses occuring simultaneously. His choice was more than appropriate, it was classic.[20]

French academic theory had traditionally stressed not only that the painter had a single instant in which to show all and make all understandable but also that the favorable moment was to be an expressive one.[21] Fragonard's *Coresus* spotlights that expressive moment by referring to a controversial eighteenth-century example: the *Sacrifice of Iphigenia* (1757, Potsdam: Sanssouci New Palace; figure 3), executed by Carle Van Loo, Fragonard's teacher at the Ecole Royale. Indeed, we can conjecture that the tragedy of Coresus and Callirhoe was chosen from the stock of unrepresented themes because of its obvious similarities to the story of Iphigenia.[22]

The two share the basic motif of the imminent sacrifice of a young girl forestalled by an unforeseen event. In the one it is the intervention of

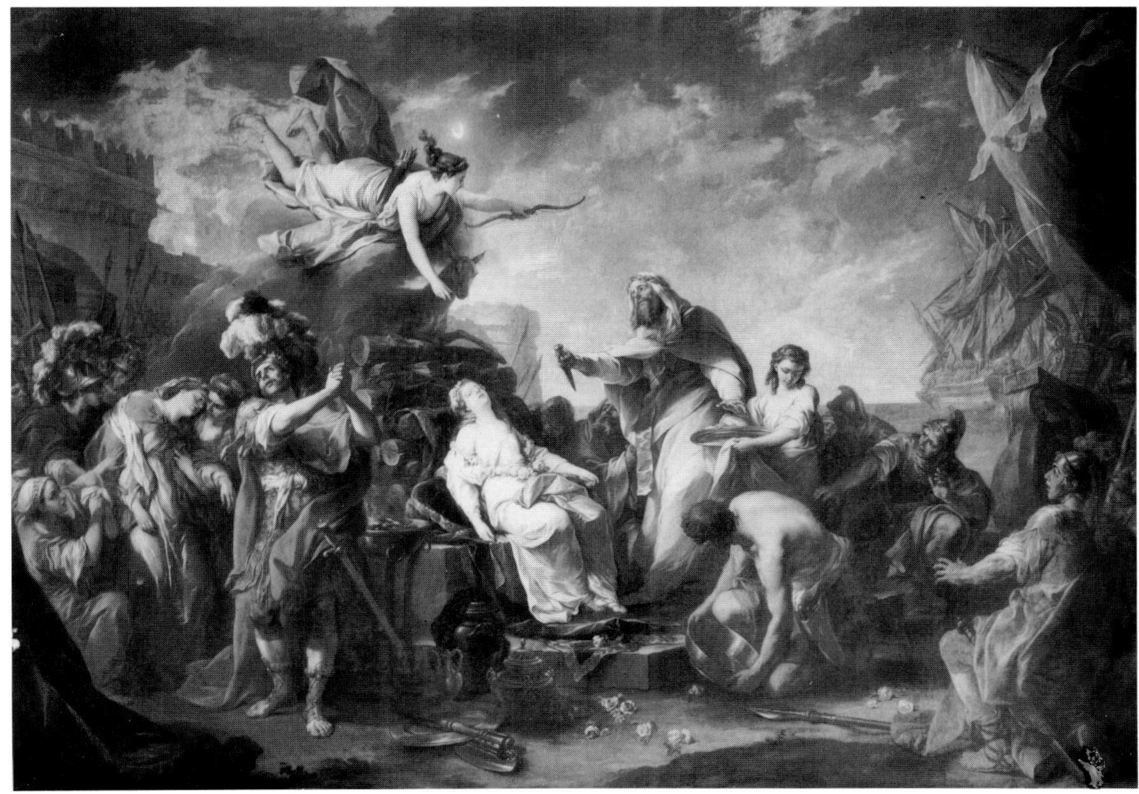

Figure 3 Carle Van Loo, *The Sacrifice of Iphegenia*, 1759. Potsdam, Sanssouci.

a goddess, in the other the suicide of a priest. Although Diana's sudden appearance in the Iphigenia story is miraculous where the suicide of Coresus is tragic, the *génie infernal* surging ominously over the events in Fragonard's scene substitutes for the goddess Diana, who soars heroically across Van Loo's canvas. Fragonard's Callirhoe, however, is herself the most significant quotation from Van Loo. Not only does her attitude imitate that of Iphigenia (knees bent, head turned to one side, arms limp and hanging), but also her faint, described neither in Pausanias' text nor in the two eighteenth-century stage productions of the theme, evokes Van Loo's passive figure.[23] But in referencing Van Loo's much-discussed composition, Fragonard's *Coresus* also references a whole range of paintings that critical thinking associated with that work.

French artists, writers, and critics had been continually interested in the Iphigenia theme during the hundred years preceding Van Loo's work, and this interest was sparked by the ancients' accounts of the inventive painter Timanthes.[24] His lost *Iphigenia*, known through literary texts, exemplified the expressive moment and raised the issue of the artist's ability to invent adequate responses for the characters. Pliny recorded that Timanthes represented the *Sacrifice of Iphigenia* with all onlookers shown in various stages of grief. The face of Agamemnon, however, he veiled: "Having thus exhausted every presentment of grief, he has veiled the face of her father for which he had reserved no adequate expression."[25] In the *Orator* Cicero imbedded his account of Timanthes in a discussion of decorum, concluding that "it was quite impossible to represent such grief as his [Agamemnon's] with a paint brush."[26] And Quintilian cited Timanthes within a discussion of the orator's ability to invent creative solutions to aesthetic dilemmas:

> the artist had depicted an expression of grief on the face of Calchas and of still greater grief on that of Ulysses, while he had given Menelaus an agony of sorrow beyond which his art could not go. Having exhausted his powers of emotional expression, he was at a loss to portray the father's face as it deserved and solved the problem by veiling his head and leaving his sorrow to the spectator.[27]

Although for the ancients (in particular, Quintilian) Timanthes might have been an example of *ingenium,* French writers found that their accounts allowed for several possible readings: (1) that the representation of Agamemnon's grief was above the means of Timanthes' art; (2) that the representation of such grief was above the means of all art; it could only be suggested to spectators who could then represent it in their imaginations; (3) that extreme grief, especially that of a king, could not be represented decorously. There was another interpretation available from the ancients, as well, for Eustathius had suggested that Timanthes veiled Agamemnon in emulation of Homer, who had used the device to describe the grief of Priam.

The argument that Timanthes covered Agamemnon's head in order to preserve decorum was not emphasized in France, even in the seventeenth century when the classical tradition stressed the observation of *bienséance.*[28] Early in the eighteenth century Du Bos, who believed that art should arouse the emotions of the spectator, explained that Timanthes covered the face of Agamemnon to help the audience appreciate the excess of feeling. Comparing Timanthes' work to Poussin's *Death of Germanicus* (c. 1627; Minneapolis: Minneapolis Institute of Art), he wrote:

> Poussin was able to use the idea of the Greek painter [Timanthes] who had represented Agamemnon with veiled head at the sacrifice of Iphigenia in order to better convey the excess of grief of the victim's father. Poussin was able to use this feature to express the same thing by representing Agrippina who hides her face with her hands in the painting of the death of Germanicus.[29]

Later eighteenth-century writers particularly stressed what moved the spectator, and in 1745 Dézallier d'Argenville again compared Poussin with Timanthes as he described how Leonardo, in painting his *Last Supper* (1495–98; Milan: Sta. Maria delle Grazie), might have expressed the utter hideousness of Judas:

> He [Leonardo] should have readily followed the Greek painter Timanthes, who, in the *Sacrifice of Iphigenia* unable to express her father Agamemnon's grief, covered his face in order *to allow it to be inferred by the spectator* [emphasis added]. So must a painter who is a great poet proceed. Poussin has done as much in the *Death of Germanicus*.[30]

Dézallier, and to a lesser extent Du Bos, exemplify the eighteenth-century reading of the Timanthes story as a lesson in evoking viewer response. Because both writers wanted to praise Poussin, who followed Timanthes, they interpreted the ancient precedent in a favorable way, stressing that veiling Agamemnon would increase the expressive power of the work by activating the viewer's participation. However, those who wanted to vaunt the *Sacrifice of Iphigenia* executed by Carle Van Loo had to read the Timanthes story differently because Van Loo displayed to the spectator Agamemnon's response. In commending Van Loo, the suggestive power of Timanthes' device would have to be ignored in favor of explanations that called up other ideas present in French theory.[31]

One of these relied on the notion that the ability to invent superior expressions indicated natural talent raised to its highest power because expression could not be taught by the rules of art. By midcentury expression was associated with genius in Watelet's *L'Art de peindre* (1760) and Dandré-Bardon's *Traité de peinture* (1765), and both authors described it as the "poetic" part of invention. The importance of expression led Caylus to establish in 1759 a prize that would encourage young painters to concentrate on developing this crucial aspect of their art. The first competition took place in 1759. Dandré-Bardon selected the topic of admiration mixed with joy. Academicians believed that the mixed emotions presented a more difficult problem because they required that one passion be nuanced by another, that closely related passions be differentiated, or that opposing emotional states be reconciled.[32] In relation to the Iphigenia theme, the problem of rendering Agamemnon lay in the mixed character of his expression. In the interpretation of many French critics, Fréron, for example, Timanthes simply lacked the art for so difficult a task and despaired of expressing Agamemnon's grief. Fréron found Van Loo more admirable for rendering with success what Timanthes did not dare to do.[33]

Although some writers suggested that Van Loo's solution simply indicated the superiority of his "genius," others believed that his treatment was more appropriate to painting. This second argument did not assume that Timanthes was deficient in expressive power but rather that he wanted to be true to his literary source, which the French took to be Euripides (not Homer). Although suited to a written or spoken text, Agamemnon's veil seemed absurd in painting where the language of the passions could always be displayed. Here is the Comte de Caylus' analysis of Timanthes' device:

> This procedure so praised by the orators and by the poets, and whose application can be, in effect, very useful to rhetoric and poetry, seems to me a contradiction in painting and, if I dare say it, an absurdity. Each passion has its expression and its language, but its nuances are infinite and these nuances, most of which are inaccessible to rhetoric and poetry because language is more suited to express the opinions of the mind [*vues de l'esprit*] than to render the movements of the soul, have, in painting, resources and means that no artist will ever be able to exhaust.[34]

Several important characteristics of the expressive moment emerge from reading eighteenth-century discussions of Timanthes and criticism of Van Loo's *Iphigenia*. Although artists selected their moments from texts, they were free to imagine them in a way appropriate to a spatial art. Strong or complex emotions were not to be avoided either because they broke decorum or because they were beyond the means of art. On the contrary, the ability to portray strong or mixed emotions was a mark of the artist's genius. And finally, when expression was suppressed (as in the case of Timanthes, Leonardo, or Poussin), it was justified as more easily engaging the imagination of the spectator and insuring an active participation in the work of art.

Fragonard's *Coresus*

Because it renders an expressive moment with all figures responding to a central event, Fragonard's *Coresus* belongs to the class of images that includes Van Loo's *Iphigenia,* Poussin's *Germanicus*, Leonardo's *Last Supper*, and the lost painting of Timanthes to which they were related. In the *Coresus*, however, all the spectators were imagined by Fragonard; for Pausanius, unlike Euripides, neither indicated who (if anyone) witnessed the event nor described any immediate responses to it. The inclusion of spectators suggests that Fragonard altered the scene to meet the demands of the expressive moment, a moment of action and response, conceived in a way appropriate to painting.[35] Fragonard thus places himself within a tradition, inviting comparison (but not direct competition) with those earlier paradigms. His *Coresus* is most closely related to Van Loo's *Iphigenia,* not only because the figure of Callirhoe references that of Van Loo, but also because Fragonard's solution exemplifies the aesthetic premises of history painting in the mid-eighteenth century.

The moment chosen by Fragonard posed problems of expression similar to those faced by an artist who rendered the *Sacrifice of Iphigenia*. For example, each had to show variations of the same emotion. In the traditional theme the challenge was to show different degrees of grief varied according to a character's relationship to Iphigenia, and mixed with other psychological states (Agamemnon expressed the grief of a father and the nobility of a king). In the *Coresus* Fragonard imagined that each spectator showed some mingling of surprise and fear, which were combined in different proportions according to age, sex, and rank. For example, the young women in the foreground shrink from the spectacle, while the older priest in the background expresses surprise, in an expansive and dignified revision of Le Brun's conventional pose. This differentiation was handled in accord with the academic law of *convenance*, which legislated that actions and gestures be appropriate to the character making them. As a general principle, *convenance* applied to all aspects of the work (drawing, color, brushwork, light effects, disposition, etc.) and tried to guarantee that the "truth" of nature (and not only the artist's manner) was expressed in the painted forms.[36]

It was the compelling and "truthful" nuancing of the mixed emotion combined with effective contrast that so impressed Diderot:

> Everything denotes sadness and fright. . . . Those two old priests, whose cruel looks have feasted so often on the steam of the blood with which they have watered the altars, have not been able to refrain from expressing sorrow, empathy, fright; they pity the unfortunate priest, they suffer, they are frightened. This woman by herself, leaning against one of the columns, seized with horror and fright, suddenly recoils, and this other one, who had her back against a stone, is also thrown over, one of her hands covers her eyes and her other arm seems to repel this frightening spectacle away from her.[37]

Fragonard's onlookers, who express fright and surprise in various ways, exemplify for the real audience the range of emotions that might be felt while contemplating the painted spectacle; at the same time, their expressive presence encourages the viewer to participate in the scene. Eighteenth-century writers (Du Bos, for example) discussed how viewers responded to represented events as if they were real. This response was not provoked because they mistook artifice for reality but because artificial passions were excited within them by the contemplation of artificial events.[38] There was thus an analogy between modes of response; real objects provoked real responses as artificial objects provoked artificial ones. In terms of Van Loo's *Iphigenia* and Fragonard's *Coresus*, the arousal of artificial emotions helped the artist bridge the gap between viewer and painting. The degrees of grief represented in the *Iphigenia* intensify until they climax in the figure of Agamemnon. The relationship established among the represented responses (that is, within the artificial) is one of proportion, and so viewers can position their artificial responses to the event represented (as well as their response to the responses) on the continuum displayed. In allowing viewers to place themselves on the emotional scale, the artist facilitates their identification with and projection into the fictive world of the painting.[39] The same principle operates in Fragonard's *Coresus* where the most intense emotion is figured in the dying priest.

In addition to the proportional relation that rules the expressions in Fragonard's *Coresus*, the variety of types (different ages, ranks, and sexes) combined with their anonymity encourages the real beholder's identification with the painted counterparts, many of which seem more like outside observers than characters in the story. The association of real and painted viewers is suggested by the stationing of some internal spectators outside the main scene, which is demarcated by two painted boundaries (the massive columns and platform edge) and one real one (the top of the canvas).[40] These outsiders are enchained in a virtual S-curve that begins at the baby on the woman's knee, passes through the darkened forms behind her, and extends to the lighted figure leaning over the altar. Although he reaches toward the main scene, he does not appear to enter it; he touches (or appears to touch) the column just where a crescent of light completes the curve by leading away from the main action. Thus the painting implies three levels of viewers: those directly in the scene framed by the columns, those outside the columns but in the picture, and those standing outside the picture (the Salon audience).

Among the surrogate viewers held apart from the main scene, two appear more important than the rest. The first is the old man who reaches toward the interior space. Intensely lit and sensuously colored, he has a key place in the composition, which is structured into a grid of horizontals and verticals by elaborate framing devices. The strongest edges are the vertical columns and the horizontal step. These are varied in adjacent serpentine patterns that converge on the old man at the left side of the canvas. One undulation is defined by the figural group enchained together outside the left column; the chiaroscuro complements this effect as the heads of the figures are woven around an arc of light that moves up the canvas. The viewer's interest is thus attracted to the old man, and he begins another implied line that dances above the straight step in a serpentine path across the picture plane. Directing attention toward Coresus, the points on this virtual line are a series of heads seen (primarily) in profile: the old man as he looks into the scene, the priest with his head on a second priest's shoulder, the acolytes, and the kneeling youth. Thus the pivotal point of a compositional order is established by the old man; he is the surrogate spectator who responds to the events, who reaches toward them, but who can never violate the columnar frame that separates him from what he witnesses. Although his position is like that of the real viewer (responding to, yet apart from, the events), the beholder need not imagine his response; it is fully and expertly displayed.

A second important surrogate viewer is in pointed contrast to the old man. A young woman with a child on her knee, she crouches in the darkened foreground, covering her face and leaning away from the main event. Although the perspective is not rigorously constructed (figures or objects mask most of the critical junctures between planes), a few elements do suggest that the viewer take a position near her. Because the base of the column on the left side of the painting is seen from straight on and the base of the column on the right side from an angle, the viewer is encouraged to see the main scene from the left. This position is emphasized by the prominent diagonal axis of the composition established through the figure of Callirhoe and raised hand of Coresus. Thus the viewers are placed near the woman who covers her face, and like her, they see the scene from below. The young woman, moreover, recalls the Poussin-Timanthes tradition discussed by Dézallier d'Argenville. Like Poussin's Agrippina at the deathbed of Germanicus, she covers her face with a handkerchief; however, she does not hide her facial expression because she is closely related to the intended victim and hence suffers inexpressible anguish. A character added by Fragonard, this woman emulates those covered figures who stimulate the viewer's imagination and encourage projection into the painting.

Although she is shadowed in the foreground, the woman's importance in the composition is announced by her coordination with the other parts of the work. She is one of the set points—the other two being the *génie* overhead and the conspicuous urn in the right corner—from which the composition spreads out in a pyramidal shape (a practice prescribed by academic theory).[41] In addition, the woman in the left corner participates in several triangles inscribed within the major one; these connect her to the principal group and find their highest point at Coresus' head. As a surrogate viewer this woman is integrated into the composition not only because of her placement but also because she unites in her form certain aspects of the central figures. Leaning back with knees bent, she echoes the configuration of Callirhoe, and her strongly lit elbow answers that of Coresus. Surely Fragonard used such analogies to harmonize the whole composition more effectively. But the comparison also suggests a more complex role for the figure. Her gesture signals the viewer to imagine her facial expression; but in covering her face, in closing her external eyes, could she not also be portrayed as imagining?

The type of the imagining figure is similar to that of the veiled one; in each the eyes are covered. Fragonard, for example, drew the artist as an imagining figure who places his hand over his eyes in order to see floating before him the images that would inspire his work (i.e., *The Inspiration of the Painter*, Léon Genon Collection). The woman in Fragonard's *Coresus* imagines the feelings and torments of the main figures, and she betrays her identification with their dilemma in her bodily posture. This reading accords with a common academic idea: Dandré-Bardon wrote that elegant repetitions of gestures and movements worked to produce marvellous effects when they were adapted to characters who shared a similar intention, interest, or passion.[42] The paralleling of form suggests that the woman is experiencing empathetically the same feelings as the central characters. The real viewers who identify with this surrogate are then doubly projected into the painting; they imagine themselves both spectator and actor at the same moment.

If the painting's subsidiary characters encourage the viewer to imaginatively empower its emotions, the direct expression of extreme states was reserved by Fragonard for his principals, beginning with Coresus shown in the throes of death. Choosing the suicide as the most significant event, Fragonard formed Coresus, Callirhoe, and the acolyte into what academic theory called the principal group. The highest light falls brilliantly on Coresus' white robe, and it falls vertically as Dandré-Bardon had instructed.[43] The asymmetrical counterposing of the figures is accentuated by the contrast between bright and dark masses across the pictorial field, and this masterful light effect securely establishes Coresus' prominence. Responding to this figure one critic wrote in the *Mercure de France*, "one discerns at a glance the faintness, the pallor, and the first horrors of death painting themselves on Coresus' face in the instant that he has just struck himself."[44] But for Coresus, the moment of death is a moment of mixed passion because he is dying for love, and love also demands its expression.[45]

The mixture of love and death is presented by Fragonard as an orgasmic loss of consciousness, and he quotes Bernini's *Ecstasy of St. Theresa* (1645–52; Rome: Sta. Maria della Vittoria, Cornaro Chapel) in his figure of the high priest. Not only do the voluminous, agitated drapery of Coresus and the smoke surrounding him recall Bernini's presentation of the mystic saint, but with head thrown back, eyes closed, lips parted, Coresus mimics Theresa's expression in her ecstatic union with God. We can suppose that Coresus, too, is united with his god, a god who would be quieted only by human sacrifice.

Since the eighteenth century, observers have remarked that Coresus and his acolytes are decidedly androgynous, and it is through this blurring of sexual difference that the god and his devotees are conflated. There was a tradition of representing Dionysos, the dying god through whom the earth is renewed, as androgynous. Greek artists in the late classical period showed him as a beautiful, refined young man, fleshy and wide-hipped in certain renderings. Vasari described Michelangelo's *Bacchus* as a figure that showed "a marvellous blending of limbs, uniting the slenderness of a youth with the fleshy roundness of the female."[46] That Fragonard had in mind to represent the god at the sacrifice is indicated in an earlier version of the *Coresus* (Angers: Musée des Beaux-Arts), which includes a statue of Dionysos. In that earlier conception Coresus is an old priest, not unlike Van Loo's Calchas. In other sketches and in the final version, the old priest is replaced by a young, androgynous Coresus, and the figure of Dionysos is removed. We should recall that Dionysos is important to the story not only because he demands the sacrifice, but also because it is his statue that both witnessed the events in Calydon and provoked Pausanias' retelling of them. The reference to Dionysos is preserved as Fragonard's painting invokes him in the androgynous, ecstatic, self-sacrificing priest.

Callirhoe's emotional state is unquestionably the counterpart to that of Coresus, and hers is an expressive act that silences expression. A single point of rest in a composition saturated with emotions, Callirhoe is also an extreme of emotion against which every other expression can be played. It is not that the figure is inexpressive, as some contemporary critics had it, but that her unconscious state both veils and implies other more demonstrative responses to the event.[47] The viewer is left to imagine how she looked before her faint, when she feared her impending death, and what emotion her face betrayed when she realized the significance of Coresus' actions.

The contrast of the two central figures is further developed in conjunction with a third one, that of the *génie*. Callirhoe's (encoded) female traits are juxtaposed to the genius' maleness, and the drawing of each emphasizes the sexual distinctions.[48] Callirhoe's forms are continuous and flowing, the interior articulation of her body is limited to gentle roundings that suggest a fleshy softness. The male figure's musculature, on the other hand, is highly articulated, and the interior outlines are broken and fragmented. Both of these partially clad figures contrast, in turn, with the heavily draped and androgynous Coresus, who seems to resolve the two contrasting states by participating in the sexuality of each.

Though contrasted, Coresus and Callirhoe also present parallels that suggest to an informed audience not only the fate that was intended for Callirhoe but also her later actions (her subsequent suicide). Her form nestles against his, the turn of her head copies in reverse that of the high priest; and they are united in their obliviousness to the events around them (in fact, our critic for the *Mercure* described Coresus as in the first stages of fainting). Thus the figure of Callirhoe might be said to extend the expressive moment; her form suggests both what might have happened and the events to come. And her action leads the viewer (assisted by cues from the secondary figures) to imagine her expression in the preceding moments.

In narrative paintings the artist could imply temporality by selecting a moment that pointed to both the events that preceded and followed it. The viewer thus supplied what the artist could only suggest, and time unfolded in the beholder's imagination. In a story already known (*Coresus* fits this category), the painter aroused the memory and helped the audience visualize the causes and effects of the action shown. The mechanisms for viewer stimulation recognized in the eighteenth century included a careful selection of the moment, adroit expressions that carried traces of the preceding emotion, and subsidiary figures who acted as premonitions of future events or reminders of past ones.[49] Through these means the expressive moment, so adapted to the spatiality of painting, could also be used to expand its temporal bounds.

In regard to time, the figure of Coresus is even more complex than that of Callirhoe. As Pausanias told, he stabs himself just as his rage has given way to love. The theme required that the artist render a change of emotional states. Thus, if the artist showed the pallor of death mingled with the ecstasy of love, the range of emotions could be completed by including traces of the anger that had just passed. Fragonard does not represent Coresus' rage by leaving its traces on his visage; there is no room for it in his abandonment. The problem is resolved through a slightly less sophisticated means, but one that works formally. The figure of the *génie* hovering above Coresus can be taken as the high priest's other self, and through him are intimated the passions that precipitated the drama. The figure carries two attributes generally associated with the violent and heated emotions: a lighted torch and a dagger.[50] The dagger was specifically emblematic of revenge, signifying the readiness to return injury; and the lighted torch of fury or ire, signified the loss of reason at the height of passion.[51] This iconography is supported by the formal configuration; the genius' head is aligned with that of Coresus, and the two left arms are upraised one over the other. The crucial difference comes, however, in the position of right arm. That of Coresus plunges the blade into his heart. The *génie* raises his dagger and lines it up in an arc over Callirhoe's breast, thus enacting the high priest's original intention.

The theme of conflicted emotions, of anger and love set in opposition, is made visually explicit in the contrast between Coresus and his other self. The figure of Coresus, moreover, is a microcosm of the contrast that plays throughout the composition. His splayed legs and bent knees are positioned so that the vertical axis of the figure, which runs along the articulated side of his neck, can be imagined to continue through his entire body.[52] Around this axis a contrast is developed: bent vs. extended arm, curvilinear vs. vertical drapery patterns, lighted vs. shadowed areas.

The chiaroscuro that underscores Coresus' internal conflict is essential to the entire image. Because Fragonard's handling of light is, as Diderot called it, a *tour de force*, we might be tempted to consider this virtuoso display as essentially a device to capture the viewers' attention, to impress them immediately with a striking visual effect. To do so, however, would be to underestimate Fragonard's achievement and the significance it held for his contemporaries. Cochin, for example, cited the light effects as a major reason why the government should buy the *Coresus*;[53] and in his *Essay on Painting* Diderot considered them paradigmatic: "One calls an effect of light in painting [like that] you have seen in the painting of *Coresus* a true, strong and striking mix of shades and light: a poetic moment that arrests and astonishes you."[54] He goes on to contrast Fragonard's handling, his just and appropriate distribution of light and shade, with the "false" lights that other artists add "only for effect." Diderot thus acknowledged not only that Fragonard's chiaroscuro arrested the viewer but also that it was coordinated with other formal devices to express the subject effectively. In fact, in his 1765 criticism Diderot suggested how Fragonard might have conceived his composition by envisioning it in terms of light and shade. In reconstructing the painting's invention, Diderot imagined the moment before the tragedy when the sky was brilliant with the most pure light and the temple suffused by the sun's rays. The event depicted by Fragonard is heralded by an unnatural darkness that mixes with the light and produces shudders of horror through the crowd. Then the "génie infernal," creature of darkness and premonition of impending disaster, makes his entrance, and Fragonard's drama begins.[55]

In examining the light effects as they operate in Fragonard's *Coresus*, we can conclude, with Diderot, that none are gratuitous, that all are integrated into the total fabric of the composition. The overall contrast of light and shade dramatizes the theme of conflicted emotions that is at the heart of Fragonard's painting, participating in an overall structure where oppositions are harmonized, resolved, or held in tension. The crescendo of responses, also central to the painting, likewise has its counterpart in the chiaroscuro, as Fragonard disposed, across the picture plane, masses of strong light building up and diminishing rapidly, but falling most intensely on the figure of Coresus. Fragonard's effects, moreover, create the atmosphere of lugubrious mystery that has seemed appropriate to the scene since the eighteenth century. Particularly notable in this regard is his representation of the glowing flame that illuminates the two priests behind the left column. Bathed in this firelight, these figures appear insubstantial, phantomlike. We can imagine them to have contributed substantially to the impression that struck many of Fragonard's contemporaries: that the *Coresus* looked like a frightening apparition.

Fragonard's handling of light, however, does not simply reinforce theme and establish mood, it also orders the composition and directs the viewer's looking. To summarize what we have already observed: a crescent of light along the left column helps to contain a group of viewers outside of the main scene; the light falling vertically on the main group marks it as the focal point; the masses of light and shade across the pictorial field reinforce the asymmetrical balance of the composition. We can add that the light, and especially the shade, is distributed triangularly as prescribed in academic theory and that this triangular distribution harmonizes with the pyramidal ordering of the composition. Note that the deepest shadow darkening the face and chest of the old priest as he extends his arms is distributed in a distinctly triangular form, as is the shadow that falls across the legs of both Callirhoe and Coresus, blackening the rounded base of the brazier on the right of the composition.[56]

Fragonard's *Coresus* and Academic History Painting in the Eighteenth Century

In terms of the relationship between subject matter and visual effect, an analysis of Fragonard's handling of light in the *Coresus* suggests that the artist wove together the subject depicted and the formal devices used in its depiction. Diderot's comments about the artist's use of light demonstrate not only that he approved of the merger enacted by Fragonard but also that he, in large measure, demanded it. That Fragonard's *Coresus* was so acclaimed by the Academy reinforces what a reading of eighteenth-century academic theory indicates: the academicians, despite the notion of the genre hierarchy, did not think of a painting in terms of two distinct and separable aspects, one called subject matter and the other called form. They insisted that certain subjects (those drawn from texts) were superior to other subjects (those that imitated nature); but they neither explicitly nor implicitly argued that, *within* a given painting, *what* was represented could be judged apart from *how* it was represented. Simply put, traditional painting theory in the mid-eighteenth century did not ordinarily assume the false dichotomy of form and content.

Even if we look back to the theorist Félibien, who most strongly urged the genre hierarchy, we do not find a split between form and content but a division of painting into the mental conceptualization of the chosen subject and its physical execution. It was this separation of painting into an intellectual or spiritual component dominated by the head, and a physical or material one dominated by the hand, that Roger de Piles was to refute in his *Cours de peinture par principes* of 1708. Painting, he argued, could not be divided; its so-called material part was the medium through which everything was communicated and apprehended: "The hand is to painting only what the word is to poetry: They are the agents of the spirit and the conduit through which thoughts are disseminated."[58] In other words, the painter's ideas were not expressed until they were embodied in a medium, and only to that embodiment could the audience respond. De Piles thus anticipated the elevation of execution, or *le faire*, which became central to much thinking about art in the eighteenth century.

Although Puttfarken has recently argued that eighteenth-century theorists misunderstood de Piles' emphasis on visual effects and reinstated the superiority of subject matter, his conclusion is based on a kind of separation between subject and form that would have been alien to the eighteenth century. According to Puttfarken, even painter-theorists considered all formal properties merely ways to express subject. In relation to Dandré-Bardon, in particular, he argued, "Formal devices were not acknowledged as having their own interest, they were treated purely as a means of directing our eyes to the crux of an action, of concentrating attention on the subject matter."[59]

Puttfarken's claims are pertinent here because he is considering the academic program learned by young artists in general and Fragonard in particular—an academic program that largely determined the handling of the *Coresus*. If we accept Puttfarken's reading of the eighteenth-century academicians, we accept that they believed subject matter and visual effects could easily be separated one from the other, that the organic unity of the painting could be rent apart.

To some degree the issue turns on the interpretation of *convenance*, the principle stating that all visual effects (drawing, line, color, composition, brushwork) must be appropriate to the subject depicted. Puttfarken argues that *convenance* (which was, incidentally, a concept strongly urged by every academic writer, including de Piles) assumed the superiority of subject matter over visual effects by making the latter dependent on the former.[60] Yet I think the notion of *convenance* is better conceived as the coordination of subject and pictorial language. *Convenance* demanded that if an artist depicted an object having some defining characteristic(s), then the defining characteristic(s) should be expressed in the pictorial language. The artist was not totally free, however, to choose which characteristics were defining for the objects depicted. These were more or less prescribed by cultural codes. If a painter wanted to represent the traditional figure of Venus, for example, *convenance* demanded that her youth, beauty, and sexuality be expressed because those were generally assumed to be the defining characteristics proper to Venus. Similarly, artists were not free to decide for themselves which aspects of the visual language expressed what characteristics; those were codified in instituted signs. For example, academic theory established that nobility was expressed by large, grand contours and voluptuousness in serpentine curves and glistening touches of paint.[61] But to say that the artist was obliged to choose those defining characteristics and instituted signs generally accepted by the culture is not the same thing as to say that subject matter is superior to visual effects. It is logical, after all, to think that *convenance* could have worked in reverse; if an artist wanted to render dramatic visual effects of chiaroscuro, then that artist would be obliged to choose a subject that would coordinate with those visual effects.

In pressing his case, Puttfarken takes passages of eighteenth-century theory out of context. Here is a section he cites from Dandré-Bardon in which I have included in italics the line Puttfarken omits:

> One of the principal goals of the tying together of the groups *[la liaison des Grouppes]* is to lead the eye of the spectator to the heroes of the subject. It is fitting that this operation be made by a diagonal progression. *The paths of lines horizontal or parallel to the edge of the painting rarely produce picturesque effects.*[62]

The line left out affirms that in this instance the articulation of the subject matter and the creating of a pleasing visual effect are *not* considered independently of one another. Students who worked with Dandré-Bardon or read his treatise did not learn to ignore the importance of the visual effect, nor were they taught the superiority of subject matter. Rather, his students were urged to choose what was both *convenable* to the subject and useful for making a striking composition, what would both make an immediate impression on the viewer if detached from subject matter and be appropriate to the subject if detached from visual effect. Because meaning in a painting is certified by the appropriate (or *convenable*) use of picturesque *(pittoresque)* effects, it is useless to speculate about the primacy of subject matter.

Dandré-Bardon, like other eighteenth-century academic theorists, called for the right coordination of all elements to insure a painting's unity. Harmony was a key concept for the academic painter, whose task was never limited to choosing those formal devices that would focus the viewer's attention on subject matter. If all aspects of painting were to participate in the overall harmony of the composition, paint handling was no exception. To those today familiar with the free, unblended brushwork that marks many of Fragonard's paintings, the handling of the *Coresus* may seem decidedly uncharacteristic in its degree of finish. The forms are painted with a rather large stroke appropriate to the scale of the work, but the individual marks are well blended to create a smooth, even paint surface. Only in a few areas is the handling itself noticeable; for example, thick, white strokes are evident in the drapery thrown over Coresus' right arm, and his hair is visibly touched.[63]

The paint handling can be explained by the purpose and genre of the work and by the location for which it was destined. The *Coresus* was painted for the Academy and designed as a major Salon entry. Thus the work was planned for a large public space where it would be seen from afar, where the viewers could not appreciate the delicacies of touch.[64] More important, its grand subject and grand conception demanded a grand style of execution, one that avoided both the minute, highly polished finish appropriate to small-scale cabinet painting, and the free, sketchlike one suited to more preliminary works. The grand style thus was finished but not overly finished, free but not imprecise.[65]

From conceiving the subject as an expressive moment to finishing the paint surface, Fragonard shows a command of history painting conventions in his *Coresus Sacrificing Himself to Save Callirhoe*. The artist knew how to configure an expressive moment, how to locate his work within a constellation of key history paintings, how to articulate his subject in a formal language both appropriate and striking. But is he entirely successful at making a display piece that suppresses conscious display? In other words, although a *morceau d'agrément* demanded a demonstration of skill, history painting demanded that artifice be hidden and that effects seem natural to or caused by the subject represented, and not forced upon it by the artist. Diderot perceived Fragonard's light effects to be true and striking rather than false and added only for effect. But is this assessment applicable to the work as a totality? In other words, given that all parts of the painting are coordinated into a harmonious whole so that no one effect seems forced, either in relation to the other effects or in relation to the subject chosen, is it possible that the whole can nevertheless be characterized by conscious display? It is this question that a consideration of Fragonard's theatricality must address.

Fragonard's Theatricality

For the past two hundred years critics and interpreters have commented on the "theatricality" of Fragonard's *Coresus*.[66] What does and did this term mean, and how might a concept of the theatrical be appropriate to a narrative painting? In his *Ars Poetica* Aristotle defined two manners of imitation: one in which actions are described by a mediator or narrator, and a second in which all characters are presented as functioning and in action. The first mode he applied to epic poetry (it has subsequently been extended to the novel, short story, film, etc.), the second to comedy and tragedy.[67] Eighteenth-century critics were apt to compare narrative painting to action on a stage (and vice versa), because they believed that both actors and painted figures spoke through the natural language of gestures and expressions.[68] In perceiving both drama and painting as more transparent to the object of imitation than the written text, the eighteenth-century writer ignored a major difference between the two arts that moved painting closer to the written narrative. Drama represents action through action and speech through speech; that is, like imitates like. This is not the case in either the narrative text, where actions are represented by written words, or the painting, where they are represented by marks of pigment. The difference between a painting and a drama is similar to the difference between a landscape painting and a garden. If both represent the same site, neither the garden nor the landscape painting is transparent to the model; yet the gardener imitates like with like—trees with trees, water with water, and so on. The painter, on the other hand, imitates the same model with oil on canvas.

What many (but not all) paintings do have in common with Aristotle's second mode of imitation is that they seem to have no narrator. In texts narrators function as characters who mediate the action in telling the story; they have a voice (unlike the apparent or implied author) and speak in a person and tense. Many paintings are like dramas in that events seem to unfold directly, as if they were unmediated. The sense of being at the scene is enhanced in a painting because its language does not describe but depicts, and it has no easily determinable equivalents to person and tense.

Despite the associations between painting and theater drawn commonly in the eighteenth century, writers who labeled a painting theatrical did not necessarily have Aristotle's distinctions in mind. Diderot, as Fried has incisively demonstrated, used the French term *théâtral* to characterize imitation that drew attention to itself as artifice, imitation that was obviously mediated.[69] In this sense not every piece of theater was *théâtral.* If the illusion that the viewer was present at the actual event was sustained without interruption, the term did not apply; but if the illusion was broken and the artifice revealed (if, for example, the actors addressed the audience directly), the adjective *théâtral* described the effect.[70] We continue to use the English term *theatrical* to designate that which is marked by self-display, exaggerated in manner, or affectedly dramatic. In addition, there was also a looser eighteenth-century use of the term *théâtral* that coincides with the contemporary English *theatrical* and can be considered the adjectival form of the noun *théâtre* or *theater.* Thus used, the term means like, relating to, suitable for, or belonging to the theater or dramatic performance.

In discussing Fragonard's *Coresus* in his *Salon of 1765,* Diderot suggested both that the scene as depicted by Fragonard was suited to the stage, that it reminded him of a piece of theater, and that it was theatrical in the sense of drawing attention to its own artifice. In the first case he likens the set and props for Fragonard's action to the *mise en scène* of a play. After describing details such as the temple and the implements gathered there, he urges, "Behold the scene *(Voilà le théâtre)* of one of the most dreadful and touching representations that were projected on the screen in the cavern during my dream."[71] Although he does not use the adjective *théâtral*, the sense of being appropriate to the theater is evoked by his use of the term *théâtre* to mean scene or location. Diderot also recognized that the *Coresus*, which he greatly admired, was *théâtral* (that it drew attention to its own artifice), but he was willing to overlook what others might criticize. In the text Grimm, as a character in the fictive dialogue between Grimm and Diderot, remarks that there are some judges with pure taste, who believe that they sense in every composition something of the theatrical, which displeases them. Yet, he reassures Diderot, "Whatever they say about it, believe that you have fabricated a beautiful dream and Fragonard a beautiful painting."[72] Noting some display of artifice, Diderot perhaps wanted to pre-empt the observations of other critics who might find Fragonard's painting (or his own text) too flawed by the kind of effects that he himself had more than once deplored.

Fragonard's painting is theatrical—in the sense of drawing attention to artifice—precisely because it is theatrical—it looks like a scene on the stage; which is to say that a painter necessarily ruptures the illusion of truth when presenting an action in a way that recalls the conventions of another art form. Theater had its conventions for representing events as if they were real. When those conventions were represented in a painting, however, they no longer pointed to reality. Rather, they signified theatrical illusion. This transfer from theater to painting was so widely effected in eighteenth-century academic history painting that the artificiality might go unrecognized; the transferred theatrical conventions might be accepted as adequately representing the real. Although Fragonard's teacher, François Boucher, was perhaps best known (and criticized) for these effects, they could be found in the works of artists like the Coypel and the Van Loo. They appear early in Fragonard's work in his *Jeroboam Sacrificing to the Idols* (1752; Paris: Ecole des Beaux-Arts), a history painting that won him both academic approval and the Prix de Rome. Most notable in this painting is the background rendered according to the conventions of scene design; the temple is placed at a forty-five degree angle to the picture plane in emulation of the popular *scena per anglo*.[73] The theatrical effects are increased and perfected in the *Coresus* where the action is situated on an elevated platform flanked by columns that resembles the proscenium stage. The background again is like a scene painting with temple turned at a familiar angle; and the event that surprises the spectators is like a great *coup de théâtre*, with Coresus, in a grand theatrical gesture, holding center stage.

Modern writers on Fragonard have continued to apply the term theatrical to the *Coresus*, perhaps following Diderot's lead, but more often to mean that the theater influenced him, that he imitated a scene he saw in the theater. We have already seen why this proposition is false. I would like to suggest, however, that Diderot did accurately discern a play with artifice, a theatricality, in Fragonard's painting, apart from that signaled by gestures, lighting, or expressions.

Whether or not Fragonard intended it to be the case, one can detect a certain planarity that counterbalances the illusionism in the interior scene. Carefully composed, the inscribed picture could stand as an independent painting if abstracted from the whole. The columns framing it act as architectural members within the overall composition, but they also operate as abstract borders for the interior space, distinctly flattened out with clearly drawn edges marking each side. Although within this space the temple seems to recede and figures are placed behind the main characters, depth is minimized by the screen of billowing smoke that spreads across the area. Fragonard has pushed his main figures close to the secondary picture plane established by the columns, and Coresus' elbow breaks that picture plane in imitation of *trompe l'oeil* conventions. These conventions are also recalled by the flowing of Callirhoe's garment over the step that marks the bottom edge of the interior space. If the viewer focuses on the central section, looking at the event and spectators, the space seems two-dimensional. If the eyes are cast downward to the base of the columns, however, the three-dimensional illusionism is apparent, as it is if one looks to the side of the central scene where a third column lurking in the background establishes distant space. Neither the illusion of three-dimensionality nor that of planarity can be maintained.

This structure of a relatively flat composition set within a more illusionistic one is interesting in terms of how the viewers are arranged. Those in the central scene inhabit a space seemingly less three-dimensional (and hence perhaps less real) than the viewers outside that scene. Because the three-dimensional effects are concentrated outside the columns, that area seems more real than the central stage; but it is also less real than the space of the viewer outside the painting. This leveling allows the real spectators to identify more closely with their painted counterparts outside the central scene, but it thereby distances the spectators from the event to which they respond. It also calls attention to the boundaries between art and nature and allows that flickering awareness that disrupts the truth of the illusion. As Hobson has shown, this structure was typical of rococo painting where the audience enjoyed both the illusion and its awareness of the illusion.[74]

Fragonard's *Coresus*, executed according to the principles of eighteenth-century history painting, possesses a central characteristic of rococo form: a theatrical presentation. Yet even Diderot, who elsewhere condemned this aspect of the rococo, failed to chastise Fragonard on this point. Indeed, he even valorized the artist's play with illusion in his skillful literary recreation of Fragonard's painting.

Diderot's Commentary[75]

Diderot's commentary demonstrates that he recognized a play with illusion as a central conceit in Fragonard's painting, for it is this play that Diderot emphasizes when he recreates Fragonard's great work. As Fort has ably demonstrated, Diderot imitates Fragonard by evoking the painting in an *ekphrasis* that translates the artist's rhetorical strategy from the pictorial to the literary.[76] The essay is set up as a dialogue in which Diderot (the character who tells the story) reports to Grimm (the character who listens and responds to the story) that he has missed seeing the *Coresus* at the Salon. In lieu of describing the painting, Diderot discusses with Grimm a strange dream occasioned by his reading of Plato. Diderot reports that he imagined himself a prisoner in Plato's cave, compelled to look at a screen on which were projected illusions so striking that they might be (but were not always) taken for reality. One series of illusions climaxes with the representation of a high priest's suicide, which Grimm recognizes as a double of Fragonard's painting.

Diderot thus described two illusory spaces: the philosopher's cavern and the screen within it. The relationship between the fictive spectators and those imaginary sites arranged one inside the other parallels the relationships established in Fragonard's painting. In the painting some of the painted spectators are included in the scene of Coresus' suicide and others, standing outside the framing columns, are excluded from the spectacle that transfixes them. The excluded ones, however, are trapped inside the larger illusion constituted by the entire painting. Diderot's imaginary spaces do not exactly coincide with those represented by Fragonard, for the space of the *toile* inside the cavern corresponds to the whole of Fragonard's painting, not to just its interior scene. In Diderot's commentary, the *Coresus* (which includes two levels of fictive spectators within it) is represented as an illusion beheld but not entered by the prisoners chained inside the larger imaginary space of Plato's cave.

But what about the real spectators: what relation do they have to the fictive ones, and how are they represented in Diderot's text? Standing before the painting, the Salon audience constitutes a group of spectators that remains forever apart from the represented actions and reactions, separated by the boundary between nature and art. Although physically excluded from the work of art, the real viewers are encouraged by both Diderot and Fragonard to enter it imaginatively by extending the levels of spectators outward to include themselves.[77] In Diderot's commentary the spectator's surrogate is the fictive Diderot, the narrator-dreamer who can be present in the dreamspace mentally and emotionally, but not physically. In other respects the spectator's surrogate is the dreamer's imagined self, the captive in Plato's cave who responds to illusory spectacles (paintings) as if they were real. Like the other prisoners, he laughs loudly or cries profusely at scenes that seem natural and true, even when he knows they are not. But as a prisoner chained in Plato's cave, it is (physically) impossible for the dreamer to enter the space of the illusions he beholds. Diderot suggests, however, that the effects of art can penetrate these spaces (from the *toile* within the imaginary cave, through the cave in which the dreamer's imagined self is chained, to the narrator-dreamer), for the narrator-dreamer described to Grimm how he was awakened by the cries of an old man represented on the *toile*.[78]

A complex play with levels of illusion and mediation characterizes both Fragonard's painting and Diderot's eighteenth-century interpretation of it. If Diderot encourages us to mimic the prisoners in Plato's cave by responding to art as if it were real, he does so by making us aware (as did Fragonard) of the distance separating the spectator from the work of art. Although elsewhere Diderot argued that the spectator should be uninterruptedly deceived by art, the structure and commentary of his essay on Fragonard suggest that the viewer should simultaneously respond to art as if it were nature while recognizing the difference between the two.[79]

In addition to the obvious play with illusory spaces and the spectators that inhabit them, Diderot's titling of his review *L'antre de Platon* (Plato's cave) suggests that some comparison with the philosophical message of the myth was intended. Diderot clearly borrowed the allegory that opens book 7 of the *Republic.* Plato describes a subterranean cave in which men were chained facing the rear wall and unable to move or to turn their heads. Above and behind them a fire blazed at a distance, and between them and the fire was a low wall along which other men passed carrying all sorts of vessels. Able to behold only the shadows cast by the objects, the prisoners mistook those evanescent forms for reality. In Plato's allegory the cave stood for the natural world, the world of sight where one knows not being but appearances. This world is contrasted to a lighted upper realm, the world of the ideal to which the soul aspires.[80] Diderot's divergence from Plato's allegory is apparent; what are projected in his cave are aesthetic illusions, not the appearances that characterize the world as people know it. Diderot sets out the comparison with art by stressing that the illusions are projected, not on the back wall of a cave, but on a *toile*. Throughout the essay he plays on the double meaning of *toile* as screen and canvas, comparing the projected illusions generally to paintings and specifically to Fragonard's *Coresus*.[81] Thus if Plato's cave is the natural world, Diderot's cavern is the world of artifice.

It is tempting to invoke Plato's theory of mimetic art at this point. According to Plato, mimetic art was a copy of a copy, a deceptive appearance that both imitated and created illusion. In the preface to his next *Salon,* Diderot used platonic terms to distinguish between the history painter and the practitioner of the lesser genres, exemplified by the portraitist. The latter copied the particulars of nature, made copies of copies. The history painter, on the other hand, formed an ideal in the imagination and used that ideal as a model. In addressing painters of the highest rank, Diderot urged, "Admit then, that this model is purely ideal, and that it is not borrowed directly from any individual image of nature. . . . Admit then that when you make something beautiful, you make nothing that is, nothing that even can be."[82] And later, "Admit then that the difference between the portraitist and yourself, man of genius, consists essentially in the fact that the portraitist renders faithfully Nature as she is, and fixes himself in the third rank by taste; and that you who seek the truth, the first model, make a continuous effort to elevate yourself to the second rank."[83] Although such an interpretation of the ideal may not have been what Plato had in mind, it was the Neoplatonic interpretation common to many in the eighteenth century.[84] Thus history painters are distinguished precisely because they do not make appearances of appearances.

To return to Fragonard's *Coresus*, the work is a history painting, and as such it copies an ideal imagined by the artist. Diderot believed this to be the case, and he praised Fragonard by saying, "This artist constructs the ideal sublimely."[85] This notion of the ideal and its relation to painting suggests how the comparison with Plato's cave might operate. The prisoners described by Plato see only the appearances of the ideal, not its being. The prisoners in Diderot's cave, as surrogates for the spectators of

Fragonard's painting, also see the appearance of the ideal, an ideal created by the artist. Fragonard, then, is the Neoplatonic artist able to reveal his ideal in appearances. Grimm says to Diderot, "In the cavern you saw only the simulacra of beings, and Fragonard on his canvas has not showed you anything more than simulacra."[86] Although Fragonard shows simulations (of beings), it is the ideal and not the natural that stands behind his imaginary construct. Recall Diderot's directive to the history painter: "Admit then when you make something beautiful, you make *nothing that is, nothing that even can be*" (my emphasis).[87]

It is not just to projected images, simulacra, and phantoms that Diderot compares Fragonard's painting; it is also like a dream. Grimm says to Diderot, "You have had a beautiful dream; he has painted a beautiful dream."[88] And later, ". . . believe that you have fabricated a beautiful dream and Fragonard a beautiful painting."[89] The dream is not part of Plato's allegory, and it does not appear in his discussion of art later in the *Republic*. Introduced by Diderot, this comparison allows him to strengthen the association of the *Coresus* with what is imagined, with the ideal. To paint a dream was to paint the invisible; more precisely, it was to paint what was in one's imagination. The dream was commonly used as an allegory of artistic inspiration appropriate for both painters and poets; it stood for what the artist imagined.[90] Gabriel de Saint-Aubin's *The Dream or Voltaire Composing La Pucelle* (c.1778; Paris: Musée du Louvre) exemplifies this theme. Before putting brush to canvas or pen to paper, both painter and poet were required to formulate a mental conception of the work, and it was in this process of imagining that the painter became the equal of the poet.[91]

Diderot's essay, then, praises Fragonard's talent as a history painter at the same time it recognizes his play with real and illusory spaces, with real and painted spectators. These insights accord with two major aspects of the painting: *The High Priest Coresus Sacrificing Himself to Save Callirhoe* was executed to secure Fragonard's associate membership in the French Academy; and it was painted to be exhibited, to be seen by the audience that would for days on end gather in the public space of the Salon.[92] There it announced its author as a rising force in history painting. Although Fragonard was never to execute another painting to meet similar requirements, his later works, like the *Coresus*, respond to the audience and location for which they were planned. They also demonstrate that Fragonard never abandoned his academic training; he simply adapted it to new ends.

2 The Dynamics of Decoration

The Progress of Love

In moving from Fragonard's *Coresus* to the series of panels known as *The Progress of Love* (1771–73; New York: Frick Collection; figures 4–7) we move from a public to a private exhibition space and from academic to decorative painting. Although there is understandably a distance between these works—one intended for the Salon of 1765, the other for an aristocrat's garden pavilion—they come together at central points: both are audience directed, both incorporate within themselves a play of illusion and reality, both expertly interweave formal effects with subject matter.

Executed to adorn a salon in Mme Du Barry's pavilion at Louveciennes, *The Progress of Love* is composed of four large canvases now called *The Pursuit* (figure 4), *The Meeting* (figure 5), *The Lover Crowned* (figure 6) and *The Love Letters* (figure 7).[1] All the activities represented in these scenes are located in a fictive garden. *The Pursuit* depicts a young man offering his lady a rose, *The Meeting* a tryst set on a high terrace. An artist records the scene of a young girl wreathing her beloved in *The Lover Crowned*, and in *The Love Letters* an embracing couple rereads some *billets doux*. The commission went to Fragonard in 1771, but by 1773 the patron had refused the works and hired Vien to execute another series.[2] After keeping his rejected paintings for more than fifteen years, Fragonard included them as part of a decorative ensemble that he installed in his cousin's house at Grasse in 1790.[3]

Reading *The Progress of Love:* Linear Sequence or Decorative Ensemble

The Progress of Love is perhaps the only work by Fragonard that has generated a significant number of commentaries, although none as elegant as Diderot's reading of the *Coresus.* Léon Lagrange, the first writer to actually describe the series (1867), saw the panels in Grasse, where they hung with several other works that completed the Maubert decoration: a fifth large painting (now called *Abandoned*), a chimney piece, four overdoors, and four hollyhock panels.[4] His interpretation cast the paintings as a *"drame amoureux"* divided into five acts with a final *"tableau."* Although Lagrange did not consider the four paintings executed for Mme Du Barry apart from the rest, I quote his comments at length because they demonstrate a particular strategy of interpretation:

> In the first act, [we see] the meeting of the young girls and the suitor before a fountain of love; in the overdoor the god Cupid chases a dove. In the second act he has caught it, he seizes it pitilessly; and indeed the lovers converge at the foot of a statue of Psyche and exchange on an altar a vow of love seasoned with a kiss. The third act shows us the terrace where Chloe was dreaming in the soft moonlight when Tircis, enflamed with audacity, appears at the top of a ladder, and the little mischievous god savors the perfume of blooming roses. The fourth act is only a monologue of the tender victim, swooning on the steps of a monument dedicated to love, and in the air the *enfant terrible* capers, a jester's staff in his hand. Finally, with the fifth act, the dénouement: in the midst of a bosquet more filled with blossoms, more mirthful than any, on a terrace embellished with boxed orange trees and strewn with guitars, ballads, and music sheets, the happy lover, kneeling before his beloved, receives from her hands a crown of flowers. Our friend Fragonard, sitting in a corner, his sketchbook open, his pencil ready, cries to them, "Let's not move anymore!" The final painting, over the mantle, represents Hymen-Love, a torch in each hand, in the middle of a glowing sky where the Cupids with no tasks to perform frolic.[5]

Lagrange invented a pretty story by reading the panels as if they constituted an episodic narrative composed of several moments, each set into its own frame or partitioned space. Those works aligned vertically (a large panel and its corresponding overdoor) he considered to be within the same scene or temporal unit. The horizontal arrangement, on the other hand, determined the change of scenes, and Lagrange assumed a sequential viewing order, with each panel preceding the next: Episode 1, *The Pursuit;* Episode 2, *The Love Letters;* Episode 3, *The Meeting;* Episode 4, *Abandoned;* Episode 5, *The Lover Crowned.* Although Lagrange characterized the whole as a play in which scene followed scene, he could just have

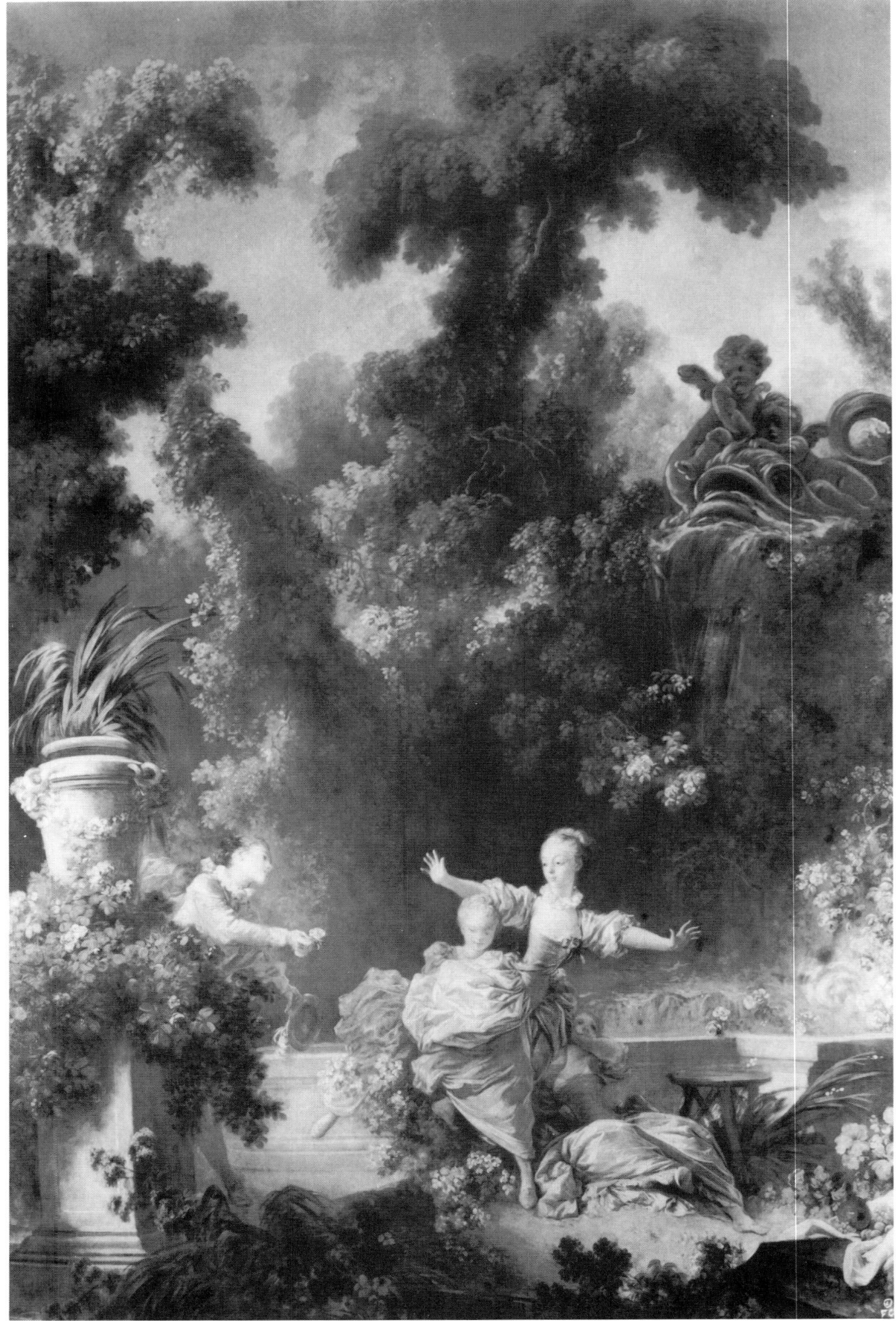

Figure 4 Jean-Honoré Fragonard, *The Pursuit,* 1771-73. © The Frick Collection, New York.

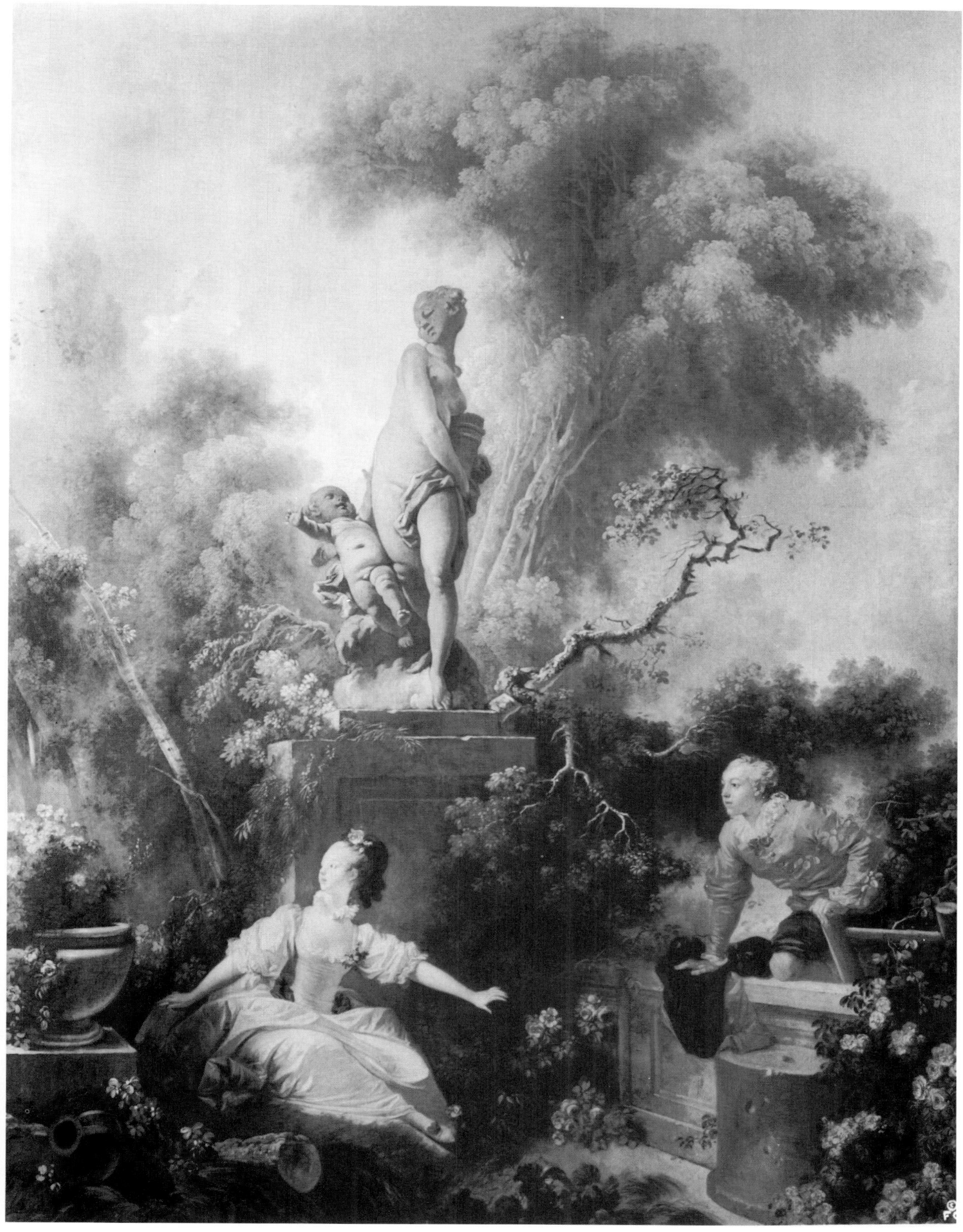

Figure 5 Jean-Honoré Fragonard, *The Meeting,* 1771-73. © The Frick Collection, New York.

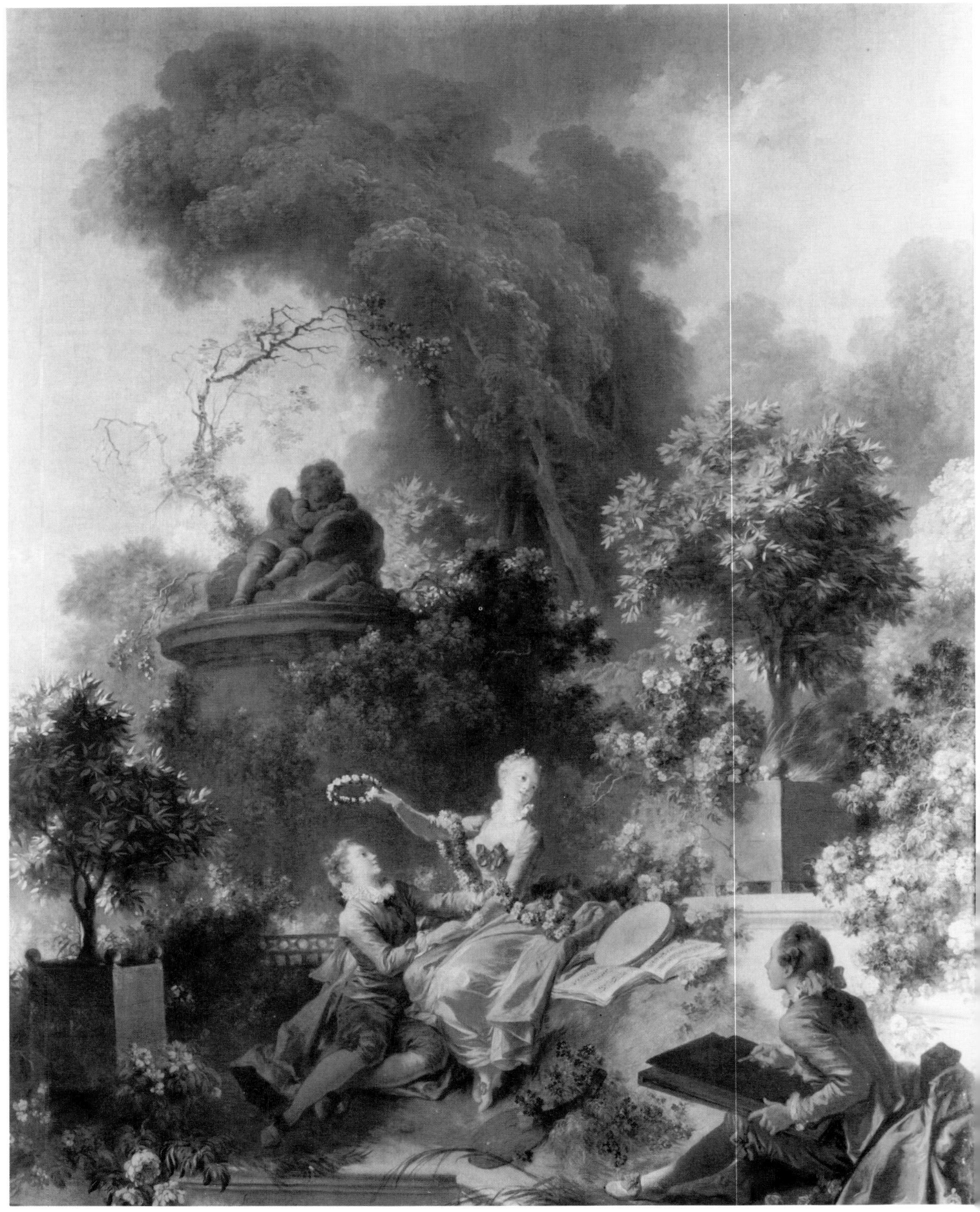

Figure 6 Jean-Honoré Fragonard, *The Lover Crowned,* 1771-73. © The Frick Collection, New York.

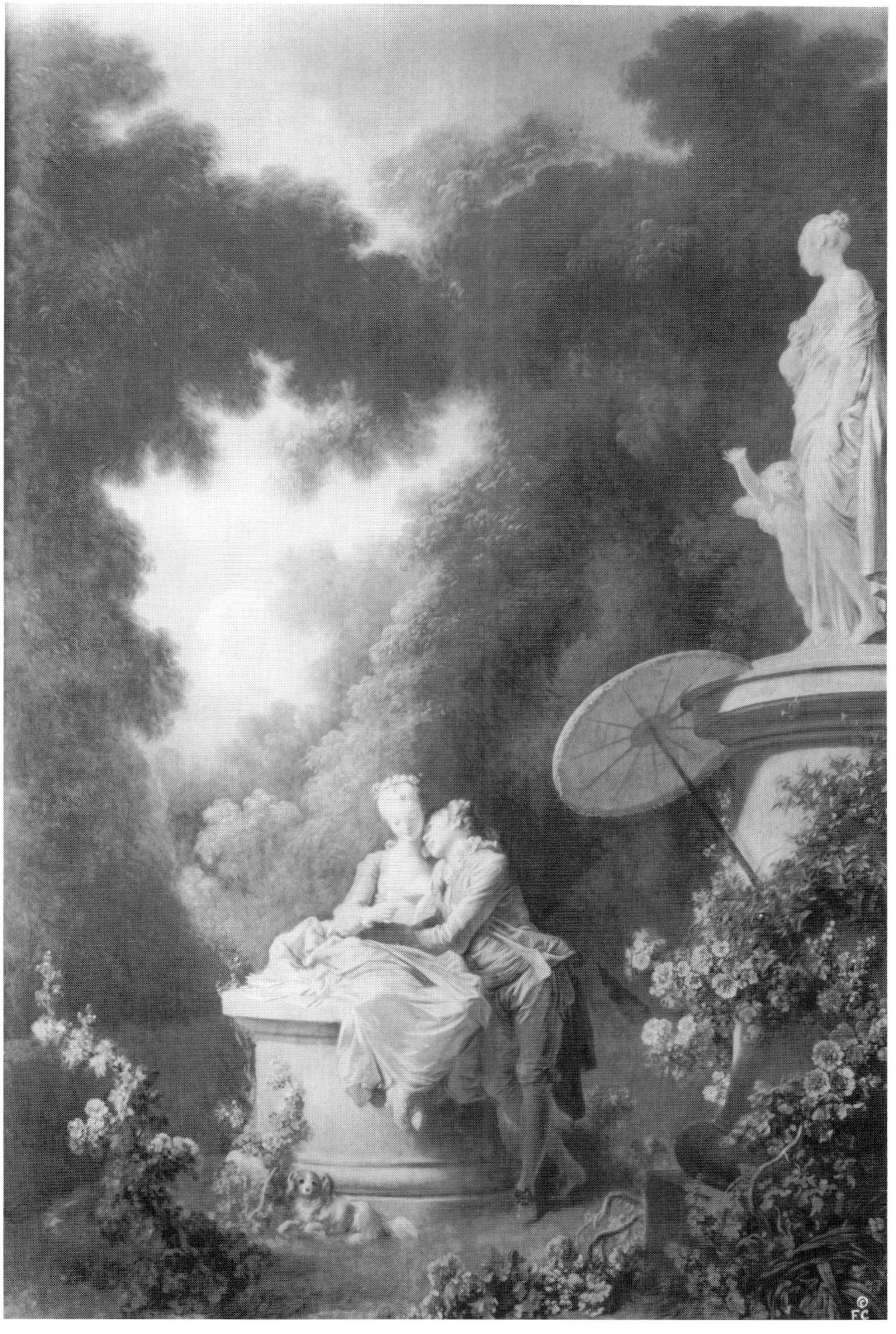

Figure 7 Jean-Honoré Fragonard, *The Love Letters,* 1771-73. © The Frick Collection, New York.

easily called it a novel in which chapter followed chapter; the reading, in other words, is based on an experience of texts.

Whether interpreters considered the works as reconstituted at Grasse or as planned for Louveciennes, they applied to Fragonard's *Progress* the model of the episodic narrative read in a determined sequence. Thus the problem of ordering the panels, of determining which scene should be looked at first, which second, and so on, has been taken as central to understanding these paintings.[6] Until 1968, however, there was no systematic investigation of how the scenes were placed in relation to one another at Louveciennes. In that year Sauerländer compared their measurements to the dimensions of the wall surfaces. Through this procedure he determined the positions of *The Lover Crowned* and *The Love Letters,* which were found to flank the door through which one entered the room from the adjoining salon. Two panels *(The Pursuit* and *The Meeting)* remained for the opposite wall, but they had identical dimensions. Sauerländer deduced their placement from Fragonard's formal organization, noting that the male figures acted as compositional brackets when *The Pursuit* was placed to the left of *The Meeting.*[7] Thus he argued persuasively for the following arrangement:

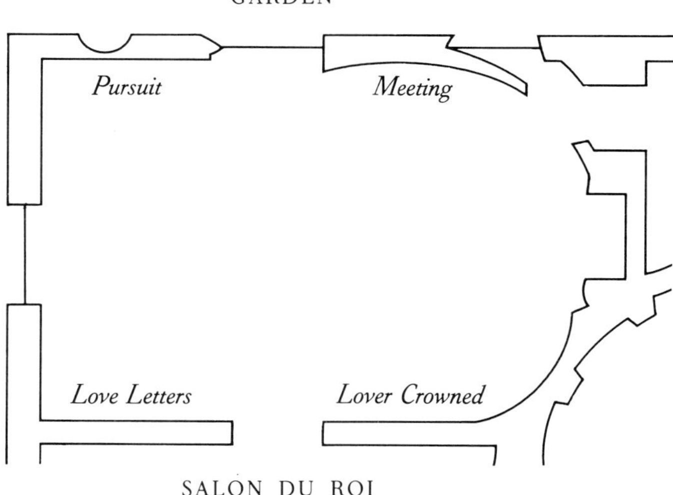

Having established the position of the panels, Sauerländer then set out to ascertain the order and meaning of the narrative. *The Pursuit* and *The Meeting,* he reasoned, were the first two scenes because they were visible on the far wall as one entered the room from the adjoining salon. But with which of those two panels did the series begin? Up to this point

Sauerländer's reasoning was guided by the principle that in decorative painting artists considered their work in reference to an architectural space. But he pursued this logic no further, relying on the assumption that the narrative moved from one scene to the next following the order of placement. He could not, however, determine the reading sequence until he had established a single starting or ending point. To accomplish that analytic task he sought the theme of the series by investigating the many iconographic details of the individual panels. His pivotal point was the identification of the statue depicted in *The Love Letters* as *Amitié* or Friendship. Investing the meaning of the entire series in the statue, he hypothesized that friendship was the real conclusion of Fragonard's love story.[8] Once the concluding scene was established, Sauerländer could designate *The Pursuit* as the opening one, since only by starting there could the viewer move in an uninterrupted sequence from one scene to the next. *The Progress,* then, should be read clockwise: *The Pursuit, The Meeting, The Lover Crowned,* and *The Love Letters.* Sauerländer thus transformed the *Progress* into a moral tale that demonstrated the inconstancy of love and the triumph of *amitié.*

Transforming Fragonard into a moralist seemed suspect to Donald Posner, who accepted the placement of the scenes suggested by Sauerländer but rejected his interpretation and order of reading. The message of friendship, Posner believed, did not fit with the tone of the paintings; and the iconography of *Amitié,* developed for Pompadour, seemed an unlikely choice for her successor's pavilion.[9] To reinstate the triumph of love as a theme, Posner re-placed *The Lover Crowned* as the final scene, arguing that the series began not with *The Pursuit* but with *The Meeting,* which he interpreted as representing an as-yet-unwilling young woman because its setting included a statue of Venus disarming Cupid.[10] By reading counterclockwise from *The Meeting* to *The Lover Crowned,* a sequential order was preserved. Although Posner proposed a more plausible interpretation of the *Progress,* like Sauerländer he treated the Louveciennes panels as an episodic narrative and assumed that there was a predetermined order of viewing. Had Posner considered further the implications of his suggestive remark that the contrasting pairs of scenes are oriented to the real garden outside, he might have reached other conclusions.[11]

The Narrative and the Decorative

Reading *The Progress of Love* is problematic because the subject is artist-created, that is, not supported by a literary text. Viewers cannot know the narrative outside of the painting(s), and they are called upon to fabricate, rather than to remember, a story line. In devising their own narratives, however, artists could, through a variety of formal and iconographic strategies, suggest reading patterns to their audience. Consider, for example, two panels that Boucher executed for Mme Geoffrin in 1765: *The Departure of the Pigeon Post* (New York: Metropolitan Museum of Art; figure 8) and *The Arrival of the Courrier* (now lost; engraved by J.F. Beauvarlet; fig-

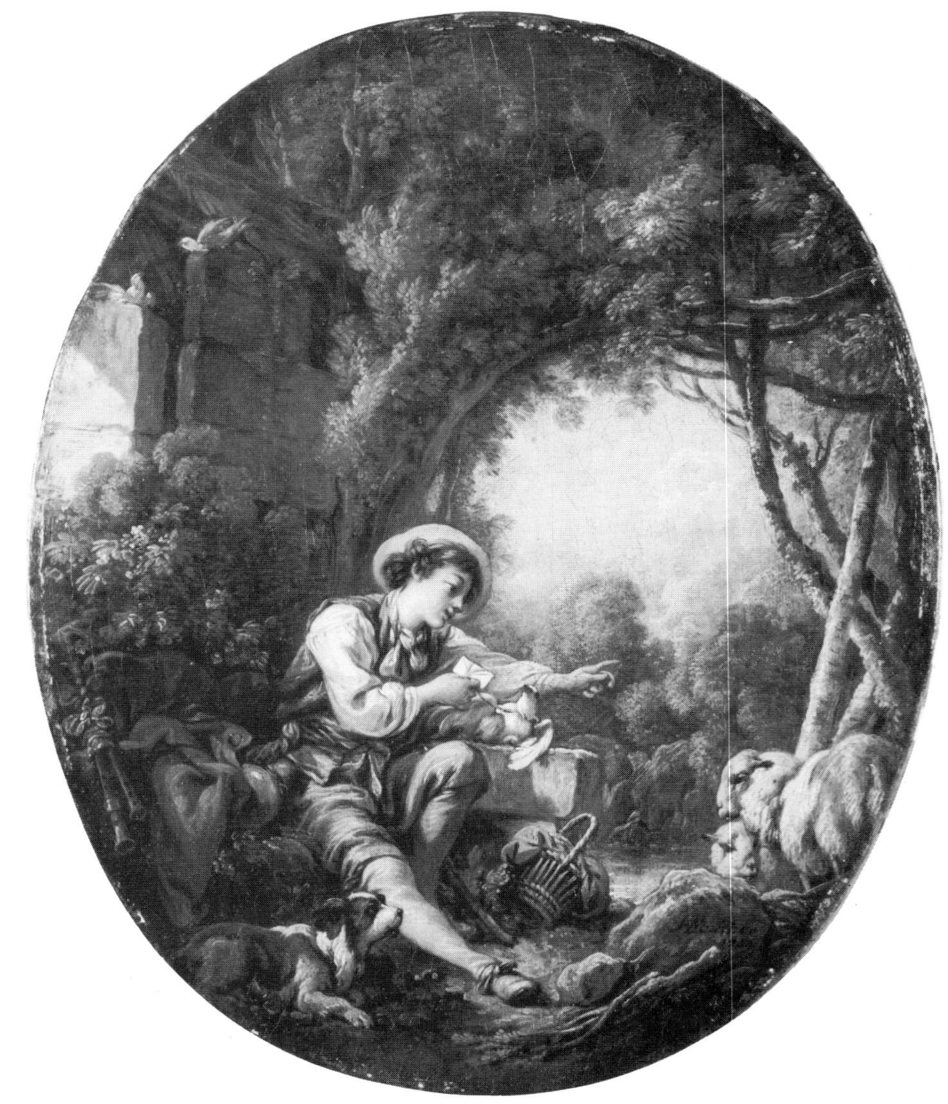

Figure 8 François Boucher, *The Departure of the Pigeon Post,* 1765. New York, Metropolitan Museum of Art. Gift of Mrs. Joseph Heine in memory of her late husband, I. D. Levy, 1944 (44.141)

ure 9).[12] In the one scene a young shepherd attaches a letter to the neck of a dove, and in the other a young girl awaits the carrier's approach. Not only does the letter-carrying dove appear in both panels, as if it had flown from one to the other, but also the two compositions are arranged to suggest a continuity when they are hung side by side. With extended leg and pointing finger the boy set to the left in the *Departure*, directs the viewer's attention to the scene of the young girl to his right.

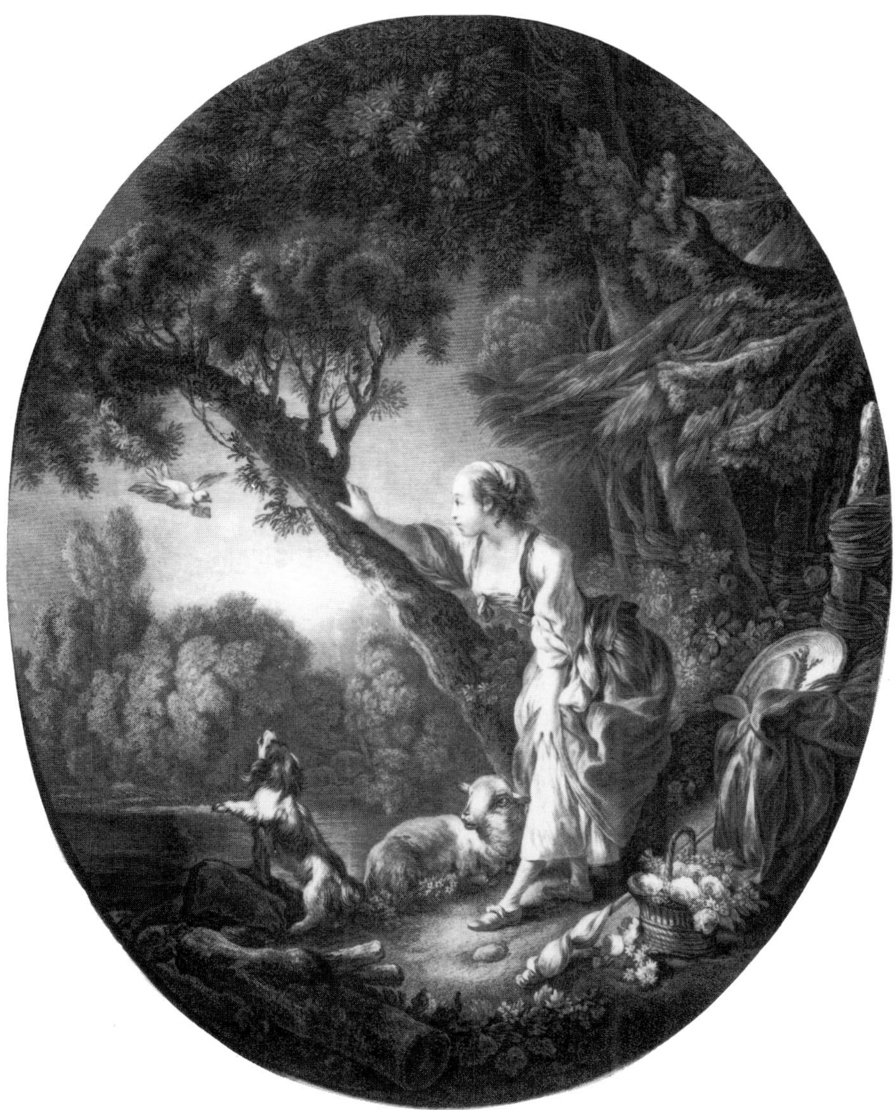

Figure 9 J.-F. Beauvarlet, after François Boucher, *The Arrival of the Courrier*, 1765 (image reversed here). Washington, D.C., The National Gallery of Art, Widener Collection.

Fragonard's Louveciennes panels, however, have no continuous action begun in one panel and completed in the next, no before and after relationship suggested in the compositional dynamics. If in *The Meeting* the figures' gestures and looks direct the viewer's attention toward the left, toward *The Pursuit,* similar devices in *The Pursuit* direct attention back toward the right, toward *The Meeting.* In the other pair of scenes the viewer's gaze is drawn to the lower right corner back into the individual compositions; in *The Lover Crowned* from artist to Cupid, in *The Love Letters* from foliage to sculpture.

Along with the continuous action and implied viewing sequence, the repetition of an iconographic motif could also connect one panel with the next; and Vien used this strategy in a series of works executed to replace Fragonard's Louveciennes panels. Two scenes, *The Oath of Feminine Friendship* (1773; Préfecture de Chambéry, Savoie) and *The Meeting with Cupid* (1773; Paris: Musée du Louvre), feature a garland of flowers held by the two female friends; and two scenes, *The Crowning of the Lovers* (1773, Paris: Musée du Louvre; figure 10) and *The Temple of Hymen* (1773; Préfecture de Chambéry, Savoie; figure 11) highlight a floral wreath crowning the lovers. More significant is that Vien repeats his cast of main characters, showing the same two female friends and the same male suitor at different places and in different dress, thus implying both a continuity of narrative and a passage of time. For Vien's series, documentary evidence supports the visual cues of narrative sequence. Two of the works were exhibited at the Salon of 1773, where reviewers consistently referred to them as part of a series depicting "the progress of love in young girls' hearts" *(les progrès de l'amour dans les coeurs des jeunes filles).*[13] It does not seem entirely coincidental that today we call Fragonard's paintings *The Progress of Love,* for the title is clearly an appropriation of that given to Vien's later series.

In Fragonard's works, however, there is no continuity of iconographic motif, and the couples (especially the women) are differentiated one from the other by physiognomy and coloring. Outside of the paintings no documentary evidence implies that the *Progress* is a sequential narrative. The single eighteenth-century reference to the series' subject is a notice in the *Mémoires secrets* recording that Fragonard depicted the "loves of the shepherds" *(amours des bergers)* at Louveciennes.[14] Although *Amours des Bergers* was cited as the series' title by Charles Blanc, for no apparent reason the Goncourts, never having seen the panels, renamed them *The Ages of Man.*[15] Some more recent interpreters (Wildenstein, for example) have followed the Goncourts' lead by calling Fragonard's series *Ages of Life.*[16]

Although none of the major twentieth-century interpretations fully accord with this notion, some writers (e.g., Wildenstein or Sauerländer) do interpret these works as the allegorical stages of love's progress or development.

The idea perhaps has appeal because the number of the panels (four) suggests a relationship with the progresses that conventionally mark time's passing—for instance, the cycle of the seasons. Among others, Boucher represented the seasons with appropriate love scenes set into landscapes differentiated according to the time of the year (*The Seasons,* 1755; New York: Frick Collection). No such tradition, however, is implied in Fragonard's paintings; in fact, there are few, if any, markers of temporal differentiation. The landscapes neither represent the various seasons nor depict the changing times of the day. The trees and foliage are not more or less grown up from scene to scene; the age of the pairs does not obviously vary. What we see is four individual sets of lovers, each with its own accessory figures, statues, and iconographic details. Located in a garden forever lush and fragrant, these couples are suspended in perpetual youth and destined to repeat, for all times and all viewers, their discontinuous moments of lovemaking.

In the Louveciennes panels Fragonard did not follow a pre-existing text, and there are few, if any, clues to either narrative continuity or temporal sequence in the paintings. What principles, then, can interpreters use in analyzing these works? For decorative paintings that, like the *Progress of Love,* are specifically designed to coordinate with an architectural ensemble, recontextualization must (ideally) precede interpretation. The theory of the ensemble extended the principle of *convenance;* conceived as both a harmonious whole and integral part of a larger system, a room was to have a decor appropriate to its use. For example, in his *Discours sur la peinture et sur l'architecture* of 1758, Duperron commented on the fitness of interior decor, differentiating the treatment of public apartments from that of private ones. The first must be "wise and grand," but in the second the artist was allowed more imaginative play.[17] Some of his descriptions might be taken as a blueprint for Fragonard's *Progress of Love:*

> Is it a question of small apartments, places where Love enjoys himself? It is there that the brush must exhaust all the seductions of sensual pleasure; myrtles, roses, groves, fields carpeted with green, the countryside where the splendor of the most vivid colors shines, these must adorn these sorts of rooms. There, the agreeable spectacle and the pleasure of a garden that art has taken care to decorate can offer itself, here it is the picture of Nature's artless charms and charming disorder.[18]

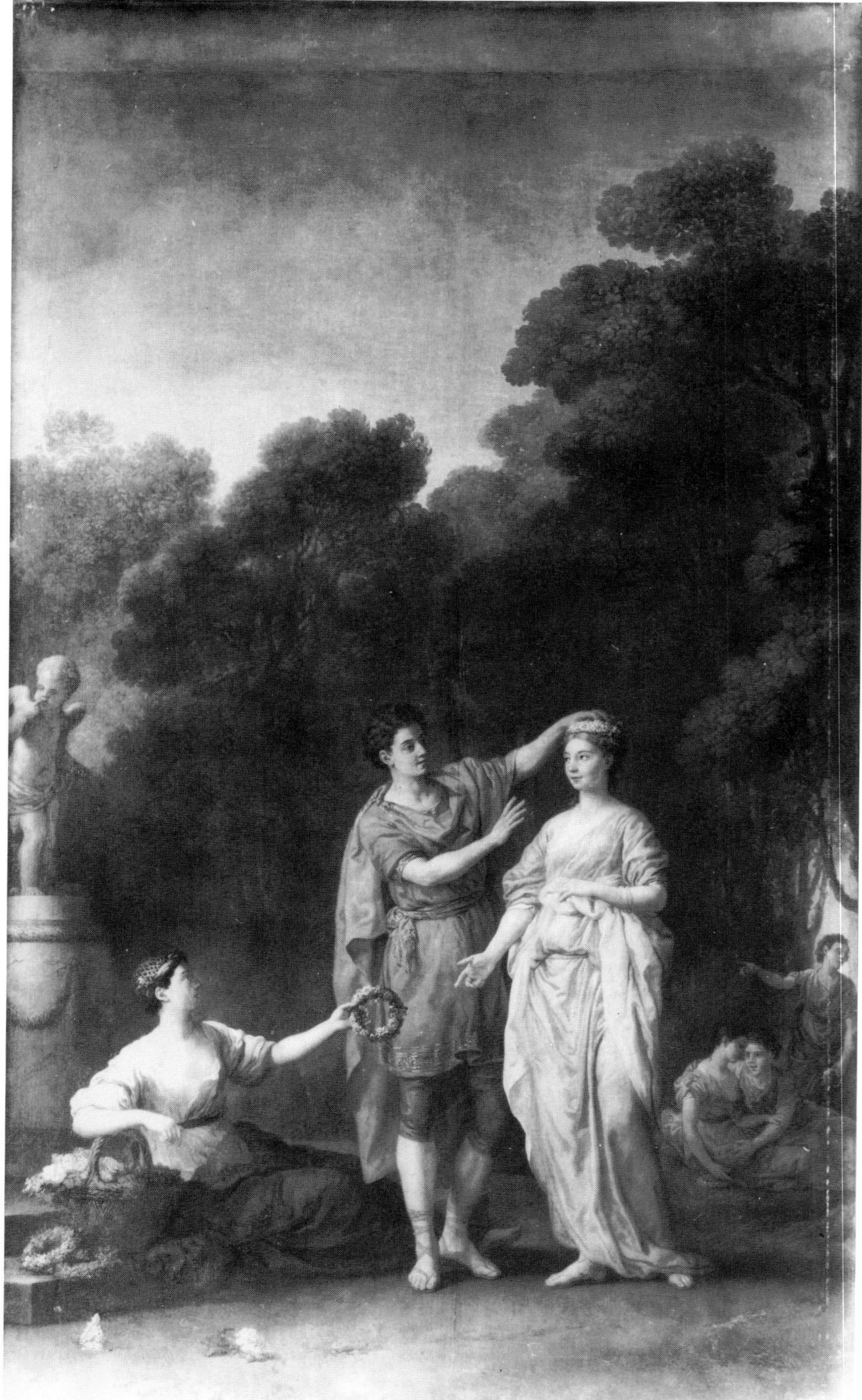

Figure 10 Joseph Vien, *The Crowning of the Lovers,* 1773. Paris, Musée du Louvre. Cliché des Musées Nationaux, Paris.

But before turning to Fragonard's *Progress,* consider the pavilion of Louveciennes in relation to its site, the location of the salon *en cul-de-four* within the pavilion, the placement of Fragonard's paintings within that salon, and the situation of the viewer in relation to the paintings.

Since the eighteenth century it has been obvious that Fragonard's love themes were appropriate for a pavilion dubbed the "sanctuary of pleasure" *(sanctuaire de volupté).*[19] Built by Ledoux for Mme Du Barry, who

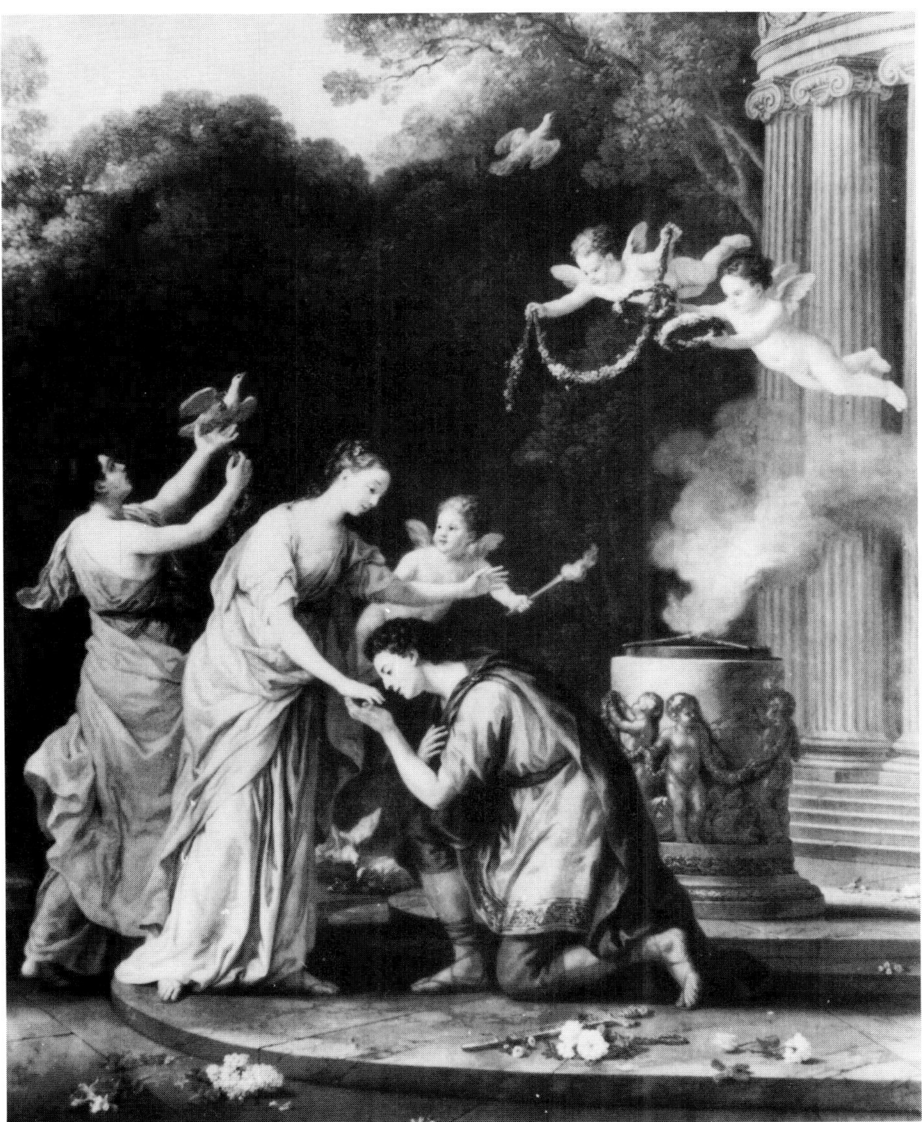

Figure 11 Joseph Vien, *The Temple of Hymen,* 1773. Chambéry, Préfecture.

was then Louis XV's titled mistress, Louveciennes seems to have been a response to Mme de Pompadour's Petit Trianon.[20] It was small, designed for private entertaining, and situated on a site "from which is enjoyed one of the most extended and richest views possible."[21]

The site was clearly as important as the building. Placed on a cliff overlooking the Seine, the pavilion was planned with particular attention to the views out from it. A grand panorama could be had from the Salon du Roi, from where one could see Saint Germain, Visinet, St. Denis, and Paris. From two other salons one could look directly into the garden, which the pavilion, like the Petit Trianon, both rested in and decorated. In fact, one could both view and enter the garden directly from the salon for which Fragonard painted his famous panels.

Not everyone, of course, could view either garden or paintings. The audience for Fragonard's *Progress* was necessarily a privileged one, since its location was accessible only to a limited few. We might categorize this group generally as the social elite and specifically as the court circle around the king and Mme Du Barry. Given that these viewers brought to the paintings a particular ideological perspective (which will be addressed below), consider at this point their physical location in Mme Du Barry's salon. Although spectators at the official Academy exhibitions may have viewed paintings by moving from one to the next, it is hardly likely that guests gathered in Mme Du Barry's pavilion would attend to Fragonard's decorative panels in the same way. As they circulated and conversed with one another, their movements would neither be regularized nor centered on the act of viewing. Their positions in relation to the entrances and exits were the only ones that the artist could count on, for although he could not control other movements in and around the salon, the doors gave some structure to the flow of traffic through it.

A guest entering the room from the Salon du Roi, either looking toward the garden or exiting into it, saw the wall on which were arranged *The Pursuit* and *The Meeting*. As Sauerländer correctly observed, these two panels were placed to create a pleasing visual design across the wall with male figures framing the two actions. But there is more. The two paintings are composed so that the triangular disposition of boy, girl, and statue in the one is mirrored (that is, seen in reverse) in the other.

The other scenes, *The Love Letters* and *The Lover Crowned,* were visible as one entered the salon from the garden or exited into the Salon du Roi. These compositions, too, are coordinated across the wall. In each Fragonard established a main diagonal axis, and these approach one another to form a V-shape at the door. In *The Lover Crowned* the elements are deployed along a virtual line that begins at the artist in the lower right corner and moves through the garden statue represented in the upper regions. A secondary axis, established from the lower left foreground roses to the orange tree above the couple, answers the first. In *The Love Letters* there is a similar balancing of major and minor diagonals. The first extends from the lower left foreground foliage to the representation of *Amitié,* and the second (which might more accurately be described as a path of vision) draws the viewer's attention from the complicated play of vines and blossoms in the right corner through the cartouche formed by the foliage behind the lovers. The parasol placed near the garden statue helps direct the eye along that path, as does the backlighting of the cartouche. Thus, the two paintings of each pair occupying a single wall were conceived to be seen simultaneously, to make an overall visual pattern. At the same time, they are metaphorically closed to one another, depicting separate and discontinuous moments. Yet there is a relationship between the adjacent scenes, a relationship based on similarity, opposition, and resolution.

Reinterpreting the Louveciennes Panels
The Meeting AND *The Pursuit*

At Louveciennes, *The Meeting* (figure 5) and *The Pursuit* (figure 6) flanked the large glass doors that allowed visitors both to see and to enter the garden, the traditional site for trysting. The interplay between the actual garden and the fictive one is thus a central element of the *Progress,* one that sets the tone for other such pairings of the real and the illusory. Both painted scenes are set in corners of an imaginary *jardin de plaisir;* and although it is clear that the two represent different locales, both are set on a terrace engulfed by irregular foliage, unclipped and overgrown almost to the point of reclaiming the architectural setting. In each case this painted foliage seems artfully arranged; a bare, angled branch in *The Meeting* contrasts with a full, leafy trunk and repeats its C-curve. Although these elements help to direct the viewer's attention to the left side of the composition, this movement is countered by the bower that bends downward and to the right, arching over the male figure. Such decorative effects suggest artifice at the same time the overgrown state signals the naturalness of the represented garden. In *The Pursuit* the luxuriant garden more successfully conceals the artful effects. The arching trees in the background still direct the viewer's attention (this time primarily toward the right), but the obviously contrived contrast between them is eliminated. Instead, the foliage forms natural cartouches to frame elements of the composition. Silhouetted against the sky, both the fountain group and urn are isolated by the irregular coming together (standing for natural growth patterns) of the trees behind.

Both *The Meeting* and *The Pursuit* thematize overture and surprise by reconstituting traditional motifs. Sauerländer associated *The Meeting* with the medieval theme of storming love's citadel, which was represented on secular objects (e.g., mirrors) and enacted as a courtly game. The lover who scaled the balcony wall in *The Meeting* seemed to Sauerländer like those knights who besieged a castle defended only by women.[22] Although overtones of this courtly game may remain attached to Fragonard's ladder motif, it is important to note the difference between his scene and the storming. In the latter women feigned an adversarial relation to their knightly lovers. Although some (Posner, for example) have argued that this is the case in Fragonard's *The Meeting,* the depicted actions of the couple do not support this claim. Rather, Fragonard represents two lovers who are on the same side of the battle, and what we see is a prearranged tryst unexpectedly interrupted.

It is not the lover climbing over the terrace who takes his beloved (and the viewer) by surprise, for he too is caught unaware. Poised atop a ladder positioned conveniently near an architectural fragment, he is a prominent element in the composition. His presence is forcefully marked because the dark pink jacket set against green breeches repeats more emphatically the complementary contrast established in the pink roses and green foliage. In an earlier conception of *The Meeting* this young lover was not so evident; underpainting now visible reveals that at one time only his head was raised over the terrace. His presence in that case was more hidden from both girl and audience, making him seem the intruder rather than the intruded upon. In the finished panel the planned meeting between two principles is obviously interrupted by a third party. Boy, girl, foliage, and statue all direct their attention (and ours) toward the unrepresented interloper whose position is suggested as outside the composition and to the left. The young woman's gesture both warns and holds off her lover, and the position of her body—twisted at the waist, head turned to the left—nearly parallels that of the statue whose duty it is to comment on the scene. The represented statue depicts Venus chastising Cupid, a theme suggesting that love's attack must be delayed. In the context of *The Meeting* it less implies that the girl is yet unwilling than that the timing is wrong. As Venus holds off Cupid, she holds off her lover until the intruder has passed. What we see, then, is the beginning of a tryst, perhaps a secret or illicit one, but not the beginning of a love affair between two people strangers to one another. Moreover, the sheet of paper held by the young woman suggests a message sent to arrange the rendezvous.

Fragonard's *The Meeting* seems a version of the interrupted meeting, a theme far more common in the eighteenth century than storming the citadel. For example, in 1750 Boucher executed *The Surprised Lovers* (now lost; engraved by Huquier), in which a rustic couple is caught in amorous adventure by a young boy peeking into the grass. De Troy's *Surprise* (1723; London: Victoria and Albert Museum) shows a servant approaching a secluded garden nook to warn courting lovers of an intruder's approach. Fragonard's painting, however, differs from both of these in that no third party (intruder or lookout) is represented. Although the identity of the intruder is left to the viewer's imagination, his or her position vis-à-vis the scene represented is not. The two lovers direct their attention across the picture plane and to the right, toward the door that leads out into the garden. Viewers might have imagined themselves the intruders as they exited through the door, or, more effectively, they might have seen another guest take the position. The barrier between the imaginary space of the painting and the real space of the salon is thus breached as real people become actors in a painted drama.

Another kind of oscillation between the real and the illusory is suggested in each panel by the resemblance established between the painted actors and the painted sculpture. The two inhabit different levels of reality—painted actors are representations of real people, painted sculptures are representations of representations. Fragonard depicts statues imitating actors—or is it that actors imitate statues—and thus obscures the distinction between what is (represented as) real and what is (represented as) representation. The interaction between figures and statues, as well as the play between painted actors and actual spectators, reinterprets the central oscillation between the real and the fictive stated in the paralleling of the outside garden with its illusory counterpart.

Turning our attention to *The Pursuit,* we notice that there the meeting seems neither prearranged nor illicit. An elegant lover surprises a young girl who romps with her friends. Doffing his plumed hat, he bows and offers her a rose, which is a central floral symbol in courtly literature.[23] In contrast to the lover made obvious by costume and position in *The Meeting,* this suitor steps out from behind a plinth, half-hidden by the cascading blossoms and nearly camouflaged because his light costume is set against a light architectural background. His presence is not immediately apparent to the viewer, who must search for the cause of the young girls' flight. If *The Meeting* thematizes surprise as a planned tryst is unexpectedly interrupted, in *The Pursuit* an unarranged meeting disrupts the young girls' play. Yet it is the expected lover represented in *The Meeting* who assumes a seemingly spontaneous pose; poised in the midst of action he balances on the balcony ledge. The pose of the unexpected lover, on the other hand, is highly artificed and belongs to the conventional language of *politesse.*

A similar kind of reversal takes place in the attitude of the female figures when seen in relation to the statue. In *The Meeting* the figure of Venus is highly mannered in a exaggerated *contrapposto.* The figure of the woman who repeats the pose is much less so, and her action seems natural to the situation. Looking toward her right, the woman's attention has been drawn by the intruder. Her eyes are wide and her mouth is slightly open. Her gesture of holding off the lover, although a little mannered, seems appropriate to the circumstances. In *The Pursuit* not only is the pose of the central figure a highly stylized representation of flight, but her attendants are placed in quite awkward and unnatural positions designed, I believe, to consciously mimic the poses of the two putti astride the dolphin above.[24] Finally, if we recall our comparison between the settings of *The Meeting* and *The Pursuit,* we can add that the more spontaneous attitudes are assumed in the more contrived setting, whereas the more conventional poses dominate the locale where artifice is more successfully concealed.

This interplay of opposites—the real and the fictive, the artificial and the natural, the calculated and the spontaneous—pervades these two scenes which generally focus on both meeting and surprise. Taken together, *The Meeting* and *The Pursuit* represent two different couples, two different settings, and two possible overtures to lovemaking, the lovemaking that the real viewer might anticipate or imagine taking place in the garden.

The Lover Crowned AND *The Love Letters*

As the guests return from the garden, the works that they see are *The Love Letters* (figure 7) and *The Lover Crowned* (figure 6), both of which again represent different locales and different couples. These two scenes have traditionally been given the responsibility of carrying the meaning of the series, and they have been contrasted according to the states of love they represent: love consummated in *The Lover Crowned* and love turned to friendship in *The Love Letters.* But as in *The Meeting,* one must consider what is overtly represented in these scenes, which have been traditionally read in accord with the demands of an assumed symbolic allegory.

Turning first to *The Lover Crowned,* interpreters have traced to the Middle Ages the motif of the lover wreathed with flowers.[25] In seventeenth- and eighteenth-century art several meanings accrued to this symbolic gesture, but the two most pertinent here are sexual consummation (as in Clodion's explicit *Satyr Enjoying a Nymph,* London: Private Collection) and marriage (as in Vien's *Temple of Hymen*). In *The Lover Crowned,* however, the couple is not simply enacting a symbolic gesture. The two figures are represented as self-consciously posing for the artist; movements are frozen rather than in the process of being made, and accoutrements are carefully arranged. One musical instrument, for example, lies with its flat face turned upward, the other is turned down showing its rounded back. In red suit and yellow dress, the lovers stand out prominently from the setting in which they have been placed, and they are framed or boxed between roses and orange tree along one diagonal, and between statue and artist along the other. Because the lovers are centered between the statue of a sleeping cupid and the depiction of the artist sketching, a comparison between the two terminal points is implied; and that comparison is emphasized by similarities between artist and amor. The mass of drapery against which the artist rests is likened to the cloud that supports the sleeping putto, and the artist's bow forms a suitable visual analogue to the amorino's wings. If cupid's work is done, that of the artist has just begun, for if the one ignites love, the other preserves and memorializes it.

The primary theme of this panel, then, is not the lover crowned but, more precisely, the *representation* of the lover crowned. The figures are cast as models for the artist who preserves the memory of love by encoding it in a traditional sign and immortalizing it through art. But as represented here the artist's act is also ironic; we see him directly copying "nature," but nature has already been ordered into a conventional pattern of art.

In most analyses of the adjacent panel, *The Love Letters,* a reading of the iconographic details has overtaken any interest in the ostensible subject. It is the statue, in this case, that has been given undue prominence. But the statue is only one element in a complex of signs. The dog, for example, is a traditional symbol of fidelity, and the embrace of the couple suggests erotic love. Put together, we see friendship, fidelity, sexual attraction. But these should enhance our understanding of the central action, not divert our attention from it.

The activity that engages this couple is rereading the letters that are piled up beside the young girl. The activity itself implies preserving and remembering the events of the affair, but it is a particular kind of preservation, one both like and unlike that depicted on the adjacent panel. Rereading letters was frequently represented in eighteenth-century French painting, and the motif should be distinguished from other kinds of letter reading, in particular that depicted in seventeenth-century Dutch paintings. In the latter we often see a note being received or opened (as in Vermeer's *The Mistress and Maid,* [1665–70; New York: Frick Collection] or Terborch's *A Lady Reading a Letter* [1660s; London: Wallace Collection]). Only one piece of correspondence is evident, and the reader is often alert, wide-eyed, perhaps even anxious. Both painted actor and real audience wonder what message the missive contains. Fragonard, on the other hand, liked to show daydreaming figures rereading letters. Such is the case in *The Letter* (New York: Metropolitan Museum of Art), where the woman, eyes half-closed and head resting on her hand, is caught in a moment of reverie. That she is remembering and reminiscing is also suggested by the pulled-out drawer filled with already received and treasured correspondence. The audience is encouraged more to wonder what is in the woman's mind than what is written in the note she holds. This representation resembles *The Love Letters* because the theme centers on the mental processes. It is unlike the larger panel, however, because in depicting only the receiver it isolates one part of the communication process.

The letter, like the epistolary novel that mimics it, was a widespread form of communication in the eighteenth century. As a representation of spontaneous emotion, the letter was inherently paradoxical; although in actuality even love letters were highly conventionalized, letters were, by agreement, often taken as genuine or natural recordings.[26] Yet even when the letter was intended strictly for personal consumption (and it often was not), it allowed lovers to write their own story and to record the affair as they wanted to remember it. The level of self-conscious manipulation contained within the love letter increased as the author rewrote. And the more the letter was read, the more the recipient reflected on and intensified a response, the more self-conscious the response became. In the mutual rereading of a group of letters by both sender and receiver, one preferred interpretation might be formalized as they shaped and molded the text that would induce pleasant reverie. The two figures we see in Fragonard's *Love Letters,* then, have created in their *billets doux* a work of art for which they are model, author, and audience—a representation of the self, by the self, and for the self.

The leafy frame behind the elegantly posed lovers is, in its self-contained paradoxes, a rococo form analogous to the love letters. Although Fragonard also used the natural cartouche in *The Pursuit,* in that work it was not as significant as in *The Love Letters,* where it is larger, more centrally placed, and more prominent flanked as it is by simple masses of foliage grouped at the sides.

If perceived in a real garden (rather than in a painted one), the natural cartouche was the visible trace of an invisible and spontaneous process: the growing together of tree branches. Yet even to designate the form as a cartouche is already to effect a transformation. We might consider the unnamed pattern a natural sign or index of growth, causally related to what it represents. In creating this sign nature is unselfconscious. When someone recognizes the pattern as artful, calling it a natural cartouche, the same pattern represents more. It also stands for culture's projecting onto natural forms (or recognizing in natural forms) its own artful structures. The natural pattern then becomes an instituted sign that represents a frame or border.

If self-representation (the unconscious self-representation of nature as art and the conscious self-representation of the couple in their letters) and its paradoxes are major themes of *The Love Letters,* then these themes are doubly represented in the courting pair. In addition to rereading their letters, these figures are depicted as having positioned themselves in elegant and conventional attitudes. Although the same could be said of almost every figure in the Louveciennes series, what is significant about the couple in *The Love Letters* is that they establish a unique relation to the sculpture represented in the scene. They are the only figures quite directly placed on or beside a pedestal, a round base that is a diminutive version of the one on which the sculpture of *Amitié* rests. At the same time, neither imitates the pose of the adjacent sculpted figures. Together these characteristics stress not so much a specific relation between the activity of the couple and the activity of the sculpture as a correspondence in their mode of being. Both are conceived as works of art, for the two lovers have become a natural or living sculpture, not unreminiscent of the small bisque figures so popular throughout the century. Although the correspondence between sculpted and real figures is developed through the other panels (especially in *The Meeting* and *The Pursuit*), it becomes expressed most emphatically in *The Love Letters,* where self-representation, specifically the self-representation of one's love, is thematized.

At Louveciennes the motif of love's self-representation that reverberates through *The Love Letters* was set against that of love's representation so evident in *The Lover Crowned.* In the latter work the figures self-consciously pose for the artist-viewer who presumably has arranged their attitudes; they are fully aware of the transformation that he will enact upon them. In *The Love Letters,* however, no represented artist has arranged the couple; they do not display themselves for any represented viewer; and they appear to be fully absorbed in their activity, which takes place in a secluded setting. Moreover, none of the subsidiary characters look at or respond to them. Venus and Cupid are preoccupied with one another, and the faithful pooch (whom we will consider below) focuses its attention outside of the represented space. The relation of these lovers to themselves-as-sculpture, then, extends their relation to their affair as story-told-in-letters. In *The Lover Crowned* they were model, artist, and audience; now they are model, artist, audience, and work of art.

The two compositions that thematize the memorializing of love through representation also suggest different relations with the real viewer and artist. *The Lover Crowned* is set out like a framed tale with the models arranged in the garden bower and analogous to the inner story. Within this structure the represented artist has a complex function. First we can compare him to the narrator of a text.[27] Like the narrator he is the character within the work of art who presents the story; in fact, we see him in the act of depicting it. There is, however, no represented audience in *The Lover Crowned* to exemplify for the real audience a range of responses. For the function of the surrogate beholder, we must turn again to the artist for he is both representing and viewing the framed interior scene. We see him at the moment when he has looked up from his work to contemplate the models before him. His dual role as narrator and surrogate viewer is emphasized by clues within the compositional structure.[28] The inner story is presented from his point of view, which corresponds with the main diagonal axis of the composition; and certain pictorial elements, the boxed orange trees, for example, are positioned so as to be seen by an observer located below and to the right of them.

As well as functioning as narrator and surrogate viewer, the represented artist is also the fictive double of the real one. In the scene represented he clearly mediates between the models and the art they will become. No spontaneous recorder of nature, this artist has carefully arranged both attitudes and accoutrements. The specific role given to the painter as a character in this scene (sketching the model) and his general function within the work (narrator-surrogate viewer) together stress the artist's role as contriver, as plot maker—in short, as fabricator of the work of art. With its highly artificed surface and complicated interplay of subject and visual effects, *The Lover Crowned* suggests that Fragonard, like his painted counterpart, was the guiding intelligence responsible for the painting; he determined the look of the scene and established the viewer's position within it.

Turning to *The Love Letters,* we are presented with an entirely different situation but one that resolves itself in a similar way. Here no narrator is represented. What we see (two figures rereading their letters) carries the fiction that the event is telling, or rather showing, itself—that we see the scene unmediated. This fiction accords well with that of the letter, which purported to present directly the feelings of the writer. In *The Love Letters,* then, there also appears to be some confluence of meaning between the scene represented and the method of representation.

This confluence seems strengthened when we notice that two other elements found in *The Lover Crowned* are pointedly missing here. First, the absence of a surrogate viewer parallels on a structural level the suggestion that the love letters represented within the painting were issued only for private consumption and therefore do not have an outside audience. In addition, the composition is more or less closed to the real beholder. No character is positioned so as to suggest a point where the viewer can easily insert himself or herself into the scene; and although the sprig of flowers in the left corner of the canvas does establish a place of entry, it clearly falls short of the mark as a substitute viewer, offering little opportunity for the psychological projection of the real beholder. Moreover, the composition gives the audience mixed messages. Although the main diagonal axis is established from the lower left corner, the obviously placed parasol is seen more from underneath and to the right. The angle of viewing Venus and Cupid is quite acute and suggests another position, one more directly below the pedestal. Thus *The Love Letters* appears to be unmediated by a narrator, unobserved by an internal viewer, and closed to the real audience to whom it offers neither entry point nor perspective.

There is, however, one element that subverts the self-containment so skillfully woven into both the theme and structure of *The Love Letters.* The betrayal is enacted by the very symbol of faithfulness: the small spaniel that lies at the lovers' feet. For it is the dog who, alert and wide-eyed, looks out of the painting to acknowledge the presence of a beholding public. This spotted fragment of *papillotage,* this breaker of illusions, is here the representative of artifice and duplicity. And the audience, alerted to the fictions of art, can then see the hand of the artist everywhere, for *The Love Letters* is perhaps even more carefully constructed than the more obviously contrived scene placed beside it.

THE LOUVECIENNES PANELS INTERPRETED

The *Progress of Love* does not unfold as four sequential stages of love. Rather the scenes are related by two kinds of logic, one of which is determined by the dynamics of the room and its relation to its exterior setting. In terms of the architecture, the subjects depicted on the two major wall surfaces coordinate with the viewer's experience of the garden. The panels seen as one goes into the garden (either by actually entering it or by looking through the doors) overtly depict possible overtures to lovemaking. In *The Meeting* the tryst has been planned by both parties, who seem to respond spontaneously to an unexpected and unrepresented intruder. In *The Pursuit* these dynamics are reversed: the intruder represented is one of the scene's protagonists, and he has apparently engineered a meeting that takes the young women by surprise. Both the suitor's courtly gesture and the stylized flight of the pursued seem contrived and mannered. With their combination of the planned and the spontaneous, the possibilities of *The Meeting* and *The Pursuit* perhaps lead the viewer to the paradoxical conclusion that, in the garden, one can anticipate the unexpected surprise. The two panels seen upon returning from the garden, *The Love Letters* and *The Lover Crowned,* are based on themes of remembering and representing. One couple holds its pose for the artist's recording, and the other rereads the self-determined text of their affair. To compensate the viewer for leaving the real pleasure garden, these two works offer the sweet pang of reminiscence.

The other logic discernible throughout the four Louveciennes panels is that of reconciled opposites, and it operates in both the structures and thematics of the panels. The overriding oppositions restate that central eighteenth-century dichotomy of art and nature: the counterfeit and the real, the calculated and the spontaneous, the mediated and the unmediated, the mannered gesture and the truthful response. These are resolved in paradoxical gestures: the sculpture animated and the figures become art; the garden naturally overgrown and the natural growth become a cartouche; letters that become a composed text and the direct rendering of a precomposed scene.

Fragonard and the *Pittoresque*

Nature and artifice: between these two terms rococo aesthetics posited an ongoing sequence of interactions.[29] In painting theory alone, the paradox of artful naturalness found endless restatements, the most significant of which was the *pittoresque*. Taken in its most general sense, the term signified what was proper to painting. Throughout the eighteenth century, however, *pittoresque* (or the English "picturesque") was applied to a variety of related concepts. For us the most familiar of these described the representation of nature, particularly in landscape painting and garden design.[30] But that use of *pittoresque* was actually a special case of the term's more general application. A painting was called *pittoresque* when its elements, wisely chosen and arranged according to the rules of art, produced a pleasing visual effect. As we have seen, in the practice of history painting the demand for pleasing visual effects (for the *pittoresque*) was inseparable from that of *convenance*. For the lesser genres where the artist (in theory) simply imitated nature, there usually was no conventional aesthetic gesture prescribed for the individual object represented; a bowl of plums, a stack of cards, a starched pinafore—these did not have the same specific requirements for representation as, say, Venus, who was always to be rendered in a visual language that bespoke voluptuousness. The general notion of the *pittoresque* did, however, contain a kind of built-in *convenance* where the depiction of nature demanded apparent naturalness. Here is Cochin's 1759 definition of *composition pittoresque:* "[It is] what is distributed so as to render natural attitudes in their most pleasing aspect without losing anything of the truthfulness of the action, to group them in such a way that they produce strong effects of light and shade unaffectedly. . . ."[31] In making a picturesque composition, then, nothing was to appear purposely arranged by the painter, and everything was to seem as if derived from the natural appearance of the object depicted.

The principle of concealed artifice also insured the natural appearance of the painting at the structural level, because a similar principle was taken to govern the operations of nature, that of basic laws hidden beneath the appearance of chance. This general belief was not the sole property of the mechanists, who posited a clockwork universe in which all was determined by the immutable laws of matter in motion. Vitalists did not embrace a nature more significantly random but one that progressed according the principles of organic growth. Although the universe did not develop, progress, or function according to blind chance, apparent chance hid the mathematical formulae of the mechanists and the developmental principles of the vitalists beneath a veil of seemingly random and haphazard phenomena.[32] Art thus imitated nature when structured according to aesthetic principles concealed beneath a seemingly artless surface.

As defined by the mid-eighteenth century, *pittoresque* art was paradoxical because it appeared both artful (i.e., organized to be visually pleasing) and not artful (naturally random) at the same time. It was perhaps more problematic when the term *pittoresque* was applied to natural things rather than art objects. When natural objects were described as *pittoresque,* the term signified what nature had incidentally (that is, by chance) made artful when acting for different ends. Watelet defined as picturesque, "Old trees whose trunks are contorted and gnawed by time, whose often-cracked bark is deeply grooved, whose branches are knotty. . . ."[33] The *pittoresque,* then, identifies not only what is artfully natural (as in the case of a landscape painting) but also what is naturally artful (as in the case of the old tree). The first is the result of calculation, the second of chance.

The paradoxes of the *pittoresque,* however, were most commonly found in garden aesthetics. Like the painter, the gardener was an artist who constructed natural effects. Watelet called the gardener a *"decorateur,"* a term that made reference to someone who ornamented the interiors of palaces and houses.[34] The natural site was the undecorated space where the gardener-decorator created artful illusions, and, if the painter invented by assembling and arranging painted objects, the gardener applied the same process to different substances—soil, water, plants. Watelet was typical of those who admired the *pittoresque* garden because it followed the rules of painting in creating an artful naturalness.[35] Constructions familiar from *pittoresque* theory emerge throughout Watelet's garden treatise. He warns, for example, that contrasts must be managed with a delicate artifice because "art that shows itself destroys the effect of art."[36]

The *pittoresque* garden, as is well known, was an artful construction contrived to seem natural through transplanted trees, "improved" contours, newly dug streams, walkways curved into "irregular" patterns. In his garden treatise of 1779, Morel noted that nature worked to the gardener's orders and thereby bent to his will. The gardener chose the sites, prescribed the forms, calculated the expressions, determined the character. Nature was only allowed the freedom to grow, and even this was limited by the initial shape the garden had been given.[37] Watelet warned decorators to design the garden with an eye to the future, to consider how the shrubs, trees, flowers might look in five, ten, or twenty years.[38] We might say that the picturesque garden was to some extent natural because nature finished and perfected the work. Some effects of negligence and disorder were produced, not by the calculated chance of art, but by the apparent chance of nature. On the other hand, nature's apparent chance worked in the service of the artist, hiding artifice.

Artists of Fragonard's generation were conversant with *pittoresque* aesthetics as applied to the making of gardens, the depiction of landscape, and the viewing of the natural scene. Although we are most familiar with the English mania for the picturesque, the French at midcentury enjoyed the same pleasures. Cochin's 1758 *Voyage d'Italie,* for example, is filled with references to scenes described as *pittoresque* because their qualities would make a good picture.[39] As secretary of the Academy, he urged students to draw landscape in Italy, particularly at those sites he identified as *pittoresque.* Here drawing after nature resembled drawing an *académie* in which the model held a conventional pose that had already been determined as artful. Copying the natural picturesque was another kind of arranged life drawing, and from it the young artist could learn how to make a pleasing landscape. The experience would prepare the painter to improve other sites or to imagine fantasy landscapes that exemplified *pittoresque* aesthetics. That many students accepted Cochin's counsel is evidenced by the numerous representations of a particularly *pittoresque* site, the Temple of the Sibyl at Tivoli.[40] Fragonard was one of those students who followed the academician's advice; he was brought to Tivoli in 1760 by the Abbé de Saint-Non, whose enthusiasm for the *pittoresque* landscape is well documented.[41]

Fragonard's play with the contradictions of art and nature in the *Progress of Love* evokes the paradoxes of the *pittoresque:* the painted narrative both takes place in a painted garden and is coordinated with a real garden visible from the decorated salon. Although at Louveciennes *pittoresque* contradiction is only one among several resolved oppositions, it becomes a major theme of two pendant landscape paintings now in the National Gallery of Art, Washington: *The Game of Horse and Rider* (figure 12) and *The Game of Hot Cockles* (figure 13). In these pendants a natural-looking garden scene contrasts with a pointedly artificial one, and the juxtaposition suggests that both the hiding and display of artifice are effects of art.

The Game of Horse and Rider is located in the untended far reaches of a park, and nearly everything about the activity of the figures suggests naturalness. It is significant that those at play are children, regarded then as spontaneous and unspoiled by civilization. They climb upon one another in a rollicking game, seeming unselfconscious and fully absorbed in their play. A couple is seated directly on the ground nearby, and the poses of both partners are deliberately unmannered, almost awkward: the woman has no artful turn to her body, the man's torso is not extended in a flowing and elegant curve. If *The Game of Horse and Rider* signifies the natural, the artificial is represented in the *The Game of Hot Cockles.* The scene is set in a cultivated part of a garden where flowers grow in beds, trees in

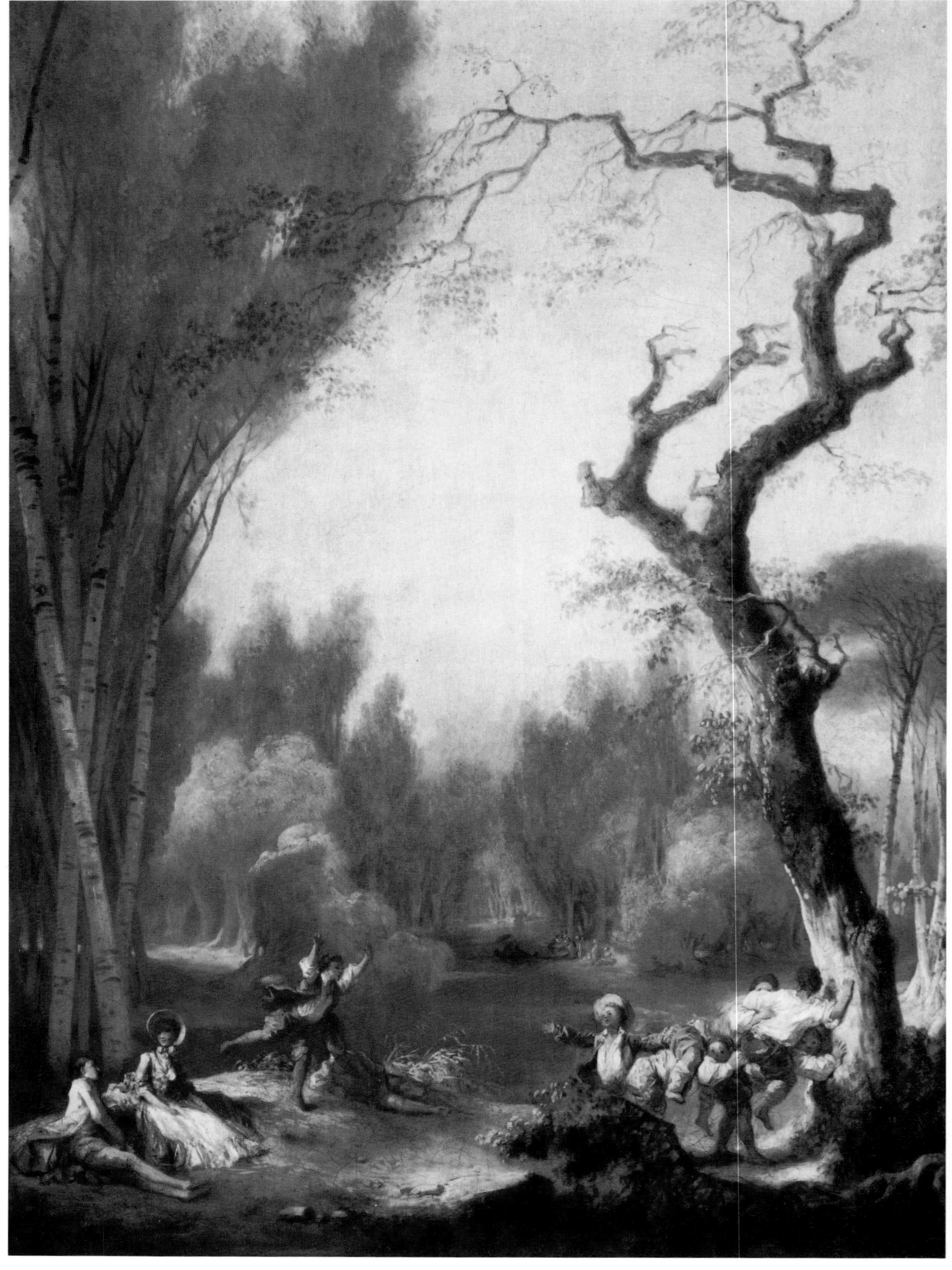

Figure 12 Jean-Honoré Fragonard, *The Game of Horse and Rider,* c. 1767. National Gallery of Art, Washington, Samuel H. Kress Collection.

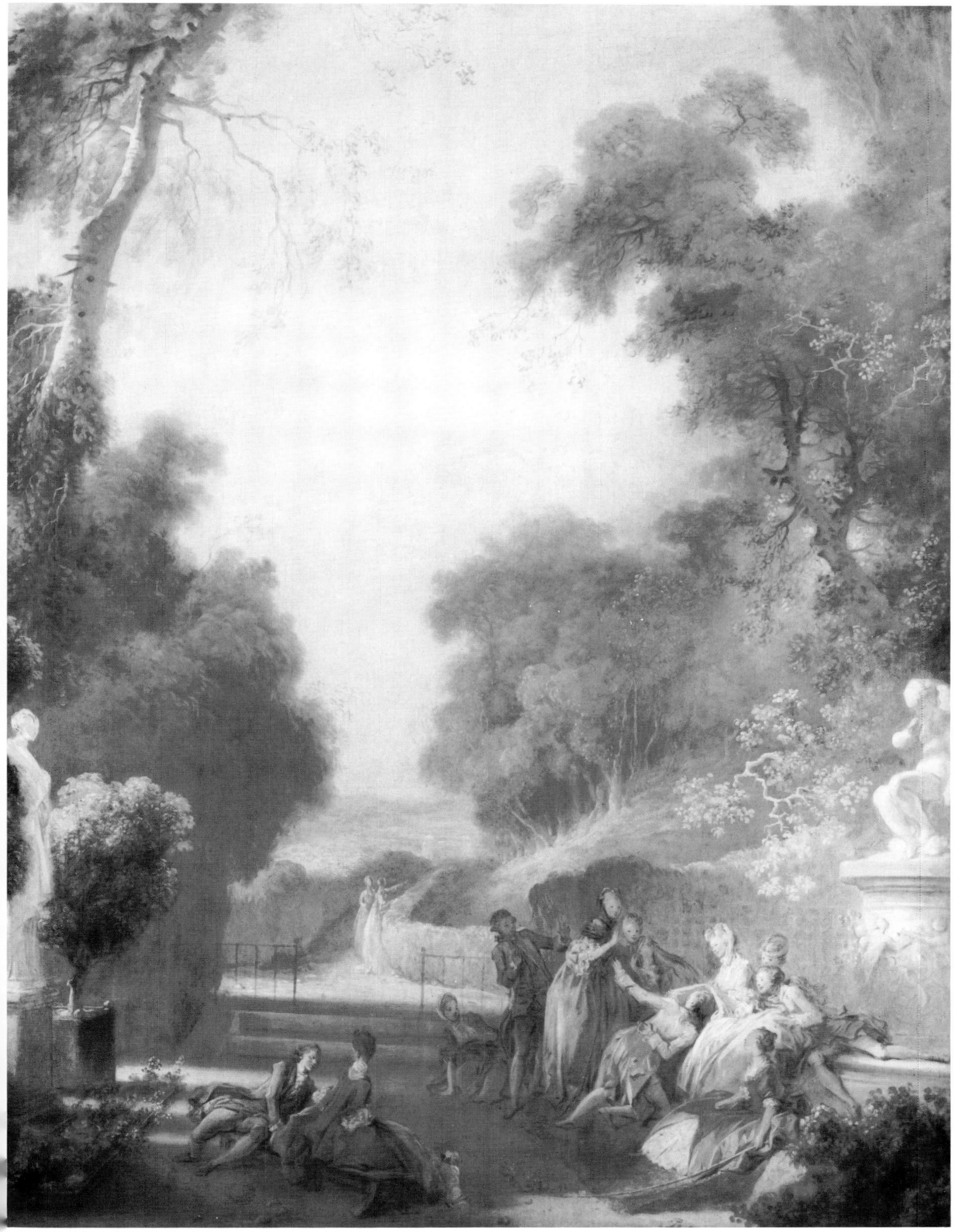

Figure 13 Jean-Honoré Fragonard, *The Game of Hot Cockles,* c. 1767. National Gallery of Art, Washington, Samuel H. Kress Collection.

boxes, and hedges in clipped rows. The game of hot cockles (blindman's buff) is played by civilized young adults rather than by children, and it is a traditional game of courtly love.[42] The contrived and mannered poses suggest conventionalized gesture, and one figure even assumes the posture that Le Brun reserved for expressing surprise. The couple sitting alone no longer lounges on the ground but on a park bench; her pose shows artful oppositions, and the line of his body forms a pleasing S-curve.

In terms of motif, the foreground scene of *The Game of Horse and Rider* is separated from the background by the natural horizontal of the river bank and underscored by the disposition of the gaming figures. In *The Game of Hot Cockles,* on the other hand, the horizontal division is effected by artificial barriers: railing and steps. Here nature is made to mimic art, for the light falls in steps and spreads across the scene in regular horizontal bands. Beyond the barriers in these two compositions, the dense landscape of the background is opened up with an element that cuts a path through it. In the natural scene it is part of the meandering stream; in the artificial one, a clipped and shaped hedgerow. Contrasting motifs are thus represented in nearly identical compositional structures. The consistency between these works extends further because in each there is an obvious division created on the canvas surface as the brushwork differentiates foregrounds from backgrounds. The foregrounds are rendered with small, choppy, and visible strokes, and the paint is laid on heavily. In the backgrounds the paint is thinner, and the colors are well blended. This differentiation is also played out in the color harmony; in each painting the unnatural blue-green color of the background contrasts with the primary triad that dominates the forground.

It hardly seems likely that this play of similarity and contrast was a matter of chance, something unplanned by the artist. It is particularly significant that one strategy remains constant: while the subjects or the motifs are contrasted, the compositional arrangements are nearly identical.[43] This phenomenon is discernible in the framing elements, as well. In *The Game of Horse and Rider* the scene is flanked left and right by trees; the straight young trunks and full foliage of those on the left are juxtaposed to the blasted trunk, jagged branches, and sparse leaves of the one on the right. In *The Game of Hot Cockles* the contrast is carried not only by trees but also by statues. Overseeing the couple's conversation, the piece on the left is a fully draped figure in the antique style. On the right is a statue familiar to Fragonard's gardens and erotic scenes, Falconet's *Menacing Cupid.* It is appropriate to its place, since in playing hot cockles the blindfolded person must guess the identity of the others. Thus the viewer must be silent and not give away the game. But not only is the *Menacing Cupid* appropriate to the scene, it is contrasted with the statue on the left, a contrast of classical and rococo, of serious and amusing, of ancient and modern. Thus when these two pendants are viewed together we see that a natural scene and an artificed one are equally artificial, a reading reinforced by the two major framing elements, one of which signifies nature (trees) and the other of which signifies art (sculpture).

Art, Love, and the Garden at Louveciennes

Pittoresque paradox, which forms the dominant theme of the Washington pendants, is an essential player in *The Progress of Love,* where the garden provides a framework for the lovemaking represented. If art reigns supreme in the *pittoresque* garden, it is also primary in Fragonard's *Progress of Love,* where it is the art of love and not its course, its uncertainty or its consummation, that is most emphatically represented.

In the Louveciennes panels the erotic, sexual elements are decidedly present but remain relatively controlled and covert.[44] The individual scenes do not have the explicitness of, say, Fragonard's *Girl Playing with Her Dog* (c. 1770; Munich: Alte Pinakotek), and the veiled sexual allusions are relatively tame and unobtrusive. Nowhere, for example, does the young man proposition his sweetheart by offering her a bunch of grapes suggestively hanging between his legs, as he does in Boucher's *Young Man Offering Grapes to a Girl* (1768; London: Kenwood House, figure 14). And when Fragonard's suitor graces his beloved with a rose, the sexual connotations of the flower are not underscored by a blatant pictorial comparison with the female anatomy.[45] Even the most potentially explicit gesture, the crowning of the lover, is dominated by art because the couple is conceived as an artist's model. This is not to deny that there is a coordination of the pleasures of art (anticipation, surprise, reminiscence) with those of love, but rather to affirm that in *The Progress* art is the dominant force that controls both love and nature.

At Louveciennes love is formed into the patterns of aristocratic flirtation that had been conventionalized in texts and images during the eighteenth century.[46] Writers and painters represented courtship as filled with codified rites and gestures; movements of the fan, turns of the head, words delivered with a particular inflection—all had their special meaning.[47] Although at times the ritual was displayed with flourish, at other times it was hidden beneath the cloak of spontaneity. Even the most nat-

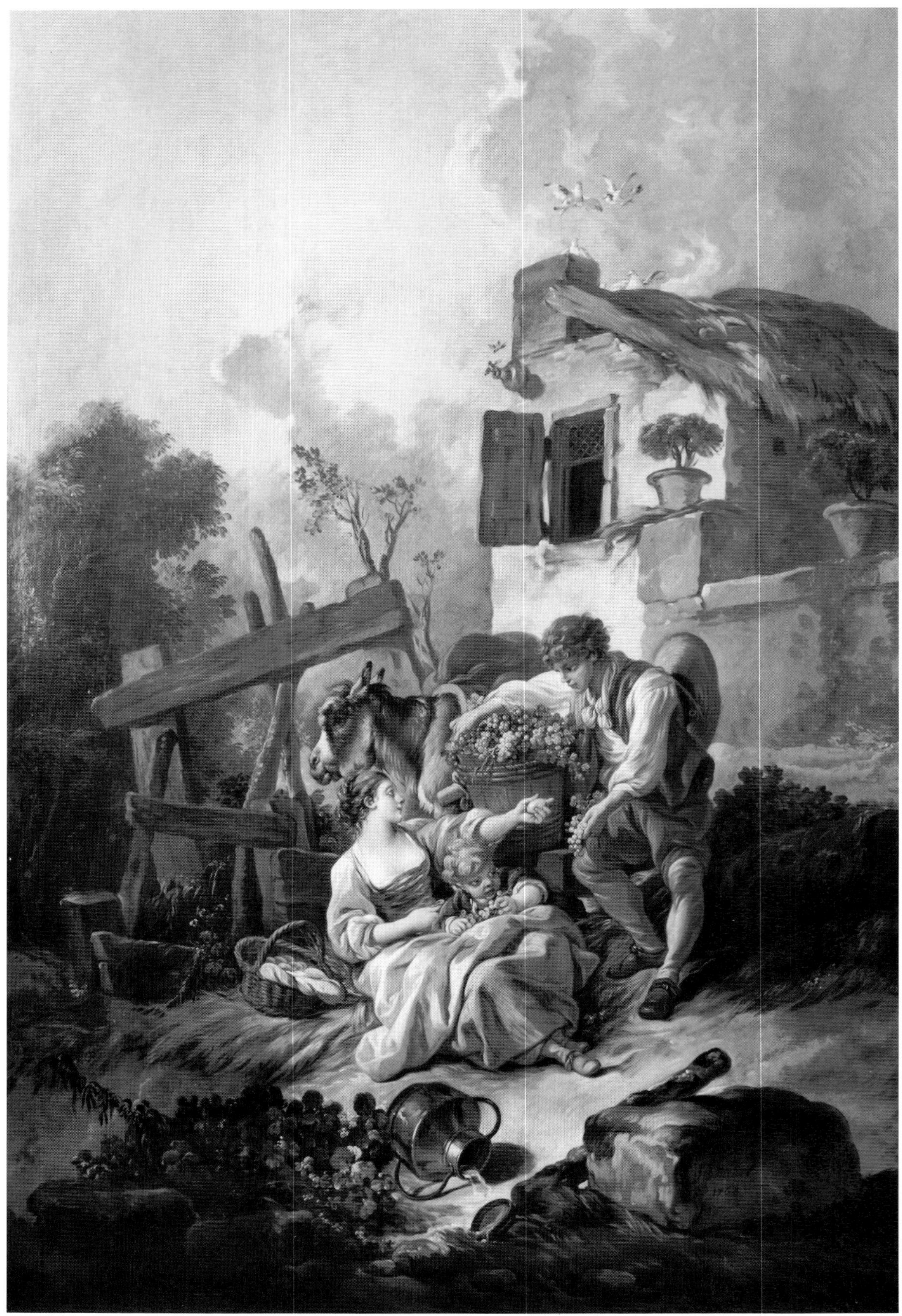

Figure 14 François Boucher, *Young Man Offering Grapes to a Girl,* 1765.
The Iveagh Bequest, Kenwood (English Heritage).

ural-seeming actions and responses, however, were revealed to the audience as carefully planned and premeditated. The arrangement of chance meetings, for example, was a well-established ploy in the art of love as depicted in theater and the novel. Sinister consequences also came from love's deceptive tactics. Laclos, for example, represented the libertine who hid his motives beneath a veneer of sincerity in *Les liaisons dangereuses,* 1782, in which the debauched Valmont wins the Presidente's heart by feigning virtue—in particular, generosity to the poor. The strategy succeeds and a modest woman falls.

Display and dissimulation, those aspects of aristocratic courtship most familiar to art, are represented with wit in the two scenes that flank the garden entrance at Louveciennes. *The Pursuit* makes a show of courtly address, whereas the seemingly spontaneous responses of *The Meeting* divert attention from the conventionalized patterns embedded in the episode.[48] The figures within these compositions, moreover, play at being contemporary versions of the knights and ladies represented in courtly literature. We have already suggested that the lover scaling the wall in *The Meeting,* at least in passing, refers to those medieval knights who stormed their ladies' citadel, and that *The Pursuit* includes the central floral symbol of courtly love literature. *The Lover Crowned* and *The Love Letters* also contain similar references. It is not just that in these panels the men seem subdued or tamed by love, but that the posture (and fiction) of male subservience was derived from medieval romances in which it was the knight's duty to serve and obey his lady, who had the power to grant or deny him her favors.[49]

This lovemaking as artful playacting is also suggested throughout the four panels in the figures' costumes and poses. Fugitives from a *fête galante,* the male suitors appear in fantasy dress.[50] The women wear costumes that suggest those of the eighteenth-century court and represent that society's ideal in their tiny waists, dainty extremities, and porcelain skin.[51] Because so many of the figures either mimic the works of art near them, or pose in stylized gestures, their attitudes and actions often seem pointedly theatrical.

The playacting in Fragonard's *Progress* is not only developed in terms of the characters represented; it also extends to the real beholder, who is offered a variety of parts. In *The Lover Crowned* the viewer is invited to enter the scene psychologically through the represented artist acting as surrogate viewer. The unrepresented intruder of *The Meeting* allows the spectator a different kind of involvement, as the painted characters seem to react to the real viewer, rather than vice versa. Although everything seems calculated to deny the beholder's presence in *The Love Letters,* the effect is undercut as the small dog affirms that someone is positioned outside the work. Finally, in *The Pursuit* the viewer must be content to remain an unacknowledged voyeur, but perhaps one who is the invisible counterpart of the visible intruder stepping out from his camouflage to offer his beloved a rose.

If the beholder's involvement oscillates between the real and the illusory while imaginatively participating in the fictive world of the painting, the swings are intensified by the paralleling of the painted garden inside the salon and the real garden outside of it. As viewers step into Mme Du Barry's salon, they also project themselves into the simulated garden, and what is seen there urges other fantasies.[52] The themes represented by Fragonard encourage the anticipation and remembrance of real or imagined events, events that could occur or have occured in a garden. Both anticipation and remembrance invite the viewer to further projection—projection out of the salon and its illusory garden, out of present time and into the (imagined or remembered) future or past. Thus, once the spectator has entered the painted garden of love, it gives way to a second illusion conjured by the imagination.

The Progress of Love and the Viewer-Created Narrative

We can now reconstitute the *Progress of Love* as a kind of narrative different from one that is sequential, linear, and artist determined. We have already seen that Fragonard presents his viewers with possibilities and choices: there are two scenes depicting different overtures to love and two others showing different ways of representing it. Within each set the artist neither suggests the temporal priority of one over the other nor establishes a compositional movement from one to the next. Not only does *The Progress of Love* break conventional narrative patterns by offering its viewers choices, it is also exceptional in that it turns the concept of the moment inside out. In representing traditional narrative time artists usually chose a scene that implied preliminary and subsequent events. Fragonard, on the other hand, leaves his viewers free to imagine the central scenes, to insert, if so inclined, their own experiences of love, to conjure fictive ones, or even to fantasize about the other guests who filled the interior space of Mme Du Barry's salon.

Not only are the observers given a choice of openings and closings (what we have called endings could even be picked as beginnings), but they are also free to relate the paintings two by two in ways other than that suggested by the sharing of a common wall. For example, when looking diagonally the viewer might connect *The Meeting* and *The Love Letters* through the full-blown statue of Venus and notice that classicism is opposed to mannerism in the sculpted figures. *The Lover Crowned* and *The Pursuit,* on the other hand, share the statue of Amour—a passive, sleeping Cupid in the one, an active attentive amorino in the other. Yet there would be other clues to relate the panels across from one another. *The Meeting* and *The Lover Crowned* both include the leafy bough juxtaposed to the jagged branch and a landscape dominated by a single overhanging tree. And although less similar to one another than the previous pair, *The Love Letters* and *The Pursuit* do share backgrounds articulated in terms of the natural cartouche, and in both scenes the foliage forms a kind of screen behind the main characters. Thus, although the sculpture suggests that *The Meeting* should be related to *The Love Letters* and *The Pursuit* to *The Lover Crowned,* the settings suggest a different pairing.

If a narrative is implied in *The Progress of Love,* that narrative is viewer created (as opposed to artist determined), and it need not necessarily encompass all four panels or be limited to them. The scenes do not so much challenge viewers to order them in the correct sequence (the sequence privileged by the artist) as invite them to participate in the creation of a narrative by using both the painted scenes and any other scenes imagined to complement them. The Louveciennes panels, then, are not a single narrative but many potential narratives, any one of which can be activated by the viewer, who is free to choose from among the many suggestive comparisons and contrasts that Fragonard planted in his illusory garden.

In many ways the process of viewing Fragonard's *Progress of Love* can be said to parallel the process of viewing a garden. A paradigm for the viewer-constructed art work, the garden left its spectators free to (re)make the work through their experiences of it. The gardener exercised some control by establishing the main alleys and walkways, and deciding where the buildings and sculptures would be placed. What could not be definitely controlled or predicted was the order of viewing, and the vantage from which the objects in the landscape would be seen. These characteristics were what distinguished painting from gardening, according to some eighteenth-century theorists. The composition of a painting seemed always the same when regarded by different viewers, for the spectator had the power to alter neither direction nor disposition within the work of art. Visitors to a park, however, could change the "intention" of the work by following their own order of viewing, by stopping more often than the gardener had envisioned, by approaching buildings and sculpture from paths other than the one foreseen.[53] The theorist Morel even objected to the comparison between painting and gardening because only the gardener had the advantage of producing effects that would be varied according to the spectators.[54] *The Progress of Love* exploits the gardener's edge; the paintings do not simply allow their own remaking, they encourage it.

At Louveciennes Fragonard created a superficially pleasing yet deeply resonant work of art. The panels both suggest a story and withhold a determined narrative order, thus engaging their audience in a lively interchange. We can only imagine that once attention was turned to the decorations, Fragonard's strategy would give the guests in Mme Du Barry's salon a focus of discussion, provoking the kind of *badinage* that, in entertaining them, would work to the artist's advantage. Because *The Progress of Love* could focus the attention of the audience on itself (that is, on its own conversation), the series could capture notice unavailable to a pat story, simply told.

Framed within this viewer-determined narrative is a discourse about the intricate relation between art and nature in courtship and in representation. Art emerges as the controlling partner even in those things—letters, gardens, surprises—that seem natural and spontaneous. And the viewer-created narrative, like naturalistic representation, is not what it seems to be. The apparent freedom afforded the beholder is determined by the artist's careful fabrication, and narrative control is ceded to a viewer whose imaginings transform themselves into a celebration of the artist's wit. What is represented in Fragonard's Louveciennes panels is less the progress of love than the triumph of artifice, artifice that shines the more brightly when its brilliance is cleverly concealed.

The Erotics of Decoration 3

Fragonard's *Progress of Love* provided an ideal opportunity for the interpreter of decorative painting; the commission came from a significant patron, and the relationships between the panels and their intended setting could be reconstructed. Other decorative works by Fragonard have been more completely severed from their original contexts, not only physically separated but also cut off by the unfortunate lack of documentary evidence. Although in many cases we know neither the names of those who commissioned the cycles nor the locations in which they were placed, we can assume that such works were intended for an elite audience of private patrons with the financial resources to hire an accomplished decorator. This is the case with four panels dated to about 1751 and held in the Detroit Institute: *The Grape Gatherer* (figure 15), *The Harvester* (figure 16), *The Wanderer* (also called *The Shepherdess*) (figure 17), and *The Gardener* (figure 18). Each non-narrative composition highlights an individual figure dressed in countrified costume and arranged in an artful pose. Of the two male figures, the Harvester pauses in the field to rest on his scythe, while the Gardener, holding a bird and a basket of flowers, poses in his *jardin de plaisir.* One young woman gathers fruit in her apron and squeezes a bunch of grapes over a child lying in the grass below *(The Grape Gatherer)*; another ambles through the landscape carrying a baby piggyback and holding a toddler at her side *(The Wanderer)*.

If we lack documentary evidence for this group of decorative figures, there is other information to compensate for our ignorance of patron and place. The Detroit panels can easily be associated with a standard iconography that incorporates within it a clear temporal sequence, the sequence

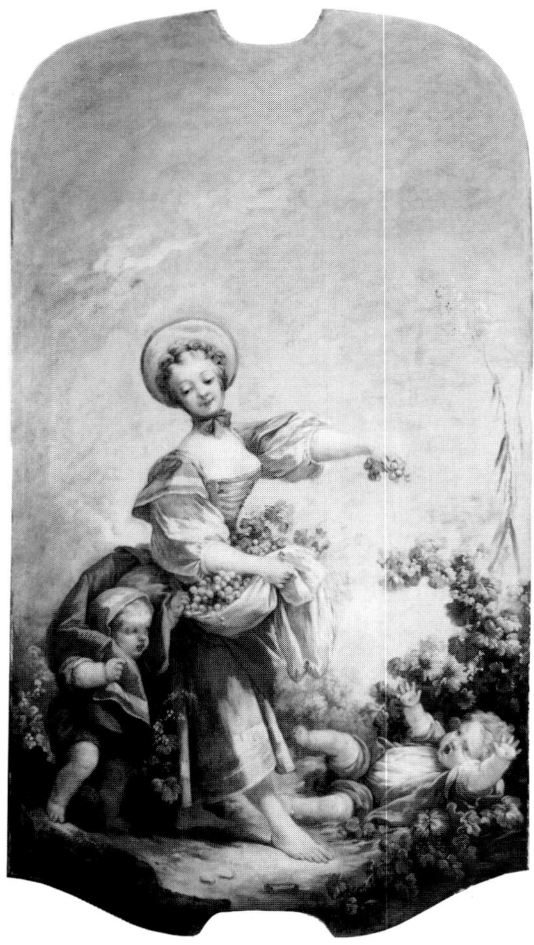

Figure 15 Jean-Honoré Fragonard, *The Grape Gatherer,* c. 1751. ©The Detroit Institute of Art, Founders Society Purchase, Mr. and Mrs. Horace E. Dodge Memorial Fund.

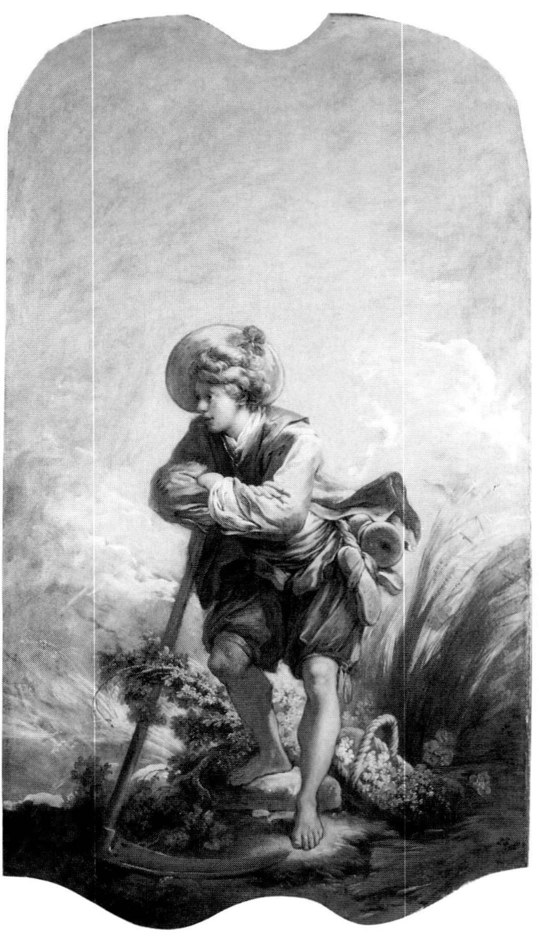

Figure 16 Jean-Honoré Fragonard, *The Harvester,* c. 1751. ©The Detroit Institute of Art, Founders Society Purchase, Mr. and Mrs. Horace E. Dodge Memorial Fund.

of the seasons. And this conventional iconography is handled in a typically rococo manner, through sexual references that enhance and embellish already decorative bodies.[1]

In comparison to the later *Progress of Love,* this early decorative series seems less exciting, less inventive, less witty. It is the sort of work that is quickly passed over as either merely imitating Boucher or repeating rococo formulae. Yet it is in those works most dependent on convention that artists sometimes show their greatest subtlety; by varying the pattern in small but significant ways, they delight an audience capable of appreci-

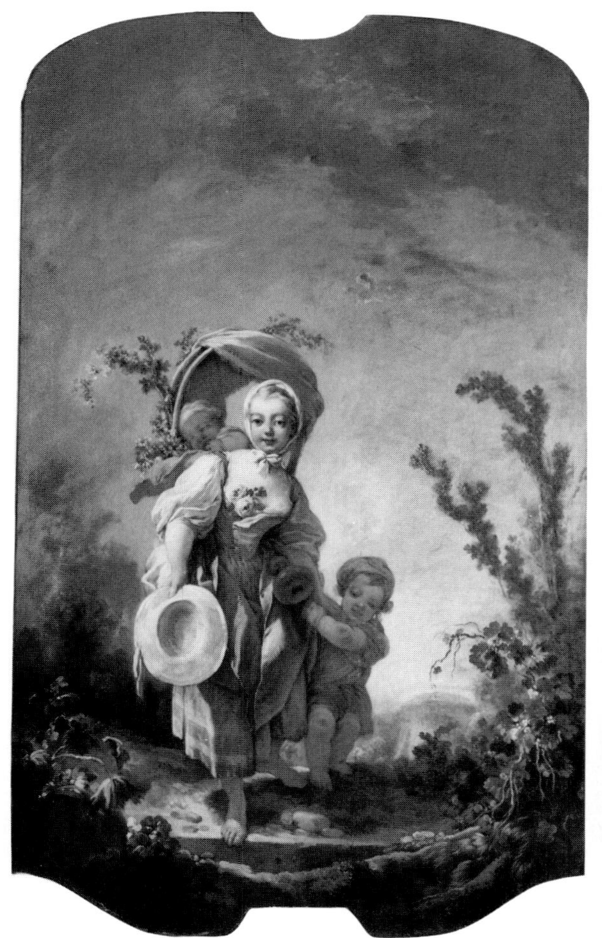

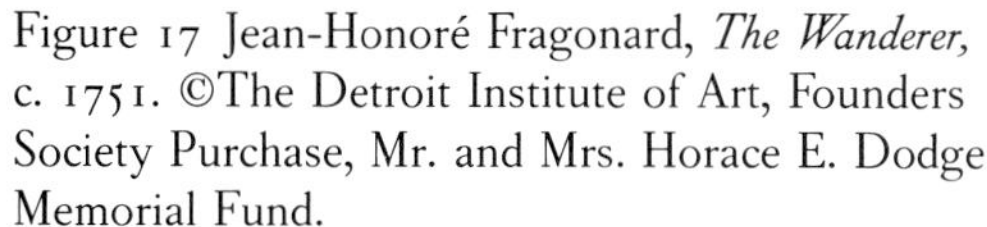

Figure 17 Jean-Honoré Fragonard, *The Wanderer,* c. 1751. ©The Detroit Institute of Art, Founders Society Purchase, Mr. and Mrs. Horace E. Dodge Memorial Fund.

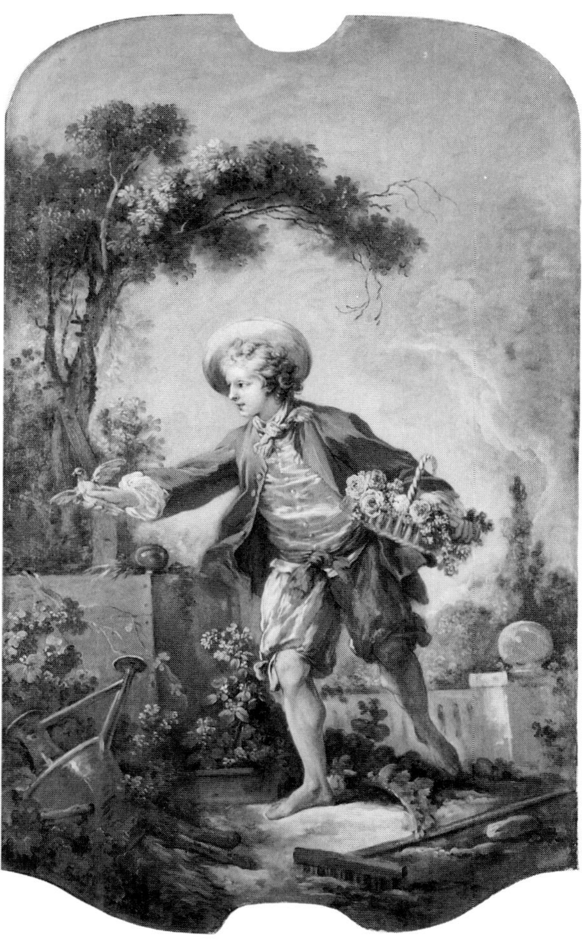

Figure 18 Jean-Honoré Fragonard, *The Gardener,* c. 1751. ©The Detroit Institute of Art, Founders Society Purchase, Mr. and Mrs. Horace E. Dodge Memorial Fund.

ating the finesse that posterity overlooks in searching the general type. For just as the Western palate has difficulty distinguishing the individual spices that flavor an Indian curry, so the twentieth-century observer does not easily appreciate the nuances that, for the eighteenth-century connoisseur, made savory the work of art. It is by interpreting both the conventional series and the innovative one, by seeking what is varied in the first and what is standard in the second, that we can come to a greater understanding of the many ways meanings could be expressed in a rococo painting. And then we can take our pleasure from the work of art.

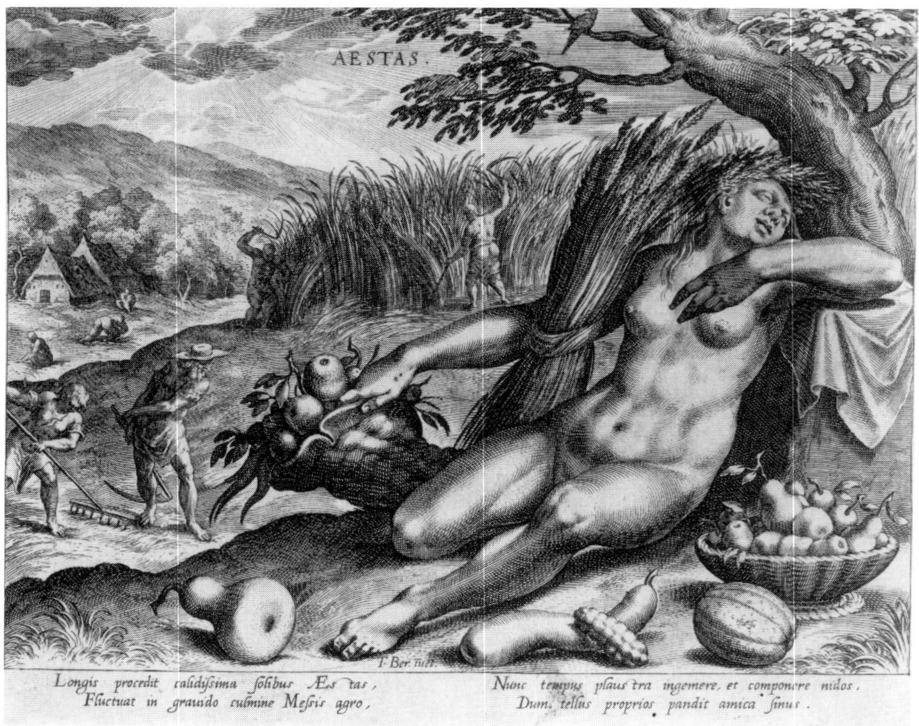

Figure 19 Jan Sadeler, after Dirck Barendsz, *Summer.* New York, The Metropolitan Museum of Art, The Elisha Whittelsey Collection, The Elisha Whittelsey Fund, 1949. (49.95.1699).

An Iconography of the Seasons in a Pastoral Mode

As representations of the seasons, three of the Detroit panels, *The Gardener (Spring), The Harvester (Summer),* and *The Grape Gatherer (Autumn),* have a very common iconography. These make legible the fourth panel, *The Wanderer (Winter),* which was invented for the occasion by Fragonard. The key signs of flower gardening, grain harvesting, and grape gathering appeared in Dutch and French examples of the Seasons from the sixteenth through the eighteenth centuries. Consider these three markedly different seventeenth-century cycles, all of which share the same basic motifs: (1) Jan Sadeler's engravings of *The Seasons* after Dirck Barendsz; (2) Charles Le Brun's designs reproduced by De Gheyn and Falck; and (3) the Crozat *Seasons* painted by Watteau and known through a suite of engravings.

Sadeler's engravings personify the seasons as gods and goddesses associated with the fecundity of the earth. The female deities Flora (flowers) and Ceres (grain; figure 19) represent spring and summer respectively; autumn is signified by the male god Bacchus (grapes). These prominent foreground figures are combined with background landscapes in which traditional activities are depicted.[2] Watteau also used Flora, Ceres (1716; Washington, D.C.: National Gallery of Art; figure 20), and Bacchus to represent the seasons, but his elegant figures are far from Sadeler's monumental nudes with their complex muscular articulation. In Watteau's works, moreover, the seasonal events are conjoined with the

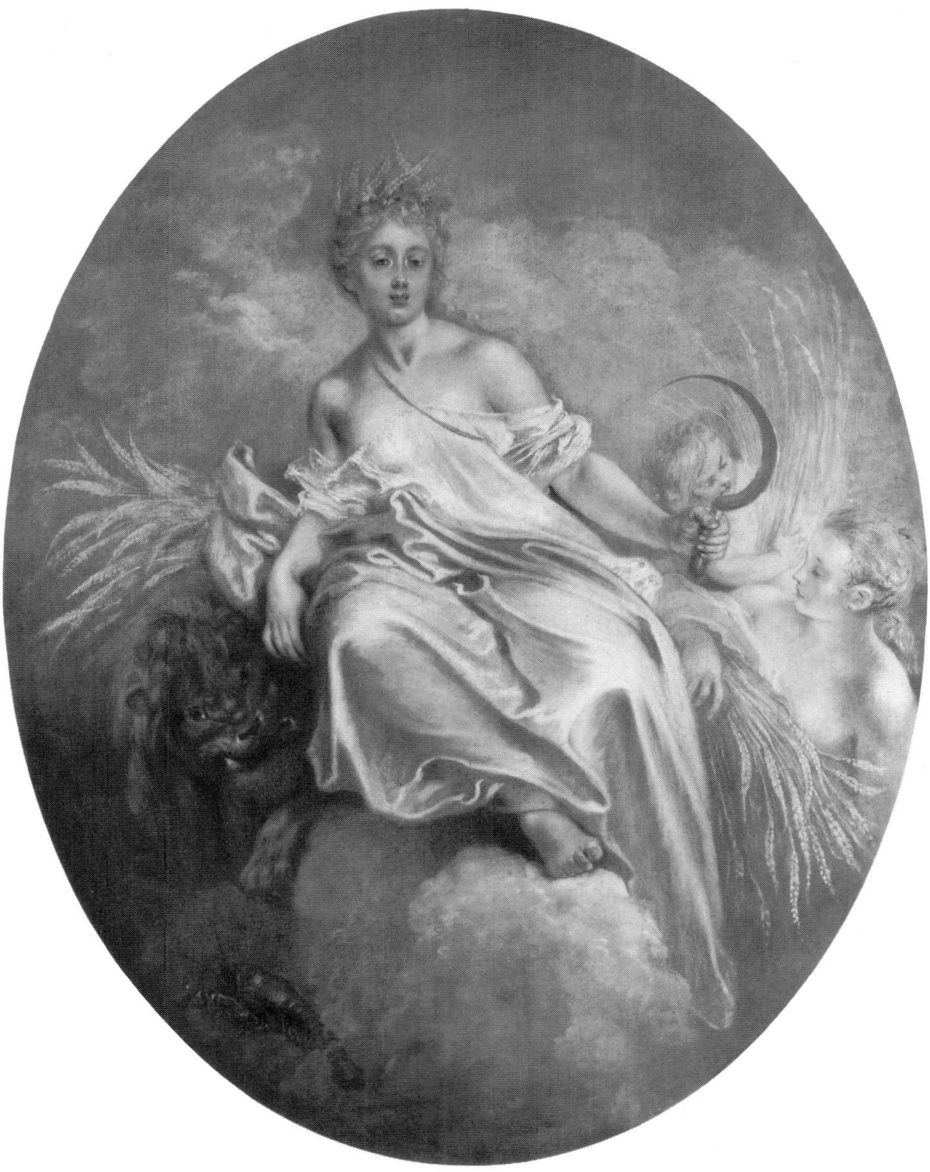

Figure 20 Antoine Watteau, *Ceres (Summer)* c. 1712. National Gallery of Art, Washington; Samuel H. Kress Collection.

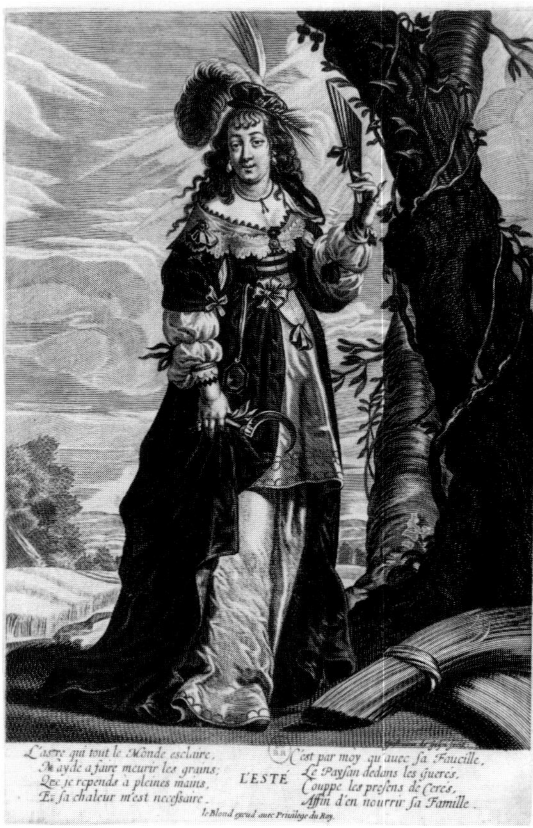

Figure 21 DeGheyn after Charles Le Brun, *Summer.* Paris, Bibliothèque Nationale.

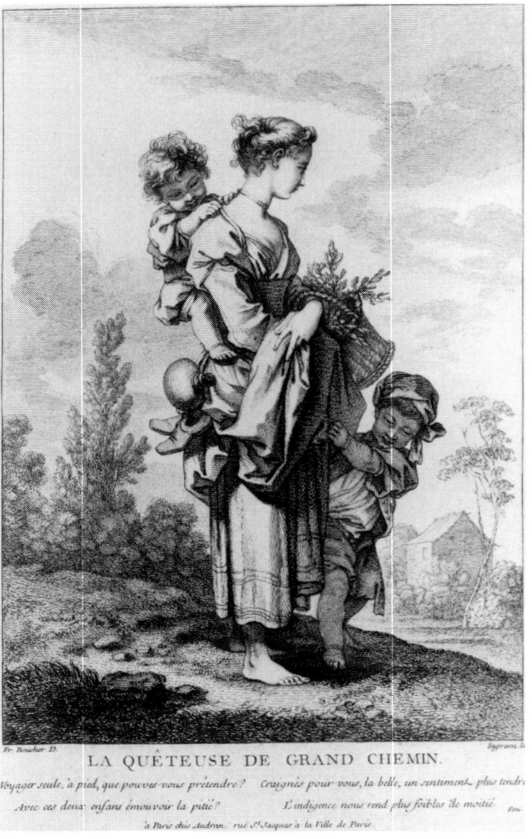

Figure 22 François Boucher, *The Beggar of the High Road.* Paris, Musée du Louvre, Cabinet des Dessins, Collection Rothschild. Cliché des Musées Nationaux, Paris.

central mythological image, and this strategy tends more to reduce the divinities to human scale than to elevate human activity to divine status.[3] Distinct from these overtly mythological allegories is the cycle by Le Brun, who prefers courtesans and shows them full length, elegantly dressed, and silhouetted against a fragment of landscape. They hold the standard attributes: a flower for Spring, a sickle for Summer (figure 21), and a basket of grapes for Autumn.

Although the objects and activities that define these images as representing the seasons remain constant, the cycles themselves vary according to the predilection of culture and audience. In particular, there are significant differences in how the idea of fecundity is encoded in the forms chosen. Perhaps the extreme is marked by Sadeler's engraving where the full-blown nude Ceres, her head thrown back, her body spread across the foreground, is surrounded by phallic-shaped fruits and vegetables. She is an allegorical representation of the season, in which nature's fecundity is cast in terms of female sexuality, a sexuality that is heroic, serious, grand. Watteau's Ceres, in contrast, looks coquettish; her form is more refined and fetching. The tenor of sexuality is different again in Le Brun's designs. His full-breasted courtesans, most of whom directly confront the viewer, present a sexuality that has been tamed and ordered by social convention. Contained in their sophisticated attire, their allure is packaged up for the viewer's delectation. In reference to such a range of possibilities Fragonard conceived his Detroit panels.[4]

But what about winter, the one season characterized by barrenness rather than fecundity? In all three cycles where flowers, grain, and grapes are primary signifiers, Winter is depicted as a figure warming hands or feet in an interior setting. Fragonard's *Winter (The Wanderer)* differs not only from these but also from other standard representations that show activities like ice skating or sledding. In Fragonard's work we see the onset of winter—something more like very late autumn than mid-January—in a landscape characterized by drooping flowers and a single forgotten pumpkin. Unlike the other three figures of the Detroit panels, the Wanderer does not step on fertile ground; rather, she is balanced on a barren ledge with her right foot slipping slightly over its edge. Before her is a cleft in the earth, and on the other side of the cleft is the last vegetation pressed to the picture plane.

To find the model for his figure, Fragonard went outside the tradition of the *Seasons* to the pastoral, to Boucher's *The Beggar of the High Road* (figure 22). In that work a young mother, identified as a traveler by her pilgrim's flask, holds one child close to her side and carries another piggyback. Fragonard imitated the compositional relation between the woman and her two children, and he specifically copied the pose of the tot walking alongside. Moreover, he preserved the idea of a wanderer by repeating in his depiction the gourd-flask that hangs at the waist of Boucher's traveler.

This direct reference to the pastoral in Fragonard's *The Wanderer (Winter)* suggests that the seasonal iconography is cast in a highly codified mode, and pastoral convention is evident not only in *The Wanderer* but also in the three other Detroit panels. As developed in literature and the visual arts since antiquity, pastoral scenes generally represented shepherds or other country folk living harmoniously in a nature both tranquil and attractive. In discussing the literary genre both Fontenelle and Pope agreed that all hardships of country life must be hidden and that figures must seem to occupy themselves with only the two most enviable human pursuits: leisure and love.[5] In eighteenth-century painting, Fragonard's teacher, Boucher, was the undisputed master of the pastoral genre, and his persistent popularity drove Diderot to lament in 1765, "will I never be rid of these damned pastorals?"[6]

The typical pastoral scene as developed by Boucher was set in a rural locale, sometimes with a long-abandoned monument; and it was inhabited by healthy, robust figures in countrified costumes. Accessories usually included the ubiquitous animals (sheep, lambs, goats, dogs), flowers, fruit, and appropriate implements (crooks, watering cans, baskets). Although Boucher's figures are shown in activities such as picking fruit or mowing hay, these toils have been drained of all association with hard work, and they are usually thinly disguised metaphors for lovemaking. More often than not, the objects surrounding the figures operate as erotic symbols and references to the sexual organs.[7]

If the fiction of leisure hides the real world of the shepherd-peasant behind the universe of pleasure presented in the pastoral, that disparity is underscored by the manner in which the subject is rendered; for the pastoral has an artificial, complex, and polished form. In poems rustic shepherds speak in elaborately perfected rhythms; in Boucher's paintings they pose and gesticulate according to the conventions of etiquette manuals. Their "rustic" bodies form elegant visual patterns and their "homespun" clothing delights the eye with a variety of coordinated colors and textures. More than a collection of country motifs and love emblems, the pastoral is an ironic form in which the disjuncture between the real and the artificial is made pointedly apparent.[8]

This disjuncture might be read as a contradiction between subject matter and manner of rendering. An artfully posed peasant is not, after all, a peasant in a natural state. Yet the subject of the rococo pastoral, as was well recognized, was not the real peasant but the beautiful fictive one who lived untouched by pain and hardship in a countryside of pleasure gardens. Thus once pastoral subject matter is recognized as quintessentially artificial, the contradiction we have been considering evaporates. Graceful and elegant peasants rendered in a graceful and elegant style are exactly appropriate to the rococo vision of pastoral life. It is not that the manner of representation contradicts the subject but that the subject represented contradicts reality.

Early in the eighteenth century, *rocaille* decorators such as Watteau seized upon the pastoral figure, that child of fantasy, as they seized upon the grotesque. Both of these embellished their designs for architectural interiors. There diminutive country maids and gents inhabited highly ornamentalized and abstract landscapes. Their stylized gestures and poses were absolutely appropriate to their decorative function.[9] Although lifted from the frame of *rocaille* ornamentation, Boucher's pastoral scenes were usually conceived with the same purpose in mind: to adorn an architectural setting. And so were Fragonard's Detroit panels.

It is clear that Fragonard inherited his mentor's command of the pastoral mode.[10] Quite obviously not in actual peasant dress, the female bodies of the Grape Gatherer (Autumn) and the Wanderer (Winter) suggest the visually pleasing lines of the corseted torso: the bosom is prominent, the waist unbelievably small, and the curves full and flowing.[11] Moreover, these young peasant women carry themselves as wellborn ladies, seeming to have learned their postures from etiquette books and dancing masters. The Wanderer, for example, walks down the steps with graceful ease. Her front foot is extended with pointed toe, her back one slightly raised to reveal a curved arch. The Grape Gatherer takes a stance common to the elegant ladies who decorated aristocratic love scenes, turning her left foot out and pointing her right foot forward.[12] Fragonard's figure, moreover, presents herself in a three-quarter view, with her head turned and tilted slightly. Etiquette books recommended this stance for women because it lent a graceful S-curve to the head, neck, and shoulders.[13] The male figures represented in the Detroit panels are as decorative as their female counterparts, and they position their legs and bodies to display their nicely shaped calves. The Gardener, posed in an arabesque of elaborate *contrapposto,* even mimics that eighteenth-century paradigm of grace, the Apollo Belvedere.

Throughout the Detroit panels the pastoral mode merges with the iconography of the seasons, a conflation not atypical of eighteenth-century practice.[14] The merger compounds contradiction. The pastoral was expected to present a fictive nature; the *Seasons,* on the other hand, traditionally represented what might be considered most real about nature: the ongoing cycle of birth and death. The mixture is further complicated because Fragonard's pastoralized seasons also imply an analogy between the natural cycle and human sexuality. Thus what is most natural about the human being and what is most real about nature are both expressed in a form designed to represent a fantasy of the natural state. Meaning in Fragonard's Detroit panels is produced when the tension between the pastoral mode and the seasonal theme collapses into a decorative eroticism expressed by covert symbols and dependent on the notions of dissimulation and disguise.

The Seasons Made Erotic

As an allegory of winter invented by Fragonard, *The Wanderer* holds a special fascination for us here. In exploring this image referring to the infertility of nature in the least hospitable of times, we can clarify that association of human sexuality with the natural fecundity which dominates all four of Fragonard's representations. We have already seen that Fragonard derived his image of Winter from Boucher's *Beggar.* The deviations from the model demonstrate how Fragonard reinvented Boucher's figure as an itinerant Venus. First, he appropriated a device from mythological history painting, the cloth of honor held above the goddess to mark her divinity.[15] In *The Wanderer* this sign is cleverly configured over the woman's head by the drapery wrapped around the basket in which the baby rides. A second deviation both identifies the figure as a traveling goddess of love and introduces an erotic iconography into the *Seasons.* In Boucher's *Beggar* the woman's bosom is completely draped; Fragonard, however, drops the bodice on his pilgrim's left side to display her breast and nipple while concealing them on the right with a corsage of roses (flower of Venus) and rose buds.

The comparison of nipple and rose bud provoked in the image capitalizes on a well-established *double entendre* translated from the written to the visual language. The French word *bouton* meant either nipple or rose bud, and the word play was illustrated visually in depictions such as Dennel's 1761 engraving after a gouache by Gabriel de Saint-Aubin, *The Comparison Between the Nipple and the Rose (La Comparaison du bouton de rose).*[16] Although in such representations the joke was quite literally spelled out as both subject and title of the work, in other images it was more deftly woven into the composition. For example, Saint-Aubin transferred the theme of overt comparison to his engraved companion pieces of 1789, *At Least be Discreet* and *You Can Count on Me.* In the first composition the woman's bodice is disarranged to display prominently a breast and nipple that point towards her lover depicted on the other canvas. In his open vest he wears a rose that is aimed back at his lady's bosom.[17] This embedding of the *double entendre* in a related subject afforded the viewer added delight in discovering references that "by chance" had found their way into the composition. Fragonard's reference to the *bouton* is also covert because it operates indirectly, suggested by formal and iconographic manipulation.[18]

If the first two modifications signal that Fragonard's Winter or Wanderer is a love goddess presented as an erotic object, two other changes even more clearly emphasize her sexuality and mark her availability to the viewer. The hat, which the young woman displays toward the audience, is the most important sexual symbol in *The Wanderer*. Like the wig *(coiffe)* and the bonnet *(bonnet)*, the hat *(chapeau)* alluded to the woman's sex; the vagina was the "chapeau enfoncé" that was pulled down on the "tête du pénis." [19] The symbol was a familiar one in the erotic vocabulary of eighteenth-century painting, used, for example, by Boucher in his pastoral scene, *Obedience Rewarded* (1768; Nîmes: Musée des Beaux-Arts; figure 23). Conspicuous is the upturned hat placed between the young boy's legs. Boucher's literal-minded use of the *chapeau* is reminiscent of the directly represented pun on *bouton*. But not satisfied with this overt ruse, Boucher saturates the painting with sexual innuendo so that the same meaning is repeatedly articulated. For example, in *Obedience Rewarded* a gourd, which signifies the male genitals, is conveniently tipped into a basket, another common symbol of the female organ; a suggestively shaped white napkin draws attention to the gourd as it enters the basket.[20] Other sexual symbols include the fountain and the empty basket held by the woman (both are representations of the female sex) and little dancing dog (which refers to male excitement or intercourse).[21] This saturation through which the figures are literally submerged in sexual content is typical of Boucher's images and Fragonard's Detroit panels. In the case of Fragonard's *Wanderer*, the meaning of the hat is reinforced in the fold of the woman's skirt, which is a visual analogue for the vaginal cleft.

Seen against Boucher's rather improbably located *chapeau*, the hat in Fragonard's *Wanderer* has a more complex function. Its soft, pink inside is directed toward the viewer, and, significantly, the Wanderer is the only one of the Detroit figures who directly confronts her public. Her position in relation to the viewer marks the fourth deviation from Boucher's beggar, who was oriented to show a side view of the body with the head turned away from the beholder. In changing the pose to one of direct audience contact, with the hat placed facing forward, Boucher's pupil created what we can consider an analogue of full frontal nudity and an image of solicitation.[22]

Up to this point we have seen how Fragonard's *Wanderer* is a sexualized image, an itinerant Venus who solicits the viewer by offering him (and I say him because this work rather strongly implies a male viewer) her empty *chapeau*. But how might this image refer to the season of winter? The hat is conspicuously empty, especially when considered in conjunction with other *chapeaux* that contain eggs to signal fertility. For example, in Fragonard's *The Happy Family* (Washington: National Gallery of

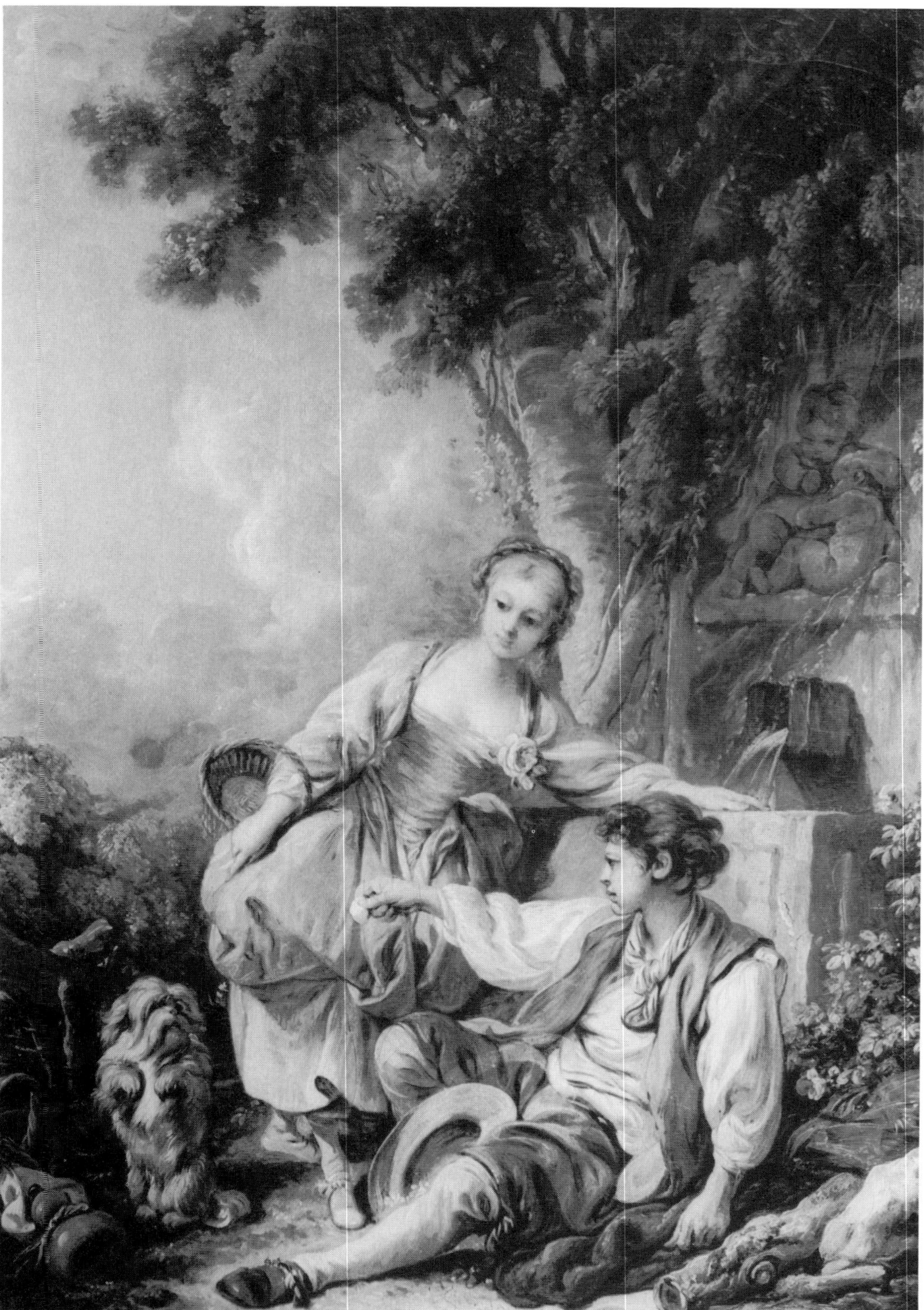

Figure 23 François Boucher, *Obedience Rewarded,* 1768. Nîmes, Musées d'Art et d'Histoire.

Art) engraved by de Launay in 1771, the egg-filled hat is emblematic of the theme suggested in the title. The absence of fertility is underscored in *The Wanderer* because, unlike the other Detroit panels, it does not include baskets of fruit, flowers, or grain; and although not completely barren, the landscape is relatively unproductive. Through this landscape the Wanderer carries the produce from past seasons (the two children), but her *chapeau* (and by extension her womb) is now empty. As Winter, the wanderer remains barren until she is again inseminated; and so the solicitation of the viewer, the male viewer, represents the promise of renewal, as does the gourd that both marks her as a traveler and reminds the audience of what is needed to rekindle the earth's fertility.

With this preliminary reading of *The Wanderer* established, let us pause before analyzing the other Detroit *Seasons* and the sexual ideology within them—pause to ruminate on the devices used by Fragonard to create sexual allusion: the parody of motifs from traditional history painting (as in the cloth of honor), the imaging of verbal puns that depend on a comparison between two objects with similar visual characteristics (as in the *bouton*), and the introduction of things that metaphorically substitute for the sexual organs (like the *chapeau*).[23]

From the various examples already cited, it should be clear that eighteenth-century erotic paintings did not use allusions drawn from only one tradition. They were, rather, an eclectic bricolage formed from the many bits and pieces available to artist and audience.[24] Once the basic ideas of *double entendre,* metaphoric substitution, and pun were established, a whole logic of signification operated; new metaphors and puns could be made if the context rendered them understandable. Artists who knew how to manipulate the elements of this code could continually manufacture new varieties of wit to delight and amuse their audiences, for sexual allusions were activated in the imagination of the beholder through association or recall. This is what happens in Fragonard's *Winter,* where the viewer's expectations are set by the context of the seasons with its common reference to the earth's fertility through human sexuality, and the context of the pastoral with its persistent use of covert erotic symbols.

We call these erotic symbols covert because sexual allusion depended on the obvious fiction that what was being seen was not sexual in content. No symbolic object was truly effective unless its presence in a representation could also be justified at a more literal level.[25] Part of the pleasure taken in the erotic symbol was the pleasure of deception; the beholders who decoded these images were pleased and amused because they could clearly perceive the sexual discourse hidden from innocent eyes. Their pleasure, then, partly depended on a probably unfounded belief in the existence of some naive viewer. Sometimes the figures represented were participants in this deception; they confronted the viewer with a sly expression or gave some other sign of cognizance. The distance between audience and work of art was thus closed as fictive characters shared secrets with real viewers. At other times, however, the figures were represented as naive, unaware of the double meaning they carried. Here the painting maintained the fiction, however slight, that the sexual symbols were accidental, that any salacious meanings were simply invented by the beholder.

This system of sexual allusion was so widespread, so appreciated, and so apparently legitimate, that it even found its way into the Salons. Jeaurat's *A Woman Convalescing,* (Private Collection) exhibited at the Salon of 1769, is a prime example; for in that work a woman masturbating was disguised as one recovering from an illness. The general type of pose was transferred from more libertine images, Baudouin's *The Reading* (Paris: Musée des Arts Décoratifs), for example, demonstrating how easy it was to slip from boudoir to salon to Salon. In the conventional depiction of masturbation (and it is significant that such a pose had its convention in the eighteenth century!), the woman holds a small book in one hand while she places the other one under her skirt or between her legs. In Jeaurat's painting the hand seems to rest innocently in her lap, but the legs splayed beneath the skirt make the reference quite clear, as does the head thrown back in a pose of abandon. The two images (Baudouin's and Jeaurat's) refer to women exciting themselves after reading those novels that Rousseau called "books read with one hand." (The theme is a variation of the reader poised in the midst of perusing a book or letter. Both stress imaginative activity.) But not only does Jeaurat transfer a type found in libertine prints to Salon painting, he also mixes it with references to high art, specifically to Bernini's *Ecstasy of St. Theresa.* And if the viewer is a little slow to catch on, nearby is a cat (or lapdog, it is not clear which) signaling sexual receptivity with arched back and erect tail.

Rarely missing the opportunity to point out such ruses, Diderot addressed the artist in his *Salon of 1769:* "This is a woman convalescing? Ah! Monsieur Jeaurat, you do not entirely know the danger of her state; she is much sicker than you think."[26] The critic's comment refers not to the physical but to the moral condition of the woman represented. Masturbation, for eighteenth-century moralists, was unnatural and disease-like, a perversion practiced for pleasure rather than procreation. Jeaurat's image might have been much more threatening to morality than Fragonard's

Wanderer because it represented (and perhaps promoted) a forbidden sexual practice.

In their veiled sexual references, Fragonard's Detroit panels would by no means have been considered (by their elite audience) particularly shocking or innovative. They do, however, reveal a particularly clever and witty use of sexual reference combined with the tradition of the seasons. To complete our analysis of the iconography, the Gardener represents spring, the season that marks the return to fertility after an unproductive winter. In his extended right hand he holds the bird, a well established image of the male genitals.[27] But again the figure is saturated, overladen with sexual symbols. Directly below the bird is another signifier of the male, the watering can with its upright spout. Although not familiar from linguistic usage, the watering can operates as a visual metaphor for the male member. Boucher, for example, often joined it with other allusions as he did in his *Gathering Cherries* (1768; London: Kenwood House), where a young man propositions his female companion by offering her his genitalia, represented by an index finger with two cherries hanging below it. A watering can is prominently displayed in the foreground.[28]

In Fragonard's *The Gardener (Spring)* the placement of the signifying objects is particularly interesting; the spout is positioned below the bird so as to point toward the young man's pubic area, which is further emphasized by the knot at his waist. We can thus discern a triangular configuration of three points—bird, spout, and knot—that converge on the erogenous zone. In addition, this area is pinned at the center of an implied diagonal line that joins the small ball adorning the edge of the planter to the larger one on the wall behind. Outside of these virtual lines, at a distance from the bird, the gardener holds a sign of the female, a basket filled with the flowers that identify the season. Although the configuration of the main symbols suggests that the actual coupling has not yet occurred, the other object lying at the gardener's feet, the rake, may point toward the activities to come: "to rake" *(ratisser)* was a euphemism for coition.[29] Finally, the entwined trees bending over the figure also suggest the impending union.[30] Their form is equally important in terms of the composition because they direct the viewer around a C-curve that is picked up at the gardener's shoulders and carried to the bird in his hand. Attention is thus focused on that most important object, but the great cycle also leads out of the composition, pointing to something outside itself. I would suggest that *Winter* or *The Wanderer* was placed to the right of *Spring.* Our itinerant Venus, then, would not only solicit the viewer but also interact with the painted figure whose outstretched bird is proffered as the antidote to her barren state. Thus there would be a closing of the cycle at that point as *Spring* would refer back to *Winter* and ahead to *Summer.*

The watering can, rake, and other implements that suggest sexual acts and organs also identify the male figure in *Spring* as one who works in his garden. This simple observation brings us to one of the basic sexual metaphors of all languages, one appropriate for the association of human sexuality with the earth and the seasons. The woman is the garden (or the field) that the man plows, plants, waters, and cultivates.[31] The woman as garden conceives of the female as a passive object on which the man, as gardener, acts. That idea is continued in *Summer,* the figure of which is likewise a worker of the field, a hay harvester. Here male sexuality is represented in terms of images that also suggest insertion. The main sign is the large blade of the scythe, an implement related to those signifiers of the penis that refer to it as an instrument used to cut, pierce, or penetrate.[32] The latter notion is played out visually as the scythe is inserted into a loop of foliage configured around it. Two other male symbols, the gourd and the shoes, are worn at the figure's waist; and all the signifiers of the male organ (the blade of the scythe, the shoes, and the gourd) point directly at that of the female, the basket filled with fruit and flowers nestled in the parted grass.[33] If *Spring* represents the proffering of the phallus, the promise of fertility, *Summer* represents the act of coupling.

We should note here that Fragonard's works differ from the standard representations of the seasons in which both sexes are included, such as those of Sadeler and Watteau. There the female goddesses represented spring (Flora) and summer (Ceres). Although woman is conceptualized in the Detroit panels as the garden or field, Fragonard reduces the female symbols in those seasons to the basket held by or set next to the male. What dominates the most fertile times is the phallus and a preoccupation with male potency. Although it may not seem unusual for male figures to signify male fertility, male potency again becomes an important motif in the female figure, *Autumn.*

The Grape Gatherer or *Autumn* climaxes the development that began with *Spring;* the young woman represents the female inseminated, and the grapes gathered in her apron allude to this state. The apron is understandable because of its location near the woman's belly and its role in depictions of the Danaë myth, where it is the container that catches Zeus' seed, symbolized as a shower of gold. Grapes also had erotic associations through mythology. In the Ovidian story of Erigone and Bacchus the god metamorphoses into a grape so that he can enter the nymph Erigone as she eats the transubstantiated fruit (see Carle Van Loo, *Bacchus and Erigone,* 1747; Atlanta: High Museum). In addition, grapes were found as visual metaphors in the pastoral tradition. Boucher's *Young Man Offering Grapes to a Girl* (1768; pendant to his *Cherry Gatherers,* London: Kenwood House; figure 14) shows a peasant boy suspending a bunch of grapes between his splayed legs as an offering to the young woman who sits nearby; she gives him an egg from her basket in exchange. In Fragonard's Detroit panel the relation between the grapes gathered in the folds of Autumn's apron and the child gathered in the drapery at her side is significant. If one suggests the fertilization of her womb, the other suggests the harvest of an earlier season. The relation between the woman and the children is like that established in *The Wanderer;* children are subsidiary figures that generally indicate female fertility. As her attributes, they are not to be construed as signifying a parent-child relationship in anything other than a strictly biological sense.[34]

The images of enfolded child and grapes are combined in *The Grape Gatherer* with a very significant gesture: the woman squeezes a bunch of grapes over a second child, who is animated by the spray. That babe, laid directly in the foliage and merged with the vegetation, seems nearly to grow out of the earth. It is brought to life by the juice of the grape, here an obvious allusion to the male fluid, the *eau de vie,* as the rest of the image makes explicit.[35]

We can now read these Detroit *Seasons* as a thinly veiled progress of love, sexual love. In *Spring* the phallus is symbolized and displayed, held out for the viewer's examination and in *Summer* it is represented specifically in terms of penetration. *Autumn* is an allegory of ejaculation and insemination. In these panels woman is either a container (an apron, a basket) or a passive medium (in particular, the soil) in which the male principle implants life. Winter's barrenness is copulation's end, yet *Winter* includes the anticipation of spring's return and, toward that end, a soliciting of the male viewer. The sexual attitudes promoted in Fragonard's Detroit panels are unsurprising; their phallocentric view of human and natural fertility glorifies the male seminal fluid. As we know, such attitudes had a long, paternal lineage.[36]

Viewing the Erotic Symbol

In proclaiming the potency of the phallus, the Detroit panels thematize the dominance of the male in the natural process of reproduction. But exactly what part does the representation of the seasons play in this theme?

If we reconsider Fragonard's Detroit panels in relation to the *Seasons* of Sadeler, Watteau, and Le Brun, it becomes apparent that the natural cycle is much less a focus in Fragonard's work. In the other three the symbols primarily reference the various seasons and seasonal activities, although certainly these are often connected to human actions and sexuality. Fragonard's symbols, on the other hand, are manipulated so that their most basic reference is to sexual encounter. Thus, in terms of the Detroit panels we might construe the seasons less as a theme and more as an element of disguise, a veil to cover the hidden meaning of the series.

The depiction of sexuality in Fragonard's *Seasons,* however, seems rather conflicted. The ornamental bodies and witty play with symbolic objects is at odds with the theme of natural process (sexual intercourse) that the paintings also represent. And here we should be careful to distinguish this coital theme from those pastoral courtships and flirtations that stress the social as much as the physical intercourse between men and women. In the Detroit panels the most intimate physical acts are represented in controlled and intellectualized symbolic gestures. This presentation of sexuality was not limited to Fragonard but held in common by those who used the covert symbol and the pastoral figure to represent decorously what could not be represented directly.

The decorative presentation of the body and the symbolizing of its sexual parts also subverts the superiority of the male generative principle posited in the phallocentric message of these panels. Men and women together are ornamentalized abstractions to be enjoyed by the viewer. Their sexual organs are emphasized, multiplied, offered to the audience, but this imaginary dismemberment is enacted through the manipulation of symbols. Thus the beholder concentrates attention not on penises and vaginas but on grapes and baskets. This part-by-part reading of the image increases pleasure because at each encounter the viewer can focus on some previously overlooked aspect of the work, skipping those that seem routine and familiar. Or, the spectator can linger over a single symbol, endlessly spinning out its associations.

The most explicit allusions, then, are enjoyed not as much for what they represent as for *how* they represent. The decorative form and play of the signifiers, the cleverness of their construction, the exercise of wit necessary for their decoding—these intellectual activities stimulate pleasure far more than any mental contemplation of the action that is referenced. In fact, the viewer's contact with what is referenced is continually delayed. The grapes gathered in Autumn's apron, for example, have multiple references—to the story of Danaë and that of Erigone, to representations of young men propositioning their lovers, to any number of texts and images that the viewer might know. It is the very multiplicity, the seemingly endless conjuring of associations, that entrances and delights viewers, who are pleased by the artist's cleverness—and also by their own. A delaying and distancing strategy also accounts for the saturation of the image that we have seen in works by both Fragonard and Boucher. In *The Gardener,* for example, the viewer is occupied with variety and repetition, with different signs that symbolize the same concept and with the many concepts symbolized within the same scene. Thus in the Detroit panels it is the signs that endlessly caress and penetrate one another; their temporary unions creating new possibilities of meaning. The site of and occasion for those unions is provided by the viewer in whose imagination the coupling and conception is continually repeated.

The representation of physical love through a play with abstract symbols does not arouse the viewer by stimulating sexual fantasies; that is a pleasure appropriate to more direct depictions of the body in sensual display. Instead, the covert symbols that insure the painting's decency divert its viewers from sexual fantasy by entertaining them with intellectual pleasures. Sexuality is thus subdued and controlled, transformed by the sophisticated badinage that produces aesthetic delight.

Towards an Erotics of the Brush

Understanding both the process of signification and the pleasures of decoding is central to an appreciation of the Detroit panels, paintings that are all too easily dismissed as merely decorative. The same can be said of *The Bathers* (1767; Paris: Musée du Louvre; figure 24), a well-admired painting where the lack of a "significant" subject has similarly deterred attempts to look beneath the surface effects. Like the Detroit panels, *The Bathers* combines the natural, the decorative, and the sexual, but the painting is at once a more subtle and more direct exploration of those themes, one that establishes a significantly different, but equally erotic, relation with the viewer.

In *The Bathers* the association of woman and nature is established not by symbolic objects but by abstract formal elements: composition, design, color, brushwork. If the coy country maids of the Detroit panels encourage a fragmented, part-by-part reading of the body symbolized, the nymphs represented in *The Bathers* initially demand that the viewer see them whole and in relation to their fictive natural setting. Their bodies are fully integrated with the reeds, water, and atmosphere, united in a single

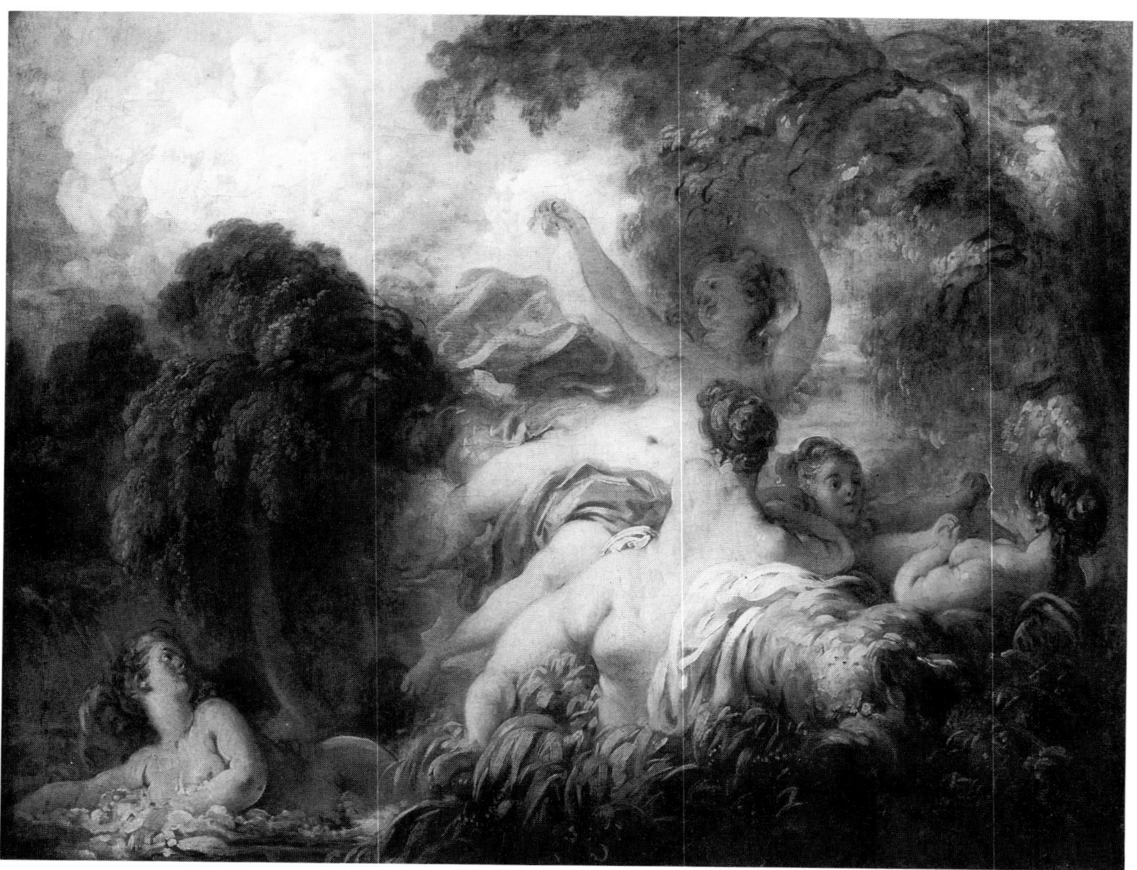

Figure 24 Jean-Honoré Fragonard, *The Bathers,* 1767. Paris, Musée du Louvre. Cliché des Musées Nationaux, Paris.

dynamic conception of nature announced at the border of the composition. That edge is formed as the apparent growth patterns of bending tree, cascading bush, and flowing reeds are joined together by the upraised arms of the central nymph, the serpentine profile of another swimming at the far left, and the back of a third immersed in the grasses at the right edge. Following the directional signals of foliage, arms, and body, the beholder reads the outer perimeter as a continuous circuit, a whirlpool or eddy, and attributes to the forms themselves the movement of his or her attention. The simulation of motion in a static painting is enhanced by the light and dark masses which, punctuated by brilliant impasto, alternate around the same perimeter. The viewer activates the frame and thereby imaginatively animates both the figures and their natural surrounds. Nature, both as lush vegetation and sensuous woman, thus seems immediately energetic, full of life and vitality.

Surrounded by the movement of this activated border, the bathers leap and glide unabashedly, their bodies displayed for the delectation of a viewer whose presence they seem not to acknowledge. Nature's vitality is extended to them, and the bodies within are as activated as the frame without. Several formal strategies used simultaneously allow the audience to imagine them in motion. The first is the momentary pose, best exemplified by the gravity-defying posture of the central bather. The second is dynamic contrast: the push-me–pull-you pose of the bathers at the right edge allows the beholder to imagine one as lunging forward and the other as reeling back. The third strategy sets up another circuit of compositional movement inscribed within that of the foliage frame. One arc is implied by the glances exchanged between the leaping and swimming bathers; the other moves up the curved back of the woman stretched out in the foreground.

The eroticism of these nymphs is immediately apparent, and it is emphasized by their vitality; theirs is a sexual energy tied to the life forces of nature. It is not only that the figures are integrated into nature by their position within the composition, but they repeat nature's rhythms, shapes, textures, and colors. It is apparent, for example, that the overarching arms of the most prominent bather are analogous to the tree branches above, and that her flowing drapery is marked with the same kind of long fluid strokes that articulate the nearby reeds. The nymph turned away from the audience displays a curvilinear left profile keyed to the pattern established by the reeds along the right side of her body, and her flesh tones (like that of her counterparts) are shadowed by the same green that colors the foliage. The coiled bun pinned at the back of her head even has the same pattern of highlighting—yellow impasto with spots of turquoise blue—as the reeds in the foreground.

The association of woman and nature represented in *The Bathers* is not unproblematic. We have seen how the formal dynamics are arranged to suggest movement, and how that movement can be taken as metaphoric of nature's growth, fecundity, and vitality. In the supple female bodies at play, nature's vitality becomes a sexuality expressed as physical energy. Our analysis of the painting has also suggested that both figures and foliage participate in an artificial construct designed to symbolize or reference nature, rather than to look natural. Extending this observation, we see that nymphs and greenery both seem artfully posed. Bodies are configured into undulating serpentine profiles, boughs bend in elegant C-curves; cloud formations rhymed with leafy masses take their place in a complicated alternation of light and dark. The bathers are opposed in pairs: looking left-looking right; facing front-facing back; leaning forward-leaning back. The rules of repetition and contrast, not of gravity and inertia, determine the configuration of the whole. Moreover, there is no pretense of correct anatomy in the depiction of the figures (witness their soft, pneumatic elbows and joints) nor any suggestion of botanical accuracy in the representation of the foliage.

At this point we can draw a parallel between *The Bathers* and the Detroit panels. Each represents some aspect of nature's vitality and woman's sexuality, but neither does so by rendering them in a naturalistic style. Clearly neither of these works feigns transparency to nature, to the object represented; in both the mode of representation is decorative (artificed) and symbolic. A major difference between them, however, is the system of signification. The Detroit panels represent sexuality through symbolic references; the nude body is never presented directly as an object of delectation, and the viewer enjoys the play of the signifiers more than the contemplation of what they signify. *The Bathers,* on the other hand, does not rely on covert sexual references. The body itself is much more fully revealed (only the genitals are covered), and the particular sexuality granted to these nymphs is represented through abstract formal configurations that associate them with nature's fecund vitality. This system of signification is like that of the Detroit panels because it, too, relies on an arbitrary code. Convention determined that hats referenced vaginas, and convention also determined that arms and branches should be associated with one another when configured in analogous patterns. Yet we can speculate that for the eighteenth-century viewer the process of decoding a work like *The Bathers* was substantially different from that of reading the Detroit panels and that this difference was primarily determined by a signifying element that we have up to now neglected: brushwork.

The Detroit panels were executed to decorate an architectural setting, and the paint handling was of necessity broad, fluid, loose, and relatively uniform because planned to be seen from a certain distance away. *The Bathers,* on the other hand, is an easel painting, i.e., a small work often designed for no particular space but best seen in a small, intimate one where its surface can be approached closely and appreciated. In the easel painting made to adorn the most intimate spaces of cabinet and boudoir, Fragonard developed an aesthetic of the brush appropriate for delighting his audience. Varied across the surface of the canvas, the brushmarks in *The Bathers* are the signs that fragment the representation, breaking it into discreet areas that detain the spectators, make them linger, dally, and delay. Above all else, it is Fragonard's brush that establishes an erotic relation with the beholder, a relation that will, for a time, distract us from the voluptuous nymphs of the Louvre canvas.

Easel Painting and the Aesthetics of Brushwork 4

The Aristocratic Brush and the Erotics of Paint Handling

Far from having a single characteristic touch, Fragonard cultivated all manners of paint handling. His capacity for variation is evident when his works are grouped together, as they are in the National Gallery of Art in Washington, D.C. A highly wrought surface built with small touches of paint and effects reminiscent of Rembrandt's chiaroscuro describe a secularized Adoration enacted by a peasant family and set in a ruined interior (*The Happy Family;* figure 25). Nearby a reader quietly absorbed in her solitary activity is brilliantly lit and vigorously brushed in large, unblended strokes that shimmer in a simultaneous contrast of yellow and violet (*A Young Girl Reading,* also called *The Reader;* figure 26). In handling she is as far from the rustic mother and child as she is from a second, more aristocratic pair (*The Visit to the Nursery;* figure 27), and these two families separated by vast social distances are represented in equally divergent manners of painting. In the *Visit to the Nursery,* areas thinly brushed and loosely sketched imperceptibly glide into high finish, and subtle transitions of light modulate colors within a limited, nearly monochromatic, tonal range. Between the reader and the aristocratic family to her left hangs one of a pair of pendant scenes, its mate placed between her and the rustic circle to her right (*The Game of Hot Cockles;* figure 13, and *The Game of Horse and Rider;* figure 12). Set in different garden locales, these two scenes point out Fragonard's command of even the most contradictory manners; in each, the background and foreground are inexorably divided by discordant handlings. The distant view is rendered in

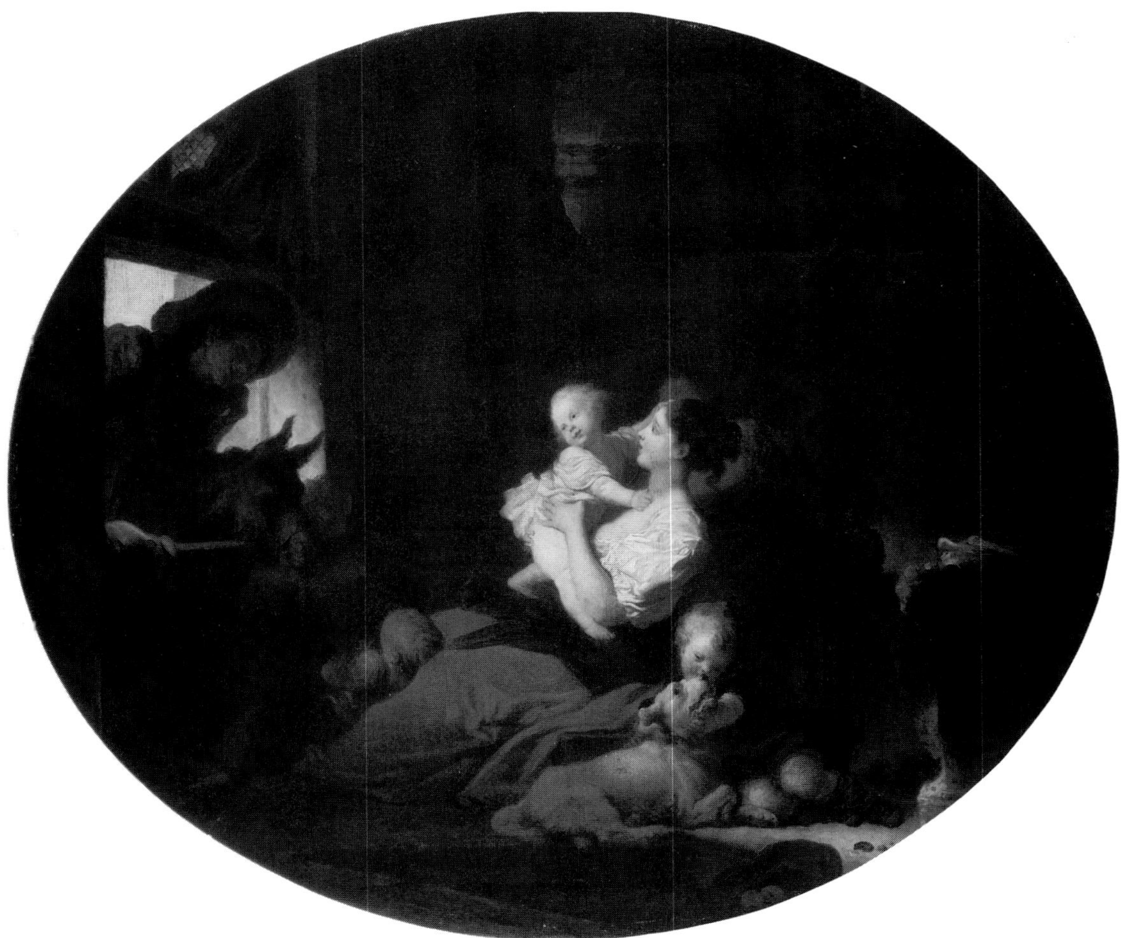

Figure 25 Jean-Honoré Fragonard, *The Happy Family,* after 1769. National Gallery of Art, Washington, Timken Collection.

thinly applied paint, with a diaphanous blending of blue and green; short, choppy paint strokes articulate elements in the foreground scenes of outdoor play.

At specific times in his career Fragonard probably preferred one manner to another, but to graph his works linearly, to make them represent a development from an early to a late style is here beside the point. That sort of analysis obscures issues more central to this argument: that Fragonard had an absolute command of technical skills, that he was able and willing to vary his manner, and that he tailored his execution to the subject, meaning, purpose, or audience at hand. Accordingly, there is no essential Fragonard who changes only with time, but rather he is an artist

Figure 26 Jean-Honoré Fragonard, *A Young Girl Reading,* c. 1770. National Gallery of Art, Washington. Gift of Mrs. Mellon Bruce in memory of her father, Andrew W. Mellon.

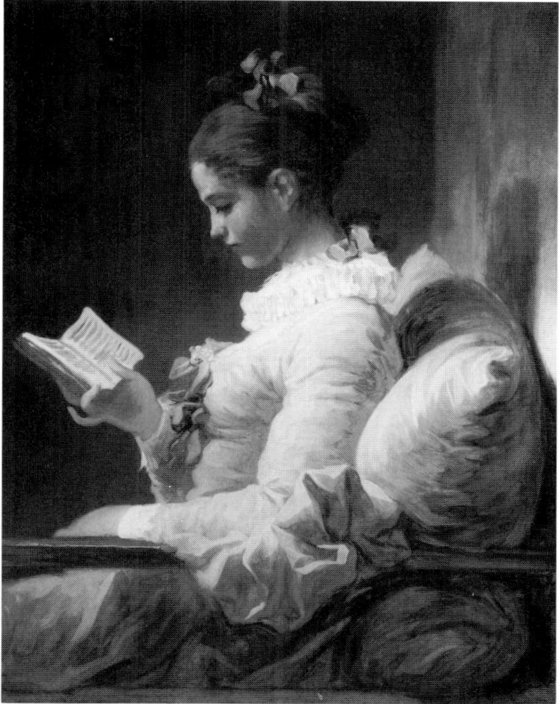

Figure 27 Jean-Honoré Fragonard, *The Visit to the Nursery,* c. 1775. National Gallery of Art, Washington, Samuel H. Kress Collection.

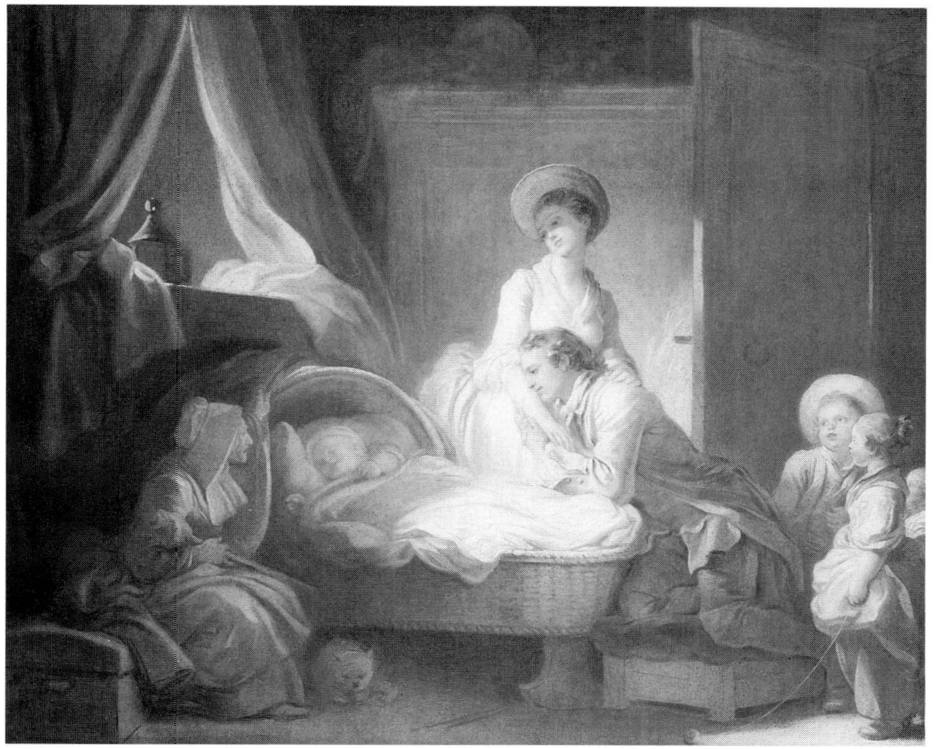

whose essence is to change. This aptitude for self-metamorphosis emerged early, and in 1758 Natoire reported to the Parisian authorities that Fragonard's astonishing ease, his ability to change handling from one moment to the next, was an undesirable talent that rendered his manner "uneven."[1] Although some might see in this description a young artist in search of his style, I prefer to imagine a nascent Proteus learning and perfecting the many guises in which he could and would appear.

Despite all the disparate manners in which Fragonard touched the canvas, he has come to be most closely associated with a free, loose, seemingly spontaneous brushwork—a sketchlike execution. Because variations of this handling do, indeed, seem to have been preferred by Fragonard, we can profitably ask why this manner was so often chosen, why it appealed to certain audiences, and what kinds of meanings it might have encoded.

EMPHASIZING *Le Faire*

During the eighteenth century brushwork assumed an increasing importance expressed in the notion of *le faire.* Charles-Nicolas Cochin, fils, articulated its centrality at midcentury, elevating execution in general and brushwork in particular. Here is how he promoted *le faire:* "No one pretends that execution *[le faire]* is the only essential part [of painting], but it is that which crowns *[couronne]* all the others."[2] What Cochin meant by "crown" we can infer from discussions of *le faire* by the secretary and likeminded theorists. In one sense, execution crowned painting because it consummated the work, not only completing it, but also bringing it to the greatest potential perfection. The term *achevé* signified the consummation particular to art, and a painting was *achevé* when it approached perfection. The *Dictionnaire des Arts,* 1792, distinguished *achevé* from words like *fini* and *terminé* because they sometimes denoted a particular manner of handling not necessarily evident in a work that was *achevé:*

> However, a painting made with fire, with enthusiasm, and without too much refinement in the *execution [le faire],* often has more right to be called a *finished [achevé]* work than one that cost the artist much time and effort.[3]

Crowning did not simply imply consummating or completing, it also suggested honoring; and, indeed, Cochin made *le faire* the perfection that ennobled all the others. Reversing the traditional view of painting as an art whose gross and mechanical parts (execution) were raised up by a poetic subject, Cochin argued that execution was a mark of authenticity, an ennobling mark that separated the master from the copyist:

It is this *faire* (as the artists call it) that distinguishes the original of a great master from the best rendered copy and that characterizes the true talents of the artist so well that a small part of the painting, even the least interesting, reveals to the connoisseur that the piece must be by a great master.[4]

Not every execution crowned, consummated, and ennobled. Cochin characterized *beau faire* in relation to ideas of *facilité, force, chaleur,* and *grace,* and associated it with spirit and taste. The following is his description of *beau faire* taken from an essay published in the *Mercure de France* in 1759:

It is this appearance of facility, of certainty, and of enthusiasm in the execution that renders even the most delicate and the most masterful details without effort, and as if by chance. It is this skillful handling of the brush or the chisel which lets one know that the artist, having a well-formed idea of what he wanted to make, has hit his mark with assurance and precision.[5]

Beau faire, then, is the appearance of facility, of self-assurance, of having been inspired; and these make the work seem as if it had been executed without effort, as if by chance. Thus execution crowns all the other parts of painting because it creates certain appearances, and these appearances directly relate to the artist's performance in making the work, to how the artist appeared to have worked.

Much of Cochin's discussion stemmed from an understanding of *le faire* as both rhetorical and aristocratic. As we shall explore below, the artist's performance corresponded to the behavioral mode prescribed for those men who would be courtiers. But other aspects of Cochin's discussion related *le faire* to a conception of execution that developed from theories of both the natural sign and the original genius.

Although Cochin acknowledged that the artist deals in appearances, he also insisted that execution was tied to state of mind. He introduced *le faire* by explaining that as one of the "greatest beauties of art," it participated little in the aims of illusion. Not based on the imitation of nature, *le faire* was only the effect of the feelings that moved the artist in painting.[6] Here Cochin implies a causal relation between execution and the emotion of the painter; he is not far from reading brushwork as an index of passion rather than as an effect of artifice. He also connected *le faire* with the *je ne sais quoi,* the unnameable something that characterized the work of genius. Describing the relation between taste and *faire,* he wrote that taste was revealed in the "lightness and graces of the manner of handling" and in the "firmness and sureness of the work," but that one "sensed" taste better than one could speak of it.[7] This last comment assures us that although the *je ne sais quoi* of taste could not be named or described, it could be perceived by a sensitive beholder. As we shall see, it is this notion of the *je ne sais quoi* that connects the models of courtier and genius at a deep level.

Cochin's concept of *le faire* makes the artist both a courtier and a genius, allows the artist to oscillate between these paradigms. Fragonard, in particular, was suspended between the two models, creating his art in the overlap, making it at the moment of their greatest intersection. As Marigny's advisor and secretary of the Academy, Cochin helped guide the young Fragonard's progress toward *beau faire* and tried to prevent what he viewed as the cooling of Fragonard's execution at the hands of Natoire, who was sent this assessment of the young painter's work:

> One fears that the excess of care might entirely cool the fire one has known in this artist. The effort shows here [in the work being judged] and one discovers none of those happy omissions nor that facility of brush that he perhaps carried to extremes before, but which he must not, however, lose entirely in discipling them. . . . All is blended, all is finished. It is time that M. Fragonard take confidence in his talents and that, working with more assurance, he recover that first fire, that happy facility he had, and which it seems that too diligent a study has restrained nearly to the point of destroying.[8]

The terms of this critique are hardly original; in chastising the young artist for not knowing when to take his hand from the canvas, the Academy is acting Apelles to Fragonard's Protogenes. Their interpretation of the ancient story accords with that given to it by Renaissance writers, by no less than Castiglione who, pointing to Protogenes, called it proverbial that excessive diligence was harmful to the painter.[9]

THE ARISTOCRATIC IDEAL OF *Le Faire:* THE ARTIST AS COURTIER

The aristocratic model of execution binds together courtier and artist in the ideal of seeming to do naturally and easily things that require art and effort. Although ancient rhetoric manuals expressed the general concept of apparent ease in the dictum that art should hide art, a complex linkage joins later theories of art and civility. David Summers describes this linkage in Renaissance Italy through a masterful analysis of critical terms. Summers argues that the Renaissance artists believed themselves ennobled by the difficulty *(difficultà)* of their work, and then he demonstrates how difficulty was reconciled with its contrary, ease *(facilità),* through nonchalance *(sprezzatura),* or the overcoming of difficulty with apparent ease. In the last term, *sprezzatura,* art theory connects with aristocratic deportment.[10]

As is well known, Castiglione introduced the term *sprezzatura* in this passage from *The Courtier* (published 1528):

> I have discovered a universal rule which seems to apply more than any other in all human actions or words: namely, to steer away from affectation at all costs, as if it were a rough and dangerous reef, and (to use a novel word for it) to practise in all things a certain nonchalance *[sprezzatura]* which conceals all artistry and makes whatever one says or does seem uncontrived and effortless.[11]

Centered on what seems to be, *sprezzatura* is an illusion that has the character of dissimulation, simultaneously hiding what it is (consciously cultivated) and presenting itself as what it is not (unpremeditated). Through its effect on an audience, *sprezzatura* can magnify ability: spectators assume that a man who performs well with ease possesses even greater skill than he actually does, and that his performance would be still more excellent if he took more pains.[12] The performance succeeds precisely because something is left to the imagination of the spectator who completes and perfects the actions. Mastery, it seems, is better imagined than displayed.

Castiglione argued that the courtier should execute all activities with *sprezzatura,* drawing his examples from weaponry, dance, music, and painting. Of the latter he wrote:

> Then again, in painting, a single line which is not laboured, a single brush stroke made with ease, in such a way that it seems that the hand is completing the line by itself without any effort or guidance, clearly reveals the excellence of the artist, about whose competence everyone will then make his own judgement.[13]

Here we can read the difference between the *sprezzatura* of the courtier and that of the painter. The first is judged according to how he performs some action, by an audience watching him; his only aesthetic product is the action itself, performed easily. The painter, on the other hand, is evaluated from the trace (the line or brushmark) that his performance leaves on the canvas; the audience sees only the results of his actions, not how he actually performed them. Logically one cannot securely judge performance from product. What appears to have been dashed off may actually have been made slowly, and what appears to have been made slowly and steadily might have progressed in fits and starts.

In describing how the courtier-painter should cultivate *sprezzatura,* Castiglione anticipated the development of similar concepts in art theory. Summers analyzed these, citing the following passages from Vasari:

"Paintings want to be done with ease and things put in their places with judgment and without a certain toil and labor that makes things hard and rude," and "[art should] always be accompanied by a grace of facility and a polished lightness of colors, and the work must be completed, not with harsh suffering, such that those who look at it must suffer the pain they see in the work." Summers stressed that for Vasari *facilità* did not mean that paintings should be unpremeditated, but that preparation should be concealed in a mastery of execution.[14]

The ideal of *sprezzatura* seems not to have made a notable impact on French painting theory until the eighteenth century. Earlier writers were not particularly concerned with seeming naturalness and *négligence,* possibly because they were preoccupied with rules. They battled to establish art as a viable intellectual discipline that could be taught and learned according to rational principles, which they avidly systematized and codified. To hide the rules under a guise of natural inclination or ease might have undermined the very notion of the visual arts they were developing. This is not to say that they advocated a labored or affected art but only that they did not stress making things with apparent ease. In fact, they did not stress the making of things (execution) at all, and this is a crucial point. To align art with the aristocratic ideal of *sprezzatura,* the theory of art must somehow privilege performance or *faire.* In the seventeenth century execution or performance had a low value; it was the base and mechanical part of painting.

Many ideas developed in eighteenth-century French art theory, however, do correspond with those presented by Castiglione and Vasari, among others.[15] Well acquainted with both their Italian and Gallic predecessors, French theorists of the eighteenth century took from them what accorded with and justified the ideal of art they were developing. Because that ideal gave increasing importance to *le faire,* considerations of performance were of interest. Those aspects of art theory closely related to courtly models attracted many eighteenth-century thinkers, who in appropriating the notion of *sprezzatura,* appropriated an aristocratic ideal. That ideal was at home among the connoisseurs, *amateurs,* and artists who made, bought, sold, and wrote about painting in the eighteenth century.[16]

Throughout the eighteenth century *facilité* and *négligence* were used in academic parlance to describe aspects of apparent ease, and each term had both a positive and negative meaning. At the negative pole, artists who displayed *facilité* or *négligence* had not attended to their work; the terms pointed out things made carelessly, without art, effort, or premeditation. When used for approbation, however, *facilité* described the appearance of speed and ease in the execution. Neither slapdash nor natural, this ease was cultivated through years of training, study, and practice. A painting praised for its air of *négligence* included *laissés* or imperfections arranged according to some artful plan. In this sense *négligence* was a calculation of art whereby effects seemed wrought *comme par hazard,* that is, as if by chance.

Below are two quotations from Antoine Coypel's influential *Conférence* of 1722. The first associates the excess of facility with neglect and its absence with lifelessness. It implies that the right amount of facility will animate the work: "If it is necessary, then, to control the excess of facility that makes [one] careless in [one's] works, it is necessary to animate the painstaking slowness that renders what one makes monotonous, cold, and, without energy."[17] The second quotation explicates calculated *négligence* and, using the examples of Rembrandt and Correggio, argues that both the visibly touched execution, and the one that hides itself, result from infinite care and ability:

> It is often necessary to neglect certain areas in order to develop others, but in this appearance of brusqueness, of casual negligence that must come from art, I repeat again, it is necessary to avoid disagreeable and disconnected strokes. . . . The works of Rembrandt that seem the most touched and even the most rough are the result of infinite care and are painted with as much suavity and harmony as those of Correggio where the touch is imperceptible.[18]

Surely Coypel's writing brings Italian ideas to mind, and it should not be surprising that in the same *Conférence* he quotes the story of Apelles and Protogenes cited by Castiglione, drawing from it the lesson that "most of painting is knowing what is enough." He echoes Vasari in criticizing overly finished works as difficult for the spectator to contemplate because they call to mind the painful effort exerted in producing them.[19]

Although Caylus assumed similar distinctions between artful and untutored facility in his lecture on *"La légèreté de l'outil"* presented to the Academy in 1755, he insisted that his *légèreté* was not the contrary of effort. According to Caylus, the master of *légèreté* finished his work thoroughly and then applied the final touches, the light touches, to hide the labor. He cited the example of François Lemoine, who spent much time finishing his works but even more in stroking them lightly to hide the pains of production.[20] Here aesthetic deception seems not to distress Caylus. In developing his discussion of *légèreté,* the *amateur* compared the artist touching his canvas lightly to the wise and enlightened writer who convinced his readers by reviewing briefly—lightly—the arguments he had established. At that moment, the writer flatters the vanity of his audience: by avoiding a detailed and distasteful repetition, he lets the sophisticated imagine for themselves what he has only suggested. In reading this final, lightly-touched recapitulation, the audience is positioned both to remember and forget the earlier, more detailed arguments: remember because those arguments are called to mind by the final touches of the author, and forget because concentration is focused on the last, seducing remarks.[21] The art of painting, however, does not unfold in time. Although the audience sees simultaneously the complex groundwork and the final overlay of touches, the light touches are physically laid over the more clearly labored ones to camouflage the signs of effort. For Caylus, the last touches applied are like the concluding remarks because each relieves the audience of the intricate argument or structure that lies beneath or behind them. In the case of painting, the audience agrees not to concentrate on what supports the finishing touches. Or keeping both underlying structure and finishing touches in mind, the viewer enjoys the tension between the two.

Caylus' light touches succeed because they allow the audience to perfect what the artist has only suggested. Complicit in its own deception, the audience is pleased to participate in making the work of art. Here is a direct link with the earlier notion of *sprezzatura,* which allowed the audience to complete and perfect the courtier's performance. And like the *sprezzatura* that entered into all the actions of the courtier, the light touches made every aspect of the painting blossom, "I would think that one can define the product of taste, spirit, and brushwork by saying that it is *the final touches which, directed by an exquisite sensibility, make all parts of a painting flower.*"[22]

Not only does Caylus' definition of *légèreté* contain key aspects of the earlier *sprezzatura,* but the term itself was frequently used to describe the style of the French salonist. For example, in *Les Confessions du comte de* *** (1741), Duclos characterized salon conversation as an elegant *bon ton* or *esprit,* which he equated not with intellectual analysis but with facility, brilliance and lightness *(légèreté)* of expression.[23] As the author of many *oeuvres badines,* Caylus could hardly have been unaware of this connotation and use of the term.[24] In fact, twice in his lecture to the Academy he drew comparisons with conversation. Early in the analysis Caylus claimed that the painter's *légèreté* was predicated on those omissions *(laissés)* analogous to the innuendos and the *mots suspendus* that comprised the grace *(l'agrément)* of conversation. And later, in arguing that Lemoine's *"légèreté de l'outil"* blinded the viewer to his faults (in particular, his incorrectness of drawing), Caylus equated the painter with the *homme du monde* whose graceful conversation created an "illusion" of flawlessness, even though his speech was neither pure nor exact.[25]

Notions dependent on the Italian ideal of *sprezzatura* developed in French painting theory during the first half of the eighteenth century, and writers found congenial the ideas of Castiglione, Vasari, Boschini, and the like. It is hardly surprising that Coypel, Caylus, and Cochin shared the same aristocratic aesthetics; they moved in privileged circles and supported elitist institutions (the Academy, for example). These and other theorists of a similar bent, however, certainly differed as to the degree of *facilité* and *négligence* they found acceptable in the finished work. How much freedom each writer allowed the artist was often proportional to how deeply his thinking was permeated by the rising ideology of genius. But before we turn to that ideology and the differences it provoked, there are still other aspects of the courtly tradition that warrant our attention.

Plaire AND THE EROTICS OF BRUSHWORK

Facilité and *négligence* were quite clearly derived from, and remained close to, the Italian *sprezzatura.* Yet they also acquired a more decidedly French accent when associated with the ideal of *plaire,* which moved between the discourses of art and *honnêteté.* J. P. Dens has demonstrated how deeply seventeenth-century French literary theory was indebted to the theory of *honnêteté* and how literature was tied to salon life where *honnêteté* was nurtured.[26] Some of these notions, for example that of *bienséance,* were also transferred to contemporaneous painting theory. By the end of the seventeenth century, however, the *honnête homme* was becoming an *homme du monde,* an *homme d'esprit,* or an *homme aimable* whose primary goal was to please. Defined as essential to the courtier-aristocrat in the writings of the Chevalier de Méré, *to please (plaire)* was at the heart of that author's conception of *honnêteté.*[27]

Although pleasure had been included among the rewards of art since antiquity, many cultures—and seventeenth-century France was one of them—subordinated this goal to that of instruction. The early eighteenth century, however, stressed pleasing and allied pleasure with notions of *le faire, facilité,* and *négligence.* We are all familiar with the writings of Du Bos, who early in the eighteenth century set out that the goal of art was to please. Du Bos is significant as heir to and mediator of the classical literary theory of *plaire* in its application to painting. More significant to painting theory per se was Roger de Piles' emphasis on *plaire* because he developed it in the context of practical advice for young artists. De Piles believed that a painter's first obligation was to attract and to please the spectator, and he repeatedly argued that the aim of painting was to "seduce the eyes."[28] Like other theorists after him, de Piles never denied the importance of instruction, nor even that it was the greater (read, more intellectual) merit. But it is clear, from the focus and attention given to pleasing, that pleasing was the privileged partner.

Whether placed in the first or second rank, the ideal of *plaire* was associated with a conception of the *pittoresque* related to, yet distinct from, its association with artfully contrived naturalness. *Pittoresque* often denoted visual effects that delighted the eye, and writers labeled as *genres pittoresques* the so-called lesser genres deemed incapable of pleasing the mind because they lacked a didactic subject. The artist's command of the *métier* completely determined the excellence of such works. A painting that instructed the mind by representing a historical or literary narrative, however, might also be *poétique* if it expressed effectively the conventional meaning of its subject.[29] The categories of the *pittoresque* and *poétique* restated in terms of the beholder the dichotomy of mind and hand that Félibien had applied to the creative process. The *poétique* was related to the intellectual pleasures of instruction, the *pittoresque* to the sensual pleasures of visual delight.

Late in the century Lévèsque, recapitulating much of Watelet's earlier writing, summarized in the *Dictionnaire des arts* (1792) attitudes toward the *pittoresque.* There he associates the *style pittoresque* with the *style ornamental,* and both are considered suitable for decoration but not for instruction. Introducing a third synonym, the *style sensuel,* Lévèsque justified the appellation by reminding the reader that what was *pittoresque* was merely flattering to the senses.[30] He went on, however, to associate the *pittoresque* with the seductive as well as with the sensual, arguing that its masters insinuated themselves *(s'insinuer)* into the favor of the audience, that they enchanted the eyes *(enchanter les yeux),* and, that "they have genuine merit because they produce pleasurable delights *[jouissances].*"[31]

This association of pleasing with enchanting, insinuating, and other terms charged with erotic connotations has its analogue in Méré's earlier explication of *honnêteté.* For Méré the courtier's essential characteristic, that of pleasing, was closely tied up with sexual encounter and conquest. The courtier enraptured, charmed, and conquered the other through insinuation, which implies not direct aggression but a circuitous and serpentine seduction. Flattery or appeals to the *amour propre* of others was a primary weapon. The *honnête homme* adapted himself to every situation and audience so as to force a surrendering to his charm.[32]

Within the theories of art and *honnêteté* the aim of pleasing was conceived in both sensual and erotic terms; and when specifically applied to painting, *plaire* was associated with the *pittoresque.* It is through the *pittoresque* that we return to the notions of *facilité* and *négligence,* both in their general application and as they related to *le faire.* The French theorists conceived a *pittoresque de l'execution,* and Watelet's formulation was typical in associating such a handling with a brush that was *"facile, badin, ragoutant".*[33] Moreover, he called picturesque execution, "A happy chance *[hasard heureux]* of the artist's hand that rendered as picturesque what was not already."[34] Similar to the constructions *négligences heureux* or *laissés heureux, un hasard heureux* signified an artfully contrived chance common to both meanings of *pittoresque* that we have discussed.

Recall that the decorator arranged elements in the *pittoresque* garden to imitate the spontaneous patterns of nature. Garden writers (Watelet and Morel) conceived the *pittoresque* as a pleasing naturalness achieved primarily in terms of composition. A *pittoresque* execution, on the other hand, was calculated to seem as though the artist had neither planned the placement of the brushmarks nor exerted effort in applying them. In rococo painting, however, both the *pittoresque* composition and the *pittoresque* execution could demonstrate the erotics of *plaire.*

If elements in the *pittoresque* landscape were arranged to signify the chance of nature, those in the interior scene were often composed to achieve a *beau désordre.* This beautiful disarray was, of course, a calculation of art. A room was represented as if chance events had left it in a pleasing visual pattern. Although not strictly limited to such scenes, *beau désordre* could be found where beautiful women (be they sophisticated ladies or country mothers) were represented as objects of delectation.[35] Thus, the delight of beholding an artfully disarranged setting augmented the spectator's pleasure in contemplating the feminine charms. In some cases, Boucher's *La Toilette* (1742; Lugano: Thyssen-Bornemisza Collection; figure 28) for example, the dishevelment of the room matched that of the provocative young woman represented within it. *Beau désordre* there is analogous to erotic *négligence* where a suggestive but delicate indecency of pose or dress disguises itself as inattention.[36] Such *négligence* was represented by novelists and playwrights throughout the eighteenth century. For example, the hero in Lamorlière's 1746 play *Angola, histoire indienne ouvrage sans vraisemblance* describes how his beloved received him in a fetching posture: she lounged carelessly, her coy dishabille allowing him to see some of her charms while increasing desire by hiding the others.[37]

Beau désordre, then, can be associated with that aspect of *négligence* analogous to the suggestive dishabille of the coquette. The room artfully disarranged not only pleases the viewer's sight, it also provides the occasion for erotic imaginings. Even the slightest disorder provokes this effect. For example, in Fragonard's *The Lock* (c.1778–80; Paris: Musée du Louvre; figure 29) a chair has been knocked over, and a piece of drapery (an article of clothing?), once thrown thoughtlessly over its back, now lies on the floor atop it. At the other end of the table a small overturned jug rests on a wad of fabric flung in a heap on the table top. This disorder is artful because the placement and direction of each object has been calculated in terms of the painting's compositional dynamic. This is also the case for the small bunch of flowers that seems tossed so serendipitously to the other side of the room. This effect of beautiful disarray is further enhanced by the artfully random twists and turns of the bed drapes. In *The Lock* the *beau désordre* entices the viewer to imagine what is not seen and cannot be seen: the preliminary events, the causes of the upheaval.

At the same time that the beautifully disheveled interior provokes, the

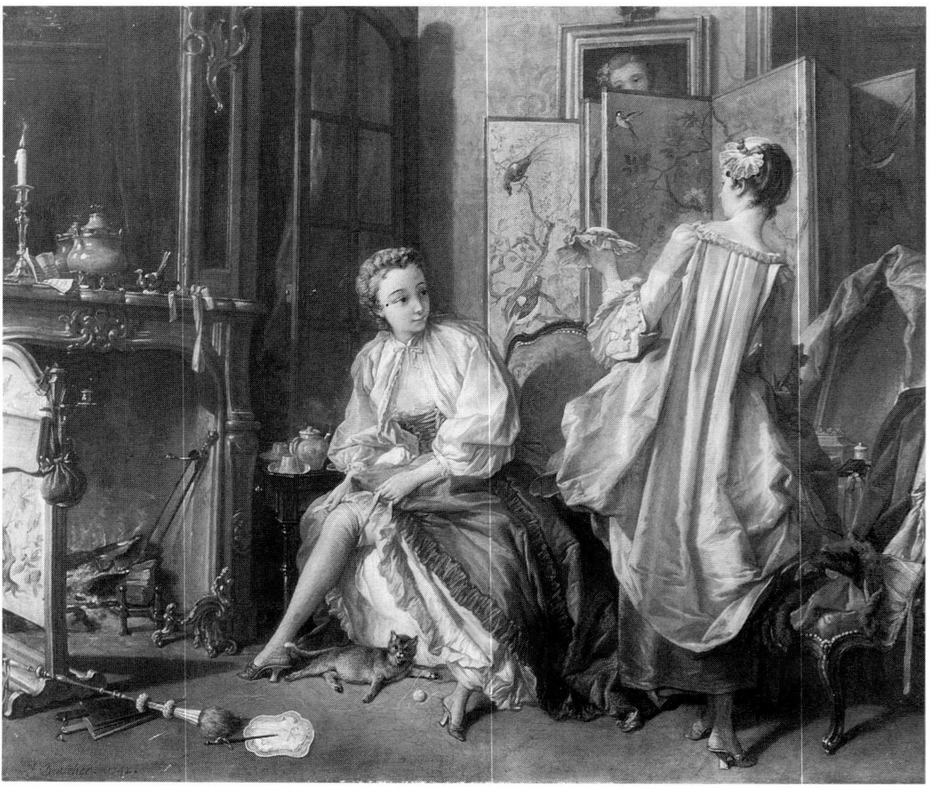

Figure 28 François Boucher, *La Toilette,* 1742. Thyssen-Bornemisza Foundation, Lugano, Switzerland.

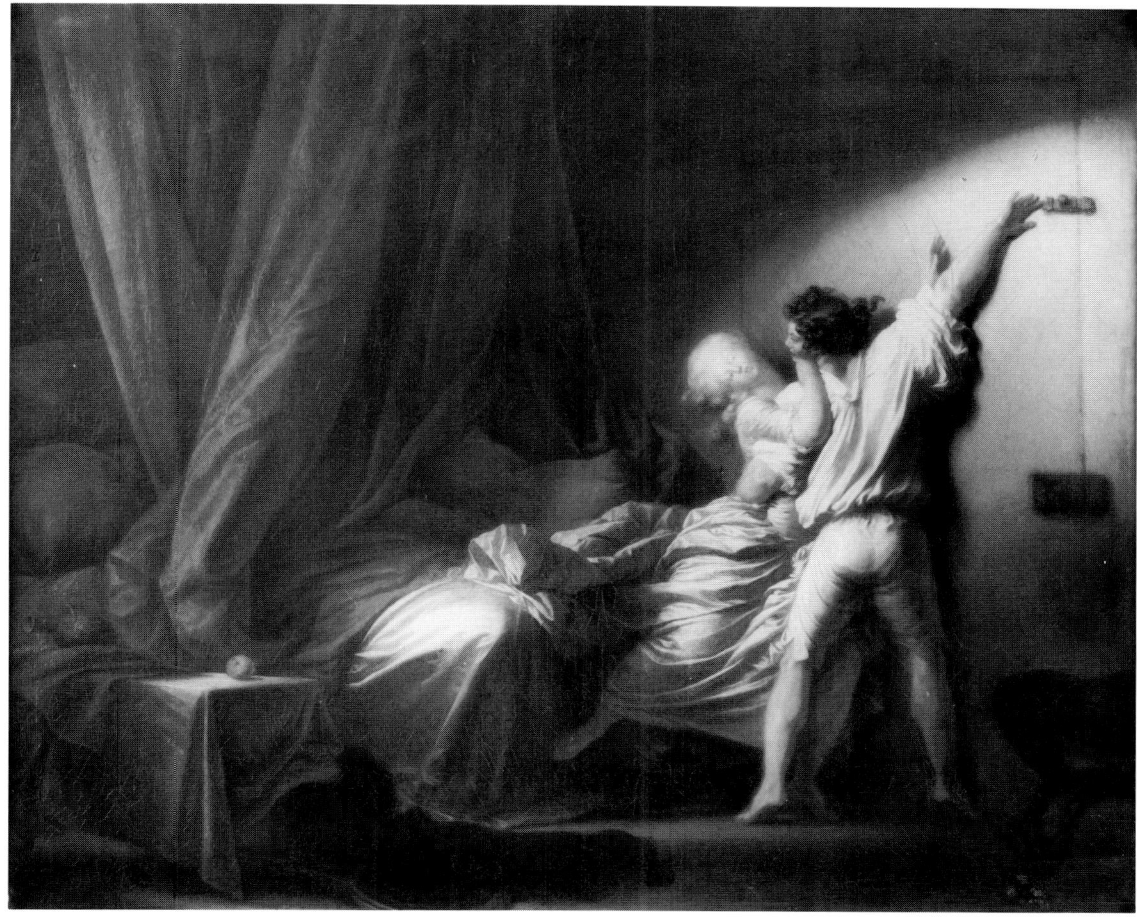

Figure 29 Jean-Honoré Fragonard, *The Lock,* c. 1778-80. Paris, Musée du Louvre. Cliché des Musées Nationaux, Paris.

pittoresque execution entices with its *légèreté, facilité,* and *négligence.* We have already seen in Caylus' writing how the painter's *légèreté* was compared to the seductiveness of salon conversation. Caylus also identified *légèreté* with a "seductive delicacy" that allowed the spectator to sense the artist's presence in all parts of a painting.[38] Cochin likewise transferred to the maker qualites that he found in the making. Luca Giordano, for instance, was the most "alluring" of all painters because "his execution shows the finest facility."[39] And Cochin also associated allure with *négligence,* specifically praising the Carracci for "that appearance of negligence which is one of the most pleasant seductions of art."[40] The secretary, moreover, did not confine his discussion of brushwork's seductive appeal to individual cases. Describing the effect of *le faire* in a more general way, Cochin noted that the paint handling of a great master has "warmth" and excites the audience. The execution of a mediocre painter, on the other hand, leaves the beholder "cold." But for Cochin it is the connoisseur who most enjoys touches that are free and facile. Such a handling gives to this cultured viewer pleasure of a kind that "nothing can replace."[41]

Part of the connoisseur's pleasure we have already considered: the pleasure of completing or participating in the work of art. By the eighteenth century this enticement, too, was associated with the notion of *plaire,* as it had been in Méré's discussion of *honnêteté.*[42] In allowing the viewer to participate in the painting, the artist emulated the courtier who seduced his audience by appealing to its vanity. Dandré-Bardon explained to young artists why they should engage the spectator's imagination; and although his comments were not made in reference to brushwork, they articulate the general principle that was widely applied to *le faire:*

> Great is the art that procures for the spectators the means to engage their imaginations. Their self-esteem is grateful to an artist who persuades them that they are in part the authors of that which their imagination adds to the painting, and they truly enjoy the pleasure *[ils jouissent réelement du plaisir]* of having a hand in the work. In this regard the man of talent is the equal of the man of spirit *[homme d'esprit]* who lends spirit to others.[43]

In Dandré-Bardon's conception the man of talent is likened to the *homme d'esprit.* The artist, however, could also play the *coquette* or *galant,* because execution was often associated with a light, flirtatious seduction through the terms *badinage* and *ragoûtant.* The *ragoût* was defined as "a sort of teasing, it testifies to the facility of the artist who is capable of playing with his brush, of toying with the greatest difficulties of the métier."[44] If a painting is *ragoûtant,* it demonstrates that its maker was able to control even the most demanding aspects of art, displaying absolute mastery by disguising it as playful dalliance. *Ragoûtant* here does not describe an execution suitable to express great pathos but one that is like the clever banter appropriate to salon seduction.

Le Faire AND THE ELITE AUDIENCE

In the aristocratic model *le faire* is associated with an ease of performance that pleases or seduces its viewer. This performance, however, was not tuned to any viewer but to those who were of the elite, those who knew the codes in which the artist spoke. But painting open only to the knowledgeable presented something of a theoretical problem because painting was commonly held to be a natural language open to the literate and illiterate alike. Painting could be reserved for the elite, however, by focusing attention on either arcane subjects or *le faire.* Most *hommes d'esprit* (and Caylus is a notable exception here) would find the second path more congenial, for they shuddered at pedantic depictions of minor incidents from obscure literary texts.

Elite art addressed itself especially to one branch of *le monde,* that comprised of connoisseurs and collectors. Theoretically only they could recognize the master's hand in a work of art and judge the painting's aesthetic value. Recall that Cochin addressed his comments on *le faire* to the connoisseur, whom he believed *le faire* pleased in a unique way. In another essay published in 1759, Cochin argued that although anyone could evaluate subject matter, the *composition pittoresque* must be left to experts instructed in the principles of art and conversant with the acknowledged masterworks.[45]

Cochin's view of who could evaluate painting was significantly different from that expressed by some other academic artists and writers. De Piles, for example, had insisted that any *homme d'esprit* could be a good judge of art even if he did not know the rules, and Charles-Antoine Coypel reiterated that claim in his *Dialogue sur la connoissance de la peinture* of 1726.[46] Cochin, however, was led to argue that the critic must be an *amateur* or *connoisseur,* in response to the arrival of *littérateurs* entering the business of assessing paintings and claiming for everyone the right to judge art.[47] As early as 1747 La Font de Saint-Yenne had argued that, like a book or a piece of theater, a painting in the public domain had to be evaluated by a disinterested spectator.[48] The next year Le Blanc defended the rights of the connoisseurs by calling the demi-connoisseurs (the *littérateurs*) worse than the ignorant; accusing them of attributing to the general public opinions that were their own, Le Blanc charged that the demi-connoisseurs were motivated by vanity. He reasserted the privilege of the *public éclairé* to judge, claiming that they gave their votes only to those who deserved them.[49]

In the battle between connoisseurs and *littérateurs,* the connoisseurs usually vaunted execution and the *littérateurs* subject matter. It was the latter group who called most stridently for the revitalization of history painting. Either they felt most at home with stories and allegories drawn from literature, or they were pressing for ethical or reformist goals, or both. No such motives, however, can be attributed to that other group who also ignored the subtleties of *le faire*—I am referring, of course, to the general public or the *grand public* for whom the *littérateurs* claimed to speak. Before the literary men entered the Salons, there was only one art-viewing elite, the *public éclairé,* and it is perhaps significant that the distinction between them and the general public (the *grand public* or the ignorant) could also be drawn on the issue of execution.[50]

Partisans of Chardin repeatedly called upon the notion that subject matter appealed to the "ignorant" viewer and execution to the enlightened one. The great still life painter, they said, was favored by the general public because he represented objects and situations familiar to them, while he was celebrated by the amateurs because of his marvellous *faire.*[51] Articulating the central paradox of Chardin's painting, writers argued that where naive viewers saw only nature, elite ones saw art—an art so subtle that it could not be discovered by ordinary eyes. The marketing of Chardin made evident this two-tiered appreciation. Naturally the original paintings sold to the elite (and other artists), and the engravings to a wider public.[52] Moralizing poems added to the engraved genre scenes directed attention away from formal issues toward the subject matter, thus giving the works a clear message. The codes of elite art contained in *le faire* were thereby replaced by the codes of the more widely understood emblematic tradition.[53]

Le faire was the connoisseur's domain, and the art expert preferred an execution that, leaving something to the imagination, was *facile, agréable, léger.* This handling was specifically associated with the elite viewer in Laugier's 1771 treatise *Manière de bien juger des ouvrages de peinture.* There he argued that a work without traces of the brush was the resource of those painters who could neither imagine things vividly nor produce great effects with a rapid execution. These painters reduced themselves to catching the eye by a great perfection of surface, and their cold, very finished works appealed only to the ignorant masses.[54]

This association of the skillfully unfinished with the connoisseur is closely connected to the appreciation of drawings and sketches. These, conventional wisdom had it, could only be understood by the connoisseur. *L'Idée du peintre parfait,* 1701, contained a long section devoted to the appreciation of drawing in which that appreciation was characterized as the most difficult sort of connoisseurship requiring the most practice, discernment, delicacy, and penetration.[55] Dézallier d'Argenville later contrasted those who prized drawings with those who valued only very finished works. Hitting familiar themes, he distinguished between the would-be connoisseur who always needed something finished to please his eye and the real connoisseur whose imagination was fired by the spark that burned in a drawing.[56] Although the appreciation of the sketch developed within the aristocratic concept of *le faire,* it was equally exploited by those who touted genius. Located deep in the overlap of the two models, the appreciation of drawings is situated with that quality said to distinguish both the aristocratic audience and the recognizers of genius: taste.

TASTE AND THE *Je Ne Sais Quoi*

Taste was the central endowment of the *honnête homme,* who could sense beauty or superior talent as if by instinct and without the aid of rules. For the Chevalier Méré, (*Quatrième Conversation,* 1668) taste was an undefinable sentiment, a sixth sense that acted spontaneously and with certainty. Good taste consisted in "judging well all that presents itself by a *je ne sais quel [sic]* sentiment, which works more quickly and sometimes more surely than thought."[57] Many eighteenth-century writers adopted these general ideas about taste, which was analyzed most thoroughly by the Abbé Batteux. In *Les beaux arts réduits à un même principe,* 1746, Batteux characterized taste as a gift of nature originally given to (all) people so they could judge natural things according to need and pleasure. Since the arts imitated nature, natural taste was the basis for acquired taste, defined by Batteux as a sentiment directed toward the work of art. This acquired taste was perfect when one could sense the difference between the good and the bad and between the excellent and the mediocre by a distinct impression, without confounding them or mistaking one for the other, and without knowing why or how the judgment was made.[58] Batteux, however, believed that this acquired taste had to be cultivated through knowledge of the rules and principles of a given art and through a study of those things recognized as tasteful.[59] By thus tying the exercise of taste to a familiarity with art objects and aesthetic theory, Batteux moved taste more securely into the realm of the privileged.

Important for the enlightened spectator, taste was more crucial to the artist who, before executing a work, had to judge and select, to choose from nature or from images those that could be used to make the most beautiful effects. Two aspects of taste described in the literatures of *honnêteté* and art put it at odds with other qualities of courtier and artist. First, taste was seen as an innate gift, and even when Batteux defined acquired taste he did not deny its basis in nature. Second, taste acted spontaneously without the conscious control of intellect, and again this was also true of Batteux's acquired taste. Conceived as the natural ability to recognize instantaneously what was superior, taste had a problematic relation to *sprezzatura.* The first represented a real, natural spontaneity, the second a calculated, artificial one. Although many desirable characteristics of artist and courtier were rooted in affected appearance and practiced response, one of the most important—taste—was a natural endowment. The courtier model thus allowed that sometimes the artist acted by exercising his natural gifts spontaneously. Such ideas facilitated the transformation of the artist from courtier to genius.

More primary than taste in easing this transformation was the innate gift that characterized the *honnête homme* as artist and performer, the *je ne sais quoi.* Méré found that *je ne sais quoi* entered into the appearance as well as the actions of the *honnête homme;* his countenance radiated with an insinuating *je ne sais quoi,* his voice carried a certain *je ne sais quoi* that was appealing and casual.[60] Moreover, the *je ne sais quoi* placed the *honnête homme* above all the rules. When it was present, all defects were forgiven; when it was absent, all virtues were overlooked.[61]

Although its name tells us that the *je ne sais quoi* cannot be named, it was long associated and even equated with the quality of grace.[62] And grace brings us back to where we began this discussion, to Castiglione. His discussion of grace is an obvious precedent for the notion of the *je ne sais quoi:*

> If I remember rightly, my dear Count, it seems to me that you have repeated several times this evening that the courtier has to imbue with grace his movements, his gestures, his way of doing things and in short, his every action. And it appears to me that you require this in everything as the seasoning without which all other attributes and good qualities would be almost worthless. Now I admit that everyone should easily be persuaded of this, seeing that, by the very meaning of the word, it can be said that a man who behaves with grace finds it with others. You have said that this is very often a natural, God-given gift, and that even if it is not quite perfect it can be greatly enhanced by application and effort.[63]

The association of the God-given gift with the *je ne sais quoi* is an important part of the ideology of genius, and it is to this model that we must turn. But first a final note. To act as a courtier—to possess grace, taste, *je ne sais quoi* and to perform with *sprezzatura*—one did not have to be of noble birth, although certainly this good fortune gave anyone an extra luster. It was necessary, however, to be born with natural talent: "It is true that, through the favor of the stars or of Nature, certain people come into the world endowed with such gifts that they seem not to have been born but to have been formed by some god with his own hands and blessed with every possible advantage of mind and body."[64] Although such proclamations might have been a ruse to naturalize the established social order (the aristocracy of blood), they also established these favored courtiers as an elite defined by innate talent. The metamorphosis of the artist from courtier to genius was thus a change from one type of natural aristocracy to another. There was, however, a major difference between the artist as courtier and the artist as genius, for the ideology of the second tried to obliterate entirely the seeming and the affected in favor of the actual and the spontaneous. It insisted on giving priority to nature and the natural sign rather than to art and the instituted one.

Genius, Enthusiasm, and Touch

THE GENIUS

Michel Foucault has shown us how the classical age was obsessed by typology, sorting all natural creatures into phylum, family, and genus, categorizing them by their observable characteristics.[65] Man was not exempt from the classifier's zeal, and new types, such as that of the genius, found their definitions in the course of the eighteenth century. Before then there were no geniuses, only individuals who had genius. The French term *génie* referred to a mental power and came from the Latin concept of *ingenium,* which designated the ability to reason forcefully or to invent new concepts by comparing or combining existing ideas. Eventually, *génie* became synonymous with talent, inclination, or natural disposition.[66]

As to the painter's genius, seventeenth-century French theory treated it in a general way; and Roger de Piles' discussion of genius in the 1709 *L'idée d'un peintre parfait* continues this early tradition, noting only that genius was both a gift of nature and a prerequisite for all truly great artists.[67] By 1719 Du Bos wrote on genius at greater length, but his concept of it did not challenge its synonymy with talent:

> We call genius the aptitude that a man has received from nature for doing well and easily certain things that others can do only very badly, even in exerting much effort. We learn to do the things for which we have genius with as much facility as we have in speaking our natural language.[68]

Some salient features of Du Bos' discussion, however, bring to mind the perfect courtier and the language used to describe him. The words *faire* and *facilité* appear throughout the passage, which emphasizes doing or making things easily, without effort. But there is a difference. Du Bos did not write of a calculated ease, a difficulty overcome, a *sprezzatura;* his genius was an innate ability.

About midcentury the genius emerged as a type. At first he (and the genius like the courtier was assumed to be a man) made only a brief appearance alongside discussions of genius as a mental quality. Called the *homme de génie,* he entered the *Encyclopédie* in the article on *enthousiasme,* where the quality genius was conceived metaphorically as the brush with which an artist or writer fabricated a mental conception of his work upon the canvas of imagination.[69] The metaphor of brush and canvas isolated the component parts of genius, the quality, and demonstrated their operation in the creative process. The canvas is simple imagination, or as Diderot called it, "the faculty of painting absent objects as if they were present."[70] The brush (or genius) is a more complex power composed of two mental faculties: compound imagination and judgment. The first combined and recreated mental images, the second discerned and chose those things suitable for the painting. The metaphor describes the process of invention in which compound imagination and judgment work in concert to choose and combine objects proper to produce the desired expressions and effects.

Given this discussion of genius as a quality, the account of the *homme de génie* as a type may seem unexpected because it does not focus on his creativity. Rather his social persona is highlighted in the text, which described the conduct of this "singular species" as little resembling "the mode of behavior adopted in society." Totally preoccupied with their art, men of genius exhibit "a natural candor, a frank character" and, above all, "the most decided antipathy for all that has the appearance of intrigue, artifice, and conspiracy."[71] The discussion sets up the genius as a natural type apart from all others and particularly contrasts him to the social, man-made ideal of the courtier. The reader is advised against searching for genius in an author, painter, or musician who is "compliant," "servile," "evasive," and an "adroit courtier."[72] But why did the text establish so conspicuously the *homme de génie* as a contrary of the courtier? There were, as we know, clear similarities between the two types; the concepts of *je ne sais quoi* and *sprezzatura* were not far from the ideas of inborn talent and spontaneous facility that had come to be associated with genius. By 1750, however, a new ideology was being broadcast. That ideology not only privileged nature but also viewed artificial salon culture as both corrupted and corrupting.[73]

ENTHUSIASM AND TOUCH

For the writer of the *Encyclopédie* the *homme de génie* lacked an aptitude for courtly intrigue, but he was marked by an enthusiasm that insured an intense absorption in his work. Enthusiasm was an ancient concept, developed from the platonic notion of divine madness to Ficino's melancholia and the *fureur poétique* of the Pléiade.[74] By the seventeenth century enthusiasm was conceived metaphorically as fire—in particular, the heavenly fire stolen by Prometheus. A lucky few with the potential to become great artists received this divine energy at birth. Later they would use it to enliven and vivify their creations.[75]

Although most theorists of the enlightened century severed enthusiasm from its divine origin, many maintained the idea of a furor that seized the artist's imagination, suspended the usual operations of his mind, and provoked a loss of consciousness.[76] In the *Encyclopédie,* however, enthusiasm was touted as quintessentially rational even as it maintained its connections with fire, heat, energy, and loss of consciousness. Rational meant emanating from the powers of the mind, and the rational conception of enthusiasm displaced the idea that some frenzy exterior to the intellect took hold of it.[77] The author cast this rational enthusiasm as an emotion analogous to that aroused by beholding a great work. Asking his readers to envision themselves looking at an excellent painting, he presented that experience as the imperfect parallel of the artist's excitement in contemplating a newly fabricated mental picture:

> A sudden surprise arrests you, you experience a pervasive emotion. Your absorbed gaze remains in a kind of immobility. Your entire spirit focuses itself on a crowd of objects that occupy it all at once, but soon, restored to its movement, your attention wanders around the different parts of the whole that had struck it. Its heat *[chaleur]* communicates itself to your senses; your eyes obey it and anticipate it, a lively fire animates them. You perceive. You detail. You compare the attitudes, the contrasts, the light, the features of the characters, their passions, the choice of the action represented, the skill, the force, the boldness of the brush. You notice that in this circumstance your attention, your surprise, your emotion, your warmth will be more or less vivid according to how much prior knowledge you have acquired and according to how much taste, delicacy, spirit, sensitivity, judgment that you have received from nature.[78]

This image of enthusiasm divides the *homme de génie* into maker and spectator, for the genius first imagines his work and then contemplates his mental picture. Enthusiasm subsequently turned imaginer to creator as it moved his hand to execute and enliven his production:

> The impulse which has shaken him, which fills him, and which carries him away, is such that everything yields to it and that it is the dominant feeling. So, with nothing able to distract or stop him, the painter seizes his brush and the canvas is colored, the figures arranged, the dead revived; the chisel is already in the hand of the sculptor and the marble animated; the verse flows from the pen of the poet and the theater grows more beautiful from a thousand new actions which interest and astonish us.[79]

What emerges in this discussion of a reasonable enthusiasm is an artist obsessed by his own imaginative conception, one who is absorbed, arrested, even immobilized before it. Pinned in rapturous contemplation, the artist becomes excited, enflamed, and finally overpowered by a desire to create that unsettles and transports him. So strong was that entranced state that nothing could stop or dissuade the genius from his goal. It was the blissful oblivion in enthusiasm that Diderot characterized in orgasmic terms: "The poet senses the moment of enthusiasm. . . . It begins as a trembling in his chest, and passes in a wonderful and rapid way to the extremities of his body. Not only a trembling, but a strong permanent heat which embraces him, excites him, kills him, but gives spirit and life to all that he touches."[80]

If enthusiasm was marked by a display of rapture likened to sexual climax, Watelet's conception of feigned enthusiasm presented in the *Dictionnaire des arts* made an equally suggestive association of the creative urge with the erotic impulse. The *amateur* wrote that an artist affected ardor after his enthusiasm had cooled, "as women whose love is exhausted and who do not want to renounce the advantages which it procures them, seek to show it all the more by displaying it in the same proportion as they have lost it."[81]

Three aspects of enthusiasm—obsession, excitement, and transport—were fundamental traits of the enflamed artist as he was described by widely diverse writers, many of whom gave enthusiasm an erotic character. Also central to these conceptions was the division of the artist into spectator and creator. In contemplating the contents of his imagination, the artist contemplated a spectral self constituted as an object of desire. Batteux made Zeuxis the prototype of the enthused artist; to represent the ideal woman the Greek painter combines in his imagination the most beautiful natural features he could observe. Aroused by contemplating his newly created object, Zeuxis "forgets himself" and his spirit passes into what he makes.[82]

If Zeuxis was the historical prototype of the enthused artist, Pygmalion was the mythic one; and all the elements characteristic of enthusiasm are present in the story of the sculptor who falls in love with his representation of the perfect woman, the goddess Galatea.[83] Rousseau's *Pygmalion* (composed c.1762, performed 1772) began with the artist confronting his work, paralyzed and awed by his own creation, by its reflection of himself,[84] yet restless with a desire that disrupts his concentration. In his *Pygmalion* Rousseau makes certain basic assumptions about the relationship between the aesthetic and erotic impulses, and these assumptions are evident in individual statements. Pygmalion implies a correspondence between sexual arousal and enthusiasm when he speaks of "masterpieces of nature," "charming models" that "inflamed me at the same moment with the fires of love and genius."[85]

Although only the genius could achieve true enthusiastic bliss, the sensitive viewer could, through a process of transmission, vicariously participate in the artist's creative ecstasy. The *Encyclopédie* defined a second species of enthusiasm parasitic on the artist's emotion: an enthusiasm of the viewer. Though not as strong as the artist's transport, this second enthusiasm depended on the liveliness of mind, sensibility, and experience of the beholder.[86] The notion that creator and viewer mutually enjoyed the enthused state, however, was neither new at midcentury nor particular to that time. De Piles had already posited the idea and Laugier, writing later in the century, believed that the liveliness of a painting passed rapidly into the spectating soul: "Nothing can make us better aware of the graces of painting than that enthusiasm particular to sensitive souls, which makes all the fire that animates the canvas pass rapidly into us."[87] This reciprocity of enthusiasm—of the enthusiasm that creates and the enthusiasm that admires—is kin to the relation established in the aristocratic model between *je ne sais quoi* and taste. And as in the aristocratic model, the aesthetic pleasure of enthusiasm is tied to the erotic.

But in what aspect or aspects of the work was this enthusiasm carried to the viewer? If enthusiasm was the emotion that motivated the artist to pick up brush or chisel, then that emotion left its traces in the action, the play, the physical motion of hand and instrument. Many eighteenth-century writers found the most revealing indicator of enthusiasm in the way the artist touched the canvas. The term *touche,* however, had two related meanings in the eighteenth century. In a general sense, *touche* (touch) was derived from the verb *toucher;* it designated the mark of the brush as the artist applied the paint to the canvas. In a more specific sense, *touche* was a kind of accent or stress used by the artist in painting the different features of objects, and these touches enlivened or animated a representation. In applying them the artist was affected both by the nature of the object he represented (its visible appearance conditioned by lighting, movement, etc.) and by how he felt when he was making his representation. As an "instantaneous" effect of the impression that an object or idea made on the painter, the touch was conditioned by the artist's changing states of mind, and thus it could be taken to signify his thoughts, feelings, or inspiration.[88] The conception of touch, both in its general and specific sense, as an index of enthusiasm was held concurrently with a theory of execution that directed the artist to alter his brushwork consciously. On the one hand touch was deemed spontaneous and personal, and, on the other, it was taught as a controllable and conventionalized element of art.

THE AESTHETICS OF THE SKETCH

When touch was considered a true index, the kind of touching most likely to carry enthusiasm was that touch recorded when the artist first picked up brush or pencil—the touch associated with the sketch. We have already seen how the taste for sketches grew up in an aristocratic milieu where it was the connoisseur's domain. But the sketch also had meanings for those preoccupied with genius and enthusiasm; it expressed the artist's soul, as Diderot told his readers in the *Salon of 1765:* "A sketch ordinarily has a fire that a painting does not. It is the heated moment for the artist, the purest verve, without any admixture of the artifice that reflection puts on everything; it is the soul of the painter spreading itself freely on the canvas."[89]

Diderot here takes the sketch as more than a representation of the moment when the artist's mind worked quickly, spontaneously, and without reflection. The sketch, he tells us, *is* that moment, and it reveals instantaneous conception, untainted by artifice. Both immediate and unmediated, the sketch allowed direct access to the artist's enthusiasm.

And what of the pleasure afforded the viewers? Not only were they transported, but they also had the satisfaction of completing forms only suggested. We can compare those who savored the sketch to those who observed the courtier's performance: both enjoyed the work in a perfected form developed in their own imaginations. In contemplating the work as they would have it finished, beholders, like enthused artists, were aroused by a self-reflection, an extension of the self. This excitement, however, was not productive because the beholder never took up pen or brush. Diderot analyzed the pleasures of the sketch, as the quotation cited above continues:

> The vaguer the expression of the arts, the freer the imagination [of the viewer]. In vocal music one is forced to understand what is expressed. I let a well-made symphony say almost whatever pleases me, and since, through my experience of my own heart, I know better than anyone what affects me, it is rare when the expression that I give to the sounds, analogous to my current situation—serious, tender, or gay—does not touch me more than any other that would be less of my own choosing. It is nearly the same with the sketch and the painting. I see in the painting something pronounced; how many things do I imagine in the sketch that are scarcely delineated there.[90]

Making explicit the audience's infatuation with its own imaginings, Diderot theorizes that the sketch, like instrumental music, allows the appreciator's fancy to wander unconstrained.

It was not a large step for the painter to bring aspects of the sketch into the finished work, because qualities related to the sketch were already part of the artist's vocabulary. We have seen in the French tradition concepts of *négligence, facilité,* and *légèreté;* the artist had long been instructed to flatter the viewer's imagination by leaving something unfinished. The freedom of the touch perhaps only needed a little exaggeration to suggest the enthusiasm particular to the sketch. And since the viewer did not actually see the work as it was being made, the touch could be made to signify enthusiasm, whether or not that nearly mythical emotion had been felt.

An evident speed of execution was not desired for its own sake. By the mid-eighteenth century a free and loose execution was ordinarily denigrated when considered a demonstration of manual dexterity and exalted when taken as an index of the mental powers at work. The significant point is this: the enthused genius allegedly conceived of a work instantaneously, saw it complete, and rendered it impulsively.[91] A sketchlike execution implied an uncalculated work, one not planned through various studies and drawings. Yet an artist could make hundreds of studies for a work and then execute the final product quickly, even directly on the canvas. Another painter might execute the finished work slowly but make it seem to have been quickly brushed; and a third could produce a freely handled work with a little preparation, not by relying on a unique vision, but by manipulating learned conventions, memorized models, and studied types.

We can gauge the popularity of a sketchlike handling in eighteenth-century France by these remarks of the painter Liotard who worked in an entirely other manner:

> In the principal cities of Europe and above all in those where there are the most painters, there are some prejudices completely opposed to the principles or rules that I will propose and in particular to the one I have just prescribed. People never stop saying that all good painting must be facile, freely brushed, and well touched; they have persuaded those who have no knowledge of the principles of art and whom I will call ignorant.[92]

Liotard's comments raise the question of how much sketchiness was desirable in a finished work, a work not considered as a preliminary stage of another work. The answer to this question varied with the viewer's ideological stance and personal predilections, as well as with the purpose and placement of the painting. Although a Salon entry was usually more carefully finished than either an *ébauche* or a work painted for an *amateur's* cabinet, some academicians appreciated broad ranges of freedom in handling. Cochin, for example, praised artists whom others thought too extravagant or too free in their technique. He found Luca Giordano (called Fa Presto because of his apparent speed of execution) the most alluring of all painters, a man with a "very fine genius" who united all parts of painting to a high degree.[93] Writing earlier in the century, Du Bos had not been so kind to Luca, seeing in his work the merely mechanical skill of a *pasticheur.*[94] Similarly, Cochin approved of Tintoretto, whom many writers found too extravagant in his *faire.* De Piles, for example, had granted the Venetian facility but held him too excessive, and Caylus warned that many of his works had only false facility.[95] For Cochin, on the other hand, Tintoretto was tiresome when he finished too exactly but above all comparison when he worked quickly, abandoned to the heat of his genius.[96] The academician Cochin admired a free, sketchlike execution in a finished work and, as his remarks indicate, was willing to read it as a sign of the artist's mental state. Diderot's Salon comments generally indicate that although he admired the real sketch, he equivocated on a sketchlike execution. Some artists, for example Deshays, were praised for their ability to preserve the enthusiasm of the first moment in the finished work. Others, such as Hallé, were criticized even in works exhibited as preliminary versions for the "extreme license of the sketch."[97]

Although viewers disagreed on the degree of sketchlikeness allowable in the finished work, there was no doubt that the real sketch, the painter's *première pensée* was tied to the moment of enthusiasm. And there was also no doubt that a real connection was posited between brushwork and the artist's state of mind. But why did Cochin and writers like him accept the handling of a finished painting as an index of the artist's mental state even as they posited a conventionalized language of brushwork, a language that could be consciously manipulated? Could brushwork be a sign at once natural and instituted?

TOUCH AND THE NATURAL SIGN

Eighteenth-century semiotics conceived the sign broadly as "anything determined to represent something else."[98] This definition, found in the *Encyclopédie* of 1751, is consistent with Condillac's thinking in the 1746 *Essai sur l'origine des connoissances humaines,* where he distinguished and ordered three kinds of signs: the accidental, the natural, and the instituted. In the accidental sign a chance circumstance connected an object or sensation perceived (the signifier) to some absent object imagined (the signified). These signs were available even to animals who could bring to mind an absent object if (and only if) that object was connected with a present sensation. (For example, a predator might be motivated to go to where it had previously fed if the sensation of hunger happened to be connected to that place.)[99] The connection between signified and signifier differed in the natural sign, for there they were joined by natural law or necessity. Among natural signifiers were the outward physical responses (cries, gestures, facial expressions) nature established to represent the internal passions. The first time a response was elicited by a passion, however, there was no sign, only a consciousness of perception. The response became a sign through repetition as reminiscence registered that the perception had been experienced before.[100] Although natural signs were universally determined and accidental ones the result of an individual's chance encounter, neither could be conjured at will apart from a sensation. Instituted signs, on the other hand, were freed from physical objects and sensations. They contained two ideas, that of the signifier and that of the signified; and the relationship between them was purely arbitrary, i.e., determined by choice. Such signs were required for independent thought, and thus they were crucial for mental development.[101] Words were clear examples of instituted signs.

Because Condillac based his classifications on the differing connections between signifier and signified, it would seem that a response such as a scream would always be a natural sign. This was not the case. For a boy nursed by bears, a scream was only an accidental sign because he had no way of determining that the sounds natural to his passions were the proper signs of the emotions he felt.[102] The argument here implies that natural signs are always to a certain extent instituted because the signifiers have *both* a necessary (i.e., determined by nature) and a chosen (i.e., determined by human society) connection with what they signify. No clear-cut line, then, divides the natural from the instituted sign. Although Condillac seemed unaware of blurring the edges on that point, later in the text the author defined a process by which natural signifiers could become instituted. Natural cries, for example, were instituted signs when used at will to represent feelings; "then they are no longer natural signs whose character is to express in and of themselves and independently of the choice made of them, the impression that one feels."[103] Here again the line was drawn on a question of choice. However, in the first case, where the accidental is differentiated from the natural, choice refers to an act of selection, of designating an X to signify a Y (designating a scream to signify pain, for example); in the second, choice also refers to an act of willing, of consciously deciding to make a sign. In the latter example one chooses to do or to make that which has already been chosen as a signifier.

The idea of choosing to do or to make articulates the crucial difference between the instituted and the natural sign. In the latter case the signifier is spontaneously generated; it is quite literally caused by the signified (or its referent) and not controlled by choice or reason. Once the sign is instituted, however, the assurance of a cause and effect relationship is lost. It is possible that there can be only effects, only appearances. To wince noticeably when comfortable, for example, is to conjure the sign for pain without feeling pained. By exploiting the expectation of a causal connection, the natural sign, having become instituted, can create artifice. Diderot recognized this idea in his *Paradoxe sur le comédien* (written in 1773; published in 1830) where the actor creates an illusion by making signs—gestures and facial expressions—for emotions he does not feel. His talent, Diderot writes, "depends not, as you think, upon feeling, but upon rendering so exactly the outward signs of feeling, that you are deceived. . . . The gestures of his despair are memorized and have been prepared in front of a mirror."[104] In making signs the painter is like the actor; if he knows that a certain gesture made by a figure or a certain brushmark upon the canvas will be taken as a signifier, he can make the sign independently of feeling the emotion expressed by the figure or conveyed by his mark.

With its definition of the natural sign, eighteenth-century semiotic thinking inserted a causal connection between the artist's state of mind and the touch. The touch expressed enthusiasm because, like a facial expression or a gesture, it was spontaneously generated by an emotional state. Thus the move from a courtier to a genius model is also the move from a mimetic to an expressive concept of art. Diderot, however, realized that an expressive art was every bit as contradictory as a natural one. Yet he and other writers might have been predisposed to consider the touch as a natural sign because they mistakenly conceived the whole painted image as a natural sign for what it represented. A pictorial representation of say, a tree, was taken to signify (the idea of) a tree to the extent that a real tree signified (the idea of) itself. Du Bos even speculated that he spoke poorly in saying that painting used signs; rather, painting put nature herself before the viewer's eyes.[105]

If we consider art from the maker's perspective (as Diderot did in the *Parodoxe*), we see that a painting conceived is never a natural sign for the

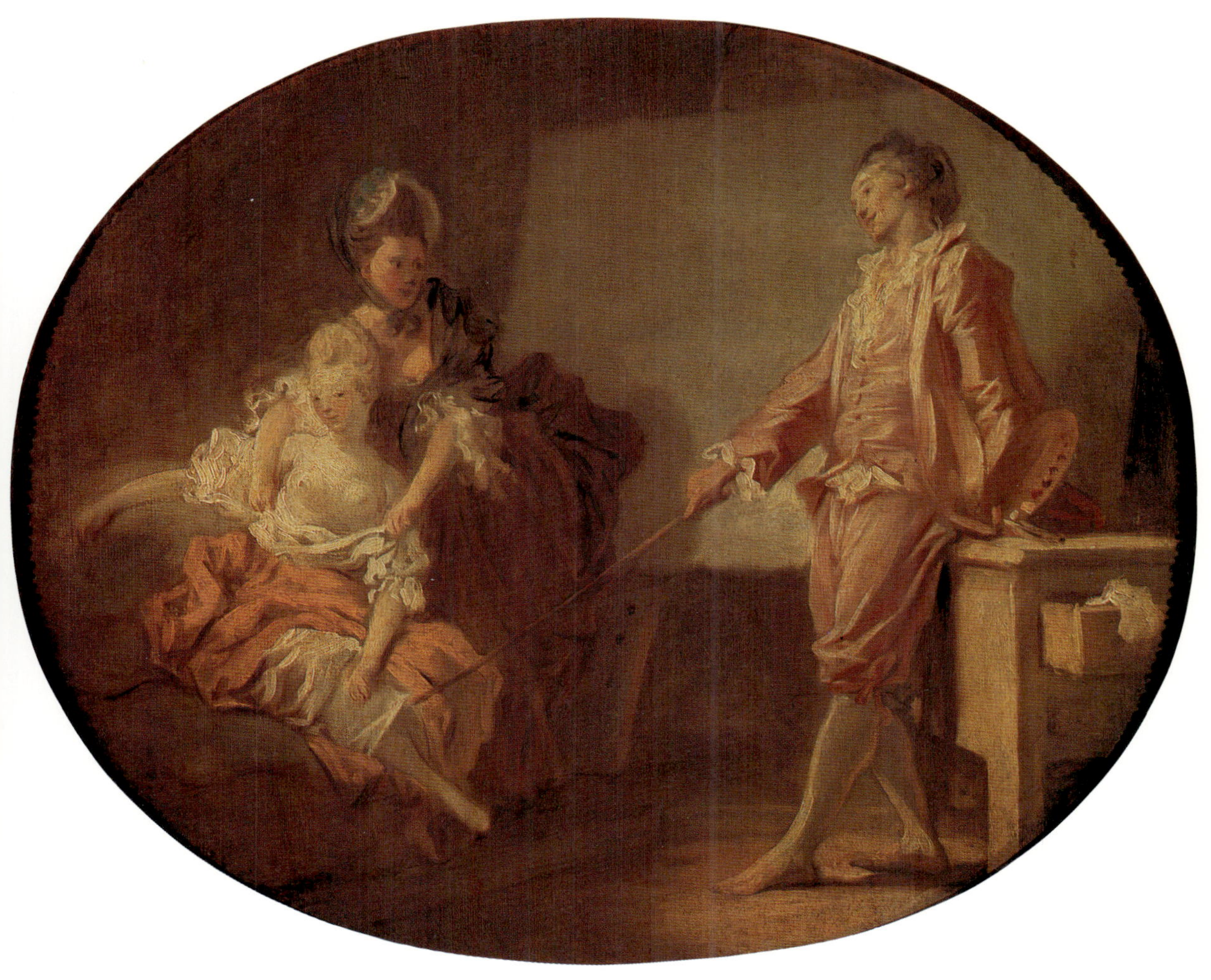

Plate 1 Jean-Honoré Fragonard, *The New Model,* 1770. Paris, Musée Jacquemart-André.

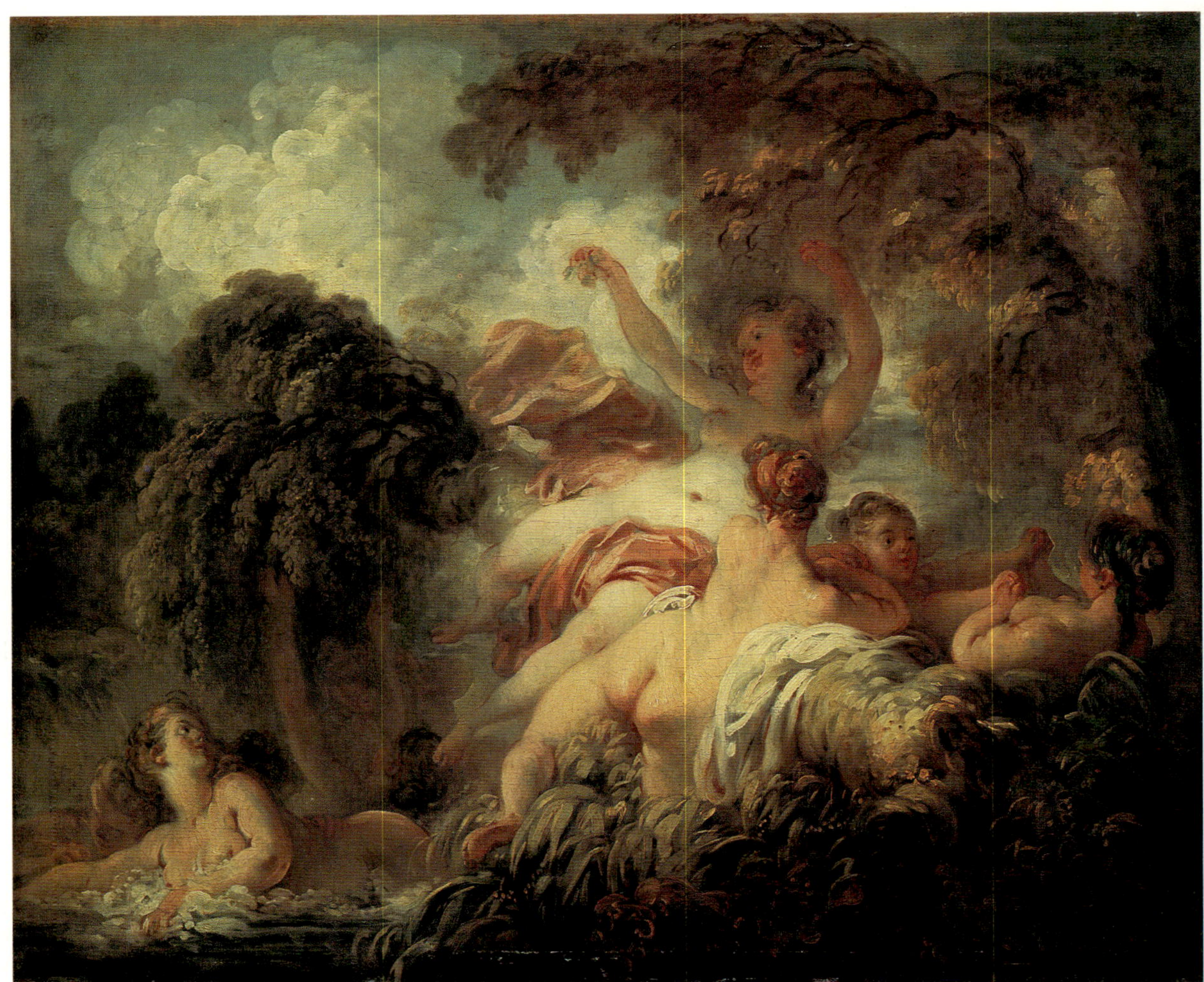

Plate 2 Jean-Honoré Fragonard, *The Bathers,* 1767. Paris, Musée du Louvre. © Réunion des Musées Nationaux.

Plate 3 Detail of *The Bathers.*

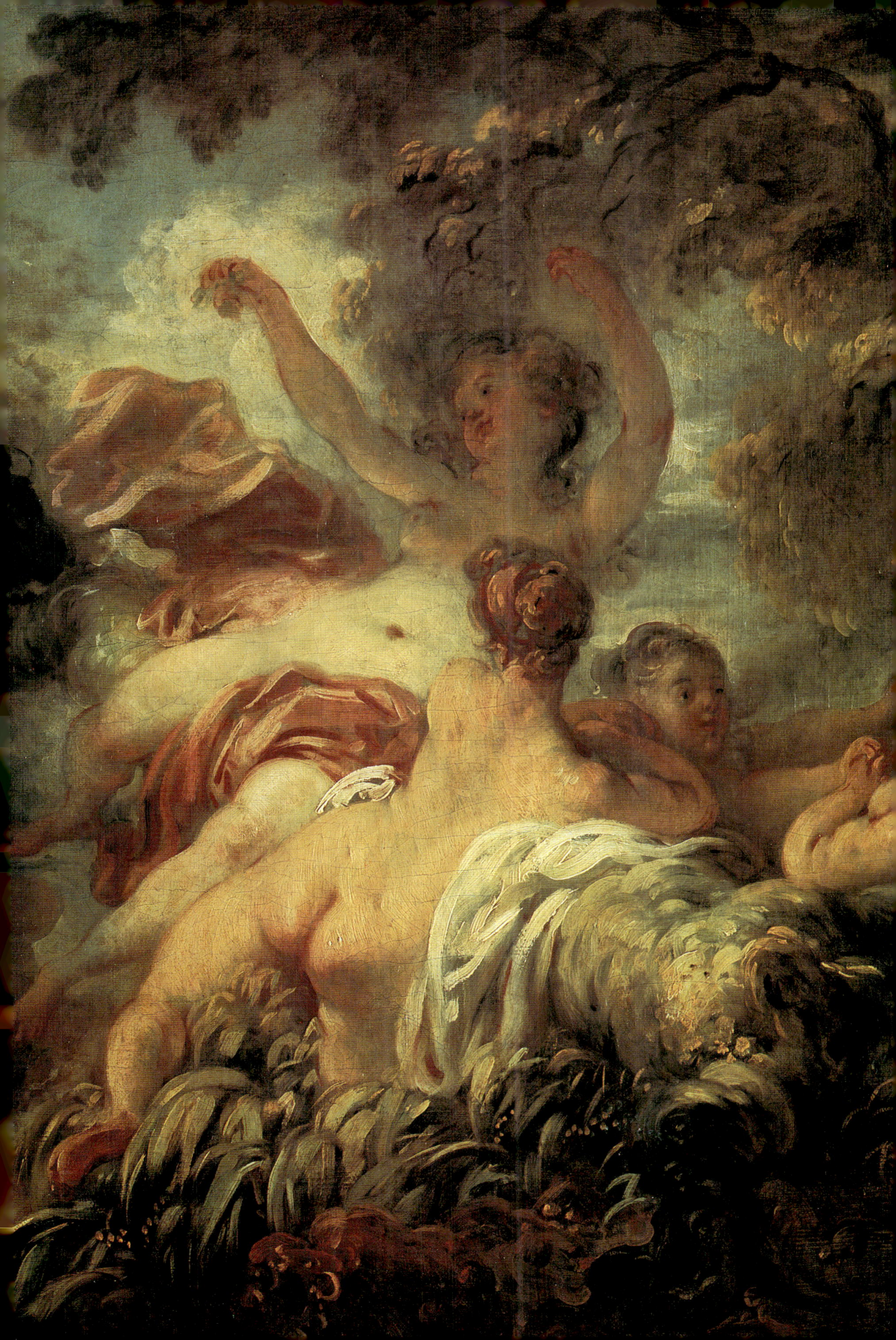

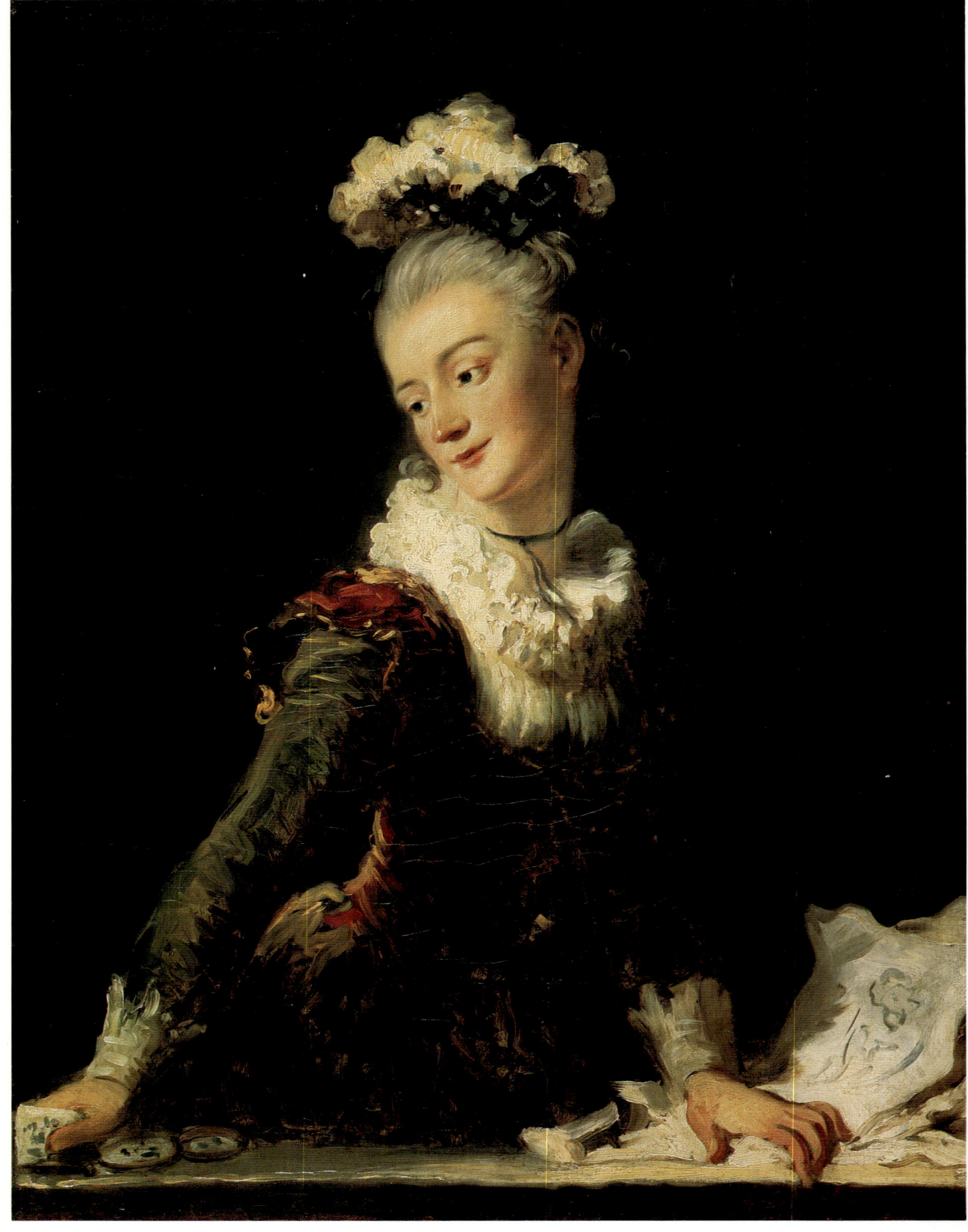

Plate 4 Jean-Honoré Fragonard, *La Guimard,* 1769. Paris, Musée du Louvre.

Plate 5 Detail of *La Guimard.*

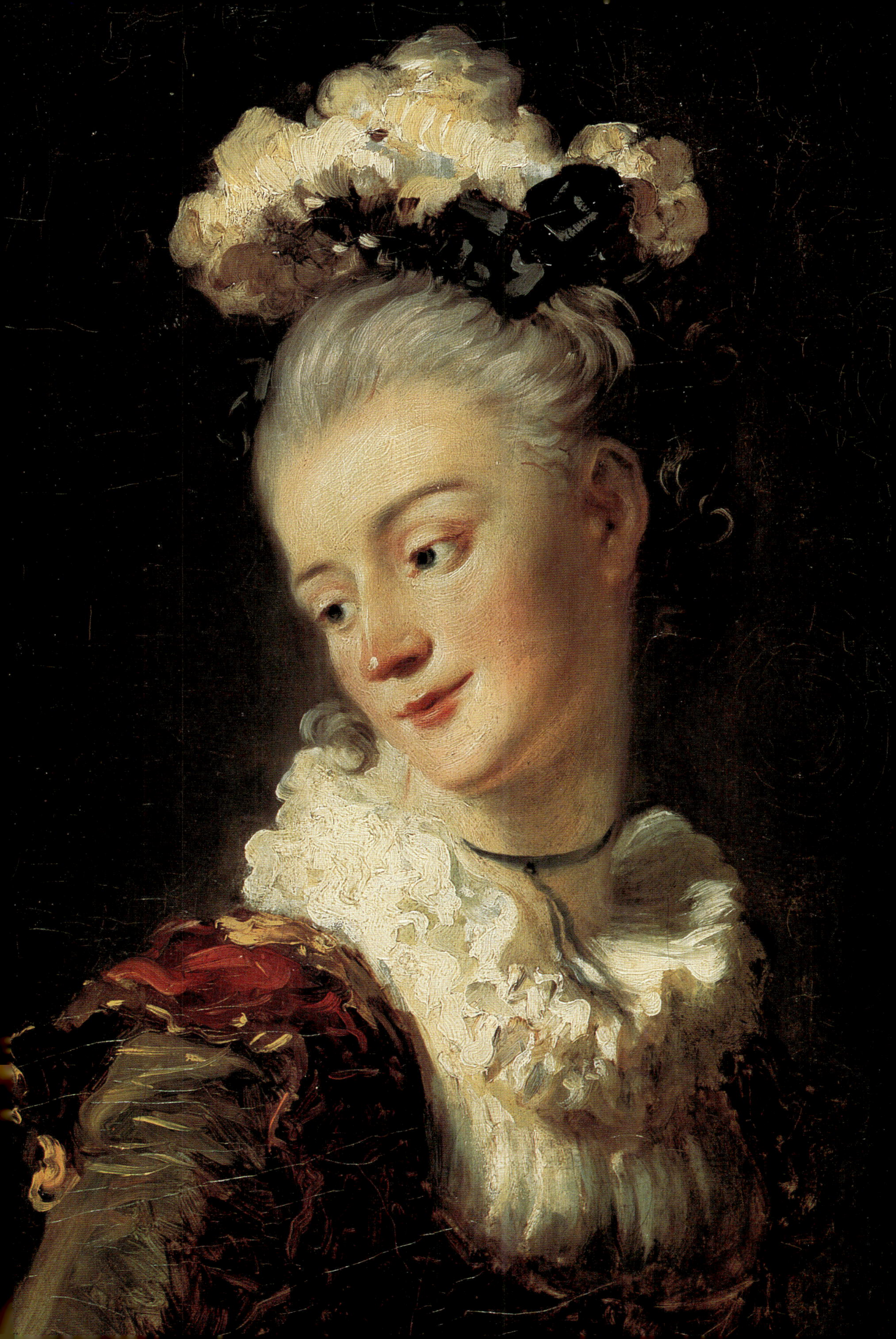

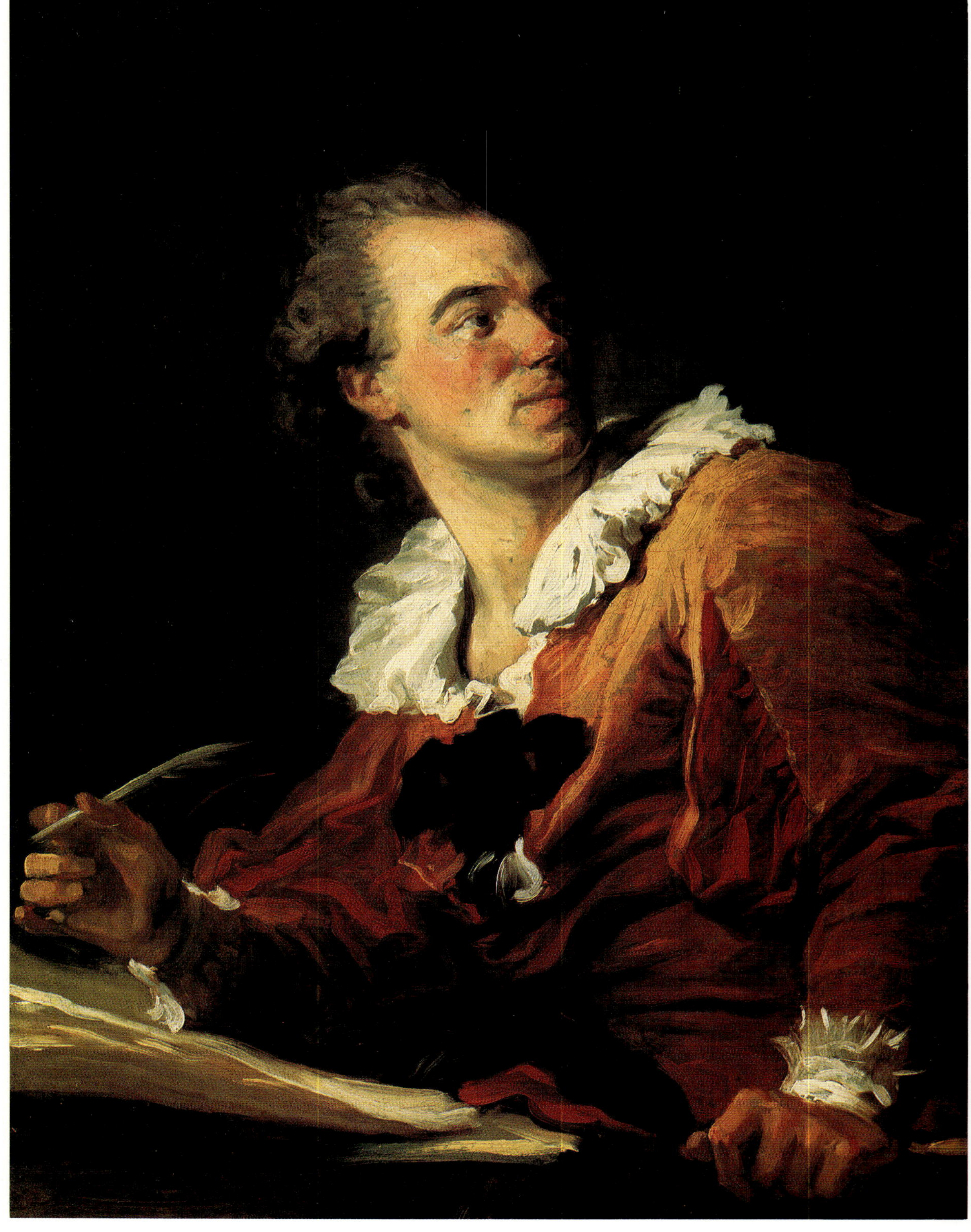

Plate 6 Jean-Honoré Fragonard, *Inspiration,* c. 1769. Paris, Musée du Louvre.

Plate 7 Detail of *Inspiration.*

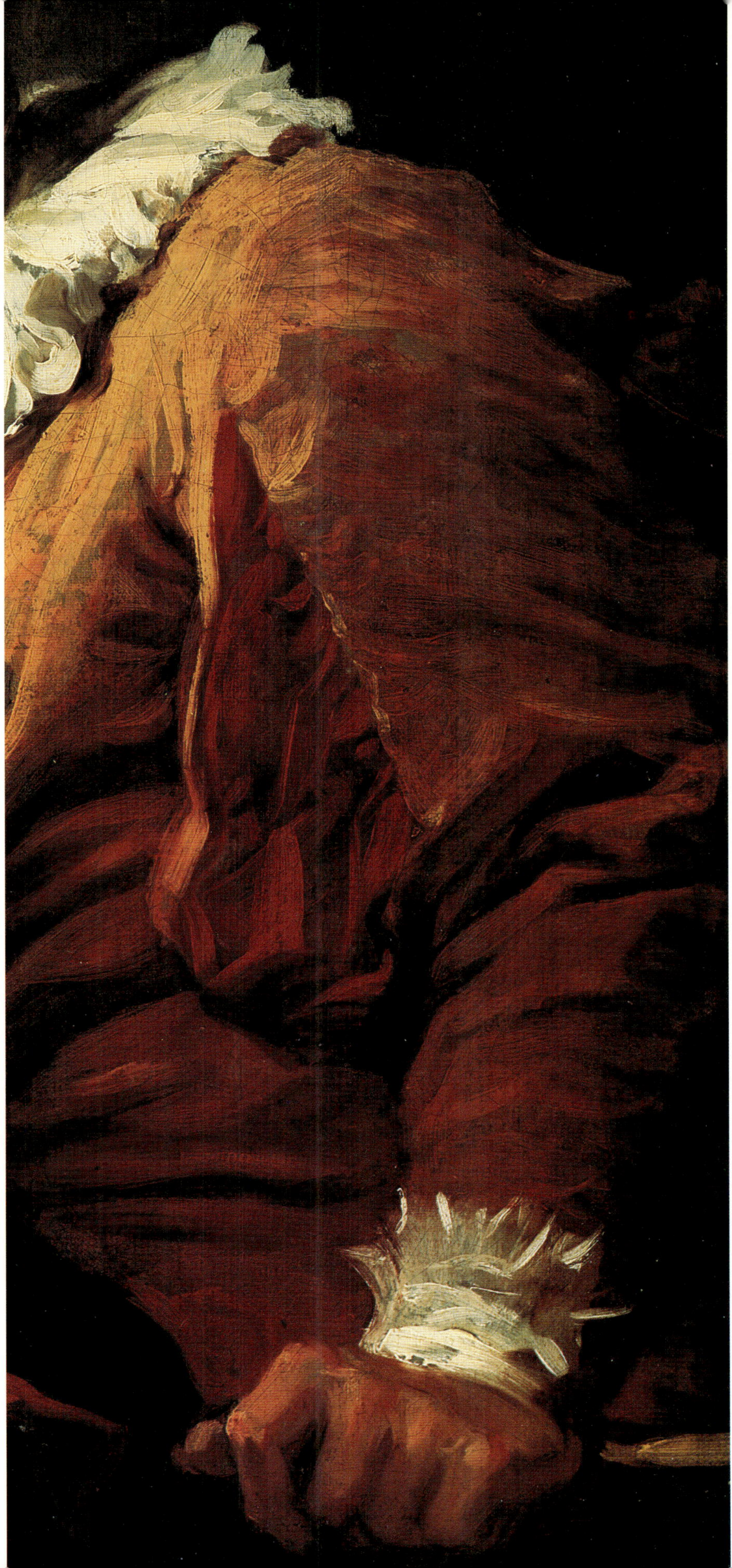

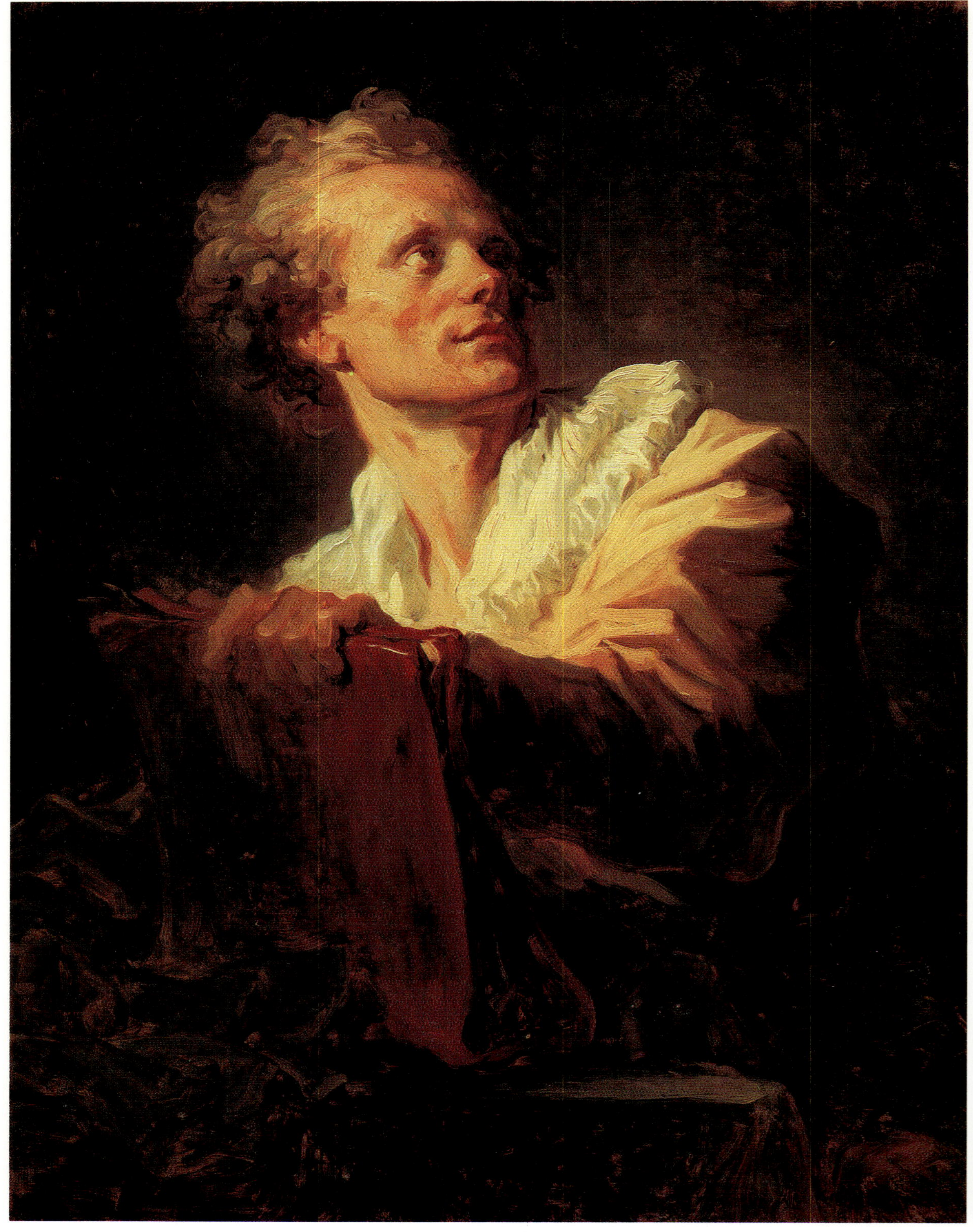

Plate 8 Jean-Honoré Fragonard, *The Young Artist,* c. 1770. Paris, Musée du Louvre.

artist who imagines and executes it. When painters choose colors, gestures, lines, touches, they use instituted signs. For the eighteenth-century academician the process of inventing the work of art was a process of choice, or more precisely of choosing things already chosen.[106] For example, painters picked from a stock of conventionalized gestures those that conveyed the ideas they wanted to express; they selected the paint handling suitable for representing the appropriate state of mind. In short, they conjured the idea of what was to be signified and imagined recognizable signifiers. These signifiers were not to be mistaken for nature; they were part of the language of art.

The confusion over the status of painting as a natural or artificial sign brings us back to the problem of touch. The brushmark had a twofold significance in the eighteenth century. Touches were marks of color denoting the appearance of bodies, and they were painted accents recreating how that appearance was conditioned by light, movement, and the like. Unlike his predecessor Du Bos, Watelet believed that in depicting an object the touch was more a sign than a precise imitation; and he outlined the two functions of that sign: touches were at once imitative signs *(signe imitatif)* drawn from nature and signs that communicated *(signe communicatif)* how the artist saw and felt in making the imitation.[107] As a *signe imitatif,* certain aspects of the touch would vary as the painter stressed or pronounced certain qualities of the object he was representing. The idea that the touch was to say something about the object it denoted had been articulated in painting theory and demonstrated in academic practice vis-à-vis the notion of *convenance.*[108] This conscious control and adjustment to the situation at hand implies that touch is an artificial sign. Although not naive about the imitative function of touch, Watelet also posited it as a natural sign, a *signe communicatif* referring to the artist's state of mind.

Watelet's discussion of *touche,* like Cochin's analysis of *faire,* typifies the divided thinking of many eighteenth-century writers. Two discourses existed side by side. The academic discourse of art theory, still tied to a rhetorical, aristocratic model, considered the artist a courtier, an actor, or a poseur; it accepted artifice and the audience agreed to be deluded by it. Alongside, and even within, that discourse, another evolved; it insisted on glorifying the natural sign. In this discourse of spontaneous expression, the artist was an enthused genius and his art was a genuine index of his emotional state; artifice was degraded and the viewer saw what was signified directly. With this second model, however, the audience could be profoundly deceived, because viewers could assume natural connections between touches (signifiers) and emotional states (signified). Although a part of the audience realized the impossibility of an unmediated representation, transparency maintained its status as the ideal state of painting.[109]

ON THE INTERPRETATION OF BRUSHWORK

There is no work of art that can be totally aligned with either the aristocratic or the genius model. As characteristics of both were mixed to a greater or lesser degree in every text about art, so every work of art lent itself to more than one reading. Fragonard formed himself in the overlap between these two models; and although his work can be interpreted according to one or the other paradigm, much of it reveals the paradoxes and contradictions of both, paradoxes and contradictions inseparable from the problems of mimesis and expression in the eighteenth century. Nothing could be either natural or artifical when the theory of representation posited the existence of natural, motivated signs and also insisted on their institutional basis.

As we explore Fragonard's easel paintings, brushwork will assume an increased importance appropriate to the fascination with making, executing, and touching that characterized much writing about art in the eighteenth century. Brushwork will be conceived as one part of the total signifying system that is the painting, and our discussion of it will be integrated into our discussion of the whole work of art. Paint handling can only be analyzed according to context since, as we have seen, brushmarks have a wide range of meanings, many of them not precisely defined. In general, the stresses will be on the three most insistent characteristics of brushwork: its association with the elite viewer, its erotic content, and its equivocal status as both calculation of art and index of enthusiasm. The following assumptions about brushwork will shape our discussion:

1. Because brushwork carries conventionally established meaning, artists can choose handlings that signify the concepts they want to express. Brushwork can say something about both the object represented and the artist who made the representation.

2. When conceived as an expressive sign, brushwork produces an effect that points to the artist and is relatively independent of the subject represented. The separation of brushwork (in its expressive function but not in its imitative one) from subject matter evolved away from a conception of execution as the mechanical part of painting to a glorification of *le faire* as an index of the artist's state of mind.

3. The same kind of brushwork can take on different meanings in different contexts. The free handling of an erotic painting, for example, may

have some connotations related to subject that are not carried by the large, visible brushmarks of a fantasy portrait.

4. Brushwork means different things to different audiences. Although a free execution could be read in one way by an *amateur* (as a signifier of genius), it could be interpreted in quite another by an advocate of strict academic classicism (as a signifier of laziness).

5. Try as we may, as twentieth-century viewers we can never see eighteenth-century paintings as those paintings were seen by their contemporary audience. A whole history of looking and interpreting stands between us and rococo painting, a history whose layers cannot be entirely stripped away to reveal the original, pristine meaning(s) of brushwork. We cannot easily slough off our own habits of viewing, no matter how self-conscious we become. The interpretation of brushwork, like any interpretation, is necessarily a mediated one.

READING FRAGONARD'S *Bathers*

Returning to the Louvre *Bathers* (figure 24) we can now more fully analyze the dynamic that operated between the painting surface and those who beheld it. To analyze that dynamic, particularly its erotic components, I will work through the ideal audience implied by the painting, an audience of connoisseurs and cognoscenti—but also an audience of male viewers.[110]

The variety and contrast of the parts within the unified whole insured for *The Bathers* two kinds of reading. In his first contact with the painting, the beholder ideally concentrates on the entire composition, attending to how bathers and surroundings are successfully integrated. The general effect is enhanced by the overall freedom of touch that characterizes the paint surface. This first stage of considering the painting corresponds with that described by J.-L. de Cahusac in his analysis of enthusiasm. Arrested and absorbed by the work, the beholder focuses on the whole. The more sensuous looking, however, is the second looking, in which the viewer diverts his attention to the parts, concentrating on their variety and contrast. It is this looking that fragments the surface, detains the viewer, and changes from beholding to beholding.

Above all other compositional elements, the brushmarks help the viewer focus on the individual parts, for these brushmarks articulate, associate, distinguish, and differentiate the separate forms. The viewer, encouraged by different but equally sensuous paint handlings, enjoys the bodies of Fragonard's nymphs one by one; his violating eye lingers on a different attribute of each bather. What seduces the beholder most effectively are the emphatic touches collected around the most alluring parts of the female body. The nymph at the left side of the composition is posed for erotic display; surely it is not natural buoyancy that supports her elegant *contrapposto!* The position of her body, breasts and belly exposed, in itself provokes, but the viewer is invited to further enjoyment by the adroit positioning of the paint touches. A collection of thickly applied, eye-catching strokes plays over the water's surface to caress the figure's entire frontal torso; they are particularly dense and emphatic around her floating breasts. To complete the invitation, Fragonard has represented the bather as being touched, for the hands of her companion rest on her arm and hip.

Having experienced one bather's delights, the viewer can move on to her companion reclining in a pose popularized by Boucher's nymphs and odalisques. Seen from behind, this figure offers her buttocks and parted thighs for the viewer's delectation. The proposition is made more explicit by the foliage executed in long strokes of paint. These touches run along the length of her curvilinear right profile and, more importantly, fill the area between her parted legs. The beholder takes his pleasure in this lush foliage and moves on to the third nymph, whom he sees in a frontal view. Again her legs are parted, but here the pubic area is modestly covered with a drapery that winds between her legs to flutter behind. This drapery is like the covert symbol because it reveals while pretending to hide; at the same time that it covers her sex, it draws attention to that location, allowing the viewer to imagine what lies beneath. And the cloth, executed in a beautiful and free paint handling, tempts the viewer to linger there and to slide with it along the length of her extended limbs.

Although the viewer can enjoy the paint handling specifically as it draws attention to different parts of the female body (to what is represented), he can also enjoy it as an independent erotic element apart from what is represented. For example, the paint handling exemplifies the visual pleasure of contrast throughout. The thickness of the touch varies as areas of heavily applied, almost sculpted strokes (for example, the reeds in the foreground) are set in contrast to very thinly brushed ones (for example, the figure to the far left of the canvas). The shape of the marks changes as well and isolates one built-up area from the next: long, fluid strokes represent the reeds; shorter, choppier ones the water's surface. Applied on top of these are dots of color that add both sparkle and excitement over the entire pictorial area and establish a surface of small, quick, seemingly haphazard touches. Other elements of contrast attributable to the brush include wet, glistening areas set against more dryly brushed ones, and very abbreviated forms juxtaposed to those more clearly articulated.

The brushwork of *The Bathers* signaled the *style sensuel* or the *style pittoresque.*[111] The *négligence* necessary to the erotic enjoyment of surface is exaggerated throughout *The Bathers,* where some forms are scarcely defined (the face of the bather at the far left corner), others are abbreviated to touches of color (the left foot of the bather whose back is to us), and still others are nearly indistinguishable from the surrounding ground (the arms of the background bather reaching up toward the bush). Although its paint handling would probably have been too unrestrained for Caylus' taste, *The Bathers* demonstrates a strategy similar to that of *légèreté.* The surface seems spontaneously, almost haphazardly, executed, but the calculated composition and light effects, as well as the general orchestration of "random" touches, belie that appearance. There is much, then, to be enjoyed in Fragonard's *négligence,* not the least of which is the tension between the paint surface and the underlying structure.

Upon first looking, however, *The Bathers* seems closed to the viewer. The attention of all the major characters is absorbed by their own activities. The nymph with upraised arms exchanges glances with her sister swimming below, and the bather with her back to the audience concentrates on the scene behind. In the right corner two nymphs attend to one another. The other figures, most of which are barely visible, look in various directions, but none makes contact with the viewer. Held apart from the scene, the viewer is a voyeur who intrudes, an unpunished Acteon spying on the chaste nymphs of Diana.[112] Yet even if the composition makes no room for him, the paint handling involves the viewer as a participant in the work, for it is only through his beholding that forms are completed and realized. At the points where the touches least articulate the form, the viewer must complete what the artist has left merely suggested, adding his own vicarious touches. Thus he imagines stroking the bathers in two ways, as the artist who lays the pigment on the canvas and as the lover projected into the fictive world of the painting. These correspond respectively to the sensuous pleasure derived from touches as acts of the artist and to the erotic enjoyment of touch in its relation to the object represented.

It is the artist's paint handling that allows the viewer to enter a composition from which he is excluded, inviting him to touch both canvas and bather. It is also the artist's paint handling that suggests to him an appropriate emotional state, for when Fragonard made this work in 1767 many already considered brushwork to be an index of the artist's enthusiasm, or ardor. That enthusiasm, as we have seen, was equated with sexual desire; the fever pitch in which the artist created was a lover's abandonment. When transmitted in the touch, this dual aspect of enthusiasm could also enflame the viewer, who focused his energy on two objects of desire: the art work itself and the objects represented in the artwork. He thus vicariously experienced the artist's urge to create as both inspiration and sexual arousal.

Although one could argue that the erotic meaning of *The Bathers* is signaled by the motif of the female nude in and of itself, it is important to remember that not every representation of the unclothed woman emphasizes a sexual or titillating meaning. It is the handling of the nude that cues the viewer, and in *The Bathers* there are sufficient signals even apart from brushwork (display poses, for example) to suggest an erotic reading. Once these clues are perceived, the viewer can consider brushwork part of the total system and can isolate, from among the various meanings that brushwork can carry, those that best coordinate with other aspects of the painting. With this in mind we can move from a work where the artist's enthusiasm carried in his touch is best read in terms of sexual metaphor to a group of portraits in which touch is more forcefully presented as an index of the painter's genius.

Representing Genius

Fragonard's *Portraits de Fantaisie*

5

The Fiction of Enthusiasm

From *amateur* to *philosophe,* eighteenth-century writers were fascinated by the enthused state. Painters were not immune to its appeal, and geniuses gripped by enthusiasm became familiar figures to the visual arts. They could be found in the works of François Boucher (*The Young Draughtsman,* 1739; Private Collection), Gabriel de Saint-Aubin (c. 1778; *The Dream or Voltaire Composing La Pucelle,* Paris: Musée du Louvre), Jean-Bernard Restout (*Portrait of Lebrun-Pindare,* 1780; Dijon: Musée des Beaux-Arts), and Elisabeth Vigée-Lebrun (*Mme de Staël as Corrine,* c. 1808; Geneva: Musée d'art et d'histoire). The *amateur* La Live de Jully represented himself as the inspired writer in an engraving of 1760. Within Fragonard's *oeuvre* the enthused artist appears frequently, in drawings such as his undated *Ariosto Inspired by Love and Folly* (Besançon: Musée des Beaux-Arts) and in the following paintings: *A Young Woman Inspired by Cupid,* (now lost but engraved in 1783 by Halbou as *The Favorable Inspiration*), *St. Jerome Reading* (c. 1765; Hamburg: Kunsthalle; figure 32), *Portrait of Diderot* (c. 1769; Paris: Musée du Louvre, figure 37), *Inspiration* (c. 1768; Paris: Musée du Louvre; figure 30), and *The Young Artist* (c. 1770; Paris: Musée du Louvre, figure 31).

Those of Fragonard's paintings that thematize enthusiasm occasion provocative analyses of brushwork, because the artist could exploit touch as both an imitative and expressive sign. Consider, for example, Fragonard's *Inspiration* (figure 30), a painting that belongs to a group of works known as his *portraits de fantaisie.*[1] The figure portrayed is familiar within

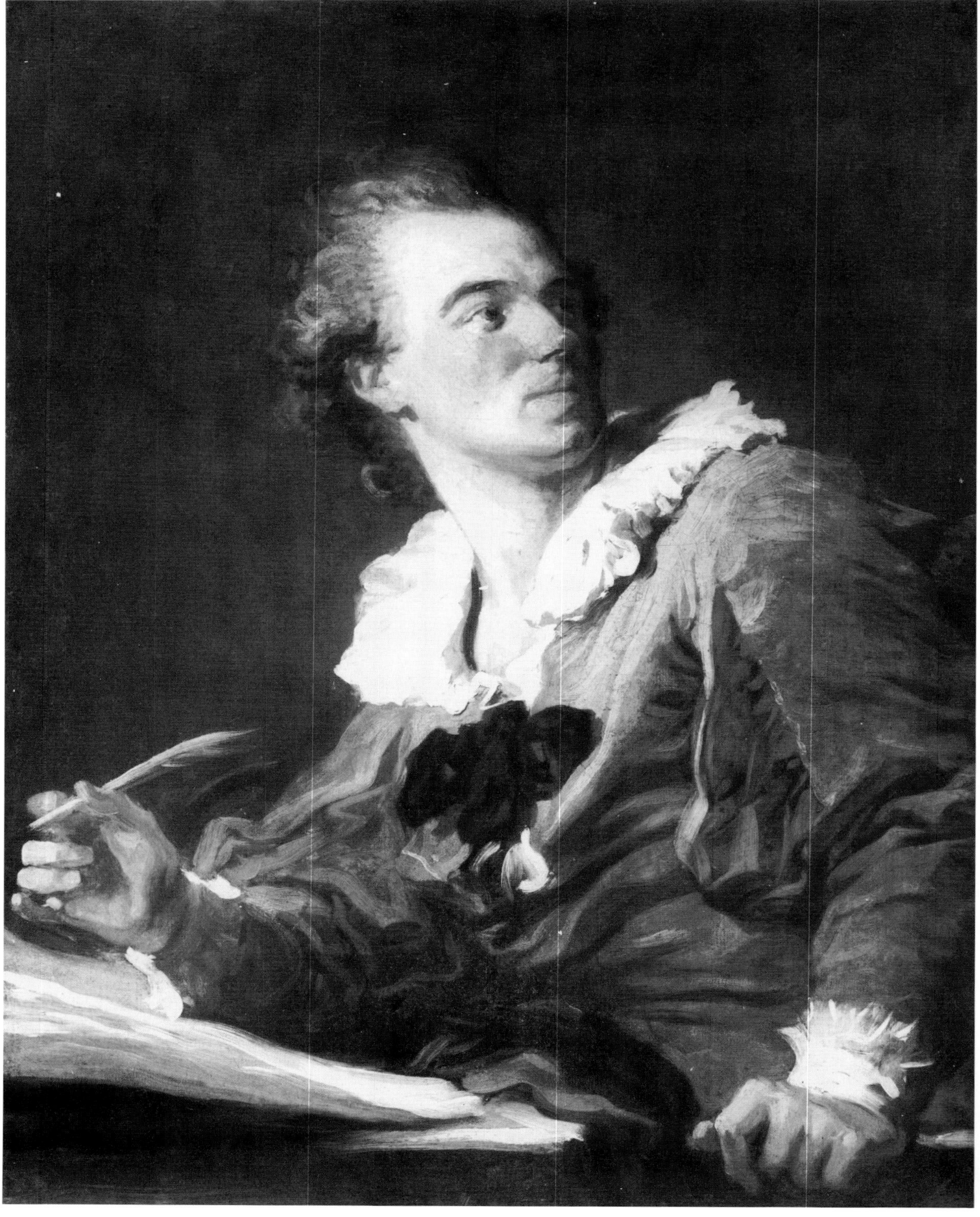

Figure 30 Jean-Honoré Fragonard, *Inspiration,* c. 1769. Paris, Musée du Louvre. Cliché des Musées Nationaux, Paris.

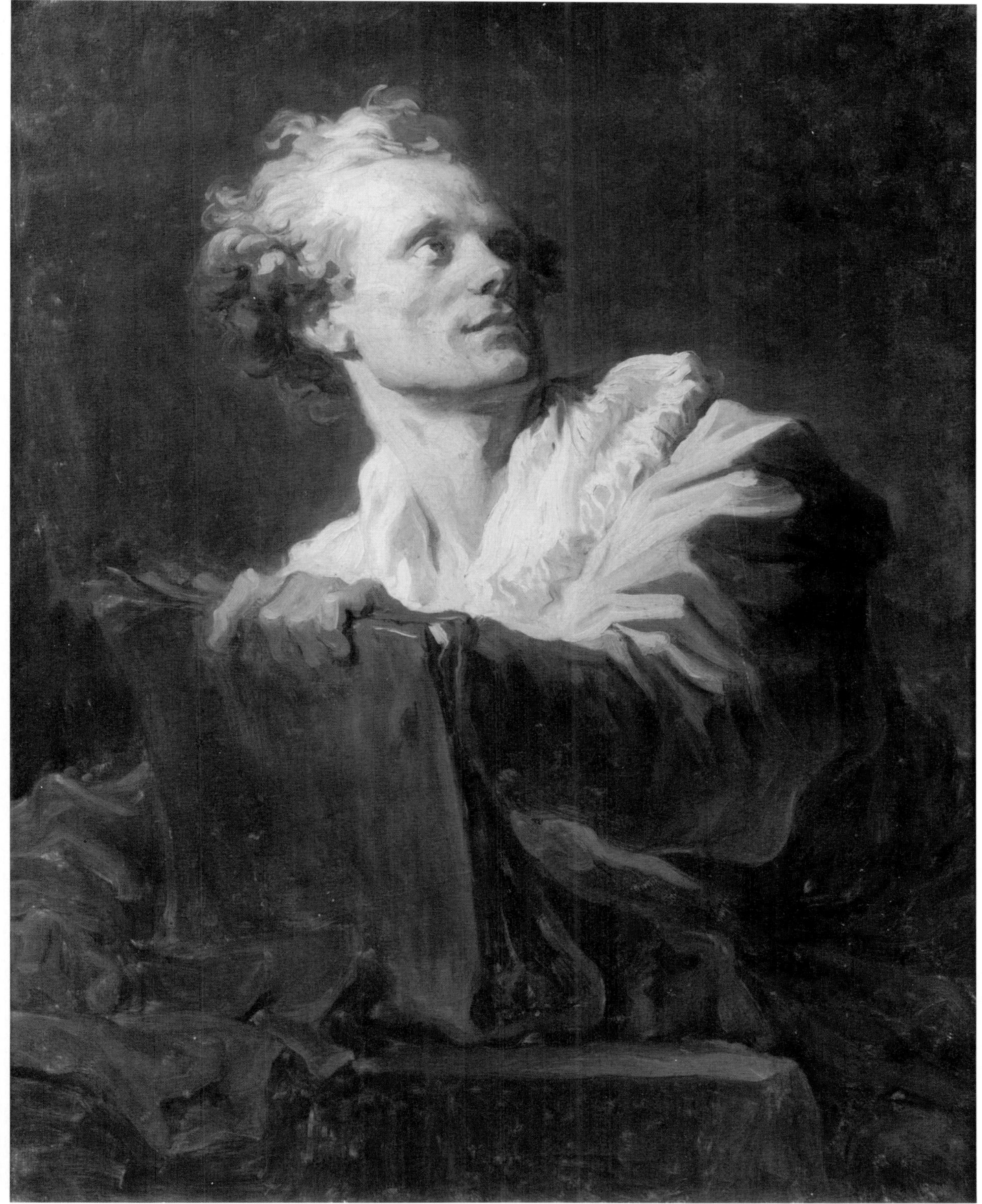

Figure 31 Jean-Honoré Fragonard, *The Young Artist,* c. 1770. Paris, Musée du Louvre, Bestuigui Collection. Cliché des Musées Nationaux, Paris.

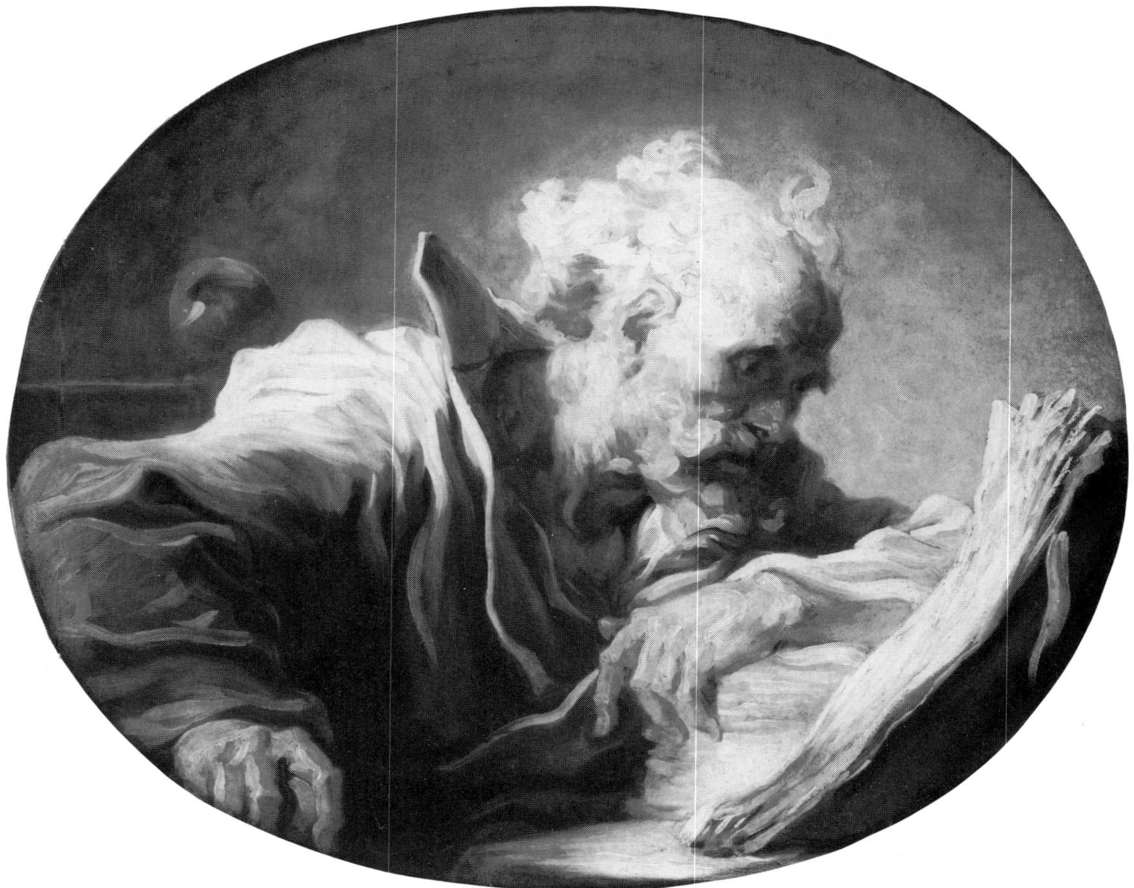

Figure 32 Jean-Honoré Fragonard, *St. Jerome Reading,* c. 1765. Hamburger Kunsthalle.

the context of our representational heritage. He mimics (representations of) the inspired gospel writer turning from his work to face a divine messenger. Although the angel of God has been banished from this secular representation, the moment of enthusiasm evidently is upon the writer. He has lifted his pen from the page and turned from his work to lose himself in a new imagining. An intense energy agitates his hair and costume, his face is strongly illuminated, his clothing blazes with red, orange, and yellow. These are the visual equivalents of a metaphoric fire, the internal force of enthusiasm activated within him. But enthusiasm extends beyond the subject here, for as surely as the painting depicts a writer who is inspired, it expresses the inspiration of the painter who depicted him. Or does it? Upon further consideration, the alliance of subject and technique with enthusiasm dissolves. When read together, the two deny the possibility of inspiration by suggesting that it is rationally constructed, manufactured through signifying gestures. Thus, if the painting seemed at first an attempt to correspond closely to the ideal of transparent signification, upon analysis it emerges as a fiction executed by a consummate actor who could make the appropriate signs.

In reference to subject matter, the most recognizable signifier of enthusiasm in Fragonard's *Inspiration* is the conventional pose that characterizes the young writer: head turned to look over his shoulder, pen poised in midair. This posture had been part of the visual language since the Middle Ages, when platonic madness had been converted to Christian inspiration, when God spoke to his elect through supernatural messengers. Representations of saints visited by angelic intermediaries range from St. John of the ninth-century Ebbo gospels to Caravaggio's *St. Matthew* (1602; Rome: Contarelli Chapel, S. Luigi dei Francesi), a work Fragonard copied in Rome. Sometimes in these depictions the angel was absent and the turning writer was illuminated by an intense light signifying the inspiring force of the divine, as in Valentin's *St. Jerome* of 1620 (Camerino: Sta. Maria in Via). In depictions of saints, enthusiasm was conceived as Christian fervor, but in secularized representations of artists or writers, enthusiasm was cast in terms of self-contemplation. Thus Fragonard's use of the traditional posture and intense lighting does not imply a literal belief in divine intervention but the necessity of envisioning a conventional signifier of inspiration understandable to his audience. Maintaining the traditional pose attests to the power of visual conventions both to endure and to change. These conventions are like words, like the terms *enthusiasm* and *inspiration,* whose signified meanings varied from epoch to epoch.[2]

In representing the concept of enthusiasm, Fragonard has once again saturated his painting with signifiers, delaying his viewers at that level. Some of these signifiers can be isolated by considering *Inspiration* in conjunction with two additional works by Fragonard that represent the same concept: *The Young Artist* (c. 1770; Paris: Musée du Louvre; figure 31) and *St. Jerome Reading* (c. 1765; Hamburg: Kunsthalle; figure 32). Although in the latter work the painter did not use the conventional pose that now seems so readable, his contemporaries described it as St. Jerome "reading, full of enthusiasm."[3] All three paintings share a depiction of agitated hair and drapery with free and vigorous brushwork. Referring to established signifiers of enthusiasm, this complex of signs comments on both the artist depicted and the depicting artist.

The problem of representing enthusiasm was identical to that of representing any mental or emotional state: to externalize what is experienced internally. As we have seen, the physical movements caused by the passions (gestures and facial expressions) were considered natural signs that became instituted when acknowledged by society. During the seventeenth century Charles Le Brun rigidly codified the depiction of those signs in a language of frozen gesture. In the process of systemization, Le Brun chose from already instituted signs those signifiers of particular emotions that he preferred over others.[4] The eighteenth-century painters often deviated from Le Brun's system because it drained the passions of life by rendering them static. Rather, they depicted the signs as if in the process of being made, sometimes using the postures sanctioned by Le Brun, sometimes referring to paradigmatic representations by other artists. But whether or not artists used Le Brun's system, they were called upon to choose and imagine the signifiers of an emotional state they wished to portray.

In Fragonard's *Inspiration,* as in his *St. Jerome* and *The Young Artist,* the agitated drapery and streaming hair refer the viewer only to other representations of enthusiasm, for nowhere in nature did anyone see an artist working in a whirlwind of drapery and tresses. Energy itself had to be externalized to signify the power of enthusiasm, an emotion engaged by the invisible mental activity of imagination and judgment. Fragonard represented the concept of pure mental energy in depicting his enthusiastic subjects as having transfixed eyes. This expression was conventional; it assured the viewer that the figure was unconcerned with immediate physical realities.[5] The transfixed eyes signaled attention to an interior state; the moving drapery and hair signified the nature of that state. With no natural force or physical movement to cause the turmoil, the mind's activity is thereby registered.

Despite the animated hair and drapery, Fragonard's enthused writer is depicted in a moment of stasis, as if totally arrested and immobilized by the mental picture that absorbs him. This motionlessness that renders the figure of *Inspiration* suspended in contemplation was already encoded in the conventional pose. With the head turned strongly away from the body, the attitude creates a self-canceling double directionality further emphasized by the compositional dynamics. The major axis of *Inspiration* directs the viewer's attention from the figure's hand falling at his side, through the center of his face, to the licks of his curling hair. This view across the canvas from lower right to upper left is reinforced by the unnaturally long and straight line of the writer's neck and by the left sleeve inset, whose triangular form acts as an arrow to control the beholder's looking. Although the viewer's eye is encouraged to move along this path, it is simultaneously urged to look from lower left to upper right, from the writer's poised hand to his lighted shoulder. The pen whose feather points across the canvas and the stretched-out brushmarks of the costume emphasize this secondary movement. The sense of motion and agitation is thus attached to a figure immobilized within a structured composition. This formal language fulfills the accepted description of the enthused state, as the writer is indeed arrested in the midst of his mental turmoil. The same is true for *The Young Artist,* where the turning of the head away from the body is even more emphatic. The immobilized turn is staged in the upper zone of the composition. Again the line of the neck stresses a diagonal oriented from lower left to upper right, and the countering line runs from lowered right shoulder to raised left one.

The motion implied most emphatically, however, is that of the brush. To depict a writer in the midst of creative thought, the signifiers of enthusiasm—that energy most proper for an inspired writer—could be implanted in the touch itself. In the *Inspiration* the brushwork that defines the drapery of the writer also recalls the conventional mode of depicting fire, operating along with the color to establish the well-known metaphor. The touches represent fiery motion as it had been instituted in painting since the sixteenth century when described by Lomazzo. Fire was depicted by strokes continually striving upwards and drawn together in points. Although ascending in a uniform movement, the motion was often interrupted by agitation.[6] The brushmarks that render the garments of Fragonard's young writer rise in the composition from lower left to upper right. Their general ascending path is punctuated by energetic marks particularly noticeable in the zigzag strokes defining the red slashes of the sleeves. Drawn to itself, the agitated brushwork coalesces in points at the end of the slashes and at the peaks of drapery on the left shoulder. The edges of collar and cuff rise in acute, irregular triangulations and repeat the flickering movement of flames, as described by Lomazzo.[7] As the motion rises to a climax, the color intensifies from red to a glowing yellow.

Throughout the composition the combination of red and yellow, the warm colors, is distinctly pronounced and nearly overstated. Most apparent in the costume, the red-yellow is repeated in the facial tones and in the hands. There is an arbitrary placing of yellow strokes next to red ones at the bottom center of the composition, where the color has only a loose association with the depiction of objects (the yellow might denote the lighted top of the desk, the red the underside of the drapery).

The enthusiastic writer is rendered in fiery touches and fiery colors; he is figuratively on fire. And so is Fragonard. If touch could signify the artist's emotional state in making the work, then here Fragonard, the apparent artist, is represented as a painter who can invent and execute spontaneously, a painter overcome with the desire to create. His touches signal the spontaneously invented sketch; they are facile, suggestive, and abbreviated. *Inspiration* appears to have been quickly brushed with unblended strokes, seemingly unplanned, placed one next to the other. Such marks do not fully spell out forms. For example, the short, rapid touches that define the cuffs make no pretense of imitating the intricacies of fabric. The pen is rendered with a quick stroke for the shaft, a few touches for the feathers, and a spot of black for the point. Shadows are handled similarly with little regard for blending the half-tones, and distinct irregular brown strokes articulate the darkened area beneath the ruff. Complexly agitated lines, converging at the center of the composition, underscore facility and record a rapid motion of the hand.

A similar strategy is evident in *The Young Artist* where the colors are also hot and glowing. The red portfolio dominates the center of the composition, and the color again moves up to brilliant yellow and white in the highest light. The brushmarks, however, do not obviously represent the motion of fire. The chevron-shaped strokes on the young artist's sleeve do coalesce to form low broad triangles, but the brushwork lacks the emphatic ascending zigzag movement and the flickering points so evident in *Inspiration.* In other ways, however, the representation of enthusiasm is heightened, even exaggerated. When compared to *Inspiration* where the brushwork is loose and suggestive, *The Young Artist* is much more freely touched—so freely touched, in fact, that it is difficult in the lower zone to separate the forms from the undifferentiated mass of brushwork. There touches are most definitely emphasized as touches. The observer can see where individual strokes stop and start, and within those strokes the traces of the bristles are evident. Thick lines of paint indicate where the color accumulated on the edge of the brush. Although the paint stroke nearly loses its imitative role in that mélange of touches, after some concentration on the lower left of the canvas, one can discern a table top, a green cloth resting on the table top, and a hand, clawlike in its abbreviation, resting on the green cloth. The lower right side of the canvas, however, remains indecipherable.

What is one to make of those undifferentiated touches in *The Young Artist,* the most extravagantly painted of all the *portraits de fantaisie?* The argument that Fragonard simply left the painting unfinished (that he never completed the work as he had intended) ignores the signifying role of brushwork. The paint handling in *The Young Artist* is the single most important element that differentiates the work from *Inspiration,* which it closely resembles in other ways. More than any change of attribute or costume, it is the brushwork that characterizes these paintings as different inventions. To be sure, in each case the brushwork signifies enthusiasm, but in each case the handling allows a reading adapted to its specific subject.

We saw *Inspiration* dominated by the metaphor of fire; and although that association is still carried in *The Young Artist,* it is not the primary rhetorical device. In observing the paint surface of *The Young Artist,* one notices not only the very sketchy handling in the lower zone but also the great contrast with the more finished areas in the upper zone. The contrast is not simply one of finish but also of plasticity: the lower areas of the composition are comparatively flat with little three-dimensional illusion, whereas the forms in the upper area, for example the artist's white collar, are strongly modeled. Here, again, *The Young Artist* is substantially different from *Inspiration,* where the level of finish and plasticity generally seems to be all of a piece, even though the face is more clearly defined than the costume.

The contrast of handling in *The Young Artist* parallels the intense chiaroscuro that also divides the composition. It is possible to consider the different levels of finish as a function of light effects: less distinct forms in darkened areas below, more clear ones in the illumination above. But this explanation alone does not account for either the extreme freedom of the brush or the metaphoric use of light that here signifies the artist's mental energy. However, if we read the two zones together, it is evident that the composition rises from a darkened, undifferentiated mass of touches to forms clarified in the light of inspiration. Thus the (fictive) process of making a painting is enacted on the surface of a canvas depicting a young painter. It is enthusiasm that "gives life" to what the artist creates, enthusiasm that allows him to mimic the Supreme Creator in dividing light from dark and bringing form out of chaos.

Self-referentiality in *The Young Artist* can thus be construed on two levels: the subject matter depicts the process by which the painting itself was made, and Fragonard's enthusiasm (that is, the enthusiasm of the apparent artist) is carried in the touch. Both *Inspiration* and *The Young Artist* allow the audience to read the maker's enthused state from the brushwork, allowing the viewer to sense and be moved by the artist's excitement and ardor. Insofar as that excitement has an erotic component, the surface of the painting is an erotic surface for the viewer whose enjoyment is centered on those touches.

Like *Inspiration, The Young Artist* purports to be a depiction of an inspired artist by an inspired artist—of one who creates naturally and spontaneously by one who creates naturally and spontaneously. Our analysis of these works demonstrates how specific elements are coordinated in their reference to instituted signifiers of enthusiasm. But such an analysis also reveals that paradox is at the heart of these paintings. At the same moment that the works seem to be rendered spontaneously, they also seem to be the product of careful forethought, planning, and calculation. The poses, gestures, colors, paint handling, indeed every element—all are orchestrated so that the viewer is led to the conclusion that spontaneous inspiration has depicted spontaneous inspiration. And thus the technique that appeared to reveal the subject, now contradicts it, suggesting that all spontaneity is consciously created. One does not, then, see enthusiasm itself but only the art of manufacturing a fiction about enthusiasm.

The Portrait and the *Portraits de Fantaisie*

The analyses of *Inspiration* and *The Young Artist* demonstrate how these works manipulate both the conventions of art and the expectations of their audience, how they disguise *sprezzatura* as the enthusiasm of genius. Their audience was most likely a collection of *amateurs* and connoisseurs who would have been amused and delighted by observing such interplay. Similar strategies are used throughout that group of paintings with which both *Inspiration* and *The Young Artist* are identified, the *portraits de fantaisie.* These works collectively have been taken as fancy dress portraits of Fragonard's friends and patrons. *Inspiration,* for example, is usually identified as depicting the Abbé de Saint-Non, and *The Young Artist* is associated with a painter called Naigeon because the work may have belonged to his family. Diderot, the dancer La Guimard, the Duc d'Harcourt, and Saint-Non's brother La Brèteche are among the other persons said to be represented on these canvases.[8]

Despite their traditional identification with Fragonard's friends and patrons, the *portraits de fantaisie* can hardly be called face paintings. Not only are they raised above ordinary fare by superb invention and technique, but more significantly, they are marked by a display of creative prowess so insistent that the artist's self-presentation virtually eclipses his depiction of the sitters. Far from being face paintings, the *portraits de fantaisie* seem to deviate from even the fundamental charge of portraiture, that of imitating the appearance and personality of a particular individual. The dazzling brushwork alone makes it evident that the *portraits de fantaisie* stress the artist's fabrication; and the costumed figures with exaggerated poses, gestures, and expressions make no pretense of being exact resemblances. Why, then, have interpreters insisted that these are real portraits, and why do they search after the identity of the sitters? If *The Young Artist* and *Inspiration* are fictions about enthusiasm, could they not also be fictions about portraiture?

We actually have very little evidence for considering these paintings portraits. Fragonard never exhibited the works, and his contemporaries neither commented upon them nor named them as portraits. The sales catalogues that reference one or two of the *portraits de fantaisie* describe them generally as, for example, "a young woman, seen at half-length" or "a young girl seated holding a book."[9] In some cases, however, interpreters connected paintings with sitters because they did not evaluate critically certain kinds of evidence. For example, many conclude that the *Fantasy Figure in Blue* (c. 1769; Paris: Musée du Louvre; figure 33), like *Inspiration,* depicts Fragonard's patron Saint-Non because an inscription on the canvas lining reads, "Portrait of the Abbé de Saint-Non painted by Fragonard in an hour's time."[10] The inscription, however, is a later addition, as is evidenced by another in the same hand added to that *portrait de fantaisie* called *Music* (1769; Paris: Musée du Louvre; figure 34). It identifies the painting as a portrait of M. La Brèteche, brother of Saint-Non, "Portrait of La Brèteche painted by Fragonard in 1769 in an hour's time."[11] Originally, however, the inscription stated ". . . painted by Fragonard in 1780." The date was changed so that it would correspond with that written on the front of the painting (1769). Such tampering suggests that we are not dealing with an authentic inscription but one added at least after 1780, and probably in the nineteenth century. Moreover, we cannot take the "painted in an hour's time" at face value. Painting portraits quickly was a legendary talent. De Piles recorded how Sebastian Bourdon won a wager with a friend, betting that he could paint twelve life-size heads from life in one day.[12] Perhaps these inscriptions were added to increase the sale value of the works, first by associating them with a notable tradition and then by giving a name to the portraits. In the same way that buyers prefer a work by, say, the Master of the Madonnas to one executed by an anonymous painter, they find comfort in knowing they own a portrait of so-and-so, rather than one of "a woman" or "a banker."

Along with these dubious inscriptions, scholars have found confirmation of these identifications in Saint-Non's inventory, which lists pastel copies after some "têtes de fantaisie" by Fragonard. But what did eighteenth-century recorders mean when they wrote the term *tête de fantaisie?* In eighteenth-century usage *tête de fantaisie* and *portrait de fantaisie* both signified an imagined figure not made from a specific model. In the *Encyclopédie* under the entry for *fantaisie,* one reads, "A painter makes a fantasy portrait that is after no model whatsoever," and in his *Salons* Diderot clearly distinguished the *tête de fantaisie* from the *tête réelle.*[13] Perhaps this confusion of terminology has prompted the search for sitters, since twentieth-century commentators have incorrectly assumed that *portraits de fantaisie* (and the equivalent *têtes de fantaisie*) are inventive portraits rather than depictions of imagined figures.[14]

The search for sitters, however, has also been provoked by the consistent references to other portraits or portrait conventions within the *portraits de fantaisie* and by the belief that a real person can be seen behind the painting. The presence of attributes that signal an occupation or rank for each figure has further encouraged the belief that these paintings are portrayals of real and identifiable individuals. These factors have made welcome any documentary evidence (no matter how tenuous) indicating that Fragonard's paintings are portraits. Just the opposite phenomenon occurs, however, when a painting does not look like a portrait (does not follow portrait conventions) but documentary evidence associates it with that genre. For example, we read that Saint-Julien commissioned *The Swing* (1767; London: Wallace Collection) from Fragonard as a depiction of his mistress and asked that he be represented in the grass below, positioned to look up the young girl's skirts.[15] *The Swing,* however, is never investigated as a portrait; commentators have not interested themselves in identifying Saint-Julien's mistress or in discussing the degree of resemblance that marks the portrait of the baron. The absence of portrait conventions deters observers from applying the standard method of comparing work to sitter; *The Swing* simply does not look like a portrait and that takes precedence, it seems, over the documentary evidence.

It is not surprising that *The Young Artist* (figure 31) and *Inspiration* (figure 30) have been considered portraits, for many eighteenth-century painters used the inspired-artist pose in depicting talented contemporaries. Among those works cited at the beginning of this chapter, Saint-Aubin's *Voltaire,* Restout's *Lebrun-Pindare,* and Vigée-Lebrun's *Mme de Staël* are portrayals of real, identifiable persons. Yet other works, for instance, Boucher's *Young Artist* and Fragonard's *Young Woman Inspired by Cupid,* are not. The use of a convention no more guarantees that the work is really a portrait than the appearance of facile touches insures that the painter was enthused. Artists can fabricate marks to signify enthusiasm because they know how enthusiastic marks are believed to look; and they can fabricate a work that signifies a real portrait because they know that genre's conventions and how to simulate an individualized physiognomy.

Securely identifying a sitter is usually a risky business unless there is a clear and specific marker (a famous object, a distinctive scar, or the like) in the painting. At best we can say that the portrait resembles other portraits or literary descriptions, but these are not reliable guides to exact likeness, for every portrait deviates from its model. Nevertheless, in the absence of documentary evidence, the sitter must be named—the painted representation connected with its referent in nature—to prove that a work is, in fact, a portrait. In the eighteenth century the genre was defined by the relation between representation and referent, and that relation turned on the notion of resemblance. The *Dictionnaire des Arts,* for example, explained that in making a portrait the artist imitates a specific sitter and renders faithfully "the characteristic resemblance so that it can be easily recognized as that of the person whose features one has intended to render."[16]

As the principal quality of the portrait, resemblance required a good rapport of the painted features with those of nature and that sitters should be readily recognizable to their familiars.[17] Resemblance, moreover, distinguished the portrait from both the life study (in which the model was regarded as anonymous) and the imagined figure. It also limited those who could evaluate the portrait; relative to the eye (or mind) of the beholder who recognized, resemblance allowed only those who actually knew the sitter to be called as judges. Thus the portrait's essence is imperceptible to most who, over time, view the painting.

Are *Inspiration* and the *Fantasy Figure in Blue* portraits, specifically portraits of the Abbé de Saint-Non, or do they depict imagined figures? No reliable records connect these works to Fragonard's major patron, and no identifying mark (e.g., the representation of a text written by Saint-Non) clearly associates the paintings with that individual. We do not know what Saint-Non looked like, and we can not be sure of what his contemporaries believed he looked like. Moreover, the identified portraits of Saint-Non differ significantly from one another in the particulars of the physiognomy they represent.[18] On the basis of the visual evidence we clearly cannot determine whether these works represent Saint-Non or, for that matter, anyone else.

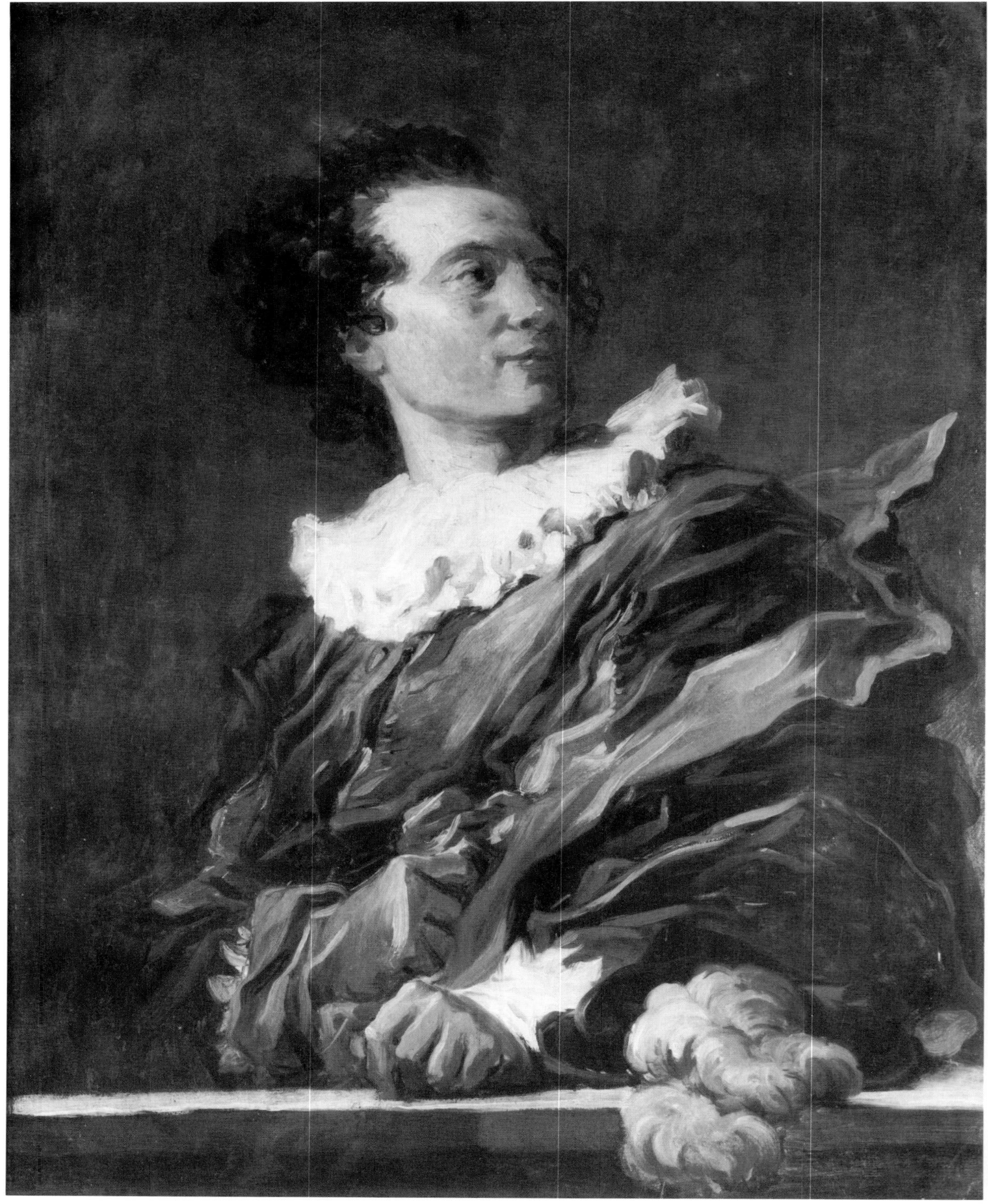

Figure 33 Jean-Honoré Fragonard, *The Fantasy Figure in Blue,* 1769. Paris. Musée du Louvre. Cliché des Musées Nationaux, Paris.

The Play of Convention and Brushwork in the *Portraits de Fantaisie*

Although we cannot securely determine if either *Inspiration* or the *Fantasy Figure in Blue* represents Fragonard's most stalwart patron, we can certainly see that both of these works exploit portrait conventions. We have already noted how the pose of enthusiasm evident in *Inspiration* was used by many eighteenth-century artists in representing their talented contemporaries. We have also seen how in that piece paint handling and convention worked together to establish meaning. The same is true for the other *portrait de fantaisie* believed to represent Saint-Non, *The Fantasy Figure in Blue* (figure 33), which combines two standard portrait types. The first of these, a convention used in five other *portraits de fantaisie,* places the figure at the ledge; it is a *trompe l'oeil* strategy that invites the viewer to perceive the sitter as truly present physically. Indeed, one of the best-known stories of mistaking image for reality that circulated in the eighteenth century referred to such a half-length portrait by Rembrandt, which, when hung in a window, fooled passersby with its illusion.[19] If Rembrandt's portrait provoked a confusion between the thing and its representation, Fragonard's work, as we shall see, confounded the copied and the imagined.

The figure at the ledge, however, is only one of the conventions that marks the *Fantasy Figure in Blue.* His pose was derived from a portrait tradition used to depict men of rank during the seventeenth century: the body presents marked diagonal oppositions, the head is turned in strong contrast, the gaze is directed toward something outside of the painting. In attitude and expression the figure suggests a self-conscious superiority as he looks past the ordinary people who gaze upon him from below. Bernini's *Bust of Louis XIV* (1665, Versailles) is a prime example of this type; and the posture was also widely used in painting, as in Rigaud's *Portrait of Desjardins* (1692; Paris: Musée du Louvre). Among the *portraits de fantaisie,* those that also use some variation of this pose include the *Warrior* (c. 1770; Williamstown, Mass.: Sterling and Francine Clark Art Institute) and the *Portrait of the Duc d'Harcourt,* as well as the *Fantasy Figure in Blue.*

What is most striking about this posture is that its dynamic resembles that of the enthused artist, although the arrangement of head and limbs is such that one pose could not literally be mistaken for the other. The change of attributes also prohibits this confusion; pen and sketchbook have been exchanged for glove and sword, signifiers of nobility, rule, and earthly power. Yet Fragonard's fantasy figure and its cousins do express mental energy in their torqued bodies, fixed stares, and streaming hair, which reminds us that enthusiasm was not a state accessible only to artists. Batteux, for example, described the similarity between the "divinity" that inspired artists to compose and that which animated heroes in battle.[20] Yet I do not think the enthusiasm of heroes or rulers is the main point here.

None of Fragonard's inspired aristocrats has the resonance of the two enthused geniuses, and none has the brilliant synthesis of attributes, pose, light, color, and brushwork that we saw in *Inspiration* and *The Young Artist.* On the other hand, all are conspicuously painted with a brush that signifies the enthusiasm of their portrayer. Seen one or two at a time (as I believe they were meant to be), these *portraits de fantaisie* might be taken as the product of their maker's enthusiasm. Seen together, the repeated reproduction of this apparently enthused brushwork suggests its manufactured quality. Fragonard seems to have chosen portrait types that allow him to exploit the potential of his touch to signify enthusiasm—in other words, types that would coordinate well with the kind of brushmarks he wanted to make. There were, after all, guises for the artist other than that of the inspired genius (the courtier or teacher, for example), and depictions of the aristocrat often stressed elegance or opulence rather than power and energy. I am suggesting that Fragonard observed the principle of *convenance* even in nonacademic paintings, but I am also suggesting that *convenance* is governed by handling. Of course the gender and age of the figures he chose to portray limited the kind of brushwork available to the painter. In depicting youthful and mature males, however, Fragonard obviously preferred postures that, like those of the enthused genius and the powerful aristocrat, allowed for a loose, free, vigorous paint handling.

That this is the case is also suggested in the work called *Music* (figure 34). There the pose is neither that of the enthused genius nor that of the powerful aristocrat, but it does emphasize immediacy, as the figure seems to have just turned from his playing to confront the viewer. The posture, then, would be an appropriate device to showcase Fragonard's spontaneous stroke. The realization that in devising *Music* Fragonard again selected a prefabricated pose strengthens the argument for the priority of brushwork, at least in this *convenance.* The whole painting is a reinvention of Greuze's portrait of La Live de Jully (1759; Washington, D.C.: National Gallery of Art; figure 35). Placed side by side, the two paintings are striking in their resemblance. If Greuze's lively portrait of La Live de Jully engages the viewer directly, Fragonard makes his figure seem even more immediate by increasing the torsion of the pose, intensifying the light effects, and exaggerating the apparently spontaneous brushwork.[21]

Once again, however, both the pose and the paint handling bring us to the obvious question: to what extent is Fragonard's *Music* a portrait, specifically a portrait of M. La Live de Jully? Strictly speaking, not at all. It is rather a portrait of Greuze's portrait of that famous amateur, a painting whose primary reference is to an illusion, a work of art. The artist used a similar strategy in the *portrait de fantaisie* called *La Guimard* (1769; Paris: Musée du Louvre; figure 36). The figure has been taken to represent that famous dancer; the identification, however, has been based on the resemblance of Fragonard's figure to selected aspects of Mlle Guimard presented in literary portraits (some by nineteenth-century authors) and a portrait bust.[22] Just as interpreters searching for the sitter of *Music* overlooked the relation of that work to Greuze's *La Live de Jully,* in pursuing the elusive Guimard they have missed the dependence of Fragonard's figure on the central *pèlerine* of Watteau's *Embarkation to Cythera* (1719; Paris: Musée du Louvre). Although Fragonard has reversed the pose (perhaps he worked from Tardieu's 1734 engraving) and used the ledge motif to truncate the figure, the similarities with Watteau's lady are undeniable: the same extended arm, the same sharp turn of the head, the same downward stare, the same arrangement of hair and hat. This transformation differs from that worked on Greuze's *La Live de Jully,* however, in that here a fictive character taken from a well-known painting is transformed into an individualized physiognomy that may or may not portray a specific woman. If we could substantiate *La Guimard's* status as a portrait, that would not negate the reference to a fiction or an illusion. It would rather blur the distinction between the imagined and the copied, or, put in different terms, it would increase the interplay between them.

This interplay in *La Guimard* is supported by a brushwork that is every bit as contrived and artificial as the exaggeratedly enthusiastic touches of *The Young Artist* and *Inspiration.* The paint handling also has the double quality of referring both to the object imitated and to the painter who made the imitation. If, in comparison to the other *portraits de fantaisie,* areas of *La Guimard* look highly finished, it is because *convenance* demanded that the flesh tones of women be handled differently from those of men. Even the brushwork of La Guimard's garments is subdued when seen beside that used to describe the attire of, say, the Fantasy Figure in Blue; and the dynamic red-green color contrast, generally dulled to brown in the shadows, is only really visible in the highest light at her waist.

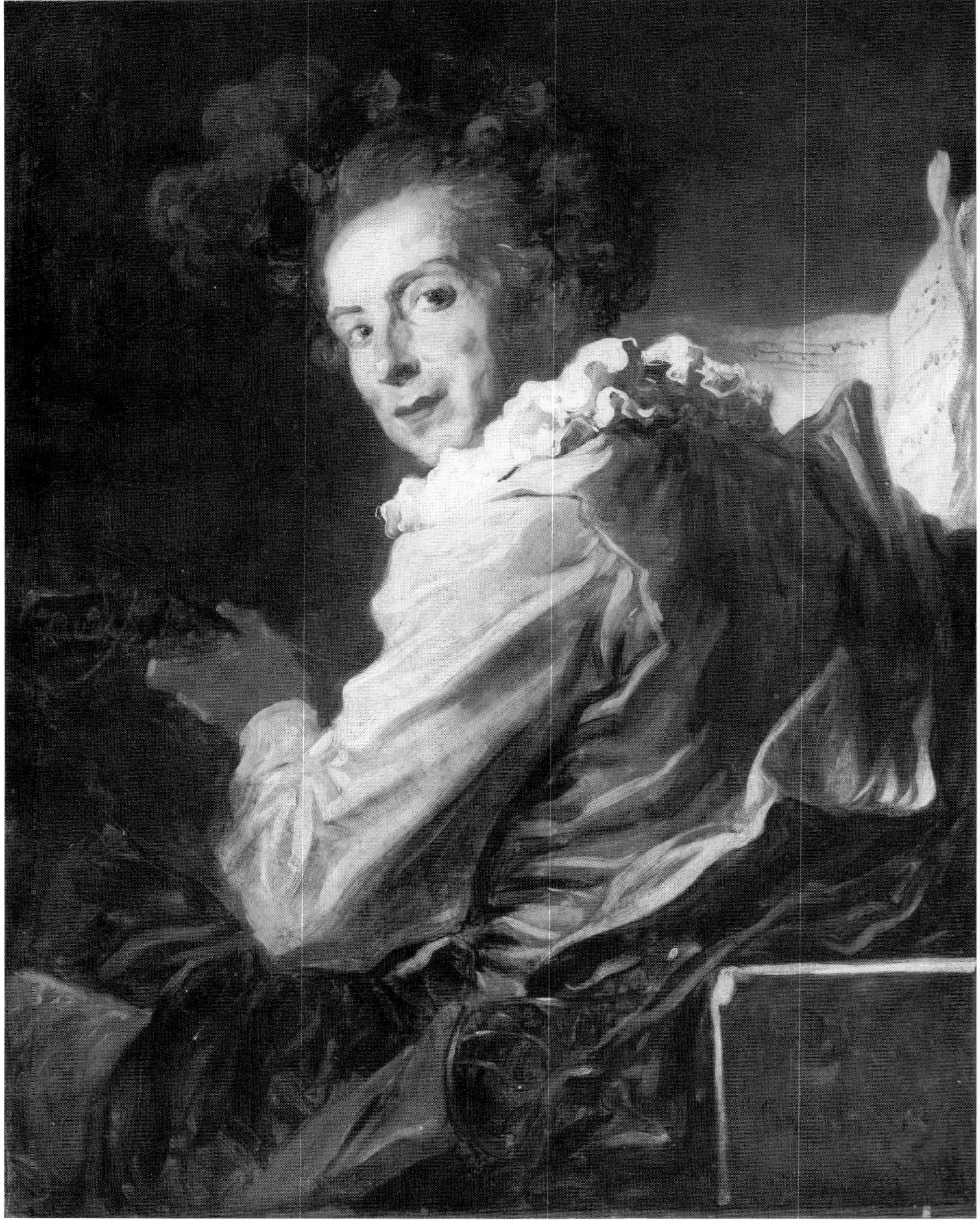

Figure 34 Jean-Honoré Fragonard, *Music,* 1769. Paris, Musée du Louvre. Cliché des Musées Nationaux, Paris.

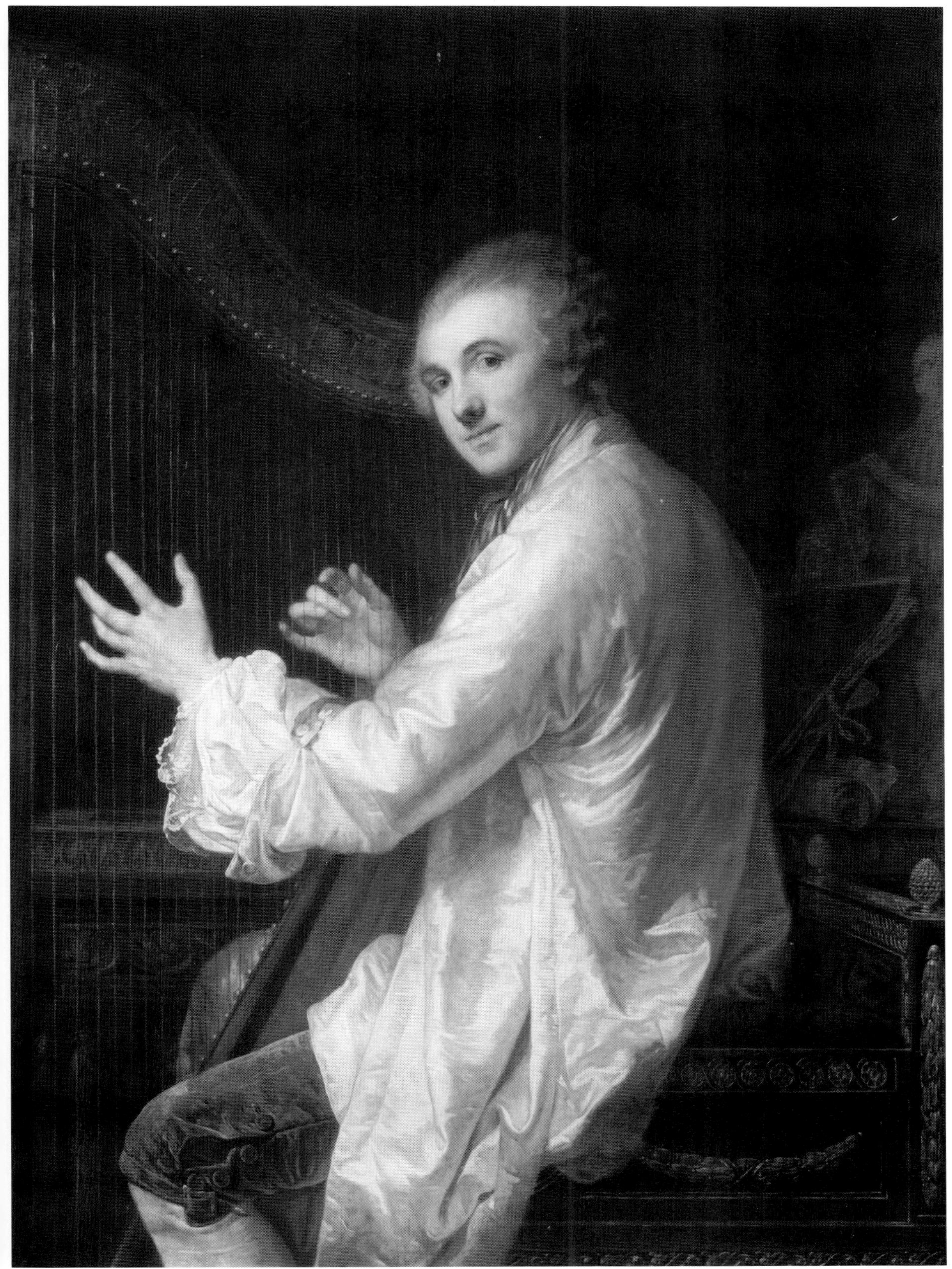

Figure 35 Jean-Baptiste Greuze, *Ange-Laurent de La Live de Jully,* 1759. National Gallery of Art, Washington, Samuel H. Kress Collection.

As the brushwork of *La Guimard* is contrived according to the object depicted, it also makes reference to another artist whose presence in the *portraits de fantaisie* has already been noted: Rembrandt. The brown and gold tones that dominate *La Guimard,* the handling of light effects, the appearance of the scumbled surface, and the brilliant handling of the white ruff that throws light on the face, all invoke the Dutch master. And Rembrandt is important in this context for at least three reasons: first, because his figure at the ledge was the most visible *trompe l'oeil* portrait in eighteenth-century France; second, because he was known for costume pieces (here the combination of Rembrandt and Watteau acquires particular piquancy); and third, because he had long been considered by French academic artists as the prototype of that painter who hid his labor under a rough and textured—a touched—surface. In *La Guimard* Fragonard disguises himself as Rembrandt, but he copies Watteau. He is the actor who plays the actor acting; he plays Rembrandt imitating Watteau. And this combination lays a particular stress on both the fictiveness of the conception and the cleverness of the artist who devised it.

The Imagined and the Copied: The *Portraits de Fantaisie* and Contemporary Portrait Debate

The *portraits de fantaisie* we have thus far considered share certain salient characteristics: apparently enthusiastic brushwork joined to a borrowed design, an adaptation of brush to subject and subject to brush, and a play with familiar portraits and conventions of portraiture. From these factors a twentieth-century observer cannot say whether these works are real portraits, but might Fragonard's contemporaries have understood these codes of representation differently?

As we have seen, resemblance was the defining feature of the portrait for an eighteenth-century audience, and it could only be assessed by those who actually knew the sitter. Thus the contemporary who could not immediately recognize the person portrayed on any given canvas was as powerless as posterity to judge if the work was or was not a portrait. Diderot suggested as much in the *Salon of 1767* when he observed that both the uninformed viewer and the connoisseur admired portraits that had the semblance of life even if they had never known the portrayed sitter. But, he wondered, why do they conclude that the works are portraits? "What difference is there between a fantasy portrait and a real portrait?"[23] When resemblance can not be determined, and Diderot clearly suggests that this is usually the case, the sitter assumes the status of an imagined figure.[24]

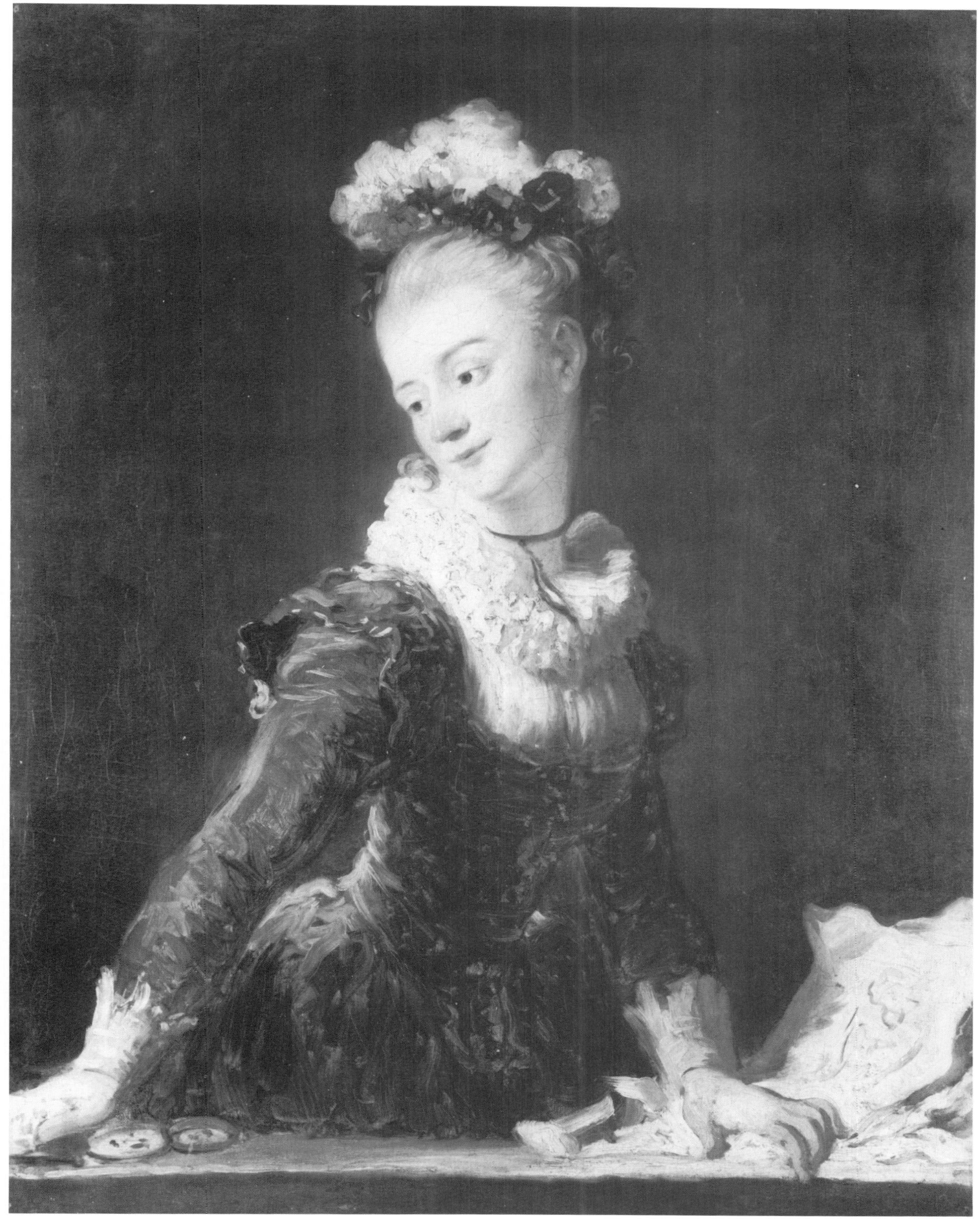

Figure 36 Jean-Honoré Fragonard, *La Guimard,* 1769.
Paris, Musée du Louvre. Cliché des Musées Nationaux, Paris.

But more importantly, Diderot's comments suggest that although resemblance may be the defining feature of the portrait, other qualities, such as liveliness, were ultimately more satisfying and convincing.

Those other qualities became a leitmotiv of Diderot's discussion of the portrait, a discussion summarizing much topical debate on the genre. In his *Salon of 1763* Diderot imagined a dispute between *gens du monde* and painters. The former praised likeness as the greatest merit of the portrait, a work made to please them by calling to mind someone who was absent (meaning the sitter, not the artist). The painters, on the other hand, wanted the portrait to please because it was beautifully handled. What does it matter, they asked, if a Van Dyck resembles or does not resemble its sitter? "The merits of resemblance are passing; it is those of the brush which astonish in their time and make the work immortal."[25] Diderot concluded from this dispute that perhaps it was necessary for the portrait to be resembling in its time but well painted for posterity. Diderot's final remarks, however, left no doubt as to which he believed the greater merit to be: "What is certain is that nothing is rarer than a fine brush, nor more common than a dauber who makes a resemblance, and when the sitter is no more, we take resemblance for granted."[26] The brush becomes a metonymy for the great painter whose presence in the work far outlives that of the sitter and who is set against the dauber, who can only copy appearances.

Although in considering individual portraits Diderot did not refrain from commenting on the degree of likeness (which he called truth), in discussing the genre of portraiture he presented himself as an enemy of resemblance, as one who expected that the artist would emphasize invention in the work and that the spectator would judge it as an artistic conception.[27] Moreover, he converted the Aristotelian distinction between historian and poet into a separation of portrait maker (whom he characterized as a dauber) and artist who makes a portrait. Like the historian, the portrait maker is concerned with the accurate description of an external object; the artist who makes a portrait, on the other hand, fabricates an internally consistent work of art, an illusion of truth. To make a good portrait, the artist must imagine and invent the sitter in much the same way as a history painter (who is not a historian but a poet) forms his characters, by showing nature not as it is but as it might be. Thus the *philosophe* calls up Artistotle's categories of the true *(vrai)* and the seemingly true *(vraisemblable)* and differentiates the portrait as history from the portrait as poetry. Diderot argued that the skilled painter made a portrait in the way Voltaire, as a poet, wrote history: "He aggrandizes, he exaggerates, he corrects the forms. Is he right or is he wrong? He is wrong for the pedant, he is right for the man of taste."[28]

This discussion suggests that although resemblance was the defining feature of the portrait, it was also its principal vice. Viewed from within the hierarchy of subjects, making a resemblance required little imagination and tied the genre to a mechanical copying of the particulars given in the external appearance of nature. The expectation of resemblance not only determined the status of portraiture but also guided how portraits were viewed, by leading the observer to concentrate on the relationship between the painted image and its referent in nature. This second consequence of resemblance proved disturbing to the *public éclairé,* who believed that only the ignorant viewer judged a painting according to resemblance.[29] The connoisseurs had other criteria. Looking behind the illusion, they prized the artist's ability to conceive a beautiful configuration of color and line, and to execute a composition with facile and suggestive handling of paint. They looked for an imaginative reconstitution of types and conventions in order to read, as it were, the history of painting in the painting. Simply put, the enlightened audience judged a work of art according to the strength of its invention.[30] In so judging a portrait, viewers shifted their attention from sitter to artist and considered the work as a representation of its maker's talent.

This continuing discussion about the portrait leads us to a basic observation: to be a great work of art, a portrait did not necessarily have to meet the criterion of resemblance; in fact, it did not even need to be a real portrait. What did characterize a great portrait was what characterized any great work of art: imaginative invention and a fine brush. As we have seen, it is these qualities that Fragonard stresses in his *portraits de fantaisie.* But this observation does not, as it might seem, obviate the question of the status of these works as portraits. On the contrary, it gives that question a renewed vigor if we realize that the whole series of *portraits de fantaisie* pose this question, that these works violate the boundary between the copied and the imagined so that the violation itself becomes a defining feature.

Through the consistent play with other portraits or portrait conventions, the *portraits de fantaisie* establish as their primary referents works of art—illusions. If this characteristic pointed to the imagined, it also signified the copied by raising the expectations of the audience, who would be encouraged to read the works as belonging to the genre of portraiture. Other aspects of the *portraits de fantaisie* effect similar confusions. The presence of attributes and seemingly individualized physiognomies tempt the viewer to see these paintings as portrayals of real and identifiable individuals, but the figures are costumed. Their garb does not copy contemporary theatrical or historical dress but is comprised of picturesque elements culled from other paintings and imaginatively synthesized. Do the *portraits de fantaisie* represent real sitters in fantasy dress or imagined characters dressed in the conventions of real portraits? Or are both possibilities contained within the same group? In pondering the masquerade, however, we recognize the artist as the real hero of these portraits—a realization that clarifies the persistent questions, because we understand that their posing is part of Fragonard's invention, his ability to play cleverly with traditions, conventions, and definitions of genre. It is only by seeing the series in this light that we can appreciate how the almost grotesquely comic *Lady with a Dog* (c. 1770; New York: Metropolitan Museum of Art) belongs to the same species as the brilliantly executed *Fantasy Figure in Blue.* By varying the variations, that is, by reinventing contemporary portraits, revitalizing standard types, even perhaps mixing real sitters with fictive ones, Fragonard refuses to confine his imaginative play to a predictable pattern.

Portraying the Portrait Critic: Fragonard's Fictive Diderot[31]

Thus far we have examined those *portraits de fantaisie* that indirectly comment on the debate over the portrait; I say indirectly because they do not focus on a portrait specifically involved in that debate. One *portrait de fantasie,* however, makes direct contact with the continuing discussion of the genre: Fragonard's so-called *Portrait of Diderot* (1769; Paris: Musée du Louvre; figure 37). We have already seen the artist reinvent a contemporary portrait in *Music;* the process is complicated in the Diderot, for that work operates between two other portraits. One of these, Michel Van Loo's depiction of Diderot (Salon of 1767; Paris: Musée du Louvre; figure 38), was executed in pigments; but the other, Diderot's commentary on Van Loo's image, was rendered in words.[32]

Van Loo represented Diderot at work on his correspondence. Seated at his desk, the unwigged critic looks elegantly informal with his expensive dressing gown open at the throat. Diderot's Salon commentary on this portrait revolves around several themes: the inability of the portrait to capture the likeness of an ever-changing sitter, the necessity of creating an image suitable for posterity, the difference between how we perceive ourselves and how others perceive us. Throughout the text three Diderots interact: the Diderot who as Salon critic narrates the text, the Diderot represented in Van Loo's portrait, and the Diderot that is the narrator's self-concept.

The text opens with the critic acknowledging his identity with the Diderot represented in Van Loo's portrait, "M. Diderot. Moi."[33] After the initial acknowledgement, however, the critic describes the Diderot represented in the painting using not the first person (as in, "I am shown"), but the third person (as in, "he is shown"). The he, the other depicted by Van Loo, is compared to the critic's self-concept; the portrait captures the "good nature" and "liveliness" of the self-concept but is unlike the latter in presenting its Diderot as too young a man with too small a head, one who is "pretty as a woman."[34] Calling his self-concept a "poor man of letters," the critic notes how Van Loo's Diderot strikes a pose more appropriate for a secretary of state than a philosopher; even worse, he wears luxurious clothes. Those clothes worried the *philosophe,* who also wrote a short essay about parting with his old dressing gown after Mme Geoffrin gave him an expensive new one.[35] The new gown represented the comfortable life that Diderot enjoyed through the generosity of his rich friends. It was not merely fortuitous, then, that Diderot mentioned the *perruque* given to him by Mme Geoffrin later in his discussion of Van Loo's portrait.[36]

Although separating his self-concept from the sitter represented by Van Loo, the narrator again merges himself (as distinct from his self-concept) with Van Loo's Diderot to explain that the expression was spoiled by Mme Van Loo who sang happy songs as he sat.[37] In this reidentification the narrator-critic admits the possibility that he did, in fact, appear as Van Loo painted him, as much as he would like to protest otherwise. Later he explains that artists cannot always see him properly because his expression is constantly changing.[38] To bring the Diderot he imagines to the fore, the critic suggests that the "sensitive philosopher" might have appeared differently had Mme Van Loo either played melancholy songs or, better still, left him to his own reverie, "Then his mouth would have dropped open, his absorbed glance would have been fixed in the distance, the workings of his intensely occupied mind would have been painted on his face."[39]

Once the self-concept emerges, the narrator again enforces his own separateness from Van Loo's Diderot. He addresses his painted image, "My pretty philosopher," and tells it how he wants to consider it: as evidence of his friendship with Michel Van Loo, rather than as his accurate portrait.[40] At this point Diderot introduces a central theme that has occupied all his discussions on the portrait, the theme of posterity. What, he

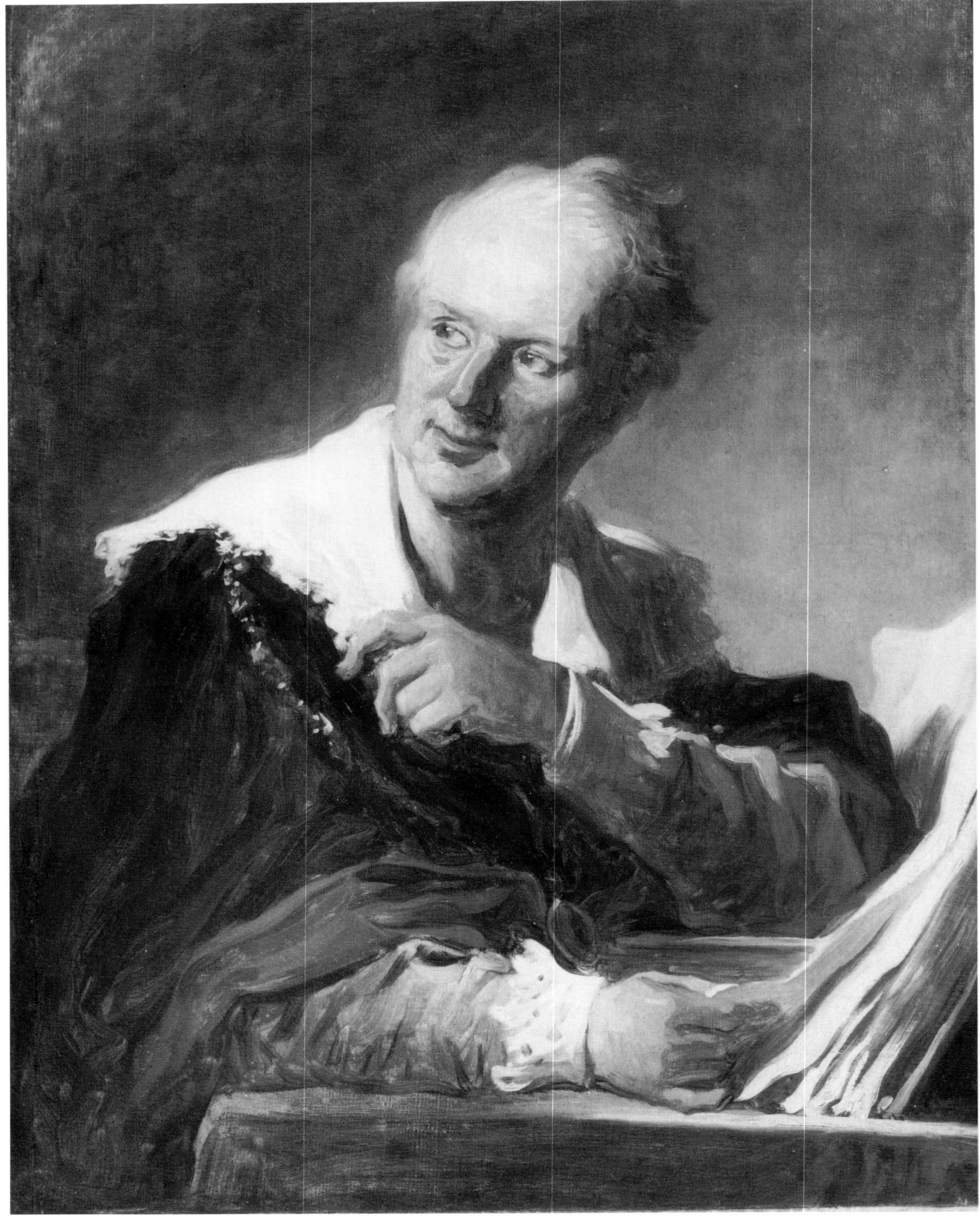

Figure 37 Jean-Honoré Fragonard, *Diderot,* 1769. Paris, Musée du Louvre. Cliché des Musées Nationaux, Paris.

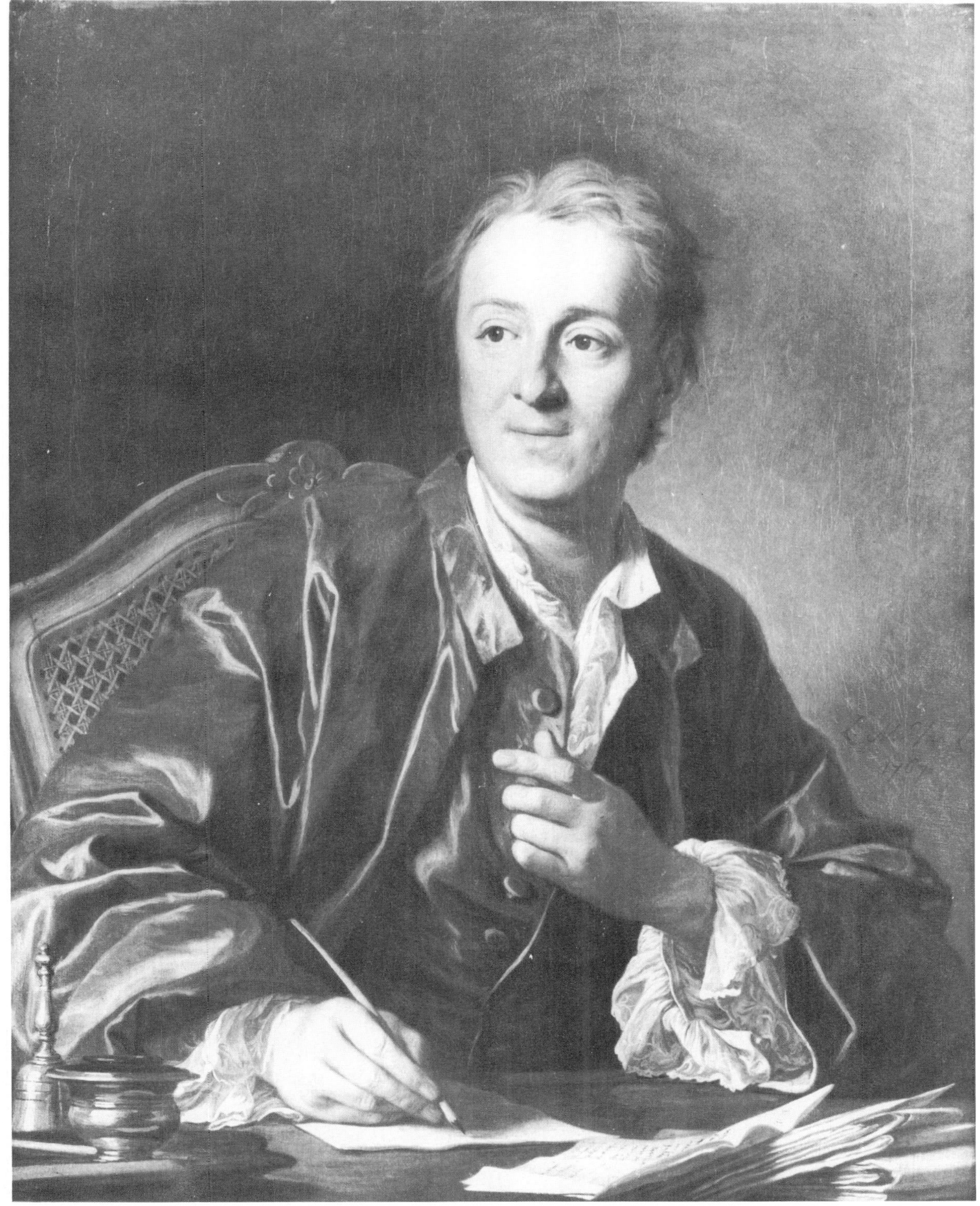

Figure 38 Michel Van Loo, *Diderot,* 1767. Paris, Musée du Louvre. Cliché des Musées Nationaux, Paris.

asks, will his grandchildren think when they compare his "sad works" with Van Loo's representation of an "old coquette"? Anxious to create his own image for posterity, an image that accords with both his self-concept and the author implied in some of his writings, the narrator-critic now says of Van Loo's Diderot, "it is not me" *(ce n'est pas moi)* in obvious contradiction to his opening statement.[41] Then, for the first time in the text, the critic merges with his self-concept, using the first person to portray himself for posterity: "I had a large forehead, very lively eyes, large enough features, a head entirely of the character of an ancient orator's, a good-naturedness very nearly approaching the simplicity, the rusticity of former times."[42]

Thus in reading the passage we move from the critic's initial identification with Van Loo's Diderot, the "Moi," to his renunciation of that identification, "ce n'est pas moi," which prepares the way for the final merger of self and self-concept. The tone of the whole passage is one of gentle self-mocking, as Diderot contradicts himself throughout—the portrait is "moi" and "pas moi," it is "quite resembling" but it is not "the truth," he admits that Mme Van Loo provoked his "laughing" expression but later claims never did he have one such as that painted by Van Loo. It is not so much that Van Loo misrepresented the real Diderot but that he did not depict Diderot as the critic would have posterity remember him.

The theme of posterity closes the piece as the critic alludes to his ongoing dispute with Falconet. He reports that Falconet destroyed a bust he had sculpted of Diderot after seeing the much finer one executed by his student Mme Collot, ". . . that Falconet, that artist so little jealous of his reputation in the future, that so determined disdainer of immortality, that man so disrespectful of posterity, [he was] delivered from the worry of transmitting to it [posterity] a bad bust."[43] And as Falconet destroyed a bust that would not do credit to his future reputation (an act that Diderot perceives as ironic), so Diderot attempted, with much self-irony, to discredit a portrayal of himself perhaps unsuited to the kind of immortality he desired. The tone of self-mocking and the highlighting of his own concern for posterity's accolades presents Diderot less as a "sensitive philosopher" and more as a man worried about his posthumous reputation. Although Diderot's self-portrait was an ironic one, in the end his strategy was successful; for when called upon to choose a representative image of the *philosophe* for an exhibition devoted to his criticism, posterity overlooked Van Loo's depiction and opted instead for one not taken from life, one that better suited both Diderot's self-concept and posterity's conception of him: Fragonard's *portrait de fantaisie.*

The similarities that link Fragonard's *portrait de fantaisie* to Van Loo's Diderot are as obvious as the differences that separate them. Although Fragonard adjusted Van Loo's pose and changed the attributes, he maintained the compositional dynamics. For example, the position of Diderot's arms is both repeated and altered by Fragonard; the gesture of grasping the shawl in the *portrait de fantaisie* is a transformation of the hand raised in Van Loo's depiction. Even the finger placement is maintained with a crooked index finger obviously separated from the other three digits.

Now the discernible changes. Diderot is no longer writing at his elegantly appointed desk; rather, he is positioned at a simple blocklike table with an open (but curiously blank) book before him. No longer young and pretty, Fragonard's Diderot has thinning hair and sagging flesh mottled with green. The rich materials and detailing that Van Loo lavished on Diderot's dress are replaced by a simple black robe and white shawl; and Fragonard's *philosophe* also wears the signs of the intellectual: the painter exaggerated the size of the forehead to accord with the standard philosopher type, and he suggested mental activity by agitating the hair and casting a bright light on the temple.

The most interesting adjustments, however, were made to a pose that, with just a little tinkering, was transformed into that of the enthused genius. Fragonard increased the torsion of the head so that Diderot appeared to look over his shoulder and represented him with lively eyes fixed in a distracted gaze. His reverie is underscored by the arranging of the arms to form a continuous inward spiral movement that suggests the self-absorption of philosophical reflection. Although the whole is executed in the sketchlike touches that we have come to associate with the *portraits de fantaisie,* the brushwork displays neither the extremely undifferentiated strokes of *The Young Artist* nor the blazing fiery ones of *Inspiration.* The agitated convulsions that mark the energized aristocrats are also missing. The brushwork of Fragonard's *Diderot* is, to be sure, loose and free, but it is also more restrained without flamboyant peaks, curls, and zigzags. Perhaps these touches are appropriate for representing an older man in whom the fires of youth have cooled.

The deviations from Van Loo's portrait evident in Fragonard's painting accord well with the alterations suggested in Diderot's commentary: the eyes are more lively because their color was changed from brown to a blue-green that contrasts with the reds in the flesh tones; the size of the head is larger; the moment chosen is one of reverie; pose and garments are appropriate for a philosopher type; the look is good-natured. Yet, the work also suggests that it is a less than serious revision of Van Loo. For example, the curiously blank book that the sitter holds—does it suggest the text about to be constructed, does it stress the imagination's unseen intellectual activity, or does it highlight the vacuity of Diderot's speculations? Or is it merely a standard feature of the *portraits de fantaisie,* appearing also in, for instance, *Study* (c. 1769; Paris: Musée du Louvre)? The garments are equally ambiguous. The humbleness of the robe is mocked by the gold chain and medallion, reminiscent of the jewelry worn by Aristotle as he contemplated the bust of Homer in Rembrandt's depiction.[44] The chain here substitutes for the expensive garments and accoutrements rendered by Van Loo. Those were gifts from Diderot's affluent friends, and in Fragonard's depiction the gold chain worn over modest garments also points to the beneficence of a patron. In a similar way the white-cuffed yellow sleeves juxtaposed to the red cape lining suggest that underneath the cover of a somber cloak there lurks another figure gussied up in a more ostentatious fancy dress, a figure who might be the author of *Les bijoux indiscrets* rather than the editor of the *Encyclopédie.* It is that hidden Diderot who meets the viewer with a wry smile.

In reinventing Van Loo's portrait, Fragonard distanced himself from any real sitter. One might envision a chain of representations with the historical Diderot at one end and Fragonard's *portrait de fantaisie* at the other. Between them we can place Van Loo's conception of Diderot and the portrait he made from that conception, Fragonard's reaction to Van Loo's portrait and his image of the *philosophe.* Like Diderot's Salon entry, Fragonard's portrait depends on an interplay among various illusions manufactured by him or by other artists. The interplay blocks reference to a real person, as does Fragonard's touch, which detains his viewers on the painting surface and occupies them with the artist rather than the sitter. The strategy evident in the so-called portrait of Diderot, then, accords well with the strategies unveiled in the other *portraits de fantaisie.*

The *Portraits de Fantaisie* and Their Audience

As portraits that question the nature of portraiture, Fragonard's *portraits de fantaisie* invite a rethinking of the genre. While refusing to distinguish the copied from the imagined, they engage other paintings in a perpetual dialogue and transform the portrait into a demonstration of the artist's invention and execution. This obvious display inverts the portrait's primary function, that of representing a sitter. If the *portraits de fantaisie* proclaim the artist's genius through a pyrotechnics of invention and brushwork, for what audience were they intended? Clearly, they were not designed for the *gens du monde* who only wanted to be admired in a good likeness. We might say that they were painted with an eye to that most demanding of judges, posterity; but this answer does not acknowledge that these works are best read as part of a discourse about the portrait that emerged within a specific cultural context. Although we do not, in every case, know the individual patron who owned Fragonard's *portraits de fantaisie,* we do know that he often worked for a specific kind of clientele: the *amateurs.* Like the Abbé de Saint-Non, they were men well versed in the history of art, well read in aesthetic theory, and thoroughly familiar with the academic conventions of picture making. They formed a sophisticated audience interested in the fashionable issues of art and fully capable of appreciating the cleverness of a painting that commented upon itself.

We know that at least some of these works were admired and owned by *amateurs.* Comte Jean-René François Almaric de Brehan, *amateur honoraire* of the French Academy, liked the paintings so well that in 1773 he copied two, the *Singer Holding a Sheet of Music* (before 1773; Private Collection) and the *Fantasy Figure in Blue.* His medium was pastel—interesting because pastel allowed sketchlike effects to be easily achieved. Two other great collectors, the Comte Du Barry and Leroy de Senneville, owned *The Reader* now in the National Gallery of Art, Washington; and Varanchan de Saint-Geniès owned a work closely related to the series, *Cavalier Seated by a Fountain* (Barcelona: Musée d'Art de Catalunya). Few of the other *portraits de fantaisie* have a secure provenance, but perhaps it is noteworthy that many of them have been consistently associated with Fragonard's most important supporter, the *amateur honoraire* Saint-Non.

The so-called portrait of the Duc d'Harcourt (1769–71; Switzerland: Private Collection) provides the most interesting case study of a patron. Rosenberg has argued most reasonably for the identification of the sitter with the Duc d'Harcourt, and based on a known connection of Fragonard with the d'Harcourt family, we can accept François-Henri as a patron, if not a sitter, of this *portrait de fantaisie.*[45] The Duc d'Harcourt fits the profile of the *amateur* and man of taste. He had a substantial reputation as a writer, published a treatise on gardening, and was elected to the Académie française in 1789. He is said to have drawn and sculpted and to have amused himself by acting in and writing plays for the *théâtre d'Harcourt.*[46] A family tradition holds that at one time Fragonard painted six figures disguised for a fête held in the *Pavillon de Fantaisie* that decorated the gardens of the d'Harcourt château. An appreciation for a costumed portrait that blurs the distinctions between fantasy and reality seems consistent with the interests of an *amateur* who performed in his own theater and regularly gave masquerade balls. And indeed the tradition might well have begun when one of his descendants noted that the portrait and the costumed fêtes represented similar interests. It does not seem totally improbable that a real, but costumed, portrait executed for the Duc d'Harcourt stimulated the whole series of works, but it is equally likely that d'Harcourt, knowing Fragonard's *portraits de fantaisie,* sought an example for his own collection.

In Fragonard's *portraits de fantaisie* we are certainly considering an elite art for a cultivated audience, an art that revels in masquerade. In these works the artist costumes himself as Rembrandt, as Watteau, as Greuze; he disguises fantasy figures as real sitters, and perhaps also real sitters as fantasy figures. And if *sprezzatura* is presented as genius, then conversely genius is presented as *sprezzatura.* For although it might have been obvious to Fragonard's privileged audience that these carefully composed and brilliantly executed works were not thrown off spontaneously in a fit of enthusiasm, it was equally obvious that they displayed a fertile imagination, a playful wit, and a consummate perfection of technique. At times Fragonard may have improvised without planning, but we are wise to remember that improvisation depends on a prior mastery of technique, a learned command of aesthetic principles, and an impressive catalogue of models stored in memory. Fragonard's virtues might not have qualified him as the mythic genius, but surely they marked him as a performer with an extraordinary talent for fabricating genius.

Art and Eroticism 6

The New Model and Her Modest Sisters

Fragonard's *The New Model* (c. 1770; Paris: Musée Jacquemart-André; figure 39) appears to be a painting of superficial effects. Its exquisitely sensuous paint handling suggests a sketch impetuously rendered by a master long familiar with images of seduction; and the theme itself, whimsical and provocative, seems a mere bagatelle. Here is how the Baron Portalis appreciated the work in 1896:

> Imagine all that you can imagine of the most blond, the most pink, the most light. Knead these tones with spirit, but with the inimitable spirit of a master, and you will have the impression as experienced [by the viewer]. The brush glides without bearing down on the faded pinks of the loose studio dress of a young painter occupied in picking up, with the end of his maulstick, the last veils of his model. This is only a sketch perhaps, but what finished painting would equal it, how could anyone dare to desire more finished these indications which say it all.[1]

At this point in our analysis of Fragonard, however, we should be wary of his disingenuous art, which hides its complexity behind erotic subjects rendered in light, easy touches. Scratching that so carefully constructed surface, we find in *The New Model* a discourse about painting and eroticism that engages a constellation of closely related works: a thought painting by Diderot presented in the *Salon of 1767*, a gouache by Baudouin shown at the Salon of 1769, and the critic's commentary on the gouache, which he takes as an attempt to embody his imagined work.[2]

Fragonard's scene is set in a painter's atelier indicated primarily by a

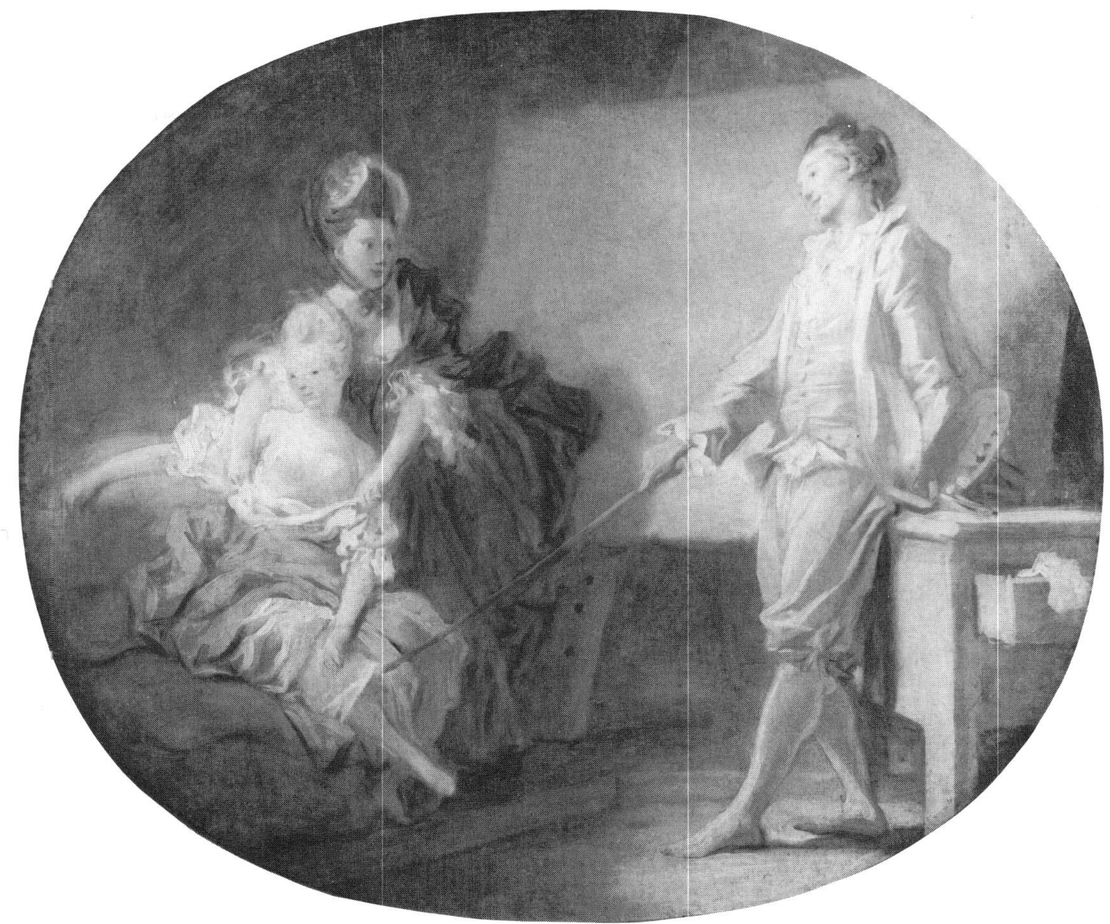

Figure 39 Jean-Honoré Fragonard, *The New Model,* 1770. Paris, Musée Jacquemart-André.

large blank canvas dominating the background. Before that *toile* a coy, nubile young model is evaluated by a painter who, one can imagine, sees her for the first time. Pulling down the girl's bodice, a chaperone looks for the painter's approval, while the painter, young and pretty as his model, raises her skirt with his maulstick. The particulars of the scene vary pointedly from that work I take as its subtext, Baudouin's *The Modest Model* (1769; Washington, D.C.: National Gallery of Art; figure 40). There a nude model has been posing for a picture of Venus and Cupid done in the manner of Boucher. With the painting on the easel nearly completed, the model seems suddenly shamed by her occupation; she covers her face with one hand and places the other between her legs, in imitation of the *Venus pudica.* Her response perhaps was precipitated by the entry of an older woman (possibly her mother) who endeavors to cover the girl with her drapery. The painter reacts to the scene in surprise and dismay, leaning from his chair with extended arms.

The differences between these two works are made meaningful by the obvious similarities that associate one with the other. First, there is the coincidence of setting the scene in the artist's quarters where we see interacting a painter, his model, and a third figure, whom we shall call the

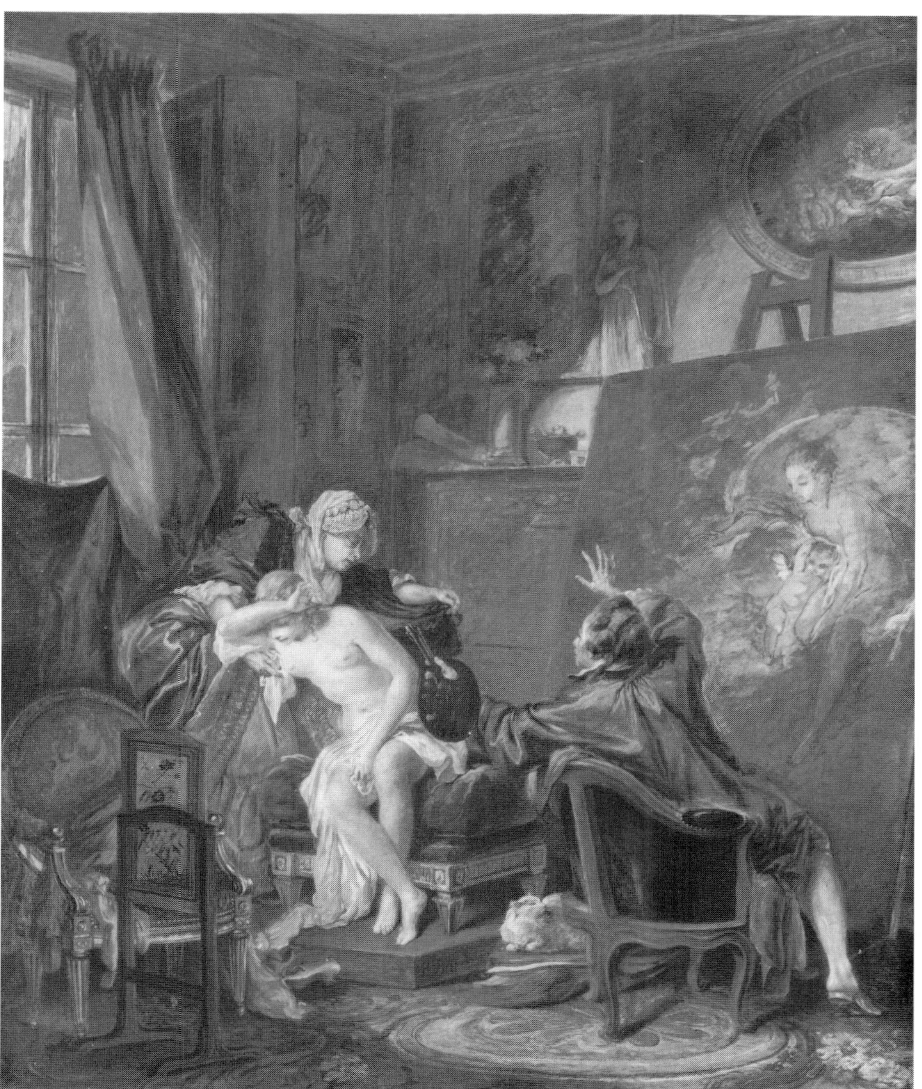

Figure 40 Pierre-Antoine Baudouin, *The Modest Model,* 1769. National Gallery of Art, Washington. Gift of Ian Woodner.

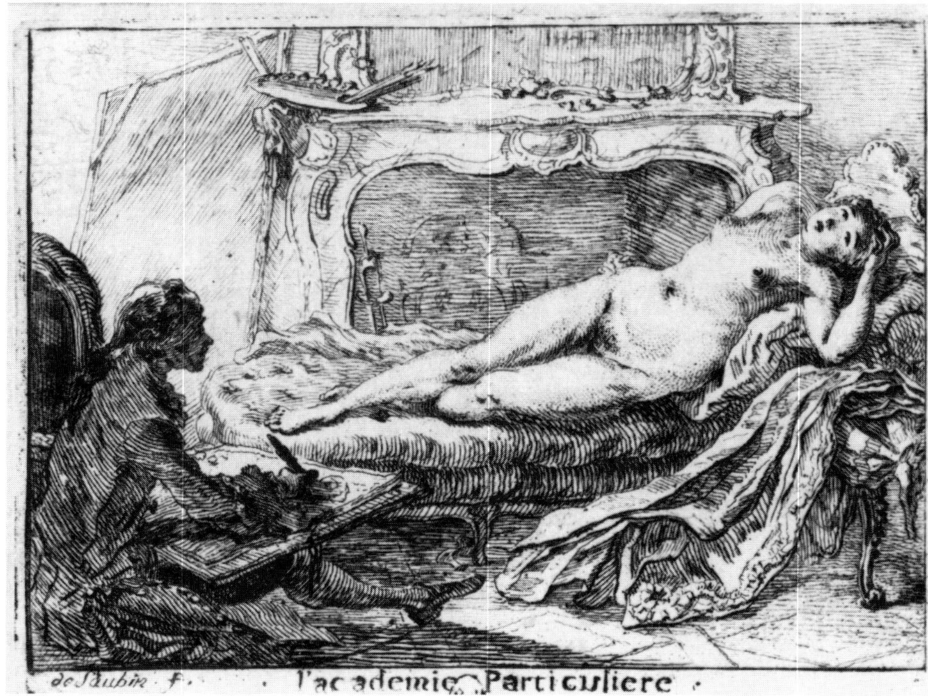

Figure 41 Gabriel de Saint-Aubin, *The Private Academy.* Paris, Bibliothèque Nationale.

chaperone.[3] The presence of these particular three characters distinguishes these two works from the other scenes of artists and models depicted in the eighteenth century. Some images, for instance Saint-Aubin's *The Private Academy* (Paris: Bibliothèque Nationale; figure 41) omit the chaperone; Boucher's illustration to Molière's *Le Sicilien ou l'amour peintre* shows artist and sitter alone in the foreground while two gentleman in the background leave the scene.[4] Depictions of Apelles and Campaspe (for example, those by Tiepolo or David) included Alexander, either alone or with a retinue of accessory figures.[5]

In more specifically comparing Fragonard's work with that of Baudouin, we see that the placement of the three figures is quite similar in each composition: the artist holding palette and brushes stands on one side apart from the two women toward whom he gesticulates. The women are set in contrast; the clothed and bonneted chaperone is juxtaposed to the undressed, bare-headed model. But Fragonard's atelier, unlike that of Baudouin, is scarcely delineated and the canvas is pointedly empty. The moment he chooses is a preliminary one, before the model has begun to sit; and the narrative action is reversed. Whereas in *The*

Modest Model the chaperone is covering her charge, in *The New Model* she is artfully revealing the young lady's charms. Fragonard established with Baudouin's painting a dynamic of similarity and reversal, which is also carried to the color tonalities. In *The Modest Model* pink punctuates the dominant blue-green, but Fragonard gives a larger role to the rosy tones while limiting blue-green to the shadows and accents.

The relationship between these two paintings cannot be adequately grasped without reference to another painting, a thought painting made by Diderot, "commissioned" by Greuze, and published in the *Salon of 1767*. Diderot's *Modest Model* is imbedded in a discussion about the ability of literary men to imagine paintings. Stressing the difficulty of composing and ordering a visual representation, Diderot argued that not every motif suitable for poetry was equally suitable for painting. Immodest about his own abilities, however, the critic assured his readers that Chardin, Lagrenée, Greuze, and others had singled him out as the only *littérateur* whose imaginings could pass onto the canvas almost exactly as they had been ordered in his head.[6] Here, then, is the painting of *The Modest Model* he imaged for Greuze:

> Greuze said to me, I would like to paint a woman totally nude without offending modesty, and I responded, make the Modest Model. Seat before you a young girl totally nude; [imagine that] her poor coverings are thrown on the ground beside her and signal her misery; that her head rests on one of her hands; that two tears from her lowered eyes run the length of her cheeks. Her expression must be one of innocence, of shame, of modesty. Her mother is next to her, with her own hands and with one hand of her daughter she covers the girl's face—or she hides her face in her hands while that of her daughter is placed on her shoulder. The clothes of the mother also reveal extreme poverty, and the artist, witness to this scene, is touched and lets drop his palette or his brush. And Greuze said, I see my painting.[7]

Although Diderot's painting was never executed by Greuze, Baudouin's gouache called *The Modest Model* appeared at the next Salon. The title was no coincidence, for the work did resemble the painting imagined by Diderot, albeit with some significant changes and additions. Nothing indicates the girl's penury or the indigence of the old woman, and neither the model's expression nor that of the artist follow those prescribed by the text. Although having the general components of Diderot's plot, Baudouin's scene is hardly clear in its meaning, and the ambiguity of the subject entranced the Salon viewers who crowded around it. Bachaumont generalized their responses in three basic questions: Why did the model resist when the work on the easel indicated many previous hours of sitting? What role did the old woman play, was she a procuress or the young girl's mother? and, What was the meaning of the inscription on the frame, *Quid no cogit egestas* or "See what poverty makes one do?"[8] The last question seemed particularly vexing.

How did Diderot respond to Baudouin's image? He was disturbed by its ambiguity, and he believed that the sensual was so mixed with the moral that one could not unquestionably determine which meaning prevailed. "And then this subject is unclear from the manner in which you have treated it, this woman is not a mother, she is a vile creature who does some villainous business."[9] As if to show Baudouin's distance from the ideal, the critic summarized the description of his imaginary painting and ended by saying, "Believe me, leave these sorts of subjects to Greuze."[10] Grimm added, "Baudouin, as libertine in his brush as with his morals, did not have in his soul the least atom necessary for the execution of a painting of this honesty and pathos."[11]

But why did Diderot and Grimm assume that Baudouin intended to preserve the *philosophe*'s didactic message in his painting of the subject? Could he not have been responding to the proposed image in some other way? After all, why would a painter who specialized in erotic scenes suddenly be inspired to represent a moral one, particularly when there was not a commission from a patron?[12] That decision would put Baudouin in somewhat the same position as the young model who after hours of nude sitting is suddenly embarrassed by her enterprise. And it seems unlikely that Baudouin's conscience was awakened, since *The Modest Model* has its erotic components and primary among them is a sensuous presentation of the female form that was evident to Baudouin's contemporaries.[13]

Returning to Diderot's *The Modest Model,* recall that he suggested the subject to Greuze because Greuze wanted to paint a nude woman without wounding modesty. The proposition itself is duplicitous—the desire to paint a sensuous subject is legitimated by cloaking it in morality. Baudouin's response to this bit of hypocrisy is ironic; in its very obvious equivocation his *The Modest Model* blatantly displays the pretense of (thinly) disguised eroticism, a pretense peculiar both to Diderot and to Greuze, the painter Diderot admired. In a larger sense, Baudouin's image may be taken as a reminder that for centuries (male) artists painted the nude female figure from motivations other than respect for virtue. In conjunction with this interpretation, it is significant that the model has sat for a representation of Venus, that she has been transformed into the enduring male symbol of female perfection. Baudouin's work suggests these questions: Why is any excuse needed to depict the nude female model, since that practice is sanctioned by the past? and, if virtue is only an excuse, then is its (i.e., virtue's) representation not hypocritical? Finally, Baudouin's decision to represent within *The Modest Model* a painting of Venus executed in the manner of Boucher only increased the scene's irony; in his choice Baudouin selected the manner that Diderot most vehemently attacked as immodest. Boucher's son-in-law and disciple Baudouin thus effectively mocked his master's most severe critic in *The Modest Model.*[14]

If we view Baudouin's painting as an ironic response to Diderot, then the equivocal meaning and the model's sudden modesty are purposeful, and so is the inscription on the frame, "see what poverty has made me do." The comment cannot logically refer to the painter we see depicted in the work, because he is living in very pleasant and comfortable surroundings. The women, as we have already noted, scarcely look indigent. But what if we take the inscription as referring to the artist who made the representation rather than to any of the figures who are represented in it? Not to the historical figure Baudouin but to the apparent creator of *The Modest Model,* who "out of poverty" (or out of desire for money) created a titillating work. The comment again would be a barb aimed at Diderot, who excused his own libertine writing because it was done in his youth and out of poverty. The motto is also appropriate as a reference to the Salon essay that contained Diderot's conception of *The Modest Model.* There the critic spoke disparagingly of Lagrenée's desire for financial reward, calling it even greater than that of Greuze, which, Diderot admitted, was saying a lot.[15]

Baudouin's *The Modest Model* resembles Diderot's conception enough to establish a reference to it and then diverges from the thought picture in specifically ironic gestures. If Diderot recognized Baudouin's mocking representation of his idea, he refused to acknowledge it as a parody, preferring instead to treat *The Modest Model* as a work that failed to translate its literary source adequately. Fragonard's *The New Model* both belongs to and expands the context of the discussion. The formal similarities to Baudouin's painting bring that theme to mind, and Fragonard's modifications suggest a change of meaning and a different relation to Diderot's vision of the artist-and-model theme. Fragonard's image is hardly equivocal, and there is no suggestion of moral purpose, as the model's body is gradually being revealed to the gazes of painter and audience. It refers to Diderot by direct contrast. Here, if you will, is the immodest model, the model who is presented as an object of delectation and who seems not to be embarrassed by it.

Fragonard's Erotic Touch

Intended for an elite audience, perhaps for those who could appreciate its relation to Baudouin and Diderot, *The New Model* is the kind of work preferred by the private patron for whom Fragonard developed his sketchlike execution.[16] These buyers often wanted a small easel painting, something for their cabinets or, in this case, their boudoirs. A work of small scale was suited to an intimate setting where it could be approached closely in order to savor the subtleties of paint handling. Paint handling here is an object of delectation, the medium through which an object of delectation is represented, and the trace of the artist's presence. *The New Model,* moreover, thematizes in its subject and iconography the interpenetration of art and eroticism evident in the paint handling. The coincidence of meaning in two fields becomes a technique in Fragonard's artistic arsenal as powerful as the disjunction of motif and handling in his *Inspiration.*

Although any subject could be treated with an eroticized paint handling in which the brushwork was intended for sensual appeal, that handling took on a more particular significance when applied to themes of love and seduction. In *The New Model,* for example, many of the qualities associated with the erotic surface are present both in what is represented and in the manner of representation. Consider, for example, *négligence,* that delicate indecency disguised as inattention. Although the term is not applicable to the model (her display, after all, is not disguised), *négligence* is evident in the painter, whose appearance is casual and artfully disheveled, with blouse open at the neck and hair slightly disarranged. Even though the furnishings in the room are decidedly sparse—limited to the prepared canvas, pillowed sofa, and small dresser—the dresser suggests (although, perhaps does not embody) that kind of *négligence* called *beau désordre,* with the disarray reduced to a white rag protruding from a partially opened drawer. Represented in the painter's dress and in the room setting, *négligence* is also evident in the paint handling where areas of the composition left unattended suggest rather than define forms. For example, anatomical features (the hands of the women or the model's right arm blending with its supporting pillow) are not rendered with clarity or precision. In the background the legs of the easel are scarcely delineated, and its top is undifferentiated from the atmosphere surrounding it. At the edge of the composition the sofa fades into the ground behind. Although there is nothing literally indecent about this kind of paint handling, it was associated with *négligence* of dress or attitude because both stimulated the viewer by provoking the imagination and appealing to the senses. Both were also calculations of art disguised as chance effects.

If we extend our discussion of *négligence* to the more general concept of suggestive incompletion, we can add that Fragonard's new model is in a state of undress more provocative than the total nudity of the woman represented by Baudouin. Fragonard plays on the titillating effect of teasing the viewer, of making him imagine what he does not see (and I am assuming a male viewer, since the eroticism of *The New Model,* as in *The Bathers,* seems directed toward that audience). Fragonard's sprightly, doll-like model, however, is in no way transparent to what she represents, and the artist eschews naturalistic effects, even those limited ones used by Baudouin. Fragonard's figure appeals because it suggests the fantasy of a sensuous woman rather than because it depicts a female body with anatomical accuracy. By abbreviating the facial features to touches of color, the artist allowed for a variety of readings that captured the mobility of fleeting but provocative glances. The multiple emotions heighten the work's erotic potential by intimating a variety of possible relationships among the three figures.

In addition to *négligence,* facility or the appearance of doing something easily and effortlessly also operates in *The New Model.* The artist represented seems to lounge against the dresser behind, and the model reclines into the sofa with one arm "carelessly" thrown over the back of the pillow. That their ease is calculated there can be no doubt. His is the ease of the courtier who relaxes in an accustomed pose with turned-out calf and pointed toe. The model arranges herself in an equally artful manner, turning so that the curves of her form are shown to their best effect; and the chaperone's arms encircling her provide a frame to display head, neck, and breasts. Just as the painted figures display calculated ease, the artist who made the painting presents his work as unlabored, exploiting the fluidity of oils. The pigment appears to stream effortlessly across the canvas in long curvilinear strokes seemingly laid down with one graceful movement of the hand, as in the drapery of the model. Elsewhere small dabs of paint quickly and deftly applied define forms such as the decorations of the bonnet. The outlines of the chaperone's dress are not exactly and meticulously drawn but are rendered in curves and countercurves that seem practiced and familiar to the hand.

Facility and negligence, apparent ease and designed inattention increase the eroticism of *The New Model.* These demand that the labor and planning be both recognized and unrecognized. To distinguish *facilité* from haste and *négligence* from carelessness, it was necessary to see both the more haphazard surface effects and the underlying structures. Although the viewer must not immediately perceive the calculation concealed beneath the paint skin, his viewing must be guided by its ordering effects, effects that both make the artless artful and increase the work's eroticism.

The New Model uses for erotic effect two ordering principles, that of *convenance* and that of reasoned contrast. The first increased sexual differentiation and hence sexual tension; the second added to the overall pleasure of visual appeal. In *The New Model* outlines delineate human forms in ways believed appropriate for the genders signified. Whereas strong curves and countercurves articulate the womens' shapes, simple and straight outlines define the painter. Punctuating this difference, the drapery winds around the female bodies (the dark shawl of the chaperone) but falls vertically over the male torso (the coat of the painter). The painter's sharply extended right arm and maulstick contrast with the relaxed pliant arm of the model, which sinks into the pillow behind; and his muscular calves oppose her dainty legs. Even the furniture participates in the system of differentiation. The hard, angular surface of the bureau supports the young artist; his model, on the other hand, leans into the softly curving form of the sofa.

But it is not simply that Fragonard differentiated the masculinity of the painter from the femininity of the model; between the two women he played oppositions suggestively. The difference in coloration is striking: the brunette chaperone with rosy flesh tones contrasts dramatically with the blond marmoreal model. More significant, the one is demurely dressed with shawl and bonnet, the other is being revealed. As masculine and feminine qualities are intensified when juxtaposed to one another, so display is exaggerated when placed against concealment.

This antonymy of male-female, clothed-unclothed was no more invented by Fragonard than was the vocabulary of *pittoresque* effects. In Boucher's *Pan and Syrinx* (1759; London: National Gallery of Art, figure 42), for example, a male satyr, tanned, brawny, and angular, contrasts with two nymphs whose nacreous flesh tones, soft bodies, and curving forms intensify sexual differentiation. The two women are also set in opposition: one is seen from the back, the other from the front; one is blond, the other brunette.[17]

Yet Fragonard embroiders, varies, and enriches the convention of doubled contrast. Absent in Boucher's works is the overriding similarity that enframes the contrast of the two women in Fragonard's painting. Alike in overall shape, with oval heads, upswept hair, and delicate fea-

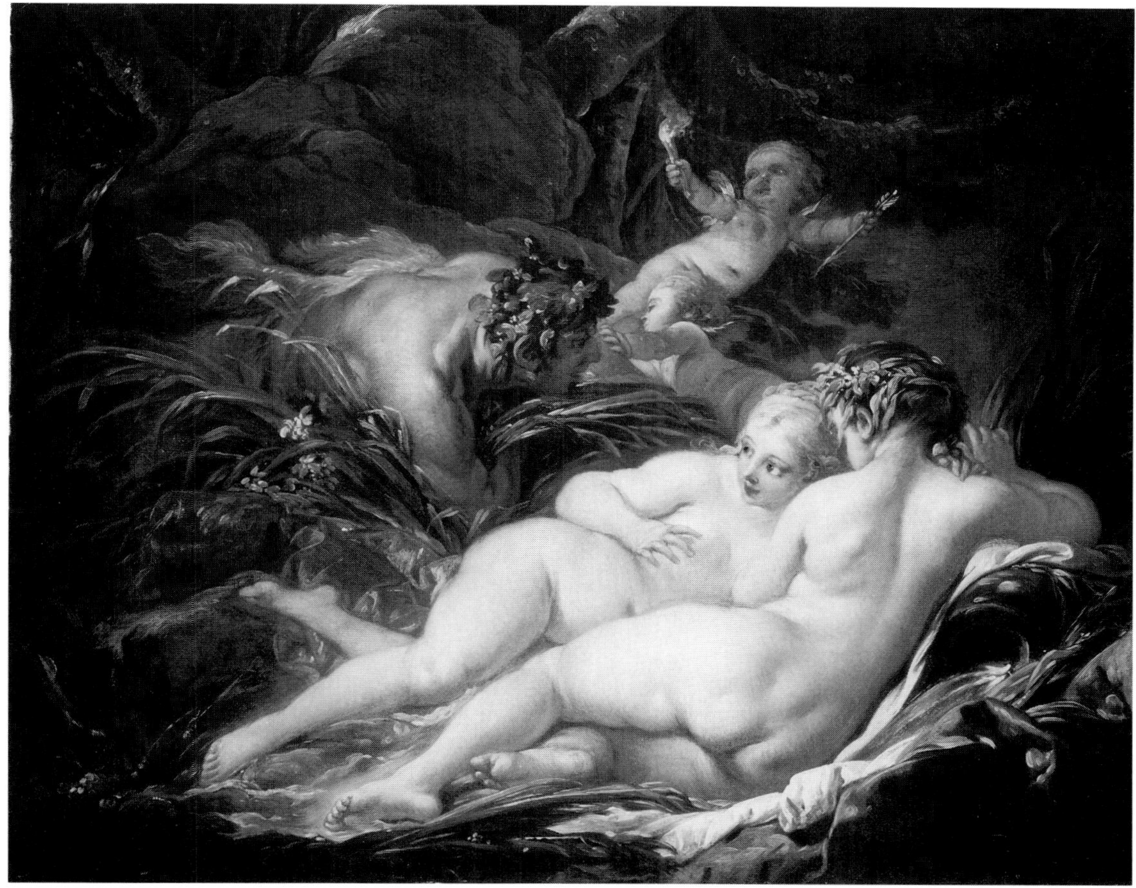

Figure 42 François Boucher, *Pan and Syrinx,* 1759. London, National Gallery of Art.

tures, the women are linked by the encircling arms of the chaperone, whose curve is repeated more openly in the arms of the model. It is easy to read the two figures as one multifaceted form suggesting two states of the same woman—or of all women—sensuality concealed beneath the mask of modesty. The idea perhaps appealed to the male fantasy in the same way that the Presidente de Tourvel appealed to the Vicomte de Valmont in Laclos' *Les liaisons dangereuses.*

Reasoned contrast also operates as a principle of visual pleasure where nonerotic objects are represented. In *The New Model* Fragonard juxtaposed the simple, geometric shapes of the easel and table to the complex drawing of the drapery. The stability and stasis established by the furnishings counterbalance the flux and dynamism of the fabric's intricate folds and undulating motion. Opposition is also the overriding color principle in *The New Model;* variations of green and red dominate the composition and a counternote of yellow enlivens the whole. The simultaneous red-green contrast has been perfectly executed; for example, the chaperone's rose-colored dress brings out the subdued green shadows of the sofa and plays against the more intense spots of blue-green in the bonnet. While the pink costume of the painter opposes the green shadows in his stockings and in the easel behind, the dabs of red on his palette highlight the contrast, at the same time balancing the lively touches of green used in the chaperone's hat. A masterful use of reflected lights harmonizes these contrasts: the model's arm slung over the sofa picks up the green shadows as well as the pink reflections from the chaperone's dress.

Brushwork also varies throughout the composition. Set against the more drily brushed areas in the background, the foreground touches marking model and painter are wet, fluid, and thickly applied. Sensuous elements within the composition such as the drapery encircling the model's bosom are treated with full, creamy strokes, but those with less erotic charge, the more modest shawl of the chaperone, for example, are rendered with a less appealingly tactile surface. Touches, however, are more than elements to be contrasted for visual appeal; and in many areas of the composition they seem less to describe objects than to present themselves as touches. In the drapery that frames the model's breasts, for example, the touches do not so much simulate the look and texture of fabric as highlight the woman's sexual characteristics and suggest the act of touching or caressing. We have already identified this strategy in Fragonard's *The Bathers.* In *The New Model,* however, touch is more obviously centralized; it becomes signifier and signified. As signifier it assumes both its imitative and expressive roles, and as signified it is represented as an erotic gesture as well as an aesthetic one.[18]

Physical contact is represented in *The New Model,* as the painter touches his model with a maulstick, an artist's tool used here as an erotic (and phallic) accessory. Thickly applied, glistening paint strokes on the artist's right cuff draw attention to his hand gripping its mechanical extension; and that hand, placed in the center of the composition, is silhouetted against the canvas' white ground. While one accentuated hand grips the maulstick to touch the model, the other balances brushes and palette. This balancing hand is scarcely visible, no more than the indication of a thumb that merges with the implements of painting. But why does the artist hold brushes and palette as he makes his initial survey of the model who has not yet posed? He is not ready to paint, he is not looking at the canvas, and the painting chair usually placed before the easel is conspicuously absent. Moreover, the palette and brushes are not placed in a working position but in one calculated for audience display. They are emphasized, in fact, by the vertical line of the dresser leg that brings attention to them.

The implements might be necessary simply as attributes of the painter, but his profession would be adequately indicated by canvas, maulstick, and situation. Yet we can suppose the palette and brush to have a symbolic value connected with their function as tools for applying pigment to the canvas. They remind the beholder of a later stage in the process of art making when the artist will transfer his vision of the model to the canvas by touching its white expanse, just as he now touches the model. The association of canvas and model as objects to be touched partially explains the extremely white flesh tones she displays; her body is nearly the color of that larger white rectangular surface positioned in the background.

Although in *The New Model* erotic and painterly touching are associated as acts of the artist, touch as the dab of paint on the canvas is also forcefully implied. The palette is spotted with pigment, and on its flat surface are arranged most of the colors used in the very painting that we see: red, pink, white, yellow. Blue-green is notably missing. It appears, however, in the touches on the chaperone's bonnet, which is associated visually with the artist's palette. Between these two an overall similarity of shape is evident, as the oval of the palette rhymes with that of the chaperone's bonneted head. The directionality established across the picture plane also encourages the comparison of the two touched objects (i.e., palette and bonnet). The chaperone looks toward the painter, and her line of sight leads the viewer to that place where the palette is located. The touches on the palette represent just what they are, touches of paint, and so fulfill the dream of totally transparent signification. But they do so only to dramatize the elusive nature of that dream because they are coordinated with those touches on the bonnet that signify what they are not, decorations arranged on a hat. The correspondence of these marks across the surface implies that the scene is an illusion fabricated from nothing but touches of paint.

Extending this last observation, we should also note that the oval palette harmonizes with the oval shape of the canvas on which *The New Model* is rendered, and that on the surface the composition is made to adhere to an oval format. Beginning at the top of the artist's head, the viewer's eye is led through his body, down to his pointing toe, and over to the toe of the model, which is coquettishly directed toward him. The position of the maulstick emphasizes the movement from artist to model. From the model's toe the forms sweep up and around to the chaperone's head, and that revealer's glance leads back to the painter. The pigments arranged halfway around the palette correspond with the sequence of the colors on the canvas surface. On the palette the colors proceed from the dots of red and pink to the spots of yellow and white; on the canvas one sees a similar order from the reds and pinks of the artist's costume to the yellow and white of his model's drapery. Again the parallel is drawn between dabs of paint unformed on the palette and dabs of paint formed on the surface of the canvas. It is the artist's hand and his act of touching that mediates, that transforms one into the other; in the same way his imagination recreated the model by envisioning a work of art.

The Imaginative Activity of Artist and Beholder

Fragonard's *The New Model* both thematizes the artist's touch and represents the imaginative process of the artist who must form a mental image of the motif or model he sees before him. Both aesthetic activities are placed within the context of an erotic encounter, which suggests a comparison between artmaking and lovemaking. As we see him, the painter is contemplating his model, but his mental conception is not made available to the viewer. The effect of the scene would be quite different if the model were already posed, as she is in Saint-Aubin's *The Private Academy* (figure 41) or Fragonard's *The Lover Crowned* (figure 7). In both of these works the beholder is encouraged to see what the artist sees, and the obviously arranged character of the scene before the artist clearly suggests the broad outlines of his vision. In each case the artist is separated from the scene as an observer and recorder, and that distance allows the viewer to imagine more easily the scene as projected by the (represented) artist. The situation is very different in *The New Model.* In that work there is no indication of a posture arranged by the (represented) artist to match his vision, and he acts as a participant in the whole rather than as the recorder of a scene within the scene.

As the viewer is encouraged to wonder what the artist sees in the new model, he is also urged to invent the outcome of the encounter. At all levels this work insists on viewer participation; the beholder completes the forms loosely defined, closes the action begun in the scene (undressing the model), and adds a second narrative episode. *The New Model* leaves the dénouement of the encounter between artist and model in doubt. The painting itself, executed according to the aesthetics of the sketch, is at once finished and unfinished, and the subject depicted is complete as a vignette but inconclusive as as story. As in *The Progress of Love,* Fragonard reverses the usual narrative situation that shows a central point in the action and asks the audience either to remember or to fabricate the preliminary and subsequent scenes. The high point of the action in *The*

New Model occurs in the mind of beholder, who is enticed to imagine the outcome of the meeting by envisioning what scene he would paint on the blank canvas behind.

Although located in the background, the blank canvas is a constant object of the viewer's attention. We have already described how Fragonard organized the surface plane of the composition to harmonize with the oval format. Another pattern, however, moves back and forth into space, tying foreground figures to background canvas. The central gesture of the painter creates the illusion that space flows from background to foreground along his extended arm and maulstick, which are aimed diagonally forward, toward the model. From where the stick touches her, the women's arms form another line leading back to the canvas. The exterior lines of the composition also direct the viewer's attention: on the far left side the outline of the two women forms a series of curves rising from the model's extended arm to the chaperone's head; from there the (represented) painter draws the viewer's attention toward him across the blank space of the canvas. On the other side of the composition, the design moves the viewer from the attention-grabbing white rag, up the artist's arm to his head, and then back across that white expanse to the figures of model and chaperone.[19]

The blank canvas that the viewer must repeatedly scan is the real stroke of genius in *The New Model.* No other depiction of artist and model contains this significant actor. In representations of Apelles and Campaspe from Vasari to Meynier, the great Greek master has already sketched on his canvas the image of his beloved sitter. Baudouin's *The Modest Model* relies on the painter's nearly-completed image to make obvious the scene's meaning in its equivocality. This equivocal meaning makes its viewers concentrate on the image before them and causes them to wonder what story the artist is telling. The viewers' freedom is also limited because the setting is very particularized and detailed. Furnishings, room, dress, accoutrements are all spelled out, as is the comparison of the model and the figure of Venus for which she has posed. We might say viewers are encouraged to interpret the image that they see but not to imagine a new one. Fragonard's image again reverses the dynamic.

The subject that Fragonard has rendered is not equivocal; it is clearly an erotic encounter between artist and model heightened by the chaperone's actions. Yet the viewer is prompted to indulge his fantasy, to imagine another scene that can be projected on the canvas behind. The unspecific location, the lack of detailed furnishings and accoutrements, the effect of the forms bleeding off at the edges, all these suggest an indeterminate site that can easily be transformed or transferred by the viewer. The blank canvas here pertains as much to the imagination of the real viewer as to that of the depicted artist; it is the place where both can project another picture, a sequel to the episode in progress. Recall here the two analogies of imagination and canvas that we have already encountered. The first was made by Diderot who, when praising Fragonard's *Coresus* at the Salon of 1767, compared imaginative activity to phantoms projected on a *toile.* Another, made in conjunction with a discussion of enthusiasm, described imagination as the *toile* on which genius painted a representation.

But in *The New Model* what relation is proposed between the viewer and the artist represented in the painting, and between the viewer and the artist who made the representation? As we have noted, the blank canvas encourages the beholder's participation in the work; he sees in his fantasy the actions he would take if he were the represented painter. Through this process the viewer vicariously acts in two possible sequels to the represented scene: in one he takes up brush and palette to render his imaginings on the canvas, and in the other he seduces the desirable model. Yet while that untouched expanse of white encourages the viewer to identify with the represented artist, the painting's structure keeps maker and beholder distinct. We have seen how Fragonard denied the viewer access to the fictive painter's conception of the model by not constructing the whole as a scene within a scene. In addition, the composition does not suggest that the beholder occupy a vantage identical to that of the artist, a tactic used successfully in *The Lover Crowned.* In *The New Model* the painter is placed to the women's left and sees them from the side; his path of vision is indicated by the line of his maulstick. The implied viewer, on the other hand, sees the model from the front, as her breasts aimed at the audience suggest. He is thus positioned near to where the maulstick touches the young woman's skirt, and his path of vision is traced by the virtual line running through the women's arms and up to the canvas. This construction places the implied viewer in a position dependent on that of the painter; within the fictive world of the painting, the artist's gesture assigns the viewer his place as it touches and controls the model.

We referred above to the unnatural whiteness of the model and its association with the canvas behind. Her marmoreal body also suggests Pygmalion's animated statue and thereby both enhances the sense of amorous adventure and highlights the priority of the artist. In *The New Model,* however, the Pygmalion story is reversed, told from the opposite direction. We see the artist confronting the real object that inspired him rather than the art object that he fabricated. But each version of Pygmalion gives the artist three roles: that of creator, that of beholder, and that of lover. In the traditional telling Pygmalion becomes infatuated with his ideal only after he sees it complete in its sensuous, artful form. Fragonard's Pygmalion, however, is enamored with what his outer and inner eye beholds when he gazes on the young girl who inspires him. She ignites both his sexual ardor and his enthusiasm, which leads him to pick up brush and palette, to transform his idea into a work of art. Like the model who can be excited by his physical caresses, the canvas will come to life under his touch.

Between the real viewer and the artist who made *The New Model* there is also an unbalanced relationship.[20] Standing outside the painting, the real viewer vicariously becomes the maker by completing in his imagination what the artist's brush merely suggested. Yet the very emphasis on touch in *The New Model* fixes the beholder in a subservient role. Although he can imagine, he cannot literally apply the pigment; he can only touch the canvas with his eyes along the paths prescribed by the painter. Although the viewer has a large share in *The New Model,* the artist remains preeminent through his physical touch, the "authentic" mark that signifies his enthusiasm and enlivens his conception.

Several subjects and themes are located in Fragonard's *The New Model.* We see first the overt subject, an erotic encounter between artist and model. The handling of that overt subject leads us to three themes: the artist's imagining of a work of art, the artist's execution of his mental image, and the association of the erotic and aesthetic urges. The overt subject also leads to an unrepresented one, the scene the viewer fabricates in his imagination; and this unrepresented subject that varies from viewer to viewer and changes from viewing to viewing denies the painting closure. But in leaving the viewer free to construct his fantasy, *The New Model* also directs him toward certain subjects. From the clues in the painting it would be difficult, for example, to imagine a moral scene following the model's introduction and easy to conjure an explicitly sexual one.

This unrepresented subject brings us back to Diderot's *Modest Model.* For those who did not know Diderot's discussion, the pleasure of fantasy would have insured that Fragonard's painting was enjoyed. For those familiar with the critic's writings, there would be further pleasure from recalling first Greuze's request for a "decent" nude and then the philosopher's boast that he could imagine subjects suitable for painting. The imagined painting was, as we have already noted, embedded in a discussion about the ability of literary men, nonartists, to invent and order a composition that could be transferred from mind to canvas. In *The New*

Model Fragonard invites, or perhaps even challenges, the viewer to project his thought picture onto the *toile* left suggestively blank.

If Greuze asked Diderot for a situation where the nude could be represented with impunity, Fragonard leads his audience to fabricate an image that could not be represented without offending modesty. Even the upright philosopher's imagination would produce a less than decent representation under the influence of Fragonard's episode. But in a more serious vein, *The New Model* suggests the crucial difference between the painter and the most imaginative beholder. It is only the painter who touches the canvas, and it is the physical making that separates painting from both imagining and writing. A writer formulates words in his or her mind and anyone can, in theory, transcribe them. If the transcription is accurate, nothing is lost in having a second party actually put the words on paper. The same cannot be said of a painting (or more correctly, it would not have been said in the eighteenth century). No one can paint the contents of an imaginer's mind in such a way that the painting remains the work of the imaginer. The painting depends on and takes its value not only from the imaginative conception but also from the individual's touch. Although this concept has been challenged by modern artists, it had wide support throughout the eighteenth century.

Baudouin's *The Modest Model* mocked Diderot's cloaking of a nude in an "honorable" subject, but Fragonard's *The New Model* subtly reminded its audience of the difference between a thought painting and one executed with oils on canvas. The work demonstrates that ideas alone do not make pictures, and that the beholder, like the model, remains subservient to the artist. The viewer admires and even imaginatively completes the canvas, but he does not touch it.

Epilogue

Having pursued Fragonard's art from the Academy's public Salon, through the private pavilion of Louveciennes, and to the intimate spaces of the *amateur's* cabinet and boudoir, it is now possible to assess the distance traveled. Clearly the itinerary was carefully selected, the stops chosen because they represented both a range and continuity of Fragonard's achievements. Regretting that some favorite landmarks escaped from view, I have tried to suggest implicitly how others might profitably explore them. Strategies have been the central focus throughout, as this essay has investigated not only the meaning of Fragonard's works but also the process of locating that meaning. Looking back, I cannot locate a dividing line between where I was simply following the trail left by Fragonard and where my thinking was guided by issues central to contemporary artists and critics. I prefer to think that this essay has helped to clarify some of the junctures where the concerns of rococo artists and theorists cross those of their twentieth-century interpreters, and that in doing so it has allowed the paintings a place in both the past and present.

Among the points of intersection, several seem particularly significant because they are so closely related. Many of Fragonard's paintings demonstrate a concern for the relation between the beholder and the work of art.[1] From the action and response of the *Coresus* to the invitingly blank canvas of *The New Model,* beholding is represented and/or thematized in Fragonard's *oeuvre.* This fascination with the viewer is a particular case of a larger preoccupation with the play between nature and art, exemplified in his work as an exploration of the limits between the real and the fictive.[2] In terms of the beholder this play is evident when Fragonard layers out surrogate viewers in the *Coresus* or when he gives real beholders parts in the painted dramas of the Louveciennes panels. These boundaries are also tested through strategies that operate in terms of the motif represented: the blurring of a distinction between the imagined and the copied in the *portraits de fantaisie,* the uncovering of *pittoresque* paradox in *The Game of Horse and Rider* and *The Game of Hot Cockles,* the confounding of painted actors and painted representations in *The Progress of Love,* the use of *beau désordre* in *The Lock.* Finally, the opposition of the spontaneous and the calculated, most closely associated with the notion of touch, also restates the problem of the real and the fictive but this time focusing on the relation between the artist and his performance in making the painting.[3] Many of Fragonard's works exploit the contradictions of *facilité, négligence,* and *légèreté,* which are themselves related to the paradoxical imperative that art should hide art. In *The Young Artist* and *Inspiration* the painter draws an especially thin line between the courtier's *sprezzatura* and the enthusiasm of genius.

As Fragonard manipulates the boundaries between the real and the fictive, his artifice becomes increasingly apparent, and the viewer's attention flickers between the illusion and the fact of the illusion. The fictiveness of the paintings is also emphasized when they overtly call up other works and especially when they establish with those works a witty repartee. The *Coresus,* for example, invokes a tradition of academic paradigms; *La Guimard* stages an interaction between Rembrandt and Watteau; the four panels at Louveciennes talk to one another. Most impressive, however, are the *Portrait of Diderot* and *The New Model,* both of which appropriate the dialogue between another man's painting and the text associated with it. Through their active participation in the intertextuality of the visual arts, Fragonard's works not only locate themselves outside of the real but also subvert the notion that art is an imitation of nature.

The style in which Fragonard's paintings engineer the oscillation between the real and the fictive gives them their particularly rococo cast. I use style here not to define a collection of formal properties such as loose paint handling or pastel colors or serpentine contours but as a way to describe an attitude or approach towards art that can be extrapolated from the paintings. (Style is here attributed to the apparent artist, although in some cases it may also belong to the real artist.) Developed to please and delight the beholder, Fragonard's style was geared to the privileged elite, frequenters of salons, where all subjects from the most banal to the most exalted were discussed with *bon ton* and wit. The style discernible in his paintings (even in those with "somber" subjects) can be termed ironic, playful, self-referential, seductive, and, at times, erotic and deceptive. *The New Model* perhaps best exemplifies all these qualities.

In exploring Fragonard's *oeuvre* I have concentrated on the themes of art and eroticism, which can be found throughout the painting and writing of the eighteenth century. While considering the first of these, recall that the Enlightenment saw the proliferation of art theory, as well as the development of aesthetics and criticism. Art itself was an issue to be taken seriously, but this did not mean that all serious discussion about art had to be couched in a didactic or pedantic style. I cite as my most important example here not Diderot's *Salons* but his *Jacques le Fataliste,* a text that should be required reading for any study of the rococo. Other works of differing ideologies and differing genres also make the point: in France Cochin's *Les Misotechnites aux enfers;* in England, Sterne's *Tristam Shandy;* and, in the visual arts, Fragonard's *The New Model.*

Equally serious was the Enlightenment's preoccupation with sexuality, although one cannot pretend that Fragonard always (or even usually) investigated this issue in a spirit of intellectual inquiry. Nevertheless, several of Fragonard's paintings (for example, *The Progress of Love* and *The New Model*) explore the relationship between the aesthetic and the erotic impulse with intelligence and insight, and others (for example, *The Bathers* and the Detroit panels) tell much about how sexuality was encoded in symbolic gestures. The point is that whoever considers what is erotic and/or sexual as unworthy of serious attention ignores an area of the human condition that was then, and remains today, a central concern of religion, philosophy, natural science, politics, and law, as well as a subject for serious artists, wags, and pornographers.

Focused on particular themes and strategies, this investigation of Fragonard's painting has revealed an art that is intelligent and subtle—an art where subject and technique play together in a harmony based on opposition and contrast. But it has certainly not exhausted the meanings that can be found in Fragonard's work, for his rich and varied *oeuvre* will lend itself to exploration from other perspectives. I say this not to underestimate the value of the conclusions reached here but to propose that the art is as resonant and complex as the century in which it was made. This essay has done no more and no less than open the door to its complexity.

But what about Fragonard, how does he emerge in this picture? Is he a courtier, a genius, an academic? A money grubber, a professional artist, a raconteur? A brilliant improviser, a master of the lesser genres, a Gallic

Hercules failed? Although the artist known as Fragonard is both all of these and none of these, the historical figure must remain as inaccessible today as he was when the Goncourts wrote a hundred years ago. And this thought is liberating, for if we stop pursuing the man, we can begin interpreting the paintings.

Notes

Introduction

1. The designation *rococo* appeared in Etienne-Jean Delécluze, *Louis-David, son école et son temps* (Paris: Didier, 1855), 82. Delécluze, who had been a student of David, noted that the term was used in the master's atelier (in particular by the group Les Barbus led by Maurice Quai) to denigrate the painting produced during the reign of Louis XV, when Mme de Pompadour was an arbiter of taste.

2. For a discussion of the persistence of the rococo, see Carol Duncan, *The Pursuit of Pleasure: The Rococo Revival in French Romantic Art* (New York: Garland, 1976), 1–38.

3. Charles Blanc, *Histoire des peintres de toutes les écoles,* 14 vols. (Paris: Jules Renouard, 1861–76), 2:1–2.

4. Pierre-Marie Gault de Saint-Germain, *Les trois siécles de la peinture en France* (Paris: Chez Belin, 1808), 232–33. Gault de Saint-Germain (1754–1842), like other critics, was willing to change his mind if it seemed acceptable or profitable to do so. By 1819 when the rococo did not seem so morally dangerous, he stressed the positive rather than the negative qualities of Fragonard's work in his review of the Salon of that year. The artist's vices are "agréable" and his fantasies "charmant."

5. Gault de Saint-Germain, 232.

6. The full title and subtitle of Gault de Saint-Germain's work is as follows: *Les trois siècles de la peinture en France ou galerie des peintres Français depuis François Ier jusqu'au règne Napoléon empereur et roi* où l'on aperçoit l'influence des moeurs, de la politique et des réputations sur les progrès et la décadence de cet art.

7. Gault de Saint-Germain, xiii.

8. Gault de Saint-Germain, 200.

9. Alexandre Lenoir, "Fragonard, Nicholas," *Biographie universelle, ancienne et moderne,* 2nd edition, 45 vols. (Paris: Mme C. Desplaces, 1854–65), 14:601–602. Alexandre Lenoir was a painter and archeologist who tried to preserve French monuments during the revolution. During the Restoration he was named administrator of

the museum at Saint-Denis. Lenoir mistakenly listed the artist as Nicholas Fragonard, and in no edition of the *Biographie* is the error corrected, which is surprising given that Fragonard's son Alexandre-Evariste was a recognized artist who lived until 1850.

10. Lenoir, 601.

11. These obituaries are collected in Georges Wildenstein, *The Paintings of Fragonard,* trans. C. W. Chilton and Mrs. A. L. Kitson (London and New York: Phaidon, 1960), 38–39.

12. "On ne peut se dissimuler que les compositions licencieuses de ce peintre n'aient souvent effarouché la vertu et alarmé la pudeur. Sous ce rapport on dira: Fragonard est coupable, et l'on ne saurait approuver, même en admirant le peintre, le génie dont le résultat allume des passions dangereuses et tend à la corruption des moeurs." Lenoir, 601.

13. Winckelmann's connection with French artists is well documented. He was an intimate of the Casa Albani circle frequented by Vien, and he was read by David when the young artist was in Rome. His *Geschichte der Kunst des Altertums* was early translated into French.

14. Johan Joachim Winckelmann, *History of Ancient Art,* trans. G. Henry Lodge, 2 vols. (Boston, 1880), 2:154.

15. Winckelmann, 1:163 and 289–97.

16. Thomas Crow provides an extended, far-ranging, and subtle discussion of the various complex interactions of social attitudes, political position, and aesthetic theory in his *Painters and Public Life in Eighteenth-Century Paris* (London and New Haven: Yale University Press, 1985), especially 104–133. The account I give here is general and adapted to the larger purpose of analyzing the Fragonard biographies.

17. "Si les moeurs sont corrumpues, croyez-vous que le goût puisse rester pur? Non, non, cela ne se peut; et si vous le croyez, c'est que vous ignorez l'effet de la vertu sur les beaux-arts . . . O richesse, mesure de tout mérite! ô luxe funeste, enfant de la richesse! tu détruis tout." Denis Diderot, "Salon de 1767," in *Salons,* ed. Jean Seznec and Jean Adhémar, 4 vols. (Oxford: Oxford University Press, 1963), 3:124.

18. Rousseau described the arts as "étendent des guirlandes de fleurs sur les chaînes de fer dont ils sont chargés, étouffent en eux le sentiment de cette liberté originelle pour laquelle ils sembloient être nés, leur font aimer leur esclavage & en forment ce qu'on appelle des Peuples policés." Jean-Jacques Rousseau, *Discours sur les sciences et les arts,* intro. G. Havens (New York and London: Oxford University Press, 1946), 101–2.

19. Rousseau, 103–9. See also Philip Robinson, *Jean-Jacques Rousseau's Doctrine of the Arts* (Berne and New York: Peter Lang, 1984), 75–77.

20. Denis Diderot, *Essai sur la peinture* in *Oeuvres complètes de Diderot,* ed. J. Assézat, 20 vols. (Paris: Garnier frères, 1876), 10:502.

21. Diderot, "Salon de 1767," in *Salons,* 3:335. Diderot's discussion of mannerism was developed in his 1759 Salon criticism as a polemic against Boucher, a man who, according to Diderot, would end up spoiling everything about painting. For a discussion of this polemic, see Georges Brunel, "Boucher, Neveu de Rameau," in *Diderot et l'art de Boucher à David: Les Salons 1759–1781* (Paris: Editions de la Réunion des Musées Nationaux, 1984), 101–9.

22. Emmanuel Joseph Sieyès, *What is the Third Estate?,* trans. M. Blondel (New York and London: Praeger, 1963), 56–58. For attitudes toward the tax collectors, see Louis-Sébastien Mercier, *Memoirs of the Year Two Thousand,* 2 vols. (1772; reprint, New York: Garland, 1974), 2:175–76, and also Charles Pinot Duclos, *Considérations sur les moeurs de ce siècle* (1772; reprint, Cambridge: Cambridge University Press, 1939), 120–29.

23. Marigny, for example, wrote to Natoire of his former pupil's reception, "Le s[r] *Fragonard* vient d'être reçu à l'Académie avec une unanimité et un applaudissement dont il y a peu d'exemple." *Correspondance des directeurs de l'Académie de France à Rome,* ed. Anatole de Montaiglon and Jules Guiffrey, 21 vols. (Paris: N. Charavay, 1902), 12:77.

24. Diderot, "Salon de 1767," in *Salons,* 3:280.

25. Charles Collé, *Journal et mémoires,* 3 vols. (Paris: Firmin Didot frères, fils et cie., 1868), 3:155.

26. "M. *Fragonard,* ce jeune Artiste, qui avoit donné, il y a quatre ans, les plus grandes espérances pour le genre de l'histoire, dont les talens s'étoient peu développés au Sallon dernier, ne figure d'aucune façon à celui-ci. On prétend que l'appas du gain l'a détourné de la belle carriere où il étoit entré, & qu'au lieu de travailler pour la gloire & pour la postérité, il se contente de briller aujourd'hui dans les boudoirs & dans les garde-robes." *Mémoires secrets pour servir à l'histoire de la république des lettres en France depuis MDCCLXII jusqu'a nos jours ou journal d'un observateur,* 36 vols. (London: J. Adamson, 1780-89) 13:32–33.

27. Denis Diderot, *Pensées detachées,* in *L'Oeuvres,* 9:124.

28. La Font de Saint-Yenne, *Réflexions sur quelques causes de l'état présent de la peinture en France* (1747; reprint, Geneva: Slatkine, 1970), 22. Mercier believed that all such portraits should be banished from the Salon. "If the painter's brush must be in the pay of idle opulence, grimacing vanity, or insolent fatuity, at least let the portrait remain in the boudoir; do not let it affront the gaze of a public in a place where the nation resorts. It is unendurable to see hung on the same line the portrait of an illustrious soldier, of a man of genius, and that of a money grubber." Louis Sébastien Mercier, *The Picture of Paris,* trans. and intro. W. and E. Jackson (London: G. Routledge & Sons, 1929), 92.

29. Crow raises these issues in *Painters and Public Life,* 11–16.

30. This problem was discussed by Candace Clements, "Making Space for Secular Narrative in Early Eighteenth-Century France: Representations of the Marseilles Plague" (Paper delivered at the meetings of the American Society for Eighteenth-Century Studies, April, 1987).

31. For a discussion of the *littérateurs'* attitude toward commercial enterprise see Rémy Saisselin, *The Literary Enterprise in Eighteenth-Century France* (Detroit: Wayne State University Press, 1979), 73–74; 116–21; 137–65. He writes, for example, of Jean-Jacques Garnier who distinguished the role of the man of letters from that of the painter. The latter worked to acquire a fortune, but the former cultivated his mind and made himself useful to society through the disinterested pursuit of knowledge. The distinction is made between exercising a profession for profit and practicing it for its own sake. See also Duclos' discussion of the *gens de lettres* in *Considérations sur les moeurs,* 135–36.

32. George Levitine, *The Sculpture of Falconet* (Greenwich, Conn.: New York

Graphic Society, 1972), 16. Diderot parodied the sculptor's avarice in his *Rêve d'Alembert* of 1769.

33. Etienne Jean Delécluze, *Les beaux-arts dans les deux mondes en 1855* (Paris: Charpentier, 1856), 280.

34. Delécluze, *Louis-David,* 124.

35. Seymour Simches, *Le romantisme et le goût esthétique du XVIIIe siècle* (Paris: Presses Universitaires de France, 1964), 15. For general discussion of the rococo revival in the nineteenth century, see also Duncan, 30–76 and Philadelphia Museum of Art, *Second Empire: Art in France under Napoleon III* (Philadelphia: Philadelphia Museum of Art, 1978), 11–16.

36. Francis Haskell, *Rediscoveries in Art* (London: Phaidon Press, 1976), 62–64. In 1867 Thoré reported that the collector Walferdin owned two to three hundred paintings by Fragonard and seven to eight hundred drawings. Even if the estimate is greatly inflated, his collection was considerable.

37. Haskell, 62.

38. Duncan, 62; *Second Empire,* 12–14.

39. Albert de La Fizelière, "L'Art et les femmes en France. Madame de Pompadour," *Gazette des Beaux-Arts* 3 (1859): 129–52, 210–29, and 292–314. La Fizelière reviewed Salons and wrote critical articles for *L'Artiste, Journal de Paris, La Patrie, Le Courrier français.*

40. She allegedly wrote, "Mon plaisir n'est pas de contempler de l'or dans mes coffres, mais de le répandre." La Fizelière, 222.

41. In 1805 Emeric-David (1753–1837) addressed the Institut des Beaux-Arts on the question of how the arts influenced the commerce and richness of a nation. He believed that one glorified the arts by showing their useful connection with industry; and in an ironic reversal of Rousseau he wrote: ". . . les arts corrompent et dégradent le peuple qui les néglige, et qui en reçoit les produits du dehors; au lieu que celui qui crée et fabrique lui-même, exerce son activité, développe ses facultés intellectuelles, et trouve même dans les lumières et dans l'aisance qui se répandent parmi toutes les classes de citoyens, une cause de liberté; car jamais on ne régira que par des lois douces et modérées des hommes généralement éclairés et riches." Toussaint Bernard Emeric-David, "De l'influence des arts du dessin sur le commerce et la richesse des nations," *Le Cabinet de l'Amateur et de Antiquaire Revue* 1 (1842):166. Emeric-David, who was born in Aix-en-Provence, was an attorney there and inherited from his uncle the position of Imprimeur du Roi et du Parlement d'Aix. He met the painters David and Peyron while traveling in Rome and became interested in the arts. In 1791 Emeric-David went to Paris where he took up writing about the arts. His two foci were Greek sculpture and the influence of painting on industry. His other writings include two *éloges* (Poussin and Pajou) and a two-volume work on Jupiter and his representations.

42. *Second Empire,* 31.

43. Fragonard's works were shown at the Salon de la Correspondance. For a discussion of that enterprise, see Emile Bellier de la Chavignerie, *Les artistes français du XVIIIe siècle oubliés ou dedaignés* (Paris: J. Renouard, 1865).

44. "Non, imbéciles, non, crétins et goitreux que vous êtes, un livre ne fait pas de la soupe à la gélatine; –un roman n'est pas une paire de bottes sans couture; un sonnet, une seringue à jet continu; un drame n'est pas un chemin de fer. . . . On ne

se fait pas un bonnet de coton d'une métonymie, on ne chausse pas un comparaison en guise de pantoufle; on ne se peut servir d'une antithèse pour parapluie." Théophile Gautier, *Mademoiselle de Maupin,* intro. Geneviève van den Bogaert (Paris: Garnier-Flammarion, 1966), 42–43.

45. Working for money or commercial ends was also criticized (as it was in the eighteenth century) by social thinkers who argued for a socially useful art; if the arts and letters served only luxury they were agents of corruption. P. J. Proudhon, for example, criticized artists for thinking only about growing rich and railed against those writers who tainted the people with their second-rate novels.

46. Discussion of these ideas can be found in Duncan, 64–65 and 73–76; Simches, 18–20; and also in the following texts: Domna Stanton, *The Aristocrat as Art* (New York: Columbia University Press, 1980); Rémy Saisselin, *The Bourgeois and the Bibelot* (New Brunswick, New Jersey: Rutgers University Press, 1984). For specific discussions of Gautier, see R. Snell, *Théophile Gautier: A Romantic Critic of the Visual Arts* (Oxford: Oxford University Press, 1982); M. C. Spencer, *The Art Criticism of Théophile Gautier* (Geneva: Droz, 1969).

47. "Il est du monde, de la plus grande société, de la meilleure compagnie, des dîners du lundi de Mme Geoffrin. . . . Il est de cette agréable et *opéradique* société de M. de la Popelinière à sa maison de Passy. Il est de l'intime familiarité du ministre Orry. Il a les plus charmantes, les plus flatteuses relations, des liaisons de grands seigneurs, de littérateurs, de savants." Edmond and Jules de Goncourt, *L'Art du dix-huitième siècle* in *Oeuvres complètes,* 45 vols. (1854–1934; reprint, Geneva: Slatkine, 1985), 1/3:295.

48. Simches, 18–20.

49. Arsène Houssaye (1815–96) published novels, plays, poetry, history, and criticism of all the arts. He was several times director of the Comédie Française and also Inspector General of the Provincial Museums and Inspector General of the Fine Arts. For many years he was director of *L'Artiste.*

50. Arsène Houssaye, "La peinture au dix-huitième siècle," *L'Artiste* 2 (1844):135.

51. Friedrich-Melchior Grimm, *Correspondance littéraire, philosophique et critique par Grimm, Diderot, Raynal, Meister, etc.,* ed. M. Tourneux, 16 vols. (Paris: Garnier frères, 1879), 10:210.

52. Arsène Houssaye, *Men and Women of the Eighteenth Century,* 2 vols. (New York: Redfield, 1852), 2:280.

53. Arsène Houssaye, *Histoire de l'art français au dix-huitième siècle* (Paris: H. Plon, 1860), 325–30.

54. Houssaye, *Men and Women,* 2:252–53.

55. "à la surintendance de M. de Marigny, frère de madame de Pompadour . . . il éprouva tant de difficultés pour la vente et le paiement de son *Corésus,* qu'il renonça aux peintures de commande et aux bonnes grâces du monde officiel. La faveur du public s'offrait à lui et devait le dédommager largement de cette rupture." Blanc, 2:8. Charles Blanc (1813–82) was an engraver and art critic, a contributor to the *Courrier français* and to *L'Artiste,* as well as the founder of the *Gazette des Beaux-Arts.* He served as Directeur des Beaux-Arts after the revolution of 1848. In 1869 Blanc was elected to the Académie des Beaux-Arts and in 1876 to the Académie française.

56. See, for example, Blanc's comments on the compensation of thirty thousand

livres Fragonard received from Bergeret for a group of his drawings. Blanc wrote, "Ce chiffre considérable pour l'epoque donne une idée de la réputation de Fragonard." Blanc, 2:8. He also reported that Fragonard earned forty thousand livres per year and depicted him as a hardworking artist painting all week in his studio (or, as Blanc describes it, his *lanterne magique*) and on Sunday taking his family to the public parks (Blanc, 2:12).

57. Blanc, 2:4.

58. Blanc, 2:11–14.

59. Jean-Baptiste, Abbé Du Bos, *Réflexions critiques sur la poësie et sur la peinture,* 6th edition, 3 vols. (Paris: Pissot, 1755), 2:228–65. For Winckelmann's adherence to the idea see Winckelmann, 1:156–62.

60. Hippolyte Taine, *Philosophie de l'art,* 2 vols. (Paris: 1904), 2:117.

61. "Tout ainsi chez lui, sa palette, son imagination, sa fleur d'idées, de sentiments, de couleurs, vient du Midi; et ne dirait-on pas que toute sa peinture a été improvisée, sous l'azur du ciel, sur un chevalet posé dans un jardin, entouré du bonheur de l'air, de la respiration de l'été." Goncourts, 4/5:217.

62. Goncourts, 4/5:231.

63. "Disons donc que la Provence ensoleillée, terre natale de Fragonard, n'a pas été sans influence sur son tempérament d'artiste, et qu'il a dû puiser dans les entrailles du sol, cette entraînante gaieté, cette chaleur communicative si caractéristiques dans ses ouvrages." Baron Roger Portalis, *Honoré Fragonard. Sa vie et son oeuvre,* (Paris: J. Rothschild, 1889), 6. Portalis also expressed his conviction of the influence of geography: "Ainsi le pays d'origine d'un artiste influe incontestablement sur sa manière de sentir et de rendre, et souvent il lui doit son tempérament froid ou bouillant, minutieux ou large." Portalis, 5.

64. "Il était difficile aussi, à son exubérante nature, de se tenir dans la voie sérieuse. Sollicité par les amateurs de sujets galants, Fragonard ne faisait que suivre son penchant naturel en cédant à leurs désirs." Portalis, 56.

65. Portalis, 70.

66. Portalis, 59.

67. "Derrière le peintre, l'homme paraît à peine. Qu'en sait-on? Presque rien. Qu'a-t-il laissé? Que reste-t-il de lui dans les mémoires et les indiscrétions du temps? . . . Les notices, les journaux, les nécrologes se taisent sur le gracieux artiste qui a trouvé la gloire sans chercher le bruit." Goncourts, 4/5:249.

68. "Trop de documents, trop de faits, pèseraient, il nous semble, sur cette mémoire légère. . . . Que son existence flotte comme dans une de ses esquisses: le demi-jour sied à cette vie de poëte, et la personnalité de Fragonard est de celles qu'il plaît de voir, ainsi qu'une ombre heureuse, ayant un doigt sur la bouche." Goncourts, 4/5:249.

69. "C'est encore la nuit, une nuit de mystère d'orage, pesant sur des arbres noirs et des massifs aux parfums lourds. Un couple couronné de roses est lancé en avant. Le vent que fendit la course d'Atalante bat la gorge de la femme et repousse sa tunique. Elle et son compagnon n'ont encore qu'un pied posé sur la margelle de marbre du bassin, —le bassin de *La Fontaine d'Amour;* et, affamés tous deux, l'oeil brûlant, ils tendent la soif et le désir de leurs lèvres à la coupe enchantée que soutiennent des amours volants ou renversés dans la vasque, mêlant leurs mains, croisant leurs doigts, trempant leurs ailes au breuvage qu'ils offrent. De la fontaine, l'eau

tombe; du bassin, le nuage monte; et ce ne sont qu'amours, amours à demi perdus dans la nuée, amours à demi trempés de pluie, amours ruisselant de lumière, amours sur les dos desquels le ruisseau qui tombe et les ondes vaporeuses qui roulent, se brisent en cascades, en gouttelettes de perles!" Goncourts, 4/5:235.

70. Representations of lovers crowned with roses are ubiquitous in eighteenth-century painting. See Anne Betty Weinshenker, "The Lover Crowned in Eighteenth-Century French Art," *Studies in Eighteenth-Century Culture* 16 (1986):271–94. For a discussion of the meaning of roses and rose crowns, see Pierre Guiraud, *Dictionnaire historique, stylistique, rhétorique, étymologique de la littérature érotique* (Paris: Payot, 1978), 555.

71. The *Sacrifice of the Rose* (c. 1780; France: Private Collection) is another of those works. Again the decor is classical as Cupid, grown to a young man, ignites a pile of rose petals placed on an antique altar. A young woman, bare breasted and provocatively (un)covered by transparent drapery, swoons beside the altar, her head thrown back, her eyes rolled upward in an expression of ecstasy. The painting can be read as an allegory of virginity's loss. The rose is a traditional signifier of the female maidenhead; to "sacrifice on the altar of Venus" was to engage in sexual intercourse. Other objects signify the male and female genitalia. Cupid's quiver of arrows, shaped like an erect phallus, draws on the then-familiar association of the arrow with the male organ; and the crown of roses, here borne aloft by a putto, was a conventional sign of female sexuality.

72. Guiraud, 342. He records the following seventeenth-century proverb, "La femme a toujours une fontaine devant elle." On *eau de vie,* see Guiraud, 294. For Boucher's use of the fountain, see below.

73. In comparing the discussion of *The Fountain of Love* in Charles Blanc's assessment of Fragonard to that of the Goncourts, one sees why the advantage has been theirs. It is not that Blanc's analysis is clumsy but that it is far less engaging. He sees in the work a successful mixing of reality and symbol that makes the painting a poetic allusion. To achieve this end, Fragonard put the allegory into the action rather than onto the actors; he never imagined abstract ideas in terms of sterile figures hung with attributes. According to Blanc *The Fountain of Love* presents an allegory of passion painted "en traits de feu dans le mouvement que font les deux fiancés pour s'abreuver à la coupe fabuleuse qui enivre les sens et le coeur." Blanc, 2:11.

74. Wildenstein, viii.

75. Wildenstein, 1.

76. Wildenstein, 43.

77. Denys Sutton, *Fragonard* (Tokyo: Yomiuri Shimbun, 1980). This assessment of Fragonard seems curious given that elsewhere Sutton saw that the emphasis on the frivolous side of the eighteenth century stemming from the Goncourts was a handicap to the re-evaluation of eighteenth-century art. See Denys Sutton, "Frivolity and Reason," in Royal Academy of Arts, *France in the Eighteenth Century* (London: Royal Academy of Arts, 1968). This essay was reprinted in *Apollo* in 1987.

78. Pierre Rosenberg's recent catalogue of the Fragonard exhibition (published as this text was undergoing its final revisions) also maintains many of the nineteenth-century prejudices typical of the Goncourts. For an analysis of Pierre Rosenberg's book *Fragonard* (New York: Metropolitan Museum of Art and Harry Abrams, 1988), see my review in the *Art Journal* 47, Winter, 1988.

79. Kendall Walton, "Style and the Process and Products of Art," in *The Concept of Style,* ed. Berel Lang (Philadelphia: University of Pennsylvania Press, 1979), 60–63.

80. For a discussion of nineteenth-century notions about temperament, see Richard Shiff, *Cézanne and the End of Impressionism* (Chicago: University of Chicago Press, 1984), 29.

81. For the most recent restatement of the temperament argument, see Rosenberg, 224.

82. Eunice Williams, *The Drawings by Fragonard in North American Collections* (Washington, D.C.: National Gallery of Art, 1978), 21.

83. For the scope of works officially commissioned by the Bâtiments in the eighteenth century, see Fernand Engerand, *Inventaire des tableaux commandés et achetés par la Direction des Bâtiments du Roi 1709–1792* (Paris: Leroux, 1709).

84. Although much work is needed to assess fully the financial aspects of the trade, Crow opened the discussion in mention of the print trade throughout his *Painters and Public Life;* see, for example, 43–44.

85. During the eighteenth century, when the Academy upheld the value system of the genre hierarchy, buyers paid as much (or more) for the physical making of the work as for the intellectual labor. Two eighteenth-century documents evidence that paintings were valued on the mundane criterion of size. Writing to Marigny in 1765, Joseph Vernet explained that his charges descended from fifteen hundred to six hundred livres as the dimensions of the paintings decreased, and assured the Surintendant that he worked best on a large scale. "Lettre à M. de Marigny sur sa manière de travailler et le prix de ses tableaux," *Le Cabinet de l'Amateur et de l'Antiquaire Revue* 2 (1843):42–43. In a similar vein, a proposal presented to Marigny for regulating the cost of paintings bought by the Bâtiment estimated the value of portraits at one hundred fifty livres the square foot. "Projet d'une sorte de tarif pour régler le prix des tableaux relativement à leur grandeur, présenté à M. le marquis de Marigny, directeur et ordonnateur général des Bâtimens du Roy, Jardins, Arts, Académies et Manufactures Royales." in Henri Stein, "L'Art tarifé au XVIIIe siècle," *Nouvelles Archives de l'Art français,* 3rd series 4 (1888), 269–71. Another clause of the document, however, indicates that it was the literal touching of the artist that was of value. Studio copies brought, "according to the usual practice," half the sum of the original; those retouched by the master commanded a greater price.

86. Crow has considered the nature of the eighteenth-century Academy at great length in his *Painters and Public Life,* especially 1–44. For a discussion of the amateur's role in the Academy, see Louis-Antoine Olivier, "Curieux, Amateurs and Connoisseurs. Laymen in the Fine Arts in the Ancien Régime," (Ph.D. diss., Johns Hopkins University, 1976).

87. Robert Darnton, "The High Enlightenment and the Low Life Literature in Pre-Revolutionary France," *Past and Present* 51 (1971):85.

88. Boucher's financial status is outlined in Crow, 11. Some artists, for example, Jean-François de Troy, produced history paintings at a much faster rate. I thank Candace Clements for this information.

89. Cochin values it at this price because Fragonard is still young. An equal work by an established artist would bring, according to Cochin, thirty-six hundred livres, and, he holds, that still isn't a great sum. *Correspondance de M. Marigny avec*

Coypel, Lépécie, et Cochin, ed. M. Furcy-Raynaud in *Nouvelles Archives de l'Art français* 20 (1904), 28.

90. They were willing, however, to commission other works and asked for a companion piece to the *Coresus.* By August 1765 Fragonard had only received six hundred livres on the already completed painting and had to wait another year for a second installment. He seems not to have undertaken the second commission.

91. *Correspondance de M. Marigny,* 11.

92. *Correspondance de M. Marigny,* 27.

93. *Correspondance de M. Marigny,* 220, 221, 247. The records note, for example, that Fragonard neglected a commission for a decorative work at Versailles because he was too busy with his commission for Mme Du Barry.

94. *Correspondance des directeurs,* 11:333–34; 359; 377–78; and especially, 338–39.

95. This is not to say, however, that such amateurs were his only patrons; he found a lucrative market, for example, among the *fermiers généraux* who collected art, and he worked for the aristocracy (e.g., Mme Du Barry) and actresses (e.g., Mlle Guimard). Other important collectors who owned works by Fragonard include: Baillet de Saint-Julien, Vassal de Saint-Hubert, the Comte Du Barry, the Marquis de Veri, and Randon de Boisset. The academic amateur, the Comte de Brehan, copied in pastel two of Fragonard's *portraits de fantaisie.*

96. Louis Courajod, *Histoire de l'Ecole des Beaux-Arts au XVIIIe siècle. L'Ecole Royale des Elèves Protégés* (Paris: J. Rouam, 1874), 33–36.

97. The rules stated, for example, that the students were to dine with the professor who was to teach them history, geography, etc. Courajod, *Histoire de l'Ecole,* 21. Fragonard extended his stay at the Ecole Royale to benefit further from Carle Van Loo's lessons in color and composition.

98. Sutton, for example, argues in his "Frivolity and Reason," that there is much to whet the appetite about the history of eighteenth-century art, not least of which is the human side. He mentions the titillating aspects, the loves and seductions of de Troy, Greuze, Vincent, Prudhon, Labille-Guiard, and concludes that the careers of many artists are as colorful as the pages of Casanova.

99. I have chosen here survey texts written by art historians who have also made contributions to the field as specialists. I use these examples to demonstrate that even scholars who have produced excellent and informed studies of particular areas of art history retain traditional (and unsophisticated) prejudices about the rococo.

100. Horst de la Croix and Richard G. Tansey, *Gardener's Art Through the Ages* (New York: Harcourt Brace Jovanovich, 1986), 781.

101. Horst Janson, *The History of Art,* revised and expanded by Anthony F. Janson, 2 vols. (New York and Englewood Cliffs, N.J.: Abrams and Prentice-Hall, 1986), 2:556.

102. Frederick Hartt, *Art: A History of Painting, Sculpture, Architecture,* 2d edition, 2 vols. (New York and Englewood Cliffs, N.J.: Abrams and Prentice-Hall, 1985), 2:754.

103. See, for example, Winckelmann, *History,* 1:305.

104. This issue was recently taken up by several speakers (Patricia Crown, Jerrine Mitchell, Paula Radisich, Candace Clements, Brian Allen) at a symposium held at the University of Missouri on "Social Implications of the Rococo Style: Images of

Women" October, 1987. Patricia Crown also discussed this issue in "Anti-Rococo Criticism and Female Sexuality" (Paper delivered at the meetings of the American Society for Eighteenth-Century Studies, Williamsburg, Va., April, 1986).

105. Sutton, "Frivolity and Reason."

106. Henri Dorra, *Art in Perspective: A Brief History* (New York and Chicago: Harcourt Brace Jovanovich), 172.

107. E. Panofsky, *Studies in Iconology* (New York: Harper & Row, 1962), 3. This work was originally published by Oxford University Press in 1939. Panofsky himself did not uphold a form/content duality; in fact his theoretical position was quite the contrary. Yet this split, unfortunately implied in his essay, has affected the way many scholars approach iconography and meaning. For a discussion of this aspect of Panofsky's thinking, see Michael Ann Holly, "The Origin and Development of Erwin Panofsky's Theories of Art," (Ph.D. dissertation, Cornell University, 1981), 193ff.

108. There are also texts about English art in the eighteenth century that promote new methods and ask new questions. For example, Ronald Paulson, *Emblem and Expression: Meaning in English Art of the Eighteenth Century* (Cambridge, Mass.: Harvard University Press, 1975); John Barrell, *The Dark Side of Landscape: The Rural Poor in English Painting 1730–1840* (Cambridge: Cambridge University Press, 1980) and Ann Bermingham, *Landscape and Ideology: The English Rustic Tradition 1740–1860* (Berkeley: University of California Press, 1986).

Chapter One

1. Diderot, "Salon de 1765," in *Salons,* 2:200.

2. Beth Wright has recently suggested that a version of the subject held in the Musée des Beaux-Arts, Angers, is the piece that Fragonard presented to the Academy on March 30, 1765. Her evidence is unconvincing. From Wildenstein's *catalogue raisonné* she cites a quotation from Bergeret's sale of April, 1786 that reads: "[this] first conception led to the artist's admission to the Academy." The meaning of this brief excerpt taken out of context is not clear, and I am highly suspicious of implications in sales catalogues where the seller is trying to attract the highest price possible. Beth S. Wright, "New (Stage) Light on Fragonard's *Coresus,*" *Arts Magazine* 60 (Summer, 1986): 54–59. Arguing for the continued identification of the Louvre painting as that judged by the Academy are the clear statement in the *Mercure de France* (October, 1765) and the final comments of Diderot on the Louvre version: "Fragonard revient de Rome. *Coresus et Callirhoé* est son morceau de réception. Il le présenta il y a quelques mois à l'académie, qui reçut l'artiste par acclamation." Diderot, "Salon de 1765," in *Salons,* 2:200. See also the comments of Mariette in *Abecedario de P.J. Mariette et autres notes inédites de cet amateur sur les arts et les artistes,* ed. Philippe de Chennevières and Anatole de Montaiglon, 6 vols. (1851–60; reprint, Paris: F. de Nobele, 1966), 2:263.

3. See Introduction, note 23.

4. La Font de Saint-Yenne, *Réflexions sur quelque causes de l'état présent de la peinture en France* (1747; reprint, Geneva: Minkoff, 1970), 14.

5. The painting is indeed larger than the typical *morceau de réception.* Compare the following dimensions: Watteau, *The Embarkation for Cythera:* 129 × 194 cm.;

Boucher, *Renaldo and Armida:* 135 × 170 cm.; Chardin, *Le Buffet:* 194 × 129 cm.; Greuze, *Septimus Severus Rebuking Caracalla:* 124 × 160 cm.; Fragonard, *Coresus:* 309 × 400 cm. Donald Posner suggested to me that the large size might indicate that Fragonard knew from the start (or had been promised) that the government would buy the work for the Gobelins tapestry manufacture. If correct, Posner's suggestion might also account for Fragonard's disappointment at the government's failure to reward him promptly.

6. Dandré-Bardon, for example, wrote of Jouvenet ". . . qu'il a réussi à prêter à ses têtes de l'esprit, du caractere, de l'expression, & qu'il a exécuté avec la plus grande vigueur des compositions aussi sublimes que ragoûtantes." Michel Dandré-Bardon, *Traité de peinture* (1765; reprint, Geneva: Minkoff, 1972), 141.

7. Although narrative paintings that represented stories were textually based, artists could and did invent new subjects in making allegories. Those allegories, however, were usually based on established motifs understandable to a contemporary audience.

8. Charles-Nicolas Cochin, fils, "Du costume dans la peinture," in *Recueil de quelques pièces concernant les arts* (1757; reprint, Geneva: Minkoff, 1972), 8.

9. Pausanias, *Description of Greece,* trans. and commentary J. G. Frazer, 6 vols. (New York: Biblo & Tannen, 1965), 1:359. In the eighteenth-century French translation of Pausanius, the text most significant to Fragonard's work reads, ". . . mais il ne la vit pas plutôt, qu'oubliant son ressentiment et n'écoutant plus que son amour, il s'immola lui-même et mourut pour elle, laissant aux hommes un exemple mémorable de l'amour le plus constant et le plus infortuné que l'on eût encore vu parmi eux." *Pausanias ou Voyage Historique de la Grèce,* trans. M. Nicolas l'abbé Gedoyne, 4 vols. (Paris: Debarle, 1797), 3:208.

10. Two seventeenth-century Italian drawings (one attributed to Pirro Ligorio and the other to Luca Giordano) have been identified with this theme (see André Pigler, "Fragonard et l'art napolitain," *Gazette des Beaux-Arts,* 6th ser., 5 (1931):192–97). Still, there is no reason to suppose that French artists in the eighteenth century considered it a subject familiar to painting.

11. Fragonard probably selected the theme; when a companion piece was commissioned from him, it was for a subject of his choice. See Engerand, 195.

12. In discussing several paintings ordered by the king of Prussia, Grimm reported that the most difficult subject, the *Sacrifice of Iphigenia,* had been given to Carle Van Loo. What made it difficult was that it had been many times executed by artists, and it had a famous ancient precedent. Grimm, *Correspondance littéraire,* 3:181.

13. Moreover, at midcentury both amateurs and critics encouraged artists to find new subjects, as did the Comte de Caylus in his *Tableaux tirés de l'Iliade et de l'Odysée d'Homer et l'Eneide de Vergile* of 1757. For a discussion of the public's dismay at hackneyed subjects, see Crow, 12–13.

14. The 1733 four-volume edition that included plates and maps was the most popular. Gedoyn noted in his preface that the taste for voyages should make Pausanias' "truthful" account particularly interesting, and he reminded his readers that the Greek author described a flourishing country rather than a site of archeological ruins. Gedoyn's translation was reissued in 1794, 1796, and 1797.

15. Robert Isherwood, *Farce and Fantasy: Popular Entertainment in Eighteenth-Century Paris* (New York and Oxford: Oxford University Press, 1986), 65–66.

16. Wright discusses this problem in "New Stage Light," 54–55.

17. La Fosse's tragedy was performed in Paris in 1703, and Destouches' opera in 1712, 1731, 1743, and 1773. It hardly seems likely that Fragonard harbored explicit memories of a stage performance for more than fifteen years; and even if he did, his *Coresus* stands beside, rather than duplicates, the two theatrical interpretations.

18. The appropriate scenes are as follows: Antoine de La Fosse, *Coresus et Callirhoé: tragédie,* act 5, scene 7; and André Cardinel Destouches, *Callirhoé: tragédie en musique* (libretto: Pierre-Charles Roy), act 5, scene 3. I thank Elizabeth Teviotdale for her thorough investigation of these texts.

19. The problem is a familiar one in eighteenth-century theoretical writings and is discussed by Caylus, Du Bos, Lessing, Harris, and Richardson. For a recent discussion of the issues, see David Wellbery, *Lessing's "Laocoön": Semiotics and Aesthetics in the Age of Reason* (Cambridge and New York: Cambridge University Press, 1984).

20. The idea of the favorable moment had a long history in French academic thinking and preceded by many years the formulations of eighteenth-century theorists (e.g., Caylus, Restout, Cochin). The idea came to France from Italy and carried the authority of Leonardo da Vinci, whose *Last Supper* (1495–98; Milan: Sta. Maria delle Grazie) was taken as a prime example of the doctrine. In his treatise on painting (which was the most frequently reprinted art treatise in eighteenth-century France) Leonardo wanted the moment chosen to be a psychological one, one that allowed for a variety of reactions to a single event. Leonardo da Vinci, *Treatise on Painting,* ed. and trans. A. Philip McMahon, 2 vols. (Princeton: Princeton University Press, 1956), 1:109–11.

21. In creating an expressive moment, the artist was instructed to present a general expression appropriate to the theme in all parts of the painting and to invent particular facial expressions that were both varied and appropriate for the figures described. Within their own tradition the French cited Poussin's *Death of Germanicus* as a paradigmatic example of the expressive moment chosen and rendered properly. See discussion below. Another example was *The Queens of Persia at the Feet of Alexander, or The Tent of Darius* (1660–61, Versailles) executed by Charles Le Brun. Using the work to illustrate the principles of painting, Félibien wrote that "il représente ce moment-là d'une maniére si sçavante, qu'il fait paroistre dans son Tableau une infinité de belles expressions, qui le rendent incomparable." André Félibien, *Recueil de descriptions de peintures et d'autres ouvrages faits pour le roy* (1689; reprint, Geneva: Minkoff, 1973), 32–33. La Font de Saint-Yenne in the eighteenth century admired Le Brun for his ability to display in a single work varied and nuanced expressions in agreement with the subject. See his *Réflexions,* 84–86.

22. Besides Van Loo's famous work, there were at least five versions of Iphigenia produced on the French stage between 1750 and 1765. For the popularity of the theme, see J. M. Glikson, *Iphigénie de la Grèce antique à l'Europe de Lumières* (Paris: Presses Universitaires de France, 1985).

23. The similarity between these two figures was pointed out by Eunice Williams, 64. Williams, however, took the borrowing as a simple "homage" to Van Loo. Fragonard alters the figure of Iphigenia in important ways. He bares the breast of his Callirhoe, both to make vulnerable the site where the dagger was to strike her and to establish a sexual contrast with the heavily draped Coresus and the uncovered male *génie* above. It can also be noted that one of the older priests who stands

amazed at Coresus' sacrifice might be Fragonard's adaptation of Calchas from Van Loo's drawing, now in the Metropolitan Museum of Art, New York. His expansive gesture reaching for the dagger has been cleverly metamorphosed into a dignified version of Le Brun's surprise.

24. For a listing of the various versions of the *Sacrifice of Iphigenia,* see Francis Dowley, "French Baroque Representations of the *Sacrifice of Iphigenia*" in *Festschrift Ulrich Middeldorf,* 2 vols. (Berlin: Walter de Gruyter and Co., 1968), 1:466–72.

25. *The Elder Pliny's Chapters on the History of Art,* trans. K. Jex-Blake, ed. E. Sellers (1967; reprint; Chicago: Ares, 1977), 117.

26. *Orations of Marcus Tullius Cicero,* trans. C. D. Yonge, 4 vols. (London: George Bell and Sons, 1879), 4:401–02.

27. *The Institutio Oratoria of Quintilian,* trans. H. E. Butler, 4 vols. (Cambridge, Mass.: Harvard University Press, 1963), 1:295.

28. Félibien barely hinted at this explanation when he noted that Poussin adapted Timanthes' device because it was the best way to express "douleur excessive." André Félibien, *Entretiens sur les vies et sur les ouvrages des plus excellens peintres anciens et modernes avec la vie des architectes* (1725; reprint, Farnsborough, Hants: Gregg Press, 1967), 221–22. Later Fuseli, who believed that the French did not understand the real motives of Timanthes, opted for the argument of propriety. He accused the French of ascribing "to impotence what was the forebearance of judgment." *The Life and Writings of Henry Fuseli, Esq. M.A. R.A.,* ed. John Knowles, 3 vols. (1831; reprint, New York: Kraus International Publishers, 1982), 2:45–59.

29. "Le Poussin a pû se servir de l'idée du Peintre Grec [Timanthes] qui avoit représenté Agamemnon la tête voilée au sacrifice d'Iphigénie, pour mieux donner à comprendre l'excès de la douleur du pere de la victime. Le Poussin a pu se servir de ce trait pour exprimer la même chose, en représentant Agrippine qui se cache le visage avec les mains dans le tableau de la mort de Germanicus." Du Bos, 2:78–79. Even as Du Bos is articulating the distinctions between painting and poetry, he cannot separate his discussion of the moment from the issue of appropriate expression. In comparing Poussin with Timanthes Du Bos was repeating an already established equation. Félibien had seen in the *Death of Germanicus* the different degrees of sorrow perfectly expressed. Poussin hid the face of Agrippina because it was difficult to understand the sorrow of a spouse. "C'est l'adresse de cet excellent Peintre, repartis-je, qui n'a pas crû pouvoir mieux exprimer une douleur excessive, qu'en couvrant le visage de cette Princesse, à l'imitation de cet ancien Peintre [Timanthes], que nous venons de nommer." *Entretiens,* 221–22.

30. "Il auroit volontiers fait comme le peintre Grec Timanthe, qui, dans le sacrifice d'Iphigénie ne pouvant exprimer la douleur de son père Agamemnon, lui couvrit le visage pour la laisser deviner au spectateur. C'est ainsi que doit agir un peintre qui est grand poëte: le Poussin en a fait autant dans la mort de Germanicus." A. J. Dézallier d'Argenville, *Abrégé de la vie des plus fameux peintres,* 4 vols. (1762; reprint; Geneva: Minkoff, 1972), 1:113 and repeated with variation 4:34.

31. The most extensive handling of Timanthes in French eighteenth-century writing can be found in Etienne Falconet, "Du tableau de Timanthe représentant le sacrifice d'Iphigénie," in *Oeuvres complètes,* 2 vols. (1808; reprint, Geneva: Slatkine, 1970), 1:159–83. Falconet argues that Timanthes copied the veiling strategy from a description in Euripides and so the device is not of his own invention. He calls it a

"trick" that conceals the most interesting part of the painting. In veiling Agamemnon, Timanthes, according to Falconet, unveiled his own ignorance. I have chosen to concentrate here on the Salon criticism from 1757, much of which runs parallel to Falconet's arguments.

32. For a discussion of the importance of expression, see J. M. Wilson, *The Painting of the Passions in Later Eighteenth-Century France* (New York: Garland, 1975). On the *prix d'expression,* see Institut de France, Académie des Beaux-Arts, "A propos d'un dessin de Cochin 'Le concours pour le prix d'expression,'" *Bulletin Semestriel* 8 (1928):153–55.

33. Elie Catherine Fréron, *L'Année littéraire* 5 (1757):337.

34. "Ce procedé si vanté par les Orateurs & par les Poëtes, & dont l'application peut être en effet fort utile à l'Eloquence & à la Poësie, me paroît dans la Peinture un contresens, &, si j'ose le dire, une absurdité. Chaque passion a son expression & son langage; mais les nuances en sont infinies, & ces nuances qui la plûpart sont inaccessibles à l'Eloquence & à la Poësie, parce que les langues sont plus propres à exprimer les vûes de l'esprit, qu'à rendre les mouvemens de l'ame, ont dans la Peinture des ressources & des moyens qu'aucun Artiste ne pourra jamais épuiser." Anne-Claude Philippe, Comte de Caylus, *Description d'un tableau représentant le Sacrifice d'Iphigénie peint par M. Carle Van Loo* (Paris: Chez Duchesne, 1757), 26–27. Caylus also contrasted to Timanthes' ploy the successful adaptation of Euripides' device in Le Brun's *Jephte.* Although there the father is represented with a mantle thrown around him so that he does not see his son's execution, he turns his face toward the spectator (Caylus, 27). There are two versions of the Iphigenia theme, one by Le Brun and the other by Coypel, that revised the literary device. Le Brun showed Agamemnon reeling backward in the act of veiling his eyes, presumably to demonstrate fear and love in conflict. Coypel's solution repeats that of Le Brun's *Jephte.* The veil is placed between father and daughter, but Agamemnon's face is turned toward the spectator. These works are illustrated by Dowley.

35. In depicting the *Death of Germanicus* Poussin added subsidiary characters who, unlike Agrippina, were not described in the text. Fragonard is perhaps emulating Poussin, whom Du Bos had praised for his ability to adapt a moment represented in the literary text to the demands of painting.

36. *Convenance* applied both to the general subject and to the individual objects portrayed. In discussing the relation between academic theory and Fragonard's work, Dandré-Bardon's *Traité de peinture* of 1765 is a good guide. It is a work that compiles the main points of French academic practice since Roger de Piles, and it is a how-to manual for artists that concentrates on the essential features of picture making. In his 1776 *Almanach historique et raisonné des architectes, peintres, sculpteurs, graveurs et ciseleurs,* the art dealer J.-B. LeBrun recommended Dandré-Bardon's treatise to all *amateurs.* (1776; reprint, Geneva: Minkoff, 1972), 15. Dandré-Bardon's writing is especially pertinent to Fragonard because the painter-theorist was a professor at the Ecole Royale when Fragonard was a student there. For his discussion of *convenance* in drawing, see Dandré-Bardon, 27.

37. "Tout marque la peine et l'effroi. . . . Ces deux prêtes âgés, dont les regards cruels ont dû se repaître si souvent de la vapeur du sang dont ils ont arrosé les autels, n'ont pu se refuser à la douleur, à la commisération, à l'effroi; ils plaignent le malheureux, ils souffrent, ils sont effrayés. Cette femme seule, appuyée contre une

des colonnes, saisie d'horreur et d'effroi, s'est retournée subitement; et cette autre qui avoit le dos contre une borne, s'est renversée en arrière, une de ses mains s'est portée sur ses yeux, et son autre bras semble repousser d'elle ce spectacle effrayant." Diderot, "Salon de 1765," in *Salons,* 2:194–95.

38. Du Bos, 1:24–33.

39. I thank Mary Pardo for pointing out to me the significance of Du Bos' remark vis-à-vis the proportional relations within the painting.

40. Bernadette Fort has discussed this aspect of Fragonard's painting in relation to Diderot's commentary. "Plato's Cave: Diderot's Art Criticism as Mimesis" (Paper delivered at the meetings of the American Society for Eighteenth-Century Studies, Williamsburg, Virginia, April, 1986).

41. Dandré-Bardon, 48.

42. Dandré-Bardon, 49.

43. Dandré-Bardon, 49.

44. "on y distingue à la première vue l'état d'évanouissement, la pâleur et les premières horreurs de la mort qui se peignent sur le visage de Coresus dans l'instant qu'il vient de se frapper." "Observations sur les ouvrages de peinture & de sculpture, etc. exposés au Louvre en 1765," *Mercure de France* (October, 1765), 165.

45. His eroticism is akin to that of seventeenth- and eighteenth-century French tragedy where antique subjects were mixed with subjects of the heart. Although Fragonard's painting does not follow either of the two contemporary dramatic versions of the Coresus myth, like them, and like Racine's *Iphigénie,* which was revived five times during the eighteenth century, it does concentrate on the human choices and reactions prompted by a tragic love. Racine often depicted sexual love as love that killed or sought to kill a rival or beloved. Beth Wright has recently remarked upon the strong Racinian tone in Fragonard's painting in "New (Stage) Light," 56–57.

46. Caroline Houser, *Dionysos and His Circle* (Cambridge, Mass.: Fogg Art Museum, Harvard University), 13. Giorgio Vasari, *The Lives of the Painters Sculptors and Architects,* ed. William Gaunt, 4 vols. (New York and London: Dutton, 1963), 4:114.

47. Diderot was one of the critics who found Callirhoe inexpressive; "Salon de 1765," in *Salons,* 2:196.

48. The display of male anatomy would have been important in a reception piece, since depiction of human anatomy, of the body in action, was central to history painting. Candace Clements has discussed male and female nude drawing in the French Academy in "The Academy and the Other: *Les Graces* and *Le Genre Galant,*" (Paper delivered at the symposium "Social Implications of the Rococo Style: Images of Women" (University of Missouri, Columbia, October, 1987).

49. These ideas are commonly expressed in eighteenth-century theoretical writings, articulated, for example, by both Caylus and Lessing. In his essay on painting Diderot argued that a complex system of being does not change all at once. On a face we are likely to find the present passion mingled with vestiges of the emotion that has passed; each moment in a story carries traces of the one before in the poses and actions of the characters. Diderot, *Essai sur la peinture,* in *Oeuvres,* 10:500.

50. Diderot identified the figure as Despair; however, the attributes of the *génie* as well as his function in the composition point to other interpretations.

51. The torch is the emblem of *Vengence* in H. Lacombe de Prezel, *Dictionnaire*

Iconologique, 2 vols. in 1 (1779; reprint, Geneva: Minkoff, 1972), 2:273. In Ripa *Furore* and *Ira* carry lighted torches. Cesare Ripa, *Iconologia,* intro. Erna Mandowsky (1603; reprint, Hildesheim: Georg Olms Verlag, 1970), 171 and 244. The dagger can be found as an emblem of both *Vengence* and *Colerique* in Charles-Nicolas Cochin, fils and H. F. Gravelot, *Iconologie par figures ou Traité complet des allegories emblemes etc.,* 4 vols. in 1 (reprint, Geneva: Minkoff, 1972), 1:64 and 1:67. See also *Vengence* in Lacombe de Prezel 2:273 and *Vendetta* in Ripa, 494. The torch when used in many eighteenth-century paintings was emblematic of love's ardor, a meaning also not inappropriate for the *Coresus.*

52. Dandré-Bardon, 39–40.

53. *Correspondance de M. Marigny avec Coypel, Lépécie et Cochin,* ed. Marc Furcy-Raynaud in *Nouvelles Archives de l'art français* 20 (1904), 28.

54. "On appelle un effet de lumière en peinture, ce que vous avez vu dans le tableau de *Corésus,* un mélange des ombres et de la lumière, vrai, fort et piquant: moment poétique qui vous arrête et vous étonne." Diderot, *Essai sur la peinture,* in *Oeuvres,* 10:474.

55. Diderot, "Salon de 1765," in *Salons,* 2:194.

56. Dandré-Bardon, 50.

57. Félibien, *Entretiens,* 92–100. Conceptualization belonged to theory or mind and referred not to the choice of the subject but to the imagining of the form in which the chosen subject should be represented. It included such tasks as envisioning the appropriate expressions, mentally arranging the figures in appropriate patterns (composing), and inventing the ideal types to represent the characters. Félibien associated execution with practice or hand; it was the physical act of transferring the mental conception to the canvas. It included ordonnance (the actual plotting of the imagined composition), drawing (the inscription of the imagined forms on the canvas), and color (the touching of the surface with pigment).

58. "La main n'est à la Peinture que ce que la parole est à la Poësie: Elles sont les Ministres de l'esprit & le canal par où les pensées se communiquent." Roger de Piles, *Cours de peinture par principes* (Paris: Jacques Estienne, 1708), 459.

59. Thomas Puttfarken, *Roger de Piles' Theory of Art* (New Haven and London: Yale University Press, 1985), 131.

60. Puttfarken, 40–41.

61. Dandré-Bardon, 22.

62. Puttfarken, 131. The quotation in French reads as follows: "Un des principaux objets de la liaison des Grouppes est de conduire l'oeil du Spectateur sur le Héros du sujet. Il convient que cette opération se fasse par une marche diagonale. *Les procédés par lignes horizontales, ou paralleles à la bordure du Tableau, produisent rarement des aspects pittoresques."* Dandré-Bardon, 48.

63. Fragonard's contemporaries also found the surface finished; when writing to secure some payment for the *Coresus* after it had been sent to the Gobelins, Cochin stressed to Marigny that the painting was "très fini." *Correspondance de M. Marigny,* 28.

64. Among other things, Dandré-Bardon argued that the touch must be adjusted "à la distance d'où la machine pittoresque doit être envisagée." Dandré-Bardon, 75.

65. In describing the kind of handling desirable for the history painter, Dandré-Bardon wrote that the touch should be precise, accurate, and varied according to the

subject, and that the finish should be generally "hardie." Explaining himself further, he concentrated on "hardiesse," or assurance, which presupposed a perfect knowledge of forms, tones, and effects. He related the concept to true facility or the ability to paint promptly but with precision. Facility did not imply that artists, at first touch, executed all the contours and forms perfectly. Citing sketches and cartoons of the old masters, Dandré-Bardon noted that indecision produced many contours thrown one over the other, but that "delicatesse" articulated one more clearly and strongly. The chosen contour was transferred to the finished work, and transferred in such a way that the sense of spontaneity associated with the initial knowing disorder of touches was maintained. Although a history painting was to be painted with precision, facility and assurance of handling were also necessary. Dandré-Bardon, 53.

66. For example, Charles Blanc calls it "une composition théâtrale," in *Histoire des peintres,* 2:6; and Fourcaud, describes the work as "comme une scène de théâtre," Louis de Fourcaud, "Honoré Fragonard," *Revue de l'art ancien et moderne* 21 (January-June, 1907): 98. A most interesting recent discussion, however, is that of Michael Fried, *Absorption and Theatricality: Genre and Beholder in the Age of Diderot* (Berkeley: University of California Press, 1980), 141–45.

67. *Aristotle's Poetics,* trans. S. H. Butcher, intro. Francis Fergusson (New York: Hill & Wang, Inc., 1961), 53–54.

68. See, for example, Du Bos, 1:386–88.

69. Fried, 100.

70. For a discussion of theater and illusion in the eighteenth century, see Marion Hobson, *The Object of Art: The Theory of Illusion in Eighteenth-Century France* (New York and Cambridge: Cambridge University Press, 1982), 139–80.

71. "Voilà le théâtre d'une des plus terribles et des plus touchantes représentations qui se soient exécutées sur la toile de la caverne, pendant ma vision." Diderot, "Salon de 1765," in *Salons,* 2:192. Fort discusses the theatrical presentation in "Plato's Cave."

72. "Quoi qu'ils en disent, croyez que vous avez fait un beau rêve, et Fragonard un beau tableau." Diderot, "Salon de 1765," in *Salons,* 2:197.

73. For a discussion of these effects in eighteenth-century painting, see Ellen Landau, " 'A Fairytale Circumstance': The Influence of Stage Design on the Work of François Boucher," *Bulletin of the Cleveland Museum of Art* 70 (November, 1983): 360–78.

74. Hobson, 42–56.

75. In the following discussion I am indebted to Bernadette Fort, who has written insightfully on Diderot's art criticism (and, in particular, about his essay on the *Coresus*) and with whom I have had many stimulating conversations.

76. Bernadette Fort, "Plato's Cave."

77. Michael Fried has discussed the relation between the spectator and the painting in Diderot's critique, Fried, 141–44. See also Fort's discussion of the spectator in "Plato's Cave."

78. Diderot, "Salon de 1765," in *Salons,* 2:195.

79. In the commentary Diderot also describes how some prisoners turn their heads to see those making the illusions. "Salon de 1765," in *Salons,* 2:189.

80. Plato, *The Republic,* intro. Charles Bakewell (New York: Charles Scribner's Sons, 1928), 273–78.

81. Fort, "Plato's Cave."

82. "Convenez donc que ce modèle est purement idéal, et qu'il n'est emprunté directement d'aucune image individuelle de Nature. . . Convenez donc que, quand vous faites beau, vous ne faites rien de ce qui est, rien même de ce qui puisse être." Diderot, "Salon de 1767," in *Salons,* 3:59.

83. "Convenez donc que la différence du portraitiste et de vous, homme de génie, consiste essentiellement en ce que le portraitiste rend fidèlement Nature comme elle est, et se fixe par goût au troisième rang, et que vous qui cherchez la vérité, le premier modèle, votre effort continu est de vous élever au second. . . ." Diderot, "Salon de 1767," in *Salons,* 3:59.

84. T. Todorov, *Theory of the Symbol,* trans. Catherine Porter (Ithaca, New York: Cornell University Press, 1982), 111–28.

85. Diderot, "Salon de 1765," in *Salons,* 2:197.

86. "Dans la caverne, vous n'avez vu que les simulacres des êtres, et Fragonard, sur sa toile, ne vous en auroit montré non plus que les simulacres." Diderot, "Salon de 1765," in *Salons,* 2:195.

87. If Diderot's commentary on Fragonard's *Coresus* is structured to emphasize the creation of illusions, the critic also highlighted the artist's chiaroscuro effects. The two are not unrelated. Barbara Stafford has recently demonstrated how eighteenth-century art theorists, concerned with picturing the fictive and the unreal, developed a sequence of cognate terms that linked darkness, shadow, obscurity, illusion, and apparition. Stafford stresses the more negative connotations of these terms—their association with wickedness, gloom, and the evil empire—which she traces to a Platonic ancestry. Barbara Maria Stafford, "From 'Brilliant Ideas' to 'Fitful Thoughts' Conjecturing the Unseen in Late Eighteenth-Century Art," *Zeitshrift fur Kunstgeschichte* 48 (1985), 329–63. Although the condemnation of illusion as devil's work has been substantially drained from Diderot's text, the critic still plays with that tradition. For example, he characterizes the *génie* as infernal, notes how he is accompanied by a "vapeur obscure," and describes a "vapeur noire" which, drawing together the main group adds "un terrible étonnant" to the scene. He also notes the lugubrious effects of the chiaroscuro and characterizes Fragonard's painted illusions as phantoms like "those of the night," phantoms that disappear at the "first sign of the cross."

88. "C'est un beau rêve que vous avez fait; c'est un beau rêve qu'il a peint." Diderot, "Salon de 1765," in *Salons,* 2:195.

89. ". . . croyez que vous avez fait un beau rêve, et Fragonard un beau tableau." Diderot, "Salon de 1765," in *Salons,* 2:197.

90. For a more scientific discussion of the role played by the imagination in dreaming, see "Songe," *Encyclopédie ou dictionnaire raisonné des sciences, des arts et des métiers,* 25 vols. (Paris: Buiasson, David l'aîné, Le Breton, Durand, 1751–65), 15:354–55.

91. But because the creative process was identical at this crucial stage, the poet could become the painter's critic. Although he could not execute a painting, he believed himself able to say how the painting should have been conceived. Thus Diderot fabricated his word pictures that so often stood in contrast to the paintings that he was describing. Those word paintings, unlike descriptions of extant works, referred to no physical object; they signified only the idea of the writer. Diderot suggests the equivalence at this level when, after describing several scenes to Grimm, he

remarks that "Ah! si j'étois peintre. J'ai encore tous ces visages-là présens à mon esprit." Diderot, "Salon de 1765," in *Salons,* 2:191.

92. I draw a distinction here between a painting such as the *Coresus* that was primarily planned for public display and a painting such as his *Groups of Children in the Sky,* which was exhibited at the next Salon but was conceived as a sketch for a decorative ceiling painting.

Chapter Two

1. Mme Du Barry was installed at court as the *maîtresse en titre* to Louis XV in 1769 and retained her position until his death in 1774.

2. Speculation as to why these panels were rejected ranges from a change of taste (Franklin M. Biebel, "Fragonard and Mme Du Barry," *Gazette des Beaux-Arts,* 6th series, 56 [October, 1960], 207–26) to a desire for a more moral and politically correct representation of love (Lynne Kirby, "Fragonard's *The Pursuit of Love,*" *Rutgers Art Review,* 3 [January, 1982]: 58–79).

3. Fragonard's relative Maubert sold the decorative series (the original four panels and those added later) *in situ* to his cousin Malvilan, who in 1806 tried to sell them to Fragonard's son. The latter refused them. They were suggested to the Louvre as early as 1857, but the institution lacked the funds necessary for the purchase. The works remained in the Midi until 1898, when they were acquired by J. Pierpont Morgan, from whom Henry Clay Frick purchased them in 1915. Wildenstein, 268.

4. Léon-Marius Lagrange (1828–68) was an art critic from Marseilles who wrote for the *Gazette des Beaux-Arts,* the *Archives de l'art français* and the *Correspondant.* His most important works were monographs on two major artists of Provence, Joseph Vernet and Pierre Puget.

5. "Au premier acte, la rencontre des fillettes et du galant devant une fontaine d'amour; en dessus de porte, le dieu Cupidon poursuit une colombe. Au deuxième acte, il l'a prise, il l'étreint sans pitié; et en effet, les amants se rejoignent au pied d'une statue de Psyché et échangent sur un autel le serment d'amour assaisonné d'un baiser. Le troisième acte nous montre la terrasse où Chloé rêvait, à la molle clarté de la lune, lorsque Tircis, bouillant d'audace, apparaît au sommet d'une échelle; et le petit dieu malin savoure le parfum des roses épanouies. Le quatrième acte n'est qu'un monologue de la tendre victime, tombée pâmée sur les marches d'un monument dédié à l'Amour; et dans les airs, l'enfant terrible cabriole, une marotte à la main. Enfin, avec le cinquième acte, le dénoûment: au sein d'un bosquet plus fleuri, plus riant que jamais, sur une terrasse garnie d'orangers *en caisse,* et jonchée de guitares, de romances, de cahiers de musique, l'amant heureux, agenouillé devant elle, reçoit des ses mains une couronne de fleurs. L'ami Frago, assis dans un coin, son portefeuille ouvert, son crayon préparé, crie au groupe: "Ne bougeons plus!" Le tableau final, au-dessus de la cheminée, représente l'Amour-Hymen, un flambeau de chaque main, au milieu d'un ciel embrasé où se jouent des Cupidons sans emploi." Léon Lagrange, "Notes de voyage, 'Les Fragonards de Grasse'" *Gazette des Beaux-Arts,* 1st series, 23 (August, 1867):190.

6. At first the order was reconstructed by interpreters who, like the Baron Portalis, examined the events depicted in the panels and from them determined a story with what they considered a logical progression. Portalis' solution remained the stan-

dard one for many years: *The Meeting, The Pursuit, The Love Letters, The Lover Crowned.* He claimed to have seen the series at Grasse, and he allegedly based his ordering on the placement there. Portalis, 100–101. Two authors, Reau and Biebel, presented another order of reading. For no apparent reason they assumed that *The Pursuit* preceded *The Meeting.* See Louis Reau, *Fragonard, sa vie et son oeuvre* (Paris: Elsevier, 1956), 74–77, 152; and also Biebel, 210.

7. Willibald Sauerländer, "Über die Ursprüngliche Reihenfolge von Fragonard's *Amours des Bergers," Münchner Jahrbuch der Bildenden Kunst* 19 (1968):138–39.

8. Sauerländer, 142–51.

9. Donald Posner, "The True Path of Fragonard's 'Progress of Love,'" *Burlington Magazine* 114 (August, 1972), 529. However, the design of the pavilion at Louveciennes refers to the Petit Trianon built for Mme de Pompadour.

10. Posner, 530.

11. Recently two interpretations of the panels have made gestures toward reading them in other ways. Kirby, for example, suggested that they constituted a narrative without closure but did not reject the idea of a determined narrative sequence: "While an ordered sequence may well have been intended for the series, what is more important is that for a particular type of spectator, the cycle would not end." Kirby, 78. Another deviation from the traditional readings was presented briefly by Marianne Roland-Michel in "Eighteenth-Century Decorative Painting: Some False Assumptions," *British Journal of Eighteenth-Century Studies* 2 (1979), 1–36. There she offered a placement of the panels different from that of Sauerländer, switching *The Lover Crowned* and *The Surprise.* For reasons that will become clear in my analysis, I find the placement she devises unconvincing. Her analysis of the compositional similarities between *The Surprise* and *The Love Letters* and between *The Pursuit* and *The Lover Crowned* seems particularly tenuous. However, her suggestion that perhaps we are dealing with two sets of love allegories, each with a beginning and a conclusion, marks a real break from the traditional readings. Unfortunately, Roland-Michel did not develop this suggestion into an analysis of the series but concluded, "What matters to us now is to show that, when we admire the paintings in their salon at the Frick, we probably do not fully understand their significance, and that at least a part of their original meaning escapes us; although this in no way detracts from the purely visual pleasure we experience in their presence." Roland-Michel, 31.

12. These two works were part of a group of four that formed a sequence. Diderot discussed the narrative in his "Salon de 1765," in *Salons,* 2:80–81.

13. For a discussion of these entries, see Biebel, 214.

14. *Mémoires secrets,* 24:161.

15. Blanc, 2:9; Goncourts, *L'art du dix-huitième siècle* in *Oeuvres,* vol. 4/5, 248.

16. Wildenstein, 268.

17. Duperron, *Discours sur la peinture et sur l'architecture* (1758; reprint, Geneva: Minkoff, 1973), 59.

18. "S'agit-il de petits Appartemens, lieux où se plaît l'Amour? C'est là que le pinceau doit épuiser tout ce que la volupté a d'attrayant; des Mirthes, des Roses, des Boccages, des Champs tapissés de verdure, des Campagnes où brille l'éclat des plus vives couleurs, doivent faire l'ornement de ces sortes de Pièces. Là, peut s'offrir le spectacle agréable & l'aménité d'un Jardin que l'art a pris soin d'orner; ici c'est le

Tableau des charmes ingénues & de l'aimable désordre de la Nature." Duperron, 60–61.

I should note here that contemporary discussions of the decoration at Louveciennes are rare. In the *Mémoires secrets* (24:161) it was noted that the ceiling of the salon across from the one decorated by Fragonard showed the "plaisirs de la campagne," which the author called a "ruris amor." The paintings by Fragonard, then incomplete, were termed, "amours de bergers," and the salon is cited as having a "ciel vague." The presence of sculpture is mentioned, but the works are not identified. A later nineteenth-century description by Dulaure names the sculpture as by Vassé, "l'un représente l'Amour et l'autre la Fourberie, tenant un masque à la main." (Michel Gallet, *Claude Nicholas Ledoux* (Paris: Picard, 1980), 265). The Goncourts noted that tapestries were hung in the Salon du Roi; they were completed in 1774 and included a *Neptune and Anymone* after Van Loo, the *Rape of Europa* after Pierre, and a *Venus and Vulcan* after Boucher. These loves of the gods were fairly soon replaced by panels commissioned from the landscape painter Vernet. The dining room, according to the Goncourts, was mirrored. [Edmond and Jules de Goncourt, *Madame Du Barry* (London: John Long, 1914)]. Finally, we should note that the constant changing of the decorations at Louveciennes seems to indicate that there was no predetermined program for either the entire building or for any one room within it. All the decorations, moreover, can be considered as appropriate to the function of the pavilion.

19. *Mémoires secrets,* 24:160.

20. Witness the similarity in scale, proportion, placement (in the garden), and exterior articulation of the facade.

21. "Le pavillon est un carré sur cinq croisées de face en tout sens, il est situé sur une hauteur considérable, d'où l'on jouit d'une des vues les plus étendues & les plus riches qu'on puisse avoir." *Mémoires secrets,* 24:160.

22. Sauerländer, 136–37. Sieges of the castle of love occured in thirteenth and fourteenth centuries, and the motif appears in Chrétien de Troyes' *Cligès.* When depicted in art, these sieges usually involved more than one couple and were associated with jousting scenes. Clifton C. Olds, Ralph G. Williams, and William R. Levin, *Images of Love and Death in Late Medieval and Renaissance Art* (Ann Arbor, Michigan: University of Michigan Press, 1975), 106–107.

23. As, for example, in the *Roman de la rose,* begun by Guillaume de Lorris about 1237 and completed and expanded by Jean de Meun about 1277. The rose was a well-used symbol in both the elite and popular culture of the eighteenth century; Piron's *La Rose ou les jardins de l'Hymen,* performed March 5, 1744, was a farce about the loss of virginity.

24. Their role in the composition is similar; the young girls are also attending amorini.

25. Weinshenker, 271–72.

26. On the letter and the epistolary novel, see Janet Altman, *Epistolarity: Approaches to a Form* (Columbus, Ohio: Ohio State University Press, 1982). I especially thank Dena Goodman for her comments on the letter as a representation of spontaneity.

27. I thank Dena Goodman for her careful critical reading of this chapter, and

for suggesting to me the appropriateness of casting the argument in terms of the narrated and the unnarrated.

28. Note that the roles of narrator and surrogate viewer are different and do not necessarily coincide. For example, imagine the sketching artist in *The Lover Crowned* placed on the top step next to the boxed orange tree, with two children seated in the grass in the right corner of the canvas. In that case the artist would still be the narrator (by virtue of the arrangement of the inner scene, etc.), but the children would be the surrogate viewers, and the story would be received from their point of view.

29. This topic is the focus for Marion Hobson's discussion of "soft illusionism" in the eighteenth century: see *The Object of Art,* 31–45. For an essay that analyzes the relation between art and nature in Hubert Robert's painting, see Paula Rea Radisich, "Hubert Robert's Paris: Truth, Artifice and Spectacle," *Studies on Voltaire and the Eighteenth Century* 245 (1986), 501–18.

30. For a compilation of the definitions of *pittoresque,* see Claude-Henri Watelet and Pierre Charles Lévèsque, "Pittoresque," in *Dictionnaire des arts de peinture, sculpture et gravure,* 5 vols. (Paris: Chez Prault, 1792), 5:73–76.

31. "qui est distribuée de maniere à mettre les attitudes naturelles dans leur aspect le plus agréable sans leur rien faire perdre de la justesse de l'action; à les grouper de telle façon qu'elles donnent lieu sans affectation à produire de grands effects de lumières & d'ombres. . . ." Charles-Nicolas Cochin, fils, "Discours sur la connaissance des arts fondés sur le dessin et particulièrement de la peinture," in *Recueil,* 179–80.

32. These issues are the subject of David Funt, *Diderot and the Aesthetics of the Enlightenment,* Diderot Studies, 11 (1968).

33. "Les vieux arbres dont le tronc est tortueux & rongé par le tems, dont l'écorce souvent interrompue est profondément sillonnée, dont les branches sont noueuses, dont pittoresque." Watelet and Lévèsque, "Pittoresque," *Dictionnaire,* 5:183.

34. Claude-Henri Watelet, *Essai sur les jardins* (1774; reprint, Geneva: Minkoff, 1972), 55, and Watelet and Lévèsque, "Decorateur," *Dictionnaire,* 1:558–60. Article signed by Watelet.

35. Watelet, *Essai,* 55.

36. Watelet, *Essai,* 61.

37. Jean-Marie Morel, *Théorie des jardins* (1776; reprint, Geneva: Minkoff, 1973), 379.

38. Watelet, *Essai,* 66.

39. Charles-Nicolas Cochin, fils, *Voyage d'Italie ou Recueil de notes sur les ouvrages de peinture et de sculpture, qu'on voit dans les principales villes d'Italie* (1758; reprint, Geneva: Minkoff, 1972). Admiring the view at Ronciglione, Cochin referred to houses with a *pittoresque* character, views agreeable to draw, and a scene forming a "machine fort pittoresque" (p. 64). At Marino he again saw views that were "très-pittoresques à dessiner" (p. 41), and at Narni he commented, "Il y a des hameaux et des maisons de plaisance, placés sur le rampant des montagnes qui presentent des aspects très beaux pour la peinture" (p. 36). The *pittoresque* was defined so that potentially every educated and sensitive viewer could be an artist; not only could beholders recognize what nature had made *pittoresque,* but they could also create the *pit-*

toresque through point of view. Knowing the principles of art, spectators could search the right vantage point for viewing a scene, or if no suitable one could be found, they could simply imagine any view as if it were *pittoresque.* A vivid imagination, an extended looking, a memory conditioned by such exercise, a rough sketch, a written description, a discussion with a companion: these would help the spectator recall the view and enjoy the conceptualized painting when far from the site.

40. Among the artists who drew this site were Hubert Robert (1758), Louis Chaix (1773), and F. A. Vincent (1773).

41. Not only did he lease the Villa d'Este when in Italy, but before his arrival there he sketched at the grounds of Watelet's new estate, Moulin Joli. Once an abandoned site, Moulin Joli had been discovered while Watelet was on a sketching tour. He was to make there one of the first gardens in France to be recognized as *pittoresque.* Fragonard's association with Cochin, Saint-Non, Watelet, and the landscape painter-gardener Hubert Robert places him firmly in the circle of those interested in the *pittoresque* in painting, landscape, and gardening. See Dora Wiebenson, *The Picturesque Garden in France* (Princeton: Princeton University Press, 1978), 19–21, and also Louis Guimbaud, *Saint-Non et Fragonard d'après des documents inédits* (Paris: Le Goupy, 1928), 140.

42. On the iconography of the games, see Colin Eisler, *Paintings from the Samuel H. Kress Collection: European Schools* (Oxford: Phaidon Press, 1977), 331–32.

43. For a discussion of a parallel strategy in Dutch seventeenth-century art, see David Smith, "Irony and Civility: Notes on the Convergence of Genre and Portraiture in Seventeenth-Century Dutch Painting," *Art Bulletin* 69 (September, 1987), 408–10.

44. This decision may have been made partly because the works were to be placed in a public room of a private pavilion rather than in the boudoir. Perhaps a certain amount of propriety had to be observed because the property would be associated not only with Mme Du Barry but also with the king.

45. See below, chap. 3.

46. For a more extended discussion of Fragonard's relation to the literary representation of lovemaking, see Jerrine Mitchell, "Le Commerce des Femmes: Sexuality and Sociability in Eighteenth-Century French Representation" (Paper delivered at the symposium: "Social Implications of the Rococo Style: Images of Women," University of Missouri, October, 1987). For a discussion of the representation of love in French eighteenth-century novels, see Philip Stewart, *Le Masque et la parole* (Paris: Librarie José Corti, 1973).

47. The use of these conventions in seventeenth-century Dutch art is discussed by Smith, 416–23.

48. For a related discussion of earlier paintings that represented courtly love in the garden, see Elise Goodman, "Rubens's *Conversatie à la Mode:* Garden of Leisure, Fashion and Gallantry," *Art Bulletin* 64 (June, 1982):247–59.

49. E. Jane Burns, "The Man Behind the Lady in Troubadour Lyric," *Romance Notes* 25 (Spring, 1985):257.

50. In his insightful discussion of Watteau, Crow has analyzed the representation of social divisions in the *fêtes galantes.* The costume and the disguise are conceived as signs of aristocracy. See Crow, 63–64.

51. For an expanded discussion of the aristocratic ideal in relation to this series, see Kirby, 58–79.

52. Michael Fried has suggested that because the viewer of Fragonard's *Progress of Love* stands surrounded by the four scenes, the whole seems a literalization of the fiction that the spectator enters the painting. See *Absorption and Theatricality,* 141.

53. Watelet, *Essai,* 55.

54. Morel, 376–77.

Chapter Three

1. In addition to these panels there is another group of works representing the seasons by Fragonard: the overdoors executed for the Hôtel Matignon, Paris (c. 1750–56; *Spring, Summer,* and *Autumn* are still in situ, *Winter* is in Los Angeles: Los Angeles County Museum). There the seasons are personified in terms of a pastoral "mother" and two children, but the iconography of the panels varies from the Detroit series, mixing scenes that make reference to the fertility of the earth, with those that show typical seasonal activities.

2. *Spring* reveals a courting couple in a garden bower; *Summer,* men harvesting grain; and *Autumn,* gatherers picking and stomping grapes.

3. In Watteau's depictions love again characterizes *Spring,* as Zephyr crowns Flora with flowers. Ceres holds the sickle of the summer harvest, and a group of tipplers enjoy the autumn wine with Bacchus.

4. In addition to the conventionalized seasons discussed above, other symbols could also be used to represent the theme. For example, a cycle by Lancret (Salon of 1738; Paris: Musée du Louvre) done in the mode of the *fête galante* exemplifies a tradition that generally focuses on the social activities of courtship appropriate to each time of the year. Although these activities are associated with love (and ultimately with sexuality), the obvious stress is on social intercourse, and the individual figures themselves are not necessarily expressive of fecundity.

5. On the pastoral, see Andrew Ettin, *Literature and the Pastoral* (New Haven and London: Yale University Press, 1984); *Survivals of the Pastoral,* ed. Richard Hardin (Lawrence, Kan.: University of Kansas Publications, 1979); Lawrence Lerner, *The Art of Nostalgia: Studies in Pastoral Poetry* (London: Chatto and Windus, 1972); and *The Pastoral Mode,* ed. Brian Loughrey (London: Macmillan, 1984).

6. Diderot, "Salon de 1765," in *Salons,* 2:82.

7. For a discussion of Boucher's pastorals, see Alastair Laing, "Boucher: The Search for an Idiom," in *François Boucher* (New York: Metropolitan Museum of Art, 1986), 56–72.

8. Crow has articulated the disjuncture between the real and the artificial in terms of that French aristocratic genre which also presented an ideal of perpetual diversion, the *fête galante.* See Crow, 55–74. For a discussion of related ideas in English art, see Bermingham, 9–54.

9. Examples of this transformation include Antoine Watteau, *The Swing,* 1708–09; Jean Mondon, fils, *The Tender Ties,* 1736; and Gottlieb Leberecht Crusius, *Capricci,* 1762. On the relation of the *fête galante* to the *rocaille* tradition, see Crow, 58–63.

10. Fragonard collaborated with Boucher on several pastoral series, as in *Blind Man's Buff* (c. 1750–56; Toledo: Toledo Museum of Art) and *The See-Saw* (c. 1750–56; Lugano: Thyssen Bornemisza Collection). Gabriel de Saint-Aubin made sketches of the works in 1777 and annotated the sheet, "Vu chez rémy 4 peintures par m[r] boucher[psseur] et m[r] fragonard élève qui ne les aime point." Alexandre Ananoff and Daniel Wildenstein, *François Boucher,* 2 vols. (Lausanne and Paris: La Bibliothèque des Arts, 1976), 2:9–10.

11. For an expanded discussion of the corset and its sexual implications in the eighteenth century, see David Kunzle, "The Corset as Erotic Alchemy: From Rococo Galanterie to Montaut's Physiologies," in *Woman as Sex Object: Studies in Erotic Art 1730–1970,* ed. Thomas B. Hess and Linda Nochlin, *Art News Annual* 38 (1972):90–105.

12. Alicia Annas, "The Elegant Art of Movement," in *An Elegant Art* (Los Angeles and New York: L.A. County Museum and Abrams, 1983), 45. On aristocratic deportment in relation to the *fête galante,* see Crow, 66–69.

13. Annas, 40–45.

14. Boucher, for example, executed a pastoral cycle of the *Seasons* (1755; New York: Frick Collection).

15. Examples of the use of this device include Boucher's *The Rape of Europa* (1747; Paris: Musée du Louvre) and his *Triumph of Venus* (1740; Stockholm: National Museum).

16. Philip Stewart, "Representations of Love in The French Eighteenth Century," *Studies in Iconography* 14 (1978):131.

17. Victor Carlson, John Ittmen, et al. *Regency to Empire. French Printmaking 1715–1814* (Baltimore: Baltimore Museum of Art, 1984), 283.

18. This issues are discussed by Stewart, "Representations of Love," 125–26 and will be taken up here below.

19. Guiraud, 180, 216, and 233. Donald Posner has discussed the iconography of the hat in "The Swinging Women of Watteau and Fragonard," *Art Bulletin* 64 (1982):85.

20. Guiraud, 475. Also *Vocabula Amatoria: A French-English Glossary* (London: Privately printed, 1896), 203.

21. On the meanings of the dog, see Stewart, "Representations of Love," 131, and also Otto Naumann, *Frans von Mieris the Elder,* 2 vols. (Doornspijk: Davaco, 1981), 1:104–105.

22. In another work attributed to Fragonard, *The Girl with a Marmot* (Cambridge, Mass.: Fogg Art Museum), the gesture of solicitation is repeated. There the young woman looks coyly at the viewer, head inclined to one side. With the same gesture as the Wanderer she holds a hat in one hand and with the other she opens a box containing the marmot, another image for the vagina. In another painting attributed to Fragonard a couple romps in the hay while the young girl holds her hat high in the air away from the boy, as if to protect her virginity. A basket lies tipped over in the foreground. See *In The Corn* (Private Collection), illustrated in Wildenstein, 201.

23. Other discussions of sexual allusion include Stewart, "Representations of Love," 129, 139, and 141; Alain Guillerm, "Le système de l'iconographie galante,"

Dix-Huitième Siècle 12 (1980):177–94; Robert M. Isherwood, *Farce and Fantasy: Popular Entertainment in Eighteenth-Century Paris,* 60–79; Robert Ellrich, "Modes of Discourse and the Language of Sexual Reference in Eighteenth-Century French Fiction," *Eighteenth-Century Life* 9 (May, 1985): 217–28.

24. The extent to which some of these symbols were the unique property of an elite picture-viewing, book-buying class is unclear. In his *Farce and Fantasy* (69–70) Isherwood discusses the variety of sexual allusions available to all in the fairs, *opéra comique,* etc. On the other hand, writers like Crébillon, fils, discuss the allusion and veiled image as a gallant code which is the "language of the well-born" spoken in the presence of the fair sex. For an exploration of this view see Stewart, "Representations of Love," 124–27, and also Philip Stewart, *La Masque et La Parole* (Paris: Librarie José Corti, 1973), esp. 1–58. Jerrine Mitchell considers this problem specifically in relation to Fragonard in "Le Commerce des Femmes: Sexuality and Sociability in Eighteenth-Century French Representation" (Paper delivered at the symposium, "Social Implications of the Rococo Style: Images of Women," University of Missouri, October, 1987); and Crow presents the mix of high and low culture symbols as a general problem in his *Painters and Public Life,* esp. 45–55.

25. Isherwood, for example, quotes the following from an eighteenth-century discussion of Piron's *La rose ou les jardins de l'Hymen,* first performed 5 March 1744: "The words *rose, rosebush, shepherd's crook,* and *garden* have caused some little thing to be thought, but they were all so fitting, as the Examiner indicated, the veil of allegory was so successfully woven that there was not the smallest hole through which one could see nudity." Isherwood, 69.

26. "Cela, c'est une femme convalescent? Ah! Monsieur Jeaurat, vous ne connaissez pas tout le péril de son état; elle est bien plus mal que vous ne pensez." Diderot, "Salon de 1769," in *Salons,* 4:72. The painting is also illustrated in that volume. I could not obtain a reproduction for this publication.

27. The association between the bird and the penis is made very explicit by Fragonard in the panel *Summer* from the Hôtel Matignon series. There a young woman (the boy's mother?) pulls up his drapery to reveal his genitals. At the same time she looks toward a bird that is emerging from its tree hung cage.

28. The significance of the extended index finger was not lost on the eighteenth-century audience. When Baudouin used the gesture in his 1765 *Gathering Cherries,* Diderot commented, "Mauvaise pointe, idée plate et grossière. . . ." Diderot, "Salon de 1765," in *Salons,* 2:138. Baudouin also uses the watering can in direct representations of seduction. For example in his *The Gardener* (Salon of 1769) a couple embracing beneath an arbor is spied upon by a young maid behind the foliage. In the right hand corner is the telltale watering can, near the couple an upturned hat.

29. Guiraud, 539.

30. For a possible Ovidian reference in the entwined trees, see Eric Zafran, *The Rococo Age* (Atlanta: High Museum of Art, 1983), 53.

31. For discussions of the ideology underlying the concept of woman as garden, see Carol Fabricant, "Binding and Dressing Nature's Loose Tresses: The Ideology of Augustan Landscape Design," *Studies in Eighteenth-Century Culture* 8 (1979):109–35; and James Turner, "The Sexual Politics of Landscape: Images of Venus in Eighteenth-Century English Poetry and Landscape Gardening," *Studies in Eighteenth-Century Culture* 11 (1982):343–66.

32. Guiraud, 29–33.

33. The gourd we have already encountered several times. The shoes are an added feature; *chausser une femme* was a euphemism for intercourse, and the *soulier* could also be used to suggest the phallus. See Guiraud, 29–33, 220, 580.

34. It has become traditional to view Fragonard's pastoral women with children as representations of the "happy mother" à la Rousseau. Images closely related to the ones we have been considering have been traditionally interpreted as representing positive, nurturing female ideals. This interpretation was presented in an article by Carol Duncan, "Happy Mothers and Other New Ideas in French Art," *Art Bulletin* 55 (December, 1973): 570–83. Articulately summarizing the new attitudes toward family life that emerged in mid-eighteenth-century France, Duncan suggested how writers and artists contributed to the creation of an ideal. However, she too carelessly tossed many works by Fragonard into a single category, reading the *Joys of Motherhood* (c. 1752; Indianapolis: Indianapolis Museum of Art) in the same way as the much later *Beloved Child* (c. 1780; New York: Private Collection), now given to Marguerite Gérard. Basic differences between the two works are ignored in favor of a generalized interpretation. "From Fragonard's atelier came a whole series of happy and good mothers. Two of these, *The Joys of Motherhood* and *The Beloved Child* celebrate with Rococo exuberence the pleasures of a peasant and a fashionable mother respectively" (583). Although the title *Joys of Motherhood* would seem to support Duncan's Rousseauian interpretation, the name does not belong to the painting; it was added at some time after the work's completion, probably in the twentieth century. The proposed date unquestionably undermines the reading, because in 1752 neither of Rousseau's influential books had appeared in print (*La Nouvelle Héloïse* was published in 1761 and *Emile* in 1762). Paintings that did represent the new Rousseauian ideals appeared only later in the 1760's (Greuze's *The Well-Beloved Mother,* 1765; Paris: Delaborde Collection, for example) and became increasingly popular in the next two decades. The Rousseauian interpretation proposed for *The Joys of Motherhood* is seriously flawed because distinctions are not made between that writer's idealizations of country life and the decorative pastoral tradition explicated above. As a result of this oversight, images are read in the wrong codes of meaning; and the relation between painting and audience is misunderstood.

35. The motif that alludes to ejaculation was altered in the work most closely related to the Detroit panel, the *Grape Gatherer* (1750–56; Paris: Private Collection). There the young woman sprinkles water from her can onto a small child lying in a basket below. In considering the two versions we can detect the synonymy of the watering can and grapes and again see the logic of sexual signification and substitution at work. Another example of this process comes in comparing two works by Boucher, *The Cage* of 1763 and *Elle mord à la grappe* (engraving by Jean Pasquier). In the first work a boy holds a bird newly released from its cage near a young girl's lips; she holds a crown of flowers, and a basket of flowers lies at her feet. In Pasquier's version the bird is replaced by a bunch of grapes held to the young girl's lips. For illustrations of these works, see Ananoff and Wildenstein, 2:224–25.

36. Two additional observations on this point: Batteux compared genius to the earth that produces nothing until it receives the seed; see Charles Batteux, *Les beaux arts réduits à un même principe* (Paris: Chez Durand, 1746), 11. Second, in France lin-

eage and legitimacy were passed only through the male, and so the seminal fluid was literally precious for its value in conferring social validity.

Chapter Four

1. "*Flagonard* [sic], avec des dispositions, est d'une facilité éthonante à changer de party d'un moment à l'autre, ce qui le fait oppérer d'une manière inégalle." *Correspondance des directeurs,* 11:232.

2. Cochin, *Recueil,* 70. Here is quoted at length the passage from Cochin's *De l'illusion dans le peinture* to which I will be referring in the following discussion: "L'une des plus grandes beautés de l'art, qui a encore moins de rapport avec l'illusion, puisqu'elle n'a pas même de fondement dans la nature, & qu'elle est uniquement l'effet du sentiment qui meut l'artiste en opérant; c'est cet art dans le travail, cette sûreté, cette facilité de maître qui souvent fait toute la différence du vrai beau, de ce beau qui excite l'admiration, avec le médiocre qui nous laisse toujours froids. C'est ce *faire* (ainsi que le nomment les artistes) qui distingue l'original d'un grand maître d'avec la copie la mieux rendue, & qui caractérise si bien les vrais talens de l'artiste, qu'une petite partie d'un tableau, même la moins intéressante, décele au connoisseur que le morceau doit être d'un grand maître" (*Recueil,* 69). He continues: "On ne prétend pas que le *faire* soit la seule partie essentielle, mais c'est elle qui couronne toutes les autres; & l'on croit pouvoir avancer que, quant au plaisir qui en résulte pour les connoisseurs, rien ne le peut suppléer" (*Recueil,* 70). And a statement from the *Discours sur la connaissance des arts fondés sur le dessin et particulièrement de la peinture* published in the *Mercure de France,* March 1759 where Cochin speaks of a merit that crowns all the others and renders them excellent, a beautiful way of painting, of handling the brush: "C'est le goût qui se manifeste par la légéreté & les graces de la manière de faire, par la fermeté & la sureté du travail; on le sent mieux qu'on ne peut l'exprimer. C'est cette apparence de facilité, de certitude, & d'enthousiasme dans l'exécution, qui rend les détails les plus fins & les plus savans, sans peine & comme par hazard. C'est ce beau maniement du pinceau ou du ciseau, qui donne à connoître que l'Artiste ayant une idée bien nette de ce qu'il vouloit faire, a frappé le but avec hardiesse et précision." *Recueil,* 189.

3. "Cependant un tableau exécuté avec feu, avec enthousiasme & sans trop de recherche du côté du *faire,* a souvent plus de droit à être nommé un ouvrage *achevé* que celui qui a coûté à l'Artiste beaucoup de temps & de soins." Watelet and Lévèsque, "Achevé," *Dictionnaire des arts,* 1:26.

4. Cochin, see note 2 above. Recall that in the valuation of paintings a studio copy brought a higher price according to the extent to which the master had touched it. See Introduction, note 85.

5. See note 2.

6. See note 2.

7. See note 2.

8. "On craint que l'excès des soins ne refroidisse entièrement le feu qu l'on connoissoit dans cet artiste. La peine s'y laisse appercevoir, et l'on n'y découvre point de ces heureux laissés [sic], ny de cette facilité de pinceau qu'il portoit peut-être cy-devant à l'excès; mais qu'il ne faut cependant pas perdre entièrement en les rectifi-

ant. . . . Tout est fondu, tout est fini. Il est tems que le s[r] *Fragonard* prenne confiance en ses talents, et que, travaillant avec plus de hardiesse, il retrouve ce premier feu et cette heureuse facilité qu'il avoit, et qu'il semble qu'une étude trop sérieuse a captivés presqu'au point de les détruire." *Correspondance des directeurs,* 11:313.

9. Protogenes was said to have been censured by Apelles for not knowing when to take his hands from the panel. By which, Castiglione explains, Apelles meant that Protogenes did not know when he had done enough, blaming him for finishing too thoroughly. Baldassare Castiglione, *The Book of the Courtier,* trans. and intro. George Bull (Harmondsworth, Middlesex: Penguin Books, 1967), 69–70.

10. David Summers, *Michelangelo and the Language of Art* (Princeton: Princeton University Press, 1981), 33–40.

11. Castiglione, 67. Castiglione has taken his cue from rhetorical theory, from the commonplace that art should hide art. He even cites the orators who, dissembling, tried to make their audiences believe that their speeches were composed according to the promptings of nature and truth rather than effort and artifice. He continues: "So we can truthfully say that true art is what does not seem to be art; and the most important thing is to conceal it, because if it is revealed this discredits a man completely and ruins his reputation" (67).

12. Castiglione, 69–70.

13. Castiglione, 70.

14. Summers, 63.

15. I have concentrated here on Castiglione and Vasari, but French eighteenth-century art writers had access to other Italian theorists who shared ideas about facility and *sprezzatura.* De Piles' ideas, in particular, were taken from Venetian theorists such as Marco Boschini, *Carta del navegar pitoresco* (Venice, 1660), and Carlo Ridolfi, *Le Meraviglie dell'arte: Ovvero Le vite degli illustri pittori veneti e dello stato* (Venice, 1648). It is not my purpose here to trace the history of these ideas from Italy to France; rather I want to concentrate on the particular inflection they were given by eighteenth-century French writers. On the relationship between French and Italian theory, see Hereward Lester Cooke, "French Eighteenth-Century Drawings: Studies in Theory and Practice," (Ph.D. diss., Princeton University, 1956).

16. By the late seventeenth century artists pursued not only the honors of the intellectual, but also those of nobility. Louis XIV, for example, had ennobled Le Brun, Mignard, Rigaud, Boullogne. The pursuit of nobility required that they present themselves not as craftsmen nor as tradesmen interested in commercial rewards but as gentlemen who undertook art for their own pleasure, and for the pleasure of others. This ennobling of the artist may also have been encouraged by the many *gens du monde* who both entered the Academy as *amateurs honoraires* and participated in writing art theory and educating young artists.

17. "S'il faut donc arrêter un excès de facilité qui fait négliger ses ouvrages, il faut animer une lenteur trop exacte qui rend ce que l'on fait triste, froid et languissant." *Conférences de l'Académie Royale de peinture et de sculpture* ed. Henri Jouin (Paris: Quantin, 1883), 261.

18. "Il faut souvent négliger de certains endroits pour en faire valoir d'autres; mais dans cet air de brusquerie et de négligence qui doit venir de l'art, je le répète encore, il faut éviter les traits durs et coupés. . . . Les ouvrages de Rembrandt qui

paroissent les plus touchés et même les plus brusqués sont d'une recherche infinie et sont peints avec autant de suavité et de rondeur que ceux de Corrège, où l'on n'aperçoit aucune touche." *Conférences,* 262.

19. *Conférences,* 261.

20. Anne-Claude-Philippe, Comte de Caylus, "De la légèreté de l'outil," in *Vie d'artistes du XVIIIe siècle. Discours sur la peinture et la sculpture. Salons,* ed. André Fontaine (Paris: Librairie Renouard, 1910), 150–57, esp. 155.

21. Caylus, 152–53.

22. "Je croirais qu'on peut définir se produit du goût, de l'esprit et du pinceau, en disant que ce sont *les dernières touches qui, conduites par un sentiment exquis, fleurissent toutes les parties d'un tableau.*" Caylus, 156.

23. Charles Duclos, *Confession du comte de* *** (Paris: Librairie Marcel Didier, 1969), 82–83.

24. On this aspect of Caylus' career, see René Godenne, "Agréable diversité des *Oeuvres Badines* du Comte de Caylus," *Dix-huitième siècle* 1 (1969):251–66.

25. Caylus, "De la légèreté de l'outil," in *Vies,* 152 and 155–56.

26. J. P. Dens, *L'Honnête homme et le critique du goût* (Lexington, Ky.: French Forum Publishers, 1981). For an extended discussion of the *honnête homme,* see Domna Stanton, *The Aristocrat as Art* (New York: Columbia University Press, 1980).

27. Chevalier de Méré, *Oeuvres complètes du Chevalier de Méré,* ed. Charles H. Boudhors, 3 vols. (Paris: Editions Fernand Roches, 1930). For example, see Méré's *Première Conversation,* 1:7–21, or his *Des Agréments,* 2:29.

28. Roger de Piles, *Cours de peinture,* 3, 20, and 41.

29. This higher, intellectual merit did not presuppose a dichotomy of subject and form; *poétique* referred to the story as a representation embedded in a particular visual form and not as a disembodied essence.

30. Watelet and Lévèsque, "Pittoresque," *Dictionnaire des arts,* 5:74–75. Here the French theorists have used Reynolds' conception of the ornamental.

31. Watelet and Lévèsque, "Pittoresque," *Dictionnaire des arts,* 5:74–75.

32. This idea is developed in terms of the *agréments* in Méré, 1:42–43 and especially 2:9ff. For an explication of this aspect of the courtier, see Stanton, 119–21 and 144ff.

33. Watelet and Lévèsque, "Pittoresque," *Dictionnaire,* 5:75.

34. Watelet and Lévèsque, "Pittoresque," *Dictionnaire,* 5:75.

35. Boucher was a master of *beau désordre.* In conjunction with depictions of women, we see this device in mythological paintings (*The Toilet of Venus,* 1751; New York: Metropolitan Museum of Art), portraits (*Madame Boucher,* 1743; New York: Frick Collection), and genre scenes (*La Belle Villageoise,* c. 1732; Pasadena: Norton Simon Collection, and *The Modiste,* 1746; Stockholm: Nationalmuseum).

36. For a discussion of *négligence,* see Stewart, *La masque,* 43.

37. Stewart, *La masque,* 44–45.

38. Caylus, "De la légèrté d'outil," in *Vies,* 155.

39. Cochin, *Voyage,* 197.

40. Cochin, *Voyage,* 185.

41. See note 3.

42. Méré even compared the *honnête homme* to the artist, saying that excellent painters do not represent all but leave something to the imagination. Méré, 1:63.

43. "C'est un grand art que de menager aux Spectateurs le moyen de laisser agir leur imagination. L'amour propre sçait gré à l'Artiste qui leur fait accroire qu'ils sont en partie les auteurs de ce que leur imagination ajoute au Tableau, & ils jouissent réellement du plaisir d'avoir part à l'ouvrage. A cet égard l'homme à talent est au pair de cet homme d'esprit qui prête de l'esprit aux autres." Dandré-Bardon, 48.

44. "Le *ragoût* est une sorte de badinage; il témoigne la facilité de l'artiste qui est capable de se jouer avec l'outil, de badiner avec les plus grandes difficultés du métier." Watelet and Lévèsque, *Dictionnaire des arts,* 5:281. *Ragoûtant* did not always imply dalliance. For example, Dandré-Bardon used the term to describe those aspects of the grand manner of painting that were pleasing to the eye. The point here is not so much the exact term used but the comparison among playing, toying, and paint handling.

45. Cochin, *Réceuil,* 179.

46. Charles Antoine Coypel, *Oeuvres* (Geneva: Slatkine, 1971), 73–85; and Roger de Piles, *Diverses conversations sur la peinture* (1677; reprint, Geneva: Slatkine, 1970), 20–21.

47. Cochin, for example, tried to suppress pamphlets of Salon criticism, and he often defended the academic artists in his own salon reviews. For an extended and provocative discussion of the public, the critics, and social hierarchies, see Crow, 105–133.

48. La Font de Saint-Yenne, *Réflexions,* 2–3.

49. Abbé Le Blanc, *Lettre sur l'exposition des ouvrages de peinture, sculpture etc. de l'année 1747,* Paris, 1747; Deloynes 26:286.

50. On the construction of the idea of the public, see Crow, *Painters and Public Life,* 105–133.

51. For a discussion of this aspect of Chardin criticism, see my essay, "Reflecting on Chardin," *The Eighteenth Century: Theory and Interpretation* 29 (Winter, 1988): 19–45.

52. This is not to suggest that no elite viewers owned engravings, but only that they were designed for a wider market (as their price would indicate), and appealed to a different taste.

53. There were reproductive techniques developed in the eighteenth century that mimicked different kinds of execution (e.g., the aquatint or the pastel engraving). Chardin's works, however, were engraved rather than executed in the more technique-oriented media.

54. Marc-Antoine Laugier, *Manière de bien juger des ouvrages de peinture* (1771; reprint, Geneva: Minkoff, 1972), 156–57.

55. De Piles, *L'Idée du peintre parfait,* 52.

56. Cooke, 191.

57. ". . . juger bien de tout ce qui se présente, par je ne sçay quel sentiment qui va plus viste, et quelquefois plus droit que les refléxions." Méré, 1:55.

58. Batteux, 57.

59. Batteux, 60–65.

60. On Méré and the *je ne sais quoi,* see Dens, 51–58, and Stanton, 208–210.

61. Stanton, 208.

62. The association of these two concepts is much more complex than this short

discussion indicates. For an extended treatment of the issue in conjunction with the notion of *agréments,* see Stanton, 203–207 and Dens, 48–52.

63. Castiglione, 65.

64. Castiglione writes a dialogue between Count Ludovico da Canossa and Gaspare Pallavicino on the necessity of noble birth. In the text it is Pallavicino who argues that the courtier need not be born to the nobility. Castiglione, 54.

65. Michel Foucault, *The Order of Things* (New York: Vintage Books, 1973), 125–65.

66. Kinert S. Jaffe, "Genius: Its Changing Role in Eighteenth-Century French Aesthetics," *Journal of the History of Ideas* 41 (October–December, 1980): 581–82.

67. The text of *L'Idée d'un peintre parfait* noted that genius was the first thing that must be presumed in a painter, that it could be acquired neither by study nor by work, and that it must be great because painting requires so much knowledge and exacts much time and application in acquiring it. De Piles, *L'Idée,* 3.

68. "On appelle génie, l'aptitude qu'un homme a reçu de la nature, pour faire bien & facilement certaines choses, que les autres ne sçauroient faire que très-mal, même en prenant beaucoup de peine. Nous apprenons à faire les choses pour lesquelles nos avons du génie, avec autant de facilité que nous en avons à parler notre langue naturelle." Du Bos, *Réflexions critiques,* 2:6.

69. Jean Louis de Cahusac, "Enthousiasme," in *Encyclopédie,* 5:720.

70. Denis Diderot, *Eléments de physiologie* in *Oeuvres complètes,* 9:364.

71. Cahusac, "Enthousiasme," *Encyclopédie,* 5:722.

72. Cahusac, "Enthousiasme," *Encyclopédie,* 5:722.

73. See below.

74. In the *Phaedrus* Plato defined a poetic mania or ecstasy that came from the muses and made possible true and great poetry. Plato, *Phaedrus,* trans. W. C. Helmbodd and W. G. Robinowitz (Indianapolis: Bobbs-Merrill, 1958), 25–26. For later ideas, see Martin Kemp, "From *Mimesis* to *Fantasia:* The Quattrocento Vocabulary of Creation, Inspiration, and Genius in the Visual Arts," *Viator* 5 (1977):366.

75. In his *De arte graphica* of 1668, Dufresnoy described what would later be called the genius as "he who is inspired at birth with some portion of that heavenly fire stolen by Prometheus." C. A. Dufresnoy, *De Arte Graphica: The Art of Painting,* trans. John Dryden (London, 1716), 10. In another legend Prometheus was established as a prototype for the artist because he fashioned man from clay and animated him with fire. Although the two myths recounted individual events, together they formed an allegory of artistic inspiration and creativity; the artist was moved by divine fire and used it to vivify his inventions.

76. De Piles found enthusiasm to be a transport of the mind that made one conceive of things in a sublime, surprising, and probable manner, and compared it to the sun in terms of its heat and vivifying influence. Yet for De Piles enthusiasm was also a state that could be rationally induced. Minds of moderate vivacity and good judgment could work themselves into enthusiasm by degrees, cultivating that ability by looking at and reading great works. De Piles, *Cours,* 114 and 118–19.

77. Cahusac, "Enthousiasme," in *Encyclopédie,* 5:719–20.

78. "Une surprise subite vous arrête, vous éprouvez une émotion générale, vos regards comme absorbés restent dans une sorte d'immobilité, votre ame entiere se

rassemble sur une foule d'objets qui l'occupent à la fois; mais bien-tôt rendue à son activité, elle parcourt les différentes parties du tout qui l'avoit frappée, sa chaleur se communique à vos sens, vos yeux lui obéissent & la préviennent: un feu vif les anime; vous appercevez, vous détaillez, vous comparez les attitudes, les contrastes, les coups de lumiere, les traits des personnages, leurs passions, le choix de l'action représentée, l'adresse, la force, la hardiesse du pinceau; & remarquez que votre attention, votre surprise, votre émotion, votre chaleur, seront dans cette circonstance plus ou moins vives, selon le différent degré de connoissances antérieures que vous aurez acquis, & le plus ou le moins de goût, de délicatesse, d'esprit, de sensibilité, de jugement, que vous aurez reçû de la nature." Cahusac, "Enthousiasme," *Encyclopédie,* 5:720.

79. "L'impulsion qui l'a ébranlée, qui la remplit, & qui l'entraîne, est telle que tout lui cede, & qu'elle est le sentiment prédominant. Ainsi, sans que rien puisse le distraite, ou l'arrêter, le peintre saisit son pinceau, & la toile se colore, les figures s'arrangent, les morts revivent; le ciseau est déjà dans la main du sculpteur, & le marbre s'anime; les vers coulent de la plume du poëte, & le théatre s'embellit de mille actions nouvelles qui nous intéressent & nous étonnent." Cahusac, "Enthousiasme," *Encyclopédie,* 5:720.

80. "Le poëte sent le moment de l'enthousiasme. . . . Il s'annonce en lui par un frémissement qui part de sa poitrine, et qui passe, d'une manière délicieuse et rapide, jusqu'aux extrémités de son corps. Bientôt ce n'est plus un frémissement; c'est une chaleur forte et permanente qui l'embrase, qui le fait haleter, qui le consume, qui le tue; mais qui donne l'âme, la vie à tout ce qu'il touche." Denis Diderot, *Second Entretien sur le fils naturel* in *Oeuvres,* 7:103.

81. ". . . comme les femmes dont le sentiment est épuisé & qui ne veulent point renoncer aux avantages qu'il procure, cherchent à en montrer d'autant plus qu'elles en ont perdu davantage." Watelet and Lévèsque, "Enthousiasme," in *Dictionnaire,* 2:162. Article signed by Watelet.

82. Batteux, 33.

83. For the popularity of this theme in eighteenth-century France see J. L. Carr, "Pygmalion and the Philosophes," *Journal of the Warburg and Courtauld Institutes* 23 (1960): 239–55.

84. De Man's provocative reading of the text analyzed *Pygmalion* in terms of the complex relation between selfhood as metaphor and the representation of selfhood as metaphor. Paul de Man, *Allegories of Reading* (New Haven: Yale University Press, 1979), 187.

85. Jean-Jacques Rousseau, *Pygmalion* in *Oeuvres complètes,* ed. Bernard Gagnebin and Marcel Raymond, 4 vols. (Paris: Gallimard, 1959–69), 2:1225.

86. Cahusac, "Enthousiasme," *Encyclopédie,* 5:720.

87. "Rien ne peut mieux nous rendre compte des grâces de la peinture, que cet enthousiasme propre des âmes sensibles, qui fait passer rapidement dans nous tout le feu qui anime la toile." Laugier, *La manière,* 48. For De Piles' discussion, see *Cours,* 115.

88. Watelet and Lévèsque, "Touche," *Dictionnaire des arts,* 5:783–88. Article signed by Watelet.

89. "Les esquisses ont communément un feu que le tableau n'a pas. C'est le mo-

ment de chaleur de l'artiste, la verve pure, sans aucun mélange de l'apprêt que la réflexion met à tout; c'est l'ame du peintre qui se répand librement sur la toile." Diderot, "Salon de 1765," in *Salons,* 2:153–54.

90. "La pensée rapide caractérise d'un trait. Or, plus l'expression des arts est vague, plus l'imagination est à l'aise. Il faut entendre dans la musique vocale ce qu'elle exprime. Je fais dire à une symphonie bien faite, presque ce qu'il me plaît; et comme je sais mieux que personne la manière de m'affecter, par l'expérience que j'ai de mon propre coeur, il est rare que l'expression que je donne aux sons, analogue à ma situation actuelle, sérieuse, tendre ou gaie, ne me touche plus qu'une autre qui seroit moins à mon choix. Il en est à-peu-près de même de l'esquisse et du tableau. Je vois dans le tableau une chose prononcée: combien dans l'esquisse y supposai-je de choses qui y sont à peine annoncées." Diderot, "Salon de 1765," in *Salons,* 2:154.

91. Antoine Coypel, for example, wrote, "Avant donc que de peindre, apprenez à penser; quand l'on pense bien, les paroles viennent d'elles-mêmes se placer; alors, plus l'on s'échauffe à parler, plus on diroit qu'il vient d'esprit, de sentiment et de ce je ne sçay quoi de naif qui semble s'attacher aux paroles. Il en est de même de la manière de peindre, qui est proprement la parole du peintre, le pinceau court et place vivement ses couleurs selon que le peintre sait penser et que les idées sont plus ou moins nettes dans son esprit." *Conférences,* 260.

92. "Dans les principales villes de l'Europe, & sur-tout dans celles où il y a le plus de peintres, il y regne des préjugés très-contraires aux principes ou regles que je propose, & sur-tout à celle que je viens de prescrire: ils ne cessent de dire que toute bonne peinture doit être facile, librement peinte, & bien touchée; ils ont persuadé à ceux qui n'ont aucune connoissance des principes de l'art, & que j'appellerai *ignorart*. . . " J.-E. Liotard, *Traité des principes et des règles de la peinture* (1781; reprint, Geneva: Minkoff, 1973), 50.

93. Cochin, *Voyage,* 198.

94. Du Bos, *Réflexions,* 2:120.

95. Roger de Piles, *The Art of Painting and the Lives of the Painters* (London: J. Nutt, 1706), 197; and Caylus, "De la légèreté de l'outil," in *Vies,* 151.

96. Cochin, *Voyage,* 14. While in Venice Fragonard frequently copied Tintoretto. Cochin had especially praised the paintings in the Scuolo di San Rocco, and Fragonard copied Tintoretto there most often.

97. For Diderot's discussion of Deshays, see *Salons,* 2:96–104; also Hallé, *Salons,* 2:86–87.

98. "Signe," *Encyclopédie,* 15:152.

99. Etienne Bonnot de Condillac, *Essai sur l'origine des connoissances humaines* in *Oeuvres complètes,* 31 vols. (Paris: Dufart, 1803), 1:76.

100. Condillac, 1:51–54 and 77–78.

101. Condillac, 1:89–90.

102. Condillac, 1:202.

103. Condillac, 1:78.

104. "Son talent consiste non pas à sentir, comme vous le supposez, mais à rendre si scrupuleusement les signes extérieurs du sentiment, que vous vous y trompiez. . . . Les gestes de son désespoir sont de mémoire, et ont été préparés devant une glace." Denis Diderot, *Paradoxe sur le comédien* in *Oeuvres,* 8:369.

105. Du Bos, *Réflexions,* 1:378–79.

106. The association of invention with choice was a standard one in eighteenth-century French art theory. In the *Dictionnaire des arts* (3:183) invention was described as not a discovery but a choice.

107. Watelet and Lévèsque, "Touche," *Dictionnaire des arts,* 5:786.

108. Dandré-Bardon, 75.

109. For a discussion of transparency, see Foucault, 58–71.

110. My purpose here is twofold: to demonstrate how the acts of making and viewing paintings were eroticized in eighteenth-century French art and to explore how erotic codes (both apart from and in conjunction with sexualized subject matter) operated in painting. The erotic paintings I am considering usually imply a male heterosexual audience. I do not focus here on issues of gender, but I will suggest simply that the paintings posit a traditional division of power between the sexes: women are objects to be looked at, men are those who look. The question of gender relations in rococo painting, however, needs a sophisticated analysis that will move us beyond the obvious division of female-object–male-viewer that I work with here. Patricia Crown has begun this analysis by suggesting how the representation of unrestrained female sexuality might have been threatening to a male audience. See Introduction, note 104. One could also ask how women responded to these works, since they were certainly seen by both sexes; but this is more difficult to discover since almost (if not) all of the theory and criticism on painting was written by men. Another line of inquiry might be to explore the differences between those rococo writers who generally eroticized aesthetics (even when considering works with nonsexual subjects), and French academic writers in the mid-nineteenth century who used aestheticization as a way to deny the eroticism of sexual subjects.

111. During the eighteenth century the painting was owned by several elite male viewers: the Comte Du Barry, M. Varanchan de Saint-Geniès, the Abbé de Gevigney.

112. In fact, the bather(s) surprised was a common theme of French eighteenth-century painting. For example, Boucher executed *The Bather Surprised* in 1742, engraved by Daullé. There a single bather is interrupted by a satyr coming out of the reeds and disguised by flowers in his hair. Gabriel de Saint-Aubin engraved another composition by Boucher, *Diana Bathing with Her Nymphs* for an edition of Ovid in 1767–71. There Acteon is shown as the voyeur.

Chapter Five

1. Sixteen paintings by Fragonard are now designated as *portraits de fantaisie,* and the group is marked by a consistency of canvas size as well as a similarity of handling. All probably date between 1767 and 1772. As far as we know, not a single contemporary writer mentioned the portraits, they were never exhibited, and Fragonard left no record of them other than the canvases themselves. The following paintings in the Louvre form part of the group: *The Young Artist, Inspiration, Diderot, Music* (dated 1769), *The Fantasy Figure in Blue, Portrait of the Duc de Beuvron, La Guimard,* and *Study.* The others are: *The Warrior* (Williamstown: Sterling and Francine Clark Art Institute), *Don Quixote* (Chicago: Art Institute), *Lady with the Dog* (New York: Metropolitan Museum of Art), *Portrait of the Duc d'Harcourt* (Private Collection), *The Actor* (Paris: Private Collection), and *The Singer* (Paris: Private Collection), *The Geographer*

(Paris: Petit Palais) and *The Reader* (Washington, D.C.: National Gallery of Art). None of these titles dates from the eighteenth century. A seventeenth work larger in dimensions has been associated with the *portraits de fantaisie: A Cavalier Seated by a Fountain* (Barcelona: Meseu d'Art de Catalunya).

2. For a related study of the changing meaning of the English term *enthusiasm,* see Susie Tucker, *Enthusiasm: A Study in Semantic Change* (Cambridge: Cambridge University Press, 1972).

3. "lisant, plein d'enthousiasme." P.-A. Hall's inventory was published in Frédéric Villot, *Hall* (Paris: Librairie française et étrangère, 1867), 144.

4. Roger de Piles contended in his *Cours de peinture* (163) that Le Brun stole from painting the variety of expression appropriate to diverse images.

5. The transfixed eyes are used to signal attention to interior states other than enthusiasm in works such as Georges de la Tour's *Magdalen* (c. 1636–38; Paris: Musée du Louvre), or Chardin's *A Philosopher Reading* (Salon of 1753; Paris: Musée du Louvre), or Greuze's *A Schoolboy at His Lesson* (Salon of 1757; Edinburgh: National Gallery of Scotland), where the silent contemplation is static. Still other works depict artists where attention to an interior state is not necessarily implied. For example, in François de Troy's *Charles Mouton* (1690; Paris: Musée du Louvre), although the figure is in the midst of playing his guitar, he is posed so as to display himself to the audience.

6. Giovanni Paolo Lomazzo, *A Tracte Concerning the Artes of Curious Paintinge, Carvinge, and Buildinge,* trans. Richard Haydocke, 5 vols. (1598; reprint, Westmead, Farnsborough, Hants: Gregg Press, 1970), 2:13.

7. Flames also had an emblematic association with genius. The representation of *Fureur ou Enthousiasme Poétique* in J. B. Boudard, *Iconologie tirée de divers auteurs,* 3 vols. in 1 (1766; reprint, New York and London: Garland, 1976), 2:37 depicted a woman with a flame emerging from her head, whose vivid eyes and rosy cheeks recalled the fire that animated her. The traditional emblems for both *Idée* (2:100) and *Génie* (2:42) also showed figures with heads ablaze.

8. Wildenstein, *The Painting,* 14–15; Charles Sterling, *Portrait of a Man: The Warrior* (Williamstown, Mass.: Sterling and Francine Clark Art Institute, 1964). The best attempt to identify the sitters is Pierre Rosenberg and Isabelle Compin, "Quatre nouveaux Fragonard au Louvre," *Revue du Louvre* 34 (1974):183–92.

9. Rosenberg, *Fragonard,* 282, 286.

10. "Portrait de l'Abbé de Saint-Non peint par Fragonard en une heure de temps." See Rosenberg, *Fragonard,* 276.

11. "Portrait de La Brèteche peint par Fragonard en 1769, en une heure de temps." See Rosenberg, *Fragonard,* 274.

12. Roger de Piles, *The Art of Painting and The Lives of The Painters* (London: J. Nutt, 1706), 368.

13. "Un peintre fait un portrait de fantaisie, qui n'est d'après modèle." See Voltaire, "Fantaisie," *Encyclopédie,* 4:403. Diderot, "Salon de 1767," in *Salons,* 3:168.

14. When Wildenstein used the term, he defined *portraits de fantaisie* as "works in which the expression of the face is not stressed," and contradicted its eighteenth-century meaning by contending that Fragonard's paintings portrayed his friends and patrons. Wildenstein, 14.

15. Collé, 3:165.

16. ". . . la ressemblance caractéristique, en sorte qu'elle puisse être aisément reconnue pour celle de la personne dont on s'est proposé de rendre les traits." Watelet and Lévèsque, "Portrait," in *Dictionnaire,* 5:145. And the portrait was categorized in the *Encyclopédie* as a work wherein the artist depicted from life the external appearance of an individual and accurately recorded his physiognomy and natural expression. "Portrait," in *Encyclopédie ou Dictionnaire raisonné,* 13:153.

17. Roger de Piles, *Cours de peinture,* 269. Although eighteenth-century writers seemed untroubled by the more complex problems raised by the notion of resemblance, modern aesthetics has addressed itself to these issues. See, for example, Nelson Goodman, *Languages of Art* (Indianapolis: Hackett, 1968), 1–5.

18. Among the alleged depictions of Saint-Non, there is a portrait engraved by Legenisel after Gabriel de Saint-Aubin in 1774 and an engraving by Seroux d'Agincourt in the 1770s. Mary Wurth Harris, "The Abbé de Saint-Non and His Pastel Copy of a Painting by Fragonard," *Apollo* 110 (July, 1979):57–61.

19. The story was recorded by Roger de Piles in his *Abrégé de la vie des peintres,* and the theorist claimed to have owned the very painting, *La Crasseuse* (now believed to be a copy of Rembrandt's *Young Girl Leaning on a Windowsill,* 1645; London: Dulwich College Gallery), that inspired such notable confusion. Roger de Piles, *Abrégé de la vie des peintres avec des réflexions sur leurs ouvrages, et un Traité du peintre parfait; De la connoissance des desseins: De l'utilité des estampes,* 2nd edition (Paris: Estienne, 1715), 423. Fragonard, in fact, copied a half-length portrait like *La Crasseuse,* Rembrandt's *The Girl with a Broom* (Leningrad: Hermitage), when it was held in the collection of Crozat de Thiers.

20. Batteux, 32.

21. Dandré-Bardon suggested the practice of competing with recognized works to young artists. By surpassing them, challengers demonstrated their imaginative powers and proclaimed their own prodigious genius. Dandré-Bardon, 63. The idea of competing with, rather than copying, a model has its roots in the ancient concept of *aemulatio.*

22. Other characteristics of the woman Fragonard depicts do not correspond to what we know of La Guimard. For example, Fragonard's figure is shown with the attributes of a painter of miniatures and expresses a shyness perhaps inappropriate for someone reputed to have consistently treated him in an imperious manner. Also undermining this identification is the tendency for commentators to attach indiscriminately the names of Fragonard's patrons to his portraits. At least three other depictions of young women have been identified as portraits of Mlle Guimard (see Wildenstein, 274, #341, #343 and #344), even though the presumed Guimards differ notably from one another in physiognomic type. For a discussion of *La Guimard,* see Rosenberg and Compin, "Quatre nouveaux Fragonards," 188–92.

23. "Quelle différence y a-t-il entre une tête de fantaisie et une tête réelle?" Diderot, "Salon de 1767," in *Salons,* 3:168.

24. Diderot's comments on the portrait reverberated into the nineteenth century, when the proliferation of resemblances angered many. For example, in 1846 Champfleury expressed similar sentiments in his tirade against the wealthy, arrogant men who commissioned portraits in order to have posterity remember their names. Have they never been to the Louvre? he asked. There they would see the portraits of *(portraits "de")* Rembrandt, Van Dyck, Rubens. Playing on the double meaning of

portrait de as either *the portrait whose sitter is* or *the portrait made by,* Champfleury reminded his audience that it was the artist who was remembered in a brilliant portrait. He went on to say that a portrait is only a portrait for a specific audience; for others it has the status of any representation: "Un portrait ne peut rester qu'à la condition d'être l'image d'un grand homme ou d'un parent, d'un ami, d'un serviteur de ce grand homme. Autrement, il perd son nom, ses qualités et ses titres. Il devient l'*homme au gant,* la *femme au singe,* le *bourgmestre.*" Champfleury, *Oeuvres posthumes de Champfleury: Salons 1846–1851* (Paris: Alphonse Lemerre, 1894), 48.

25. "Le mérite de ressembler est passager; c'est celui du pinceau qui émerveille dans le moment et qui éternise l'ouvrage." Diderot, "Salon de 1763," in *Salons,* 1:204.

26. "Ce qu'il y a de certain, c'est que rien n'est plus rare qu'un beau pinceau, plus commun qu'un barbouilleur qui fait ressembler, et que quand l'homme n'est plus, nous supposons la ressemblance." Diderot, "Salon de 1763," in *Salons,* 1:204. Grimm disagreed with Diderot on this point. He argued that the attraction of the truth was invincible and contended that the price of a Van Dyck would fall if people knew that the portrait did not resemble its sitter, "C'est que le premier mérite d'un portrait est de ressembler, quoiqu'on dise, et un grand peintre n'a qu'à faire des têtes de fantaisie, s'il n'a pas le talent de donner de la ressemblance." in Diderot, "Salon de 1763," in *Salons,* 1:204.

27. The most conspicuous example of commenting on the truth of the likeness is Diderot's commentary on his own portrait executed by Michel Van Loo and discussed below. He began that piece by stating, "J'aime Michel, mais j'aime mieux la vérité." Diderot, "Salon de 1767," in *Salons,* 3:66. Other examples include his discussion of Roslin's *Comtesse d'Egmont* in the Salon of 1763 and his comments on Greuze's portrait of M. le Dauphin in the Salon of 1761.

28. "Il aggrandit, il exagère, il corrige les formes. A-t-il raison? a-t-il tort? Il a tort pour le pédant, il a raison pour l'homme de goût. Tort ou raison, c'est la figure qu'il a peinte qui restera dans la mémoire des hommes à venir." Diderot, "Salon de 1767," in *Salons,* 3:170.

29. For example, in his discourse on portraiture delivered to the Academy in 1750, Tocqué called resemblance the part of the portrait that most impressed those who were "peu connoisseurs." Louis Tocqué, "Réflexions sur la peinture et particulièrement sur le genre du portrait," in M. Le Comte Arnauld Doria, "Le Discours de Tocqué à l'Académie 'Sur la peinture et particulièrement sur le genre du portrait,'" *Bulletin de la Société de l'Histoire de l'Art français,* (Paris, 1929), 263.

30. Because eighteenth-century theory distinguished the process of imagining the subject from that of inventing it, the portrait could be evaluated by a criterion other than resemblance. Only in history painting did the artist imagine the subject by envisioning an event never witnessed and conceptualizing the characters according to the dictates of *la belle nature.* Portrait painting never required the artist to imagine his sitter; in fact, it specifically forbade him to do so. Both portraiture and history painting, however, could require a vivid imagination (taken as the mental faculty that visualized and synthesized) in the process of invention.

31. I wish to thank both Thomas Crow and Barry Wind for the useful comments they made about this analysis after hearing a paper I read at the Midwest American Society for Eighteenth-Century Studies in Evanston, Ill., October, 1986.

32. When I suggest that Fragonard's painting operates between Van Loo's portrait and Diderot's commentary, I do not mean that Fragonard's painting is necessarily dependent on both of these works. Although I do argue that Fragonard reinvented Van Loo's portrait, I do not argue that he also reinvented Diderot's commentary, although that scenario is possible (see chapter 6, note 2). It is also possible that Diderot, knowing Fragonard's response to Van Loo, capitalized on his familiarity with the *portraits de fantaisie.* And I do not eliminate the possibility that the similarities between Fragonard's image and Diderot's commentary were unintended. I do, however, see a significant relationship among these three works, with Fragonard's image interlocking suggestively with each of the other two, mediating and augmenting the relation between Van Loo's image and Diderot's text.

33. Diderot, "Salon de 1767," in *Salons,* 3:66.

34. Diderot, "Salon de 1767," in *Salons,* 3:66–67.

35. Diderot had planned to append the essay to his next *Salon* in 1769.

36. Diderot, "Salon de 1767," in *Salons,* 3:68.

37. Diderot, "Salon de 1767," in *Salons,* 3:67.

38. Diderot, "Salon de 1767," in *Salons,* 3:67.

39. "Alors sa bouche se serait entrouverte, ses regards distraits se seroient portés au loin, le travail de sa tête fortement occupée se seroit peint sur son visage." Diderot, "Salon de 1767," in *Salons,* 3:67.

40. Diderot, "Salon de 1767," in *Salons,* 3:67; "Mon joli philosophe, vous me serez à jamais un témoignage prétieux de l'amitié d'un artiste, excellent artiste, plus excellent homme."

41. Diderot, "Salon de 1767," in *Salons,* 3:67; "Mes enfants, je vous préviens que ce n'est pas moi."

42. "J'avois un grand front, des yeux très-vifs, d'assez grands traits, la tête tout à fait du caractère d'un ancien orateur, une bonne-hommie qui touchait de bien près à la bêtise, à la rusticité des anciens tems." Diderot, "Salon de 1767," in *Salons,* 3:67.

43. ". . . ce Falconnet, cet artiste si peu jaloux de sa réputation dans l'avenir, ce contempteur si déterminé de l'Immortalité, cet homme si *disrespectueux* de la postérité, délivré du souci de lui transmettre un mauvais buste." Diderot, "Salon de 1767," in *Salons,* 3:68.

44. For an iconographic analysis of the chain in Rembrandt's work, see Julius Held, *Rembrandt's Aristotle and Other Rembrandt Studies* (Princeton: Princeton University Press, 1969), 35.

45. Rosenberg, *Fragonard,* 290. One point about Rosenberg's recent catalogue and his discussion of the *portraits de fantaisie:* he contends that these pieces could have interested only a few connoisseurs because art collectors preferred more finished works. However, the *portraits de fantaisie* are neither uniformly unfinished (compare the paint handling of *La Guimard* with that of *The Singer*), nor are they, as a group, among Fragonard's least finished works. Candidates for that honor might include the series of heads of old men probably dating from shortly before the *portraits de fantaisie* (a good example is in Paris: Musée Jacquemart-André) or the small erotic paintings (e.g., *All in a Blaze,* c. 1767; Paris: Musée du Louvre), *The Cradle* (c. 1767; Amiens: Musée de Picardie), *The Laundresses* (c. 1760(?); Rouen: Musée des Beaux-Arts). Fragonard obviously did find a market of interested buyers for these and other sketchlike works. And finally, what we do know about the owners and appreciators

of the *portraits de fantaisie* points to those whom one could surely call connoisseurs (for example, the Comte de Brehan or the Comte Du Barry, who also owned another sketchlike work, the Louvre *Bathers* of 1767).

46. For more information about the duke's life, see the introduction to the 1919 edition of his treatise written from records of the d'Harcourt family: Mgr. le Duc d'Harcourt, *Traité de la décoration des dehors, des jardins, et des parcs,* intro. Ernest de Ganay, (Paris, 1919).

Chapter Six

1. "Imaginez tout ce que vous pouvez rêver de plus blond, de plus rose, de plus clair; pétrissez ces tons avec esprit, mais avec l'esprit inimitable du maître, et vous aurez l'impression ressentie. Le pinceau glisse sans appuyer sur les roses étients du déshabillé d'atelier d'un jeune peintre occupé à soulever, du bout de son appuie-main, les derniers voiles de son modèle. Ce n'est qu'une esquisse peut-être, mais quel tableau achevé la vaudrait et comment oser désirer plus terminées ces indications qui disent tout?" Portalis, 70.

2. From the existence of Baudouin's work, which is clearly and directly related to Diderot's comments, we can suppose that artists (as well as other nonsubscribers) were familiar with at least some of the contents of the *Salons.* This does not necessarily mean that they read Diderot's manuscripts; his ideas circulated not only through manuscripts but also through salon and atelier conversation. Fragonard, like Baudouin, came from the circle of artists around Boucher, and it is not impossible that he was familiar with the contents of Diderot's criticism (at least in its general outlines or as it was popularized and circulated) through conversations with either his *amateur* patrons (Saint-Non or Bergeret, for example) or other artists (for example, Baudouin).

3. Candace Clements, "The Academy and the Other: *Les Graces* and *Le Genre Galant*" (Paper delivered at the symposium "Social Implications of the Rococo Style: Images of Women," University of Missouri, October, 1987).

4. In another version of the scene engraved by Moreau in 1773 three figures are represented: the model, who is an elegant woman fully dressed; the painter, who is seated beside a canvas on which we see a nearly complete portrait of the model, and an elegant gentleman, who stands behind the painter and looks at his work.

5. For a discussion of this tradition, see Pierre Georgel and Anne-Marie Lecoq, *La Peinture dans le peinture* (Dijon: Musée des Beaux-Arts, 1983), 51–54.

6. Diderot, "Salon de 1767," in *Salons,* 3:109: "Chardin, La Grenée, Greuze et d'autres m'ont assuré, et les artistes ne flatent point les littérateurs, que j'étois presque le seul d'entre ceux-cy dont les images pouvoient passer sur la toile, presque comme elles étoient ordonnées dans ma tête."

7. "Greuze me dit, je voudrais bien peindre une femme toute nue, sans blesser la pudeur; et je lui répons, faites le modèle honnête. Asseiez devant vous une jeune fille toute nue; que sa pauvre dépouille soit à terre à côté d'elle et indique la misère; qu'elle ait la tête appuyée sur une de ses mains; que de ses yeux baissés deux larmes coulent le long de ses joues; que son expression soit celle de l'innocence, de la pudeur et de la modestie; que sa mère soit à côté d'elle; que de ses mains et d'une des

mains de sa fille, elle se couvre le visage; ou qu'elle se cache le visage de ses mains, et que celle de sa fille soit posée sur son épaule; que le vêtement de cette mère annonce aussi l'extrême indigence; et que l'artiste, témoin de cette scène, attendri, touché, laisse tomber sa palette ou son crayon. Et Greuze dit, je vois mon tableau." Diderot, "Salon de 1767," in *Salons,* 3:109–110.

8. Louis Petit de Bachaumont, *Lettre sur l'Exposition, Salon de 1769* in *Lettres sur les peintures, sculptures et gravures de M*[rs] *de l'Académie royale, exposées au Sallon du Louvre depuis 1767–1779* (London: Adamson, 1780), 57.

9. "Et puis ce sujet de la manière dont vous l'avez traité, est obscur; cette femme n'est pas une mère, c'est une ignoble créature qui fait quelque vilain commerce." Diderot, "Salon de 1769," in *Salons,* 4:95.

10. Diderot, "Salon de 1769," in *Salons,* 4:95.

11. "Baudouin, libertin dans son pinceau comme dans ses moeurs, n'avait pas dans son âme le moindre atome nécessaire pour l'exécution d'un tableau de cette honnêteté et de ce pathétique." Diderot, "Salon de 1769," in *Salons,* 4:95.

12. Baudouin did, in fact, do some religious subjects on commission, but these are not moral/didactic genre scenes in the manner of Greuze.

13. See, for example, the review in the *L'Avant Coureur* no. 39, Monday 25 September 1769: 397–98, where the beautiful touches in the flesh of the model are praised.

14. In relation to these images there is an interesting work by Cochin, fils, engraved by Fessard and titled an imitation of Anacreon. The work depicts a painter in his studio representing a Venus and Cupid. The painting on the easel is similar (although the pose is reversed) to that in Baudouin's *The Modest Model.* A reference to this work might have strengthened the association with Boucher, who was called the Anacreon of painting.

15. Diderot, "Salon de 1769," in *Salons,* 3:108.

16. The original patron of the work is not known. Wildenstein presumes that the work corresponds to one that appeared in the Folliot sale of 1793 and was described as "un peintre dans son atelier occupé à poser le modèle, esquisse." Wildenstein, 265. Folliot was an *expert* who is known to have bought drawings by Fragonard at the sale of Bergeret de Grancourt in 1785.

17. The contrast of clothed and unclothed used so cleverly by Fragonard is also reminiscent of Boucher's *Vertumnus and Pomona* (1749; Columbus, Ohio: Museum of Art); the pose linking the two women is especially pertinent to Fragonard's later work.

18. The confluence even extends to the use of the term *toucher;* to touch the canvas was to paint, to touch a woman was not simply to caress her; it was also, in colloquial use, to have sexual intercourse with her. It is not clear, however, that this usage was widespread. Guiraud, 604.

19. Other devices also guide attention to that most important of sites. For example, on the easel leg there are three dots arranged one above the other in a vertical pattern that lead the eye from there to the canvas above them. They are the counterparts of the buttons on the painter's vest that also lead in a vertical path.

20. Here I am considering not the historical but the apparent Fragonard as the "artist who made the representation."

Epilogue

1. Fried's *Absorption and Theatricality* has been significant here.

2. Hobson, in particular, considered the theory of illusion in *The Object of Art.*

3. Richard Shiff has argued for the centrality of these notions in modern art. See, for example, *Cézanne and the End of Impressionism,* or his more recent essay, "Performing an Appearance: On the Surface of Abstract Expressionism," in Michael Auping, ed., *Abstract Expressionism: The Critical Developments* (New York: Harry N. Abrams, for the Albright-Knox Art Gallery, 1987), 94–123. Both touch and brushwork were much discussed and considered in the eighteenth century as well. I am not suggesting that the issues resolved themselves in identical patterns but that attention was focused on similar questions.

Index